DATE DUE   MAR 05

APR 05 '05			
3-25-06			
4-14-06			
JUN 0 7 2010			
GAYLORD			PRINTED IN U.S.A.

1948 AND AFTER

ISRAEL AND THE PALESTINIANS

BENNY MORRIS

CLARENDON PRESS · OXFORD

*This book has been printed digitally and produced in a standard specification
in order to ensure its continuing availability*

OXFORD
UNIVERSITY PRESS

Great Clarendon Street, Oxford OX2 6DP

Oxford University Press is a department of the University of Oxford.
It furthers the University's objective of excellence in research, scholarship,
and education by publishing worldwide in

Oxford New York

Auckland Bangkok Buenos Aires Cape Town Chennai
Dar es Salaam Delhi Hong Kong Istanbul Karachi Kolkata
Kuala Lumpur Madrid Melbourne Mexico City Mumbai Nairobi
São Paulo Shanghai Taipei Tokyo Toronto

Oxford is a registered trade mark of Oxford University Press
in the UK and in certain other countries

Published in the United States
by Oxford University Press Inc., New York

ISBN 0-19-827929-9

For Leah

PREFACE TO THE
PAPERBACK EDITION

This collection of essays serves as a complement to my study *The Birth of the Palestinian Refugee Problem, 1947–1949*, which was published in 1988. In part, these essays are based on material that I discovered or became available only after the completion of *The Birth*. They elucidate aspects of the subject not treated or only fleetingly referred to in the original work. They will, I feel, provide the reader with additional information about and insights into the Arab exodus from Palestine.

This collection was originally published in hardcover in late 1990 and consisted of nine essays. It has now been revised and expanded, largely on the basis of new documentation that has come to light. Some of the essays have undergone minor emendations. Two of the essays, 'The New Historiography: Israel and its Past' and 'The Transfer of Al Majdal's Remaining Arabs to Gaza, 1950', have been substantially expanded. To the first has been added a fairly detailed review of developments, since the original version of this book went to print, in the historiographic controversy concerning Israel's early history. The second has been expanded—in fact, doubled in size—to take account of new material, mainly from the Labour (Histadrut) Archive, which sheds fresh and important light particularly on the last stages of the transfer, in which systematic coercion was employed to obtain the Arabs' exodus to Gaza.

Most significantly, a wholly new essay has been added: 'Yosef Nahmani and the Arab Question in 1948' (Chapter 5). Nahmani, a Zionist defence activist and official for more than half a century, directed the Jewish National Fund office in Eastern Galilee. His diary for the years 1947–9, a remarkable document hitherto untapped by historians, sheds light on important aspects of the 1948 war, on Yishuv–Arab relations during the war, and on the activities of the JNF in the Galilee. In a sense, 'Yosef Nahmani . . .' complements Chapters 4 and 6 ('Yosef Weitz and the Transfer Committees, 1948–1949' and 'The Harvest of 1948 and the Creation of the Palestinian Refugee Problem') and contributes to an understanding of the causes and character of the Arab exodus.

The first essay, 'The New Historiography: Israel and its Past', is in great measure introductory. It places the collection (as well as *The Birth*) in its historiographic context and reviews the issues and arguments that have characterized the controversy sparked in Israel by the publication of *The Birth* and other 'new' histories, most notably Avi Shlaim's *Collusion Across the Jordan* (Oxford, 1988). The reader perhaps will find in some of the essays, particularly in 'Yosef Weitz . . .' and 'The Causes and Character of the Arab Exodus from Palestine: The Israel Defence Forces Intelligence Service Analysis of June 1948', answers to some of the contentions voiced by the critics of the New Historiography. He will also find, as in 'The Initial Absorption of the Palestinian Refugees in the Arab Host Countries, 1948–1949', explorations and passages that do not conform to the image of the New Historiography that these critics have tried to project.

The essays 'Mapai, Mapam, and the Arab Problem in 1948', 'The Causes and Character of the Arab Exodus . . .', 'Yosef Weitz . . .', 'Yosef Nahmani . . .', and 'The Harvest of 1948 . . .' all deal with the core questions surrounding the exodus. 'Mapai, Mapam . . .' traces what was certainly the only major ideological-ethical debate that took place in and near the corridors of Israeli power in 1948 on the question of policy towards the Arabs—and an interesting debate it was. 'The Causes and Character of the Arab Exodus . . .' analyses a unique (and, to my mind, historio-graphically decisive) intelligence document—perhaps one of the few occasions in historiography in which an intelligence document actually clarifies a major historical happening. Since the publica-tion of the original hardcover edition of this work, the identity of the document's author has also come to light—if anything, reinforcing its importance as evidence. 'Yosef Weitz . . .' traces, in great detail, almost day by day, the activities of a key Zionist official during the agrarian-demographic revolution of 1948. 'Yosef Nahmani . . .' focuses on some of these same activities, as they unfolded in Tiberias and Eastern Galilee. 'The Harvest of 1948 . . .' looks at the mechanics of the Yishuv's expropriation of the abandoned Arab lands in the course of the 1948 war.

'Yosef Nahmani . . .', 'Haifa's Arabs: Displacement and Concentration, July 1948', 'The Case of Abu Ghosh and Beit Naqquba, Al Fureidis and Khirbet Jisr az Zarka in 1948—or Why Four Villages Remained', and 'The Transfer of Al Majdal's Remaining Arabs . . .' describe the varying fates of different Arab communities during the 1948 war and in the immediate post-war period. The tales underline the variety and, often, the highly local character of what happened—despite the shared common denominators and patterns of the exodus in most places at most times. They also shed a good deal of light on the (often confused) nature of Israeli decision-making. 'Haifa's Arabs . . .' and 'The Case of Abu Ghosh . . .' highlight the interplay (and divergence) between Israel's new civilian and military authorities and the increasing restraints imposed on the IDF's power *vis-à-vis* Israel's Arab minority as the hostilities in each sector drew to a close. 'The Transfer of Al Majdal's Remaining Arabs . . .' casts some light on the thinking and manner of operation of one of Israel's most interesting politician-generals, Moshe Dayan, while elucidating the tactics of transfer once the revolutionary stage of Israeli nation-building had ended.

Lastly, 'The Initial Absorption . . .' sheds light on what happened to the exiles once they had moved to the areas under Arab rule and why they became permanent refugees.

Taken together, these essays hope to contribute to an understanding of the origins of the Palestinian refugee problem, of Israeli policies in 1948, and of the early history of Israel's Arab minority.

ACKNOWLEDGEMENTS

I would like to thank the publishers and editors of the following journals for their permission to republish the named essays:

Tikkun, where an early version of 'The New Historiography: Israel and its Past' first appeared in 1988; and the directors of Georgetown University's Center for Contemporary Arab Studies, where I delivered an earlier version of the essay as a paper at a conference in 1989.

Middle Eastern Studies, which in 1986 published 'The Causes and Character of the Arab Exodus from Palestine: The IDF Intelligence Service Analysis of June 1948' and 'Yosef Weitz and the Transfer Committees, 1948–1949'.

The Middle East Journal, which in 1986 published 'The Harvest of 1948 and the Creation of the Palestinian Refugee Problem' and, in 1988, 'Haifa's Arabs: Displacement and Concentration, July 1948'.

And the publishers Unwin Hyman, who first published 'The Initial Absorption of the Palestinian Refugees in the Arab Host Countries 1948–1949' in their volume *Refugees in the Age of Total War* (1988).

I would also like to thank Henry Hardy and the editors of OUP for seeing this collection over the hurdles of hardback publication, and Tim Barton, Janet Moth, and Dominic Byatt for their parts in the production of the paperback edition.

CONTENTS

MAPS

ABBREVIATIONS

AFSC	American Friends Service Committee Archive, Philadelphia
CP	Sir Alan Cunningham Papers, Middle East Centre Archives, St Antony's College, Oxford
CZA	Central Zionist Archives, Jerusalem
DBG	David Ben-Gurion's *Yoman Hamilhama-Tashah* (the war diary 1948–9)
DMZ	Demilitarized Zone(s)
HHA	Hashomer Hatza'ir Archives (Mapam, Kibbutz Artzi Papers), Givat Haviva, Israel
HHA-ACP	Hashomer Hatza'ir Archives, Aharon Cohen Papers, Givat Haviva, Israel
HMA	Haifa Municipal Archives, Haifa Town Hall
IDF	Israel Defence Forces
IDFA	IDF and Israel Defence Ministry Archive, Givatayim
ISA	Israel State Archives, Jerusalem
AM	Agriculture Ministry Papers
FM	Foreign Ministry Papers
JM	Justice Ministry Papers
MAM	Minority Affairs Ministry Papers
PMO	Prime Minister's Office Papers
IZL	Irgun Zva'i Leumi (National Military Organization) or the Irgun
JI	Jabotinsky Institute (IZL and LHI Papers), Tel Aviv
JEM	Jerusalem and East Mission Papers, Middle East Centre Archives, St Antony's College, Oxford
JNF	Jewish National Fund

KMA	Kibbutz Meuhad Archives
KMA-AZP	Kibbutz Meuhad Archives, Aharon Zisling Papers — Ef'al, Israel
KMA-PA	Kibbutz Meuhad Archives, Palmah Papers — Ef'al, Israel
LA	Labour Archives (Histadrut), Lavon Institute, Tel Aviv
LHI	Lohamei Herut Yisrael (Freedom Fighters of Israel) or Stern Gang
LPA	Labour Party Archives (Mapai), Beit Berl, Tzofit, Israel
MAC	Mixed Armistice Commission
NA	National Archives, Washington, DC
ND	Yosef Nahmani Diaries
PICA	Palestine Jewish Colonization Association
PRO	Public Record Office, London
CAB	Cabinet Office Papers
CO	Colonial Office Papers
FO	Foreign Office Papers
WO	War Office Papers
UN	United Nations Archives, New York City
UNTSO	United Nations Truce Supervision Organization

FIG. 1. Israel/Palestine, showing 1949 Armistice frontiers

1

The New Historiography: Israel and its Past

On 11 July 1948, the Yiftah Brigade's Third Battalion, as part of Operation Dani, occupied the Arab town of Lydda. The battalion's 400–500 troops, supported by a company from the First Battalion, took up positions around the centre of the town; the remaining population, some 30,000 Arabs, shut themselves up in their homes. There was no formal surrender, but the night passed quietly. Just before noon the following day, two or three gun-mounted armoured cars belonging to the Arab Legion, the British-led Transjordanian army, drove into town. They were either on a reconnaissance mission or were unaware that the town had already fallen into Israeli hands. A firefight ensued, and the scout cars withdrew. But a number of armed townspeople, perhaps believing that the shooting heralded a major Arab counter-attack, began sniping from windows and rooftops at their Israeli occupiers. The Third Battalion—several hundred nervous soldiers in the middle of an Arab town of tens of thousands—fiercely put down what various chroniclers, Jewish and Arab, subsequently called a 'rebellion', firing in the streets, into houses, and at the concentrations of POWs in the mosque courtyards. Israeli military records refer to 'more than 250' Arabs killed in the town that afternoon. By contrast, Israeli casualties in both the firefight with the armoured cars and in the suppression of the sniping were between two and four dead (the reports vary) and twelve or so wounded.

Israeli historians called the affair a 'rebellion' in order to justify the slaughter and the subsequent expulsion; Arab chroniclers, such as Aref al Aref, did likewise in order to emphasize Palestinian resolve and sacrifice in the battle against the Zionist invaders.

Operation Dani took place roughly midway through the first Israeli–Arab war, Israel's War of Independence. The Arab states' invasion of the fledgling Jewish state on 15 May had been halted weeks before; the newly organized and freshly equipped Israel Defence Forces (IDF) were on the offensive on all fronts, which was to be the case for the remainder of the war.

At 13.30 hours on 12 July, before the shooting in Lydda had completely died down, Lieutenant-Colonel Yitzhak Rabin, Operation Dani head of operations, issued the following order: '1. The inhabitants of Lydda must be expelled quickly without attention to age. They should be directed towards Beit Nabala. Yiftah [Brigade HQ] must determine the method and inform [Operation] Dani HQ and 8th Brigade HQ. 2. Implement immediately.' A similar order was issued at the same time to the Kiryati Brigade concerning the inhabitants of the neighbouring Arab town of Ramle, occupied by Kiryati troops that morning. There had been no shooting in Ramle that day. Ramle's notables had signed a formal surrender instrument a few hours before; no such surrender had taken place in Lydda.

On 12 and 13 July, the Yiftah and Kiryati brigades carried out their orders, expelling the 50–60,000 remaining inhabitants of and refugees camped in and around the two towns, which lie some 10 miles south-east of Tel Aviv. Throughout the war, the two towns, which sat astride the main Tel Aviv–Jerusalem road, had interdicted Jewish traffic. Moreover, the leaders of the Yishuv, Palestine's Jewish community, regarded Lydda and Ramle, at first held by Arab irregulars and, from May, by the Arab Legion, as a perpetual threat to Tel Aviv itself, a springboard from which the Arabs could attack the Jewish capital.

About noon on 13 July, Operation Dani HQ informed IDF General Staff / Operations: 'Lydda police fort has been captured. [The troops] are busy expelling the inhabitants [*oskim begeirush hatoshavim*].' Lydda's inhabitants were forced to walk eastwards to the Arab Legion lines; many of Ramle's inhabitants were ferried in trucks or buses. Clogging the roads (and the Legion's possible routes of advance westward), the tens of thousands of refugees marched, gradually shedding their worldly goods along the way. It was a hot summer day. Arab chroniclers, such as Sheikh Muhammad Nimr al Khatib, claimed that hundreds of children died in the march, from dehydration and disease. One Israeli witness described the spoor: the refugee column 'to begin with [jettisoned] utensils and furniture and, in the end, bodies of men, women and children . . .'. Many of the refugees came to rest near the town of Ramallah and set up tent encampments, which became some of today's mortar and concrete-block West Bank refugee camps.[1]

[1] A full description of the Lydda–Ramle episode is to be found in Benny Morris,

Israeli historians during the 1950s, 1960s, and 1970s were less than candid in their treatment of the Lydda–Ramle episode.

The IDF's official history of the war, *Toldot Milhemet Hako-memiyut* (History of the War of Independence), produced by the General Staff / History Branch and published in 1959, stated: 'The Arabs [of Lydda], who had violated the terms of the surrender and feared [Israeli] retribution, were happy at the possibility given them of evacuating the town and proceeding eastwards, to Legion territory; Lydda emptied of its Arab inhabitants.'[2] The official history makes no reference to the exodus of the inhabitants of Ramle or to its reasons.

A few years later, in 1961, the former head of the IDF General Staff / History Branch, Lieutenant-Colonel (res.) Natanel Lorch, published his history of the war, *The Edge of the Sword*, a slightly expanded version of *Toldot Milhemet Hakomemiyut*. In it he explained the exodus from Lydda thus: 'The residents, who had violated surrender terms and feared retribution, declared they would leave and asked for safe conduct to Arab Legion lines, which was granted.' The same sentence appears in the revised edition of *The Edge of the Sword*, published by Lorch in 1968.[3]

A somewhat less deceitful, but still misleading, description of the events in Lydda and Ramle is provided by Lieutenant-Colonel (res.) Elhannan Orren, another former officer of the IDF History Branch, in his *Baderekh el Ha'ir* (On the Road to the City), a highly detailed history of Operation Dani published by the IDF press, Ma'arachot, in 1976. Like his predecessors, Orren failed to state anywhere that what had occurred was an expulsion, and one explicitly ordered from on high. He writes:

When the police fort fell [on 13 July]—the morale of the inhabitants fell. . . . The [Lydda] notables asked that they be allowed to take with them the incarcerated menfolk, and then they would leave without delay. Their request was granted . . . and a mass evacuation of Lydda began. . . . The announcement about the exodus from Lydda was transmitted to Kiryati in

'Operation Dani and the Palestinian Exodus from Lydda and Ramle in 1948', *The Middle East Journal*, 40, 1, (Winter, 1986), 82–109.

[2] IDF General Staff / History Branch, *Toldot Milhemet Hakomemiyut* (Tel Aviv, 1959), 259.

[3] N. Lorch, *The Edge of the Sword* (Tel Aviv, 1961), 286, and revised edn. 1968, 340.

Ramle. Here, transport was provided, and the troops made [the evacuation]
easier for the inhabitants. The stream of departure, which began already
before the conquest, grew on the 12 of July.[4]

(In fact, the expulsion order had originated with Ben-Gurion,
according to the Prime Minister's first major biographer, Michael
Bar-Zohar, and most recent Israeli histories, such as Arieh Itzchaki's
Latrun).[5]

Ironically, a franker description of the episode was provided by
Yitzhak Rabin, who stated in his autobiography, *Pinkas Sherut* (in
English, *The Rabin Memoirs*), that what had occurred in Lydda and
Ramle had been an expulsion. But the relevant passage was excised
by Israeli government censors. (Subsequently, to the retired Prime
Minister's embarrassment, the offending passage was published in
the *New York Times* by Rabin's translator into English, Peretz
Kidron.)[6]

The treatment of the Lydda–Ramle affair by past Israeli historians
is illustrative of what can be called, for want of a better term, the
'old' or 'official' history. That history has shaped the way Israelis
and Diaspora Jews—or, at least, Diaspora Zionists—have seen
and, in large measure, still see Israel's past; and it has also held sway
over the way gentile Europeans and Americans (and their governments) see that past. This understanding of the past has significantly
influenced the attitudes of Diaspora Jews, as well as the attitudes of
European and American non-Jews, toward Israel over the decades,
affecting government policies concerning the Israeli–Arab conflict.

The essence of the old history is that Zionism's birth was an
inevitable result of Gentile pressures and persecution, and that it
offered at least a partial solution to the 'Jewish Problem' in Europe;
that the Zionists intended no ill to the Arabs of Palestine, and that
Zionist settlement alongside the Arabs did not, from the Jews' point
of view, necessitate a clash or displacement, but that Israel was born

---

[4] E. Orren, *Baderekh el Ha'ir*, [on the road to the city] (Tel Aviv, 1976), 124.
[5] Michael Bar-Zohar, *Ben-Gurion* (Tel Aviv, 1977), ii. 775; Arieh Itzchaki,
Latrun, ii, 394.
[6] *The New York Times*, 23 Oct. 1979. The first Israeli historian to my knowledge
to treat the Lydda–Ramle episode with relative candour, if rather briefly, was Arieh
Itzchaki, in his 2-volume *Latrun, the Battle for the Road to Jerusalem* (Tel Aviv,
1982), 392–4. But he too speaks of 'a general rebellion' of the Lydda townspeople; of
the townspeople's 'treachery', as they had 'signed a surrender' instrument before
this; and of the local dignitaries proposing the evacuation of the town.

into an uncharitable, predatory environment; that Ziónist efforts at compromise and conciliation were rejected by the Arabs; and that the Palestinians and the neighbouring Arab states, selfish and ignoble, refused to accede to the burgeoning Zionist presence and in 1947–8 attacked the Yishuv with the aim of nipping the Jewish state in the bud. The Arabs, so goes the old history, were far stronger politically and militarily than the Yishuv and were assisted in their efforts by the British, but none the less lost the war. The Haganah at first defeated the *knufiyot* (or 'gangs', the Yishuv's name for the Arab irregulars and militiamen), who were reinforced by contingents of foreign Arab volunteers (the Arab Liberation Army), and then the five (Egypt, Syria, Iraq, Transjordan, and Lebanon) invading Arab armies. In the course of that war, says the old history, in order to facilitate the invasion of the Arab armies, the Arab leaders called upon / ordered Palestine's Arabs to quit their homes: this would lay the Jewish state open to charges of expulsion and physically clear the path for the Arab armies. Thus was born the Palestinian refugee problem.

The old history—whose purest expression, incidentally, is to be found in Israeli elementary- and high-school history textbooks and in David Ben-Gurion's own 'histories' of the Yishuv and Israel's first years (*Medinat Yisrael Hamehudeshet, Behilahem Yisrael*, and so on)—generally makes the claim that in the immediate wake of the 1948 war, Israel's leaders desperately sought to make peace with one or all of the Arab states but the Arabs, hell-bent on the destruction of Israel, turned down these overtures and repaid this goodwill with continued belligerence.

The old historians, who perhaps should more accurately be called chroniclers, offered a simplistic and consciously pro-Israeli inter-pretation of the past, and generally avoided mention of anything that reflected poorly upon Israel. It was argued, with a measure of justice, that since the conflict with the Arabs was still raging, and since it was a political as well as military struggle, it necessarily involved propaganda, the good (or ill) will of governments in the West, and the hearts and minds of Christians and Diaspora Jews. Blackening Israel's name, it was argued, would ultimately weaken Israel in its ongoing struggle for survival. *Raisons d'état* often took precedence over telling the truth.

The past few years have witnessed the emergence of a new

generation of Israeli scholars and a 'new' history. These historians, some of them living or working abroad, have looked and are looking afresh at the Israeli historical experience, and their conclusions are often at odds with those of the old history.

Some critics have recently called the 'new' history 'revisionist'. I don't like the name for three reasons. First, it conjures up the faces of Ze'ev Jabotinsky and Menachem Begin, respectively the founder / prophet and latter-day leader of the Revisionist Movement in Zionism. The Revisionists, unpragmatic, right-wing deviants from the mainstream of the Zionist experience, claimed all of Palestine and the East Bank of the Jordan River for the Jews. Until 1977, their place was on the fringe of Zionist and Israeli history, though since then their vision, albeit in diluted form, has dominated the political arena in Jerusalem. To call the new history 'revisionism' is to cause unnecessary confusion and, to some, anguish.

Secondly, in western historiography, revisionism recently has denoted those, like A. J. P. Taylor, who have looked anew at the origins of either of the two world wars or both and have concluded that the blame for their outbreak must be distributed more equitably as between the Germans and the Allied Powers. And, in a minor branch of this genus, there are some who, to dilute German guilt, have even denied any Nazi wrongdoing or the Holocaust itself. A more recent wave of revisionists have sought to lessen Soviet blame for the Cold War. On this count, too, the term 'revisionism' in connection with Israeli historiography can only mislead and confuse.

Lastly, the term 'revisionism' would seem to imply that there already existed a solid, credible—if wrong-headed—body of historiography which latest fashion is bent on overthrowing, perhaps for ulterior reasons. But this is not really the case. Israel's old historians, by and large, were not really historians and did not produce real history. In reality, they were chroniclers, and often apologetic, interested chroniclers at that. They did not work from and upon a solid body of contemporary documentation and did not normally try to paint a picture that offered the variety of sides of a given historical experience. They worked from interviews and memoirs, and often from memories. They had neither the mind-set nor the materials to write real history. To call the new history 'revisionist' would, by implication, ascribe too much merit to the old history.

Two factors apply in the emergence of the new history, one relating to materials and the other to personae.

Thanks to Israel's Archives Law (passed in 1955 and amended in 1964 and again in 1981), and to its relatively liberal implementation, from the early 1980s onwards hundreds of thousands, perhaps millions, of state documents were opened to researchers. Almost all the Foreign Ministry's papers from 1948 to 1957, as well as great masses of documents—memoranda, minutes, correspondence—from other ministries, including the Prime Minister's Office (though largely excluding the papers of the Defence Ministry and the IDF), have been declassified. Similarly, the past few years have seen the organization and release of large collections of private papers and political party papers.

For the first time, therefore, historians—Israelis and non-Israelis —have been able to write studies about the first years of Israeli statehood and the first years of the Israeli–Arab conflict on the basis of a large collection of contemporary source-material.

The second factor is the nature of the new historians. Most of them, born around 1948, have matured in a more open, doubting, and self-critical Israel than the pre-1967, pre-1973, and pre-Lebanon-War Israel of the old historians. Most of the old historians, indeed, had lived through 1948 as highly committed adult participants in the epic, glorious rebirth of the Jewish commonwealth. They were unable to separate their lives from the events they later recounted, unable to distance themselves from and regard impartially the facts and processes through which they had lived. Most, if asked, will admit as much—and in this, incidentally, they share a common experience with most chronicler-participants in national liberation movements and revolutions in the modern age. The generation of nation-builders seldom casts doubt or looks frowningly back upon its handiwork.

By contrast, the new generation of Israeli historians have been capable of at least a measure of impartiality, and of sometimes more than that. Inevitably, the new historians have focused their attention on the 1947–51 period, both because the documents were available and because that first Israeli–Arab war and its aftermath were the central, natal, revolutionary event in Israeli and, perhaps, modern Jewish history. How one perceives 1948 bears heavily upon how one perceives, interprets, and understands the whole of the

Zionist/Israeli experience. For some, 1948 carries the brand of original sin; for others, it was a period marked by ineluctable savagery, but also by innocence, courage, and glory.

The past few years have seen the publication in the West and Israel of a handful of 'new' histories, including Avi Shlaim's *Collusion Across the Jordan* (Oxford, 1988); Uri Bar-Joseph's *The Best of Enemies, Israel and Transjordan in the War of 1948* (London, 1987); Ilan Pappe's *Britain and the Arab–Israeli Conflict, 1948–1951* (London, 1988); Simha Flapan's *The Birth of Israel* (New York, 1987)—not strictly a work of history, which I shall deal with presently; Yitzhak Levy's *Tish'ah Kabin* [Jerusalem in the War of Independence] (IDF Press, 1986); Yossi Amitai's *Ahvat Amim Bemivhan* [Testing Brotherhood] (Tel Aviv, 1988); Michael Cohen's *Palestine and the Great Powers, 1945–1948* (Princeton University Press, 1982); and my own *The Birth of the Palestinian Refugee Problem, 1947–1949* (Cambridge, 1988). A monumental, if controversial, work of new history, Uri Milstein's *History of the War of Independence*, has begun to appear; so far four of its projected twelve volumes have been published.

To these I would add, though slightly anticipating the 1980s, Yehoshua Porath's excellent studies of the origins of Palestinian nationalism, *The Emergence of the Palestinian–Arab National Movement 1918–1929* and *The Palestinian Arab National Movement 1929–1939* (London, 1974 and 1979).

Taken together, these works—along with a large number of articles that have appeared recently in academic journals such as *Middle Eastern Studies*, *Studies in Zionism*, and *The Middle East Journal*—significantly undermine, if not thoroughly demolish, a variety of assumptions that helped form the core of the old history.

Flapan's *The Birth of Israel* is the least historical of these books. Indeed, it is not, strictly speaking, a history at all but rather a polemical work written from a Marxist perspective. In his introduction, Flapan—the former head of Mapam's Arab Department who passed away in 1987—wrote that his purpose was not to produce 'a detailed historical study interesting only to historians and researchers', but rather to write 'a book that will undermine the propaganda structures that have so long obstructed the growth of the peace forces in my country . . .' Politics rather than historiography is the book's manifest objective.

But despite this explicitly polemical purpose, Flapan's book has the virtue of more-or-less accurately formulating some of the central fallacies—which he calls 'myths'—that inform the old history. These were: (1) that the Yishuv in 1947 joyously embraced partition and the truncated Jewish state prescribed by the UN General Assembly, and that the Palestinians and the surrounding Arab states unanimously rejected the partition and attacked the Yishuv with the aim of throwing the Jews into the sea; (2) that the war was waged between a relatively defenceless and weak (Jewish) David and a relatively strong (Arab) Goliath; (3) that the Palestinians fled their homes and villages either 'voluntarily'—meaning for no good reason—or at the behest / orders of the Arab leaders; and (4) that, at the war's end, Israel was interested in making peace, but the recalcitrant Arabs preferred a perpetual war to the finish.

PARTITION AND WAR AIMS

Because of poor research and analysis, Flapan's demolition of these myths is far from convincing. Shlaim, in *Collusion Across the Jordan*, tackles some of the myths more persuasively. The original goal of Zionism was the establishment of a Jewish state in the whole of Palestine. The acceptance of partition, in the mid-1930s as in 1947, was tactical, not a change in the Zionist dream. 'I don't regard a state in part of Palestine as the final aim of Zionism, but as a means towards that aim', Ben-Gurion wrote in 1938.[7] A few months earlier, Ben-Gurion told the Jewish Agency Executive that he supported partition 'on the basis of the assumption that after we constitute a large force following the establishment of the state—we will cancel the partition of the country and we will expand throughout the Land of Israel.'[8] To his wife, Paula, Ben-Gurion wrote: 'Establish a Jewish state at once, even if it is not in the whole land. The rest will come in the course of time. It must come.'[9]

The Yishuv entered the first stage of the war in November–

---

[7] Quoted in Shabtai Teveth, *Ben-Gurion and the Palestine Arabs* (Oxford, 1985), 188.

[8] Quoted in Benny Morris, *The Birth of the Palestinian Refugee Problem, 1947–1949* (Cambridge, 1988), 24.

[9] Quoted in Avi Shlaim, *Collusion Across the Jordan* (Oxford, 1988), 17.

December 1947 with an understanding with Transjordan's King Abdullah—'a falcon trapped in a canary's cage'—that, come the British evacuation, his army, the Arab Legion, would take over the eastern part of Palestine (now called the West Bank), earmarked by the UN to be the core of the Palestinian Arab state, and that it would leave the Yishuv alone to set up the Jewish state in the other areas of the country. The Yishuv and the Hashemite Kingdom of Transjordan, Shlaim and Bar-Joseph persuasively argue, had conspired from 1946 to early 1948 to nip the impending UN partition resolution in the bud and to thwart the emergence of a Palestinian Arab state. It was to be partition, but between Israel and Transjordan. This 'collusion' and 'unholy alliance'—in Shlaim's loaded phrases—was sealed at the now-famous clandestine meeting between Golda Myerson (Meir) and Abdullah at Naharayim on the Jordan River on 17 November 1947.[10]

Moreover, this Zionist–Hashemite understanding was fully sanctioned by the British Government, Shlaim, Milstein, Bar-Joseph, and Pappe demonstrate. Contrary to the old Zionist historiography, which was based largely on the mistaken feelings of Israel's leaders at the time, Britain's Foreign Secretary, Ernest Bevin, by February 1948 had clearly 'become resigned to the inevitable emergence of a Jewish state', while opposing the emergence of a Palestinian Arab state. And he explicitly warned Transjordan 'to refrain from invading the areas allotted to the Jews'.[11]

Both Shlaim and Flapan make the point that the Palestinian Arabs, though led by Haj Amin al Husayni, the conniving, extremist, former mufti of Jerusalem, were far from unanimous in supporting the Husayni-led crusade against the Jews. Indeed, in the first months of the hostilities, according to the Yishuv's intelligence sources, the bulk of Palestine's Arabs merely wanted peace and quiet, if only out of a healthy respect for the Jews' martial prowess. But gradually, in part because of Haganah over-reactions, the conflict spread, eventually engulfing the two communities throughout the land. In April and May 1948, the Haganah gained the upper

---

[10] Shlaim, *Collusion*, pp. 110–16; and Ilan Pappe, *Britain and the Arab–Israeli Conflict, 1948–1951* (Macmillan, 1988), 10.

[11] Shlaim, *Collusion*, p. 139; and Pappe, *Britain and the Arab–Israeli Conflict*, pp. 16–18.

hand and the Palestinians lost the war, most of them going into exile.

What ensued, once Israel declared its independence on 14 May 1948 and the Arab states invaded on 15 May, was 'a general land grab', with everyone—Israel, Transjordan, Syria, Egypt, and even Lebanon—bent on preventing the birth of a Palestinian Arab state and carving out chunks of Palestine for themselves.

Contrary to the old historiography, Abdullah's invasion of eastern Palestine was clearly designed to conquer territory for his kingdom —at the expense of the Palestinian Arabs—rather than to destroy the Jewish state. Indeed, the Arab Legion stuck meticulously, throughout the war, to its non-aggressive stance *vis-à-vis* the Yishuv and the Jewish state's territory (in part, in line with the November 1947 'understanding' and, in part, out of reluctance to commit the army in a battle in which it would be mauled. Abdullah understood that the Legion was his Kingdom's shield; without it, he would fall.)

There were two exceptions: the Legion's support for the Palestinian irregulars in overrunning the Etzion Bloc of Jewish settlements, south of Bethlehem, and the Legion's capture of the Jewish Quarter of the Old City and the probes towards West Jerusalem, at Notre Dame and the Mandelbaum Gate, in the second half of May. But the Etzion Bloc was an island of Jewish settlement inside the territory earmarked for Arab sovereignty, an island that interdicted Arab traffic along the vital Hebron–Bethlehem–Jerusalem road. And Jerusalem was an area earmarked for international rule rather than Jewish or Arab sovereignty. Jerusalem was never covered by the Yishuv–Hashemite 'understanding' and was, effectively, up for grabs throughout the war. Yet Arab Legion commander Glubb Pasha for days resisted local Palestinian importuning to advance into Jerusalem, for fear of losing his small army in costly and indecisive street battles. He moved in, reluctantly, on 17–18 May, and only after desperate appeals from the local Arab population had forced Abdullah's hand. The Legion's pushes at Notre Dame and the Mandelbaum Gate were apparently designed to relieve pressure, or expected pressure, on the Old City and Arab East Jerusalem in general, and were never pressed with determination. Conquest of Jewish West Jerusalem was never, and was never seen to be, on the cards.

Rather, in the course of May–July 1948, it was the Haganah / IDF that violated the November 'understanding' and repeatedly assaulted the Arab Legion in areas earmarked by the partition resolution for Arab sovereignty—at Latrun, Lydda–Ramle, Nabi Samwil, and so on. Abdullah and Glubb, from the start, had correctly assessed Jewish determination and military strength and had realized that their army was barely capable of seizing and controlling Arab Eastern Palestine let alone having strength to spare for offensive operations against the Jews and against Israeli territory. It is not at all clear that Abdullah and Glubb would have been happy to see the collapse in May 1948 of the fledgling Jewish republic. Certainly Abdullah was far more troubled by the prospects of the emergence of a Palestinian Arab state and of an expanded Syria and an expanded Egypt on his frontiers than by the emergence of a small Jewish state. Abdullah and Glubb desisted from an offensive strategy against the embattled Jewish state during the crucial 15 May–11 June period. Abdullah neither expected nor planned for Israel's demise; nor were the Arab Legion's operations from May onwards designed to bring this about.[12]

As to the other Arab states' hopes, objectives, plans, roles, and operations during the invasion of Palestine / Israel, Shlaim and Pappe are not completely clear. And, so long as the Arab states' archives remain closed to researchers, it is doubtful whether a clear, definitive conclusion on these matters is at all possible. Was the primary aim of Egypt, Iraq, Syria, and Lebanon in invading to overrun the Yishuv and destroy the Jewish state or was it merely or mainly to frustrate or curtail Abdullah's territorial ambitions and to acquire some territory for themselves? Or did they have both these aims—destroying Israel and frustrating Abdullah—in mind? Or were they motivated to invade mainly by a desire to appease internal pressures or expected internal pressures to come to the aid of the Palestinian brothers and to fend off threats to their own regimes stemming from this pro-Palestinian ground-swell?

Flapan argues firmly, but without evidence, that 'the invasion . . . was not aimed at destroying the Jewish state'. Shlaim and Pappe are more cautious. Shlaim writes that the Arab armies intended to bisect the Jewish state and, if possible, 'occupy Haifa and Tel Aviv'

---

[12] Uri Bar-Joseph, *The Best of Enemies, Israel and Transjordan in the War of 1948* (London, 1987), 240–5.

or 'crippl[e] the Jewish state'. Here, manifestly, we are talking about destruction. But Shlaim at the same time argues that the Arab states were driven to the invasion more by a desire to stymie Abdullah than by a wish to kill the Jews; and, partly for this reason, they did not properly plan the invasion. None of the Arab states, save Transjordan, committed the full weight of their military power to the enterprise—indicating either inefficiency or, perhaps, a less than wholehearted seriousness about the declared aim of driving the Jews into the sea. In any case, Transjordan frustrated the other Arabs' plans and intentions, and rendered their military preparations and planning ineffective.[13]

The Egyptian government during the months before May 1948 had consistently opposed participation in an invasion of Palestine / Israel. The army commanders maintained that the army was 'ill-equipped and ill-trained for such a formidable operation'. The public apparently felt otherwise, expecting the pan-Arab invasion of the Zionist entity to be a walkover. King Farouq eventually prevailed over the generals and his Prime Minister, Muhammad Fahmi an Nuqrashi Pasha, and ordered the army to march. Farouq 'probably hoped to be able to watch Abdullah's moves from close by while sharing the glory of liberating Arab and Islamic soil and preventing the creation of a communist-backed Zionist entity on the Egyptian border'.[14]

DAVID AND GOLIATH

One of the most tenacious myths relating to 1948 is that of 'David and Goliath'—that the Arabs were overwhelmingly stronger militarily than the Yishuv. The truth is more complex. It is true that the Jews fought during early 1948 and prepared for the 15 May Arab invasion believing and feeling that the Arab armies, if not the Palestinian irregulars, were stronger than they, were more numerous and professionally trained and led, and were better armed. And it is true that many in the Yishuv were gripped by a sense of foreboding, of vulnerability and of weakness, and that the Haganah / IDF victories

---

[13] Shlaim, *Collusion, passim.*

[14] Thomas Mayer, 'Egypt's 1948 Invasion of Palestine', *Middle Eastern Studies,* Jan. 1986. The question of the evolution down to 15 May 1948 of the Arab war plans, and their objective/s, has never been properly researched.

in the spring and summer of 1948 were greeted by many as nothing short of miraculous. And, to be sure, in certain engagements—as during the fall of the Etzion Bloc and Kibbutz Degania's repulse of the invading Syrian armoured column, both in May—the Haganah suffered from a significant inferiority in both manpower and weaponry.

But the truth—as conveyed by Milstein, Shlaim, Pappe, and my own work, and several recent Israeli military histories—is that the stronger side, in fact, won. The atlas map showing a minuscule Israel and a giant surrounding Arab sea did not, and, indeed, for the time being, still does not, accurately reflect the true balance of military power in the region. Nor do the comparative population figures; in 1948, the Yishuv numbered some 650,000 souls—as opposed to 1.2 million Palestinian Arabs and some 30 million Arabs in the surrounding states (including Iraq). The pre-May 1948 Yishuv had organized itself for statehood and war; the Palestinian Arabs, who outnumbered the Jews by two to one, had not. The Jews had perhaps not organized optimally, but they had organized. And in war organization, command, and control are almost everything.

During the first half of the war, from December 1947 to 14 May 1948, which was an admixture of a guerrilla and civil war, the Yishuv was better armed, and had more professional officers and better trained 'soldiers' than the Palestinians, whose forces were beefed up by several thousand 'volunteers' (some of them with military training) from the surrounding Arab states. The Haganah's superior organization, command, and control during these first months of war meant that at almost every decisive point of battle, the Jews fielded larger, better-armed, and better-trained formations than their Palestinian antagonists. When matters came to the test, during the Haganah offensives of April and early May, the Palestinian irregulars (and the 'volunteers') collapsed and fled, their redoubts —the Jerusalem Corridor, Tiberias, Haifa, Safad, Eastern Galilee —falling one after another, swiftly and in domino fashion. When one adds to this the Yishuv's superior motivation—it was a bare three years after the Holocaust, and the Haganah troops knew that it was do-or-die—one can see that the Palestinians never had a chance.

The old historiography is no more illuminating when it comes to the second half of the war, the conventional battles between 15 May

1948 and January 1949. Jewish organization, command, and control, reinforced by short, internal lines of communication, were clearly superior to those of the uncoordinated armies of Egypt, Syria, Iraq, and Lebanon; and throughout, the Haganah / IDF also had an edge in numbers. For example, in mid-May, the Haganah fielded some 35,000 armed troops as compared with the 25–30,000 of the Arab invading armies. By the time of Operation Dani, in July, the IDF had 65,000 men under arms and by December, close to 90,000 men under arms—at each stage significantly outnumbering the combined strength of the Arab armies ranged against them in Palestine. As opposed to the Haganah / IDF short lines of communications, the Egyptians and Iraqis had to send supplies and reinforcements over hundreds of kilometres of desert before these reached the front lines.

Two caveats must be entered here. First, Transjordan's Arab Legion was probably the best army in the war, and, man for man, was more effective than most of the Haganah / IDF units it faced. But it numbered only about 5,000 troops, and had no tanks or aircraft (though it had effective, gun-mounted, armoured cars). Second, in terms of equipment, during the crucial three weeks between the pan-Arab invasion of 15 May and the start of the First Truce on 11 June, the Arab armies had a clear edge in weaponry over the Haganah / IDF (the Haganah became the IDF on 31 May). The Haganah was much weaker in the air, had no artillery to speak of (only heavy mortars), and very few tanks and tracked vehicles. For those three weeks, it was 'fifty-fifty', as the Haganah / IDF chief of operations, Yigael Yadin, told the Yishuv's political leadership on 12 May. It was then that superior Jewish motivation, courage, and fortitude made all the difference, carried the day and stopped the invaders almost dead in their tracks. But during both the unconventional war before 15 May, and the renewed hostilities after the First Truce, it was superior Jewish firepower, manpower, organization, and command and control that determined the outcome of battle. (Throughout, the Arab edge in regular artillery was offset by the Yishuv's preponderance in mortars.)

The old histories tend to lay a great deal of emphasis on the Haganah / IDF's perennial shortages of weaponry and ammunition, in large measure due to Western arms embargoes against the Jewish state. The 1948 material from the British and American state archives and the new histories tend to balance this by highlighting the Arab states' grave arms and ammunition purchasing problems during 1948. They, too, suffered severely from intermittent or continuous arms embargoes and politically motivated delays in delivery. For example, one of the reasons the Transjordanians lost or failed to attempt to retake Lydda and Ramle in July was a severe shortage of shells for the Legion's 25-pounders.

It is worth adding to this that the Yishuv, by contrast with both the Palestinian Arabs and the surrounding Arab states, had a relatively advanced, if small, arms-production capacity. For instance, between October 1947 and July 1948, the Haganah's factories produced 3 million 9mm bullets, 150,000 Mills grenades, 16,000 Sten sub-machine-guns, and 210 3-inch mortars.[15]

THE BIRTH OF THE PALESTINIAN REFUGEE PROBLEM

Apart from the birth of the State of Israel, the major political outcome of the 1948 war was the creation of the Palestinian refugee problem. How the problem came about has been the subject of heated controversy between Israeli and Arab propagandists for the past four decades. The controversy has often been heated because it has been perceived as being as much about the nature of Zionism as about what exactly happened in 1948. If the Arab contention is true —that the Yishuv had always intended forcible 'transfer' and that in 1948 it had systematically and forcibly expelled the Arab population from the areas that became the Jewish state—then Zionism is a robber ideology and Israel a robber state. If, on the other hand, one accepts that the refugee exodus was essentially a result of the war, that the war was the handiwork of the Arabs, that the Palestinian masses fled by and large 'voluntarily' or at the behest of their leaders, then Israel emerges free of the taint of what some have called original sin.

In tackling the subject of the exodus historiographically, I can see no escape from recourse to my book, *The Birth of the Palestinian Refugee Problem, 1947–1949*. The only book that previously dealt with the subject in a relatively serious manner was Rony Gabbay's *A Political Study of the Arab–Jewish Conflict: The Arab Refugee Problem (a Case Study)* (Geneva and Paris, 1959). Gabbay's study,

[15] Morris, *The Birth*, p. 22.

while pioneering, inevitably suffered from 'prematurity' in the sense that the author had almost no access to contemporary (1948) documentation and perforce had to rely largely on newspaper accounts and a handful of memoirs to describe and explain the exodus. As the subject was highly sensitive, both the newspaper accounts and the recollections of participants, many of them politicians, on whom Gabbay had to rely tended to be polemical and partisan rather than factual, tendentious rather than objective or illuminating. When taking this crucial factor into account, Gabbay's study stands out as a remarkable achievement.

However, the contemporary Israeli, British, and American documentation declassified during the past few years now enables the historian to arrive at a much fuller and more accurate description and explanation of what happened. As I have set out in great detail in *The Birth*, what occurred in 1948 lies somewhere in between the Jewish 'robber state' and the 'Arab orders' explanations. While from the mid-1930s most of the Yishuv's leaders, including Ben-Gurion, wanted to establish a Jewish state without an Arab minority, or with as small an Arab minority as possible, and supported a 'transfer solution' to this minority problem, the Yishuv did not enter the 1948 war with a master plan for expelling the Arabs, nor did its political and military leaders ever adopt such a master plan. What happened was largely haphazard and a result of the war. There were Haganah / IDF expulsions of Arab communities, some of them at the initiative or with the *post facto* approval of the cabinet or the defence minister, and most with General Staff sanction—such as the expulsions from Miska and Ad Dumeira in April; from Zarnuqa, Al Qubeiba, and Huj in May; from Lydda and Ramle in July; and from the Lebanese border area (Kafr Bir'im, Iqrit, Al Mansura, Tarbikha, Suruh, and Nabi Rubin) in early November. But there was no grand design, no blanket policy of expulsion. The best illustration of this, perhaps, is the haphazardness of what happened in the Upper Galilee in late October and early November of 1948.

At the same time, at no point during the war did the Arab leaders issue a blanket call to Palestine's Arabs to leave their homes and villages and wander into exile. Nor was there an Arab radio and press campaign urging or ordering the Palestinians to flee. Indeed, I have found no trace of such a campaign, and had it taken place, had there been such broadcasts, they would have been quoted or at least left traces in the documentation. The Yishuv's intelligence services (the Shai, the Arab Division of the Jewish Agency Political Department, the IDF Intelligence Service, and the Foreign Ministry Middle East Affairs and Research Departments) and the British and American Middle East diplomatic posts all monitored Arab radio broadcasts. So did the BBC. But none of these, in the thousands of monitoring reports, ever refer to, let alone cite from, such an alleged broadcast. Not even once.

Indeed, in early May 1948, when, according to Israeli propaganda and some of the old histories, such a campaign of broadcasts urging or ordering the Arabs to leave should have been at its height, in preparation for the pan-Arab invasion, Arab radio stations and leaders (Radio Ramallah, Radio Damascus, King Abdullah, and Arab Liberation Army chief Fawzi al Qawuqji) all issued calls, in repeated broadcasts, to the Palestinians to stay put or, if already in exile, to return to their homes. Reference to and quotations from these broadcasts appear in a number of Haganah, Mapam, and British documents from early May 1948.

Certainly, local Arab commanders and politicians in a number of areas and on certain occasions ordered the evacuation of women and children from war zones or potential war zones. This happened in areas of East Jerusalem, and in certain villages in the Coastal Plain and in the Galilee in April and May. Less frequently, as happened in Haifa on 22 April, the local Arab leaders advised or instructed their communities to leave rather than stay in a potential war zone or 'treacherously' remain under Jewish rule. But there were no blanket Arab orders or campaigns to leave, neither by the Palestinian national leadership, the Arab Higher Committee, nor by the leaders of the neighbouring Arab states.

Rather, in order to understand the exodus of the 600,000–760,000 Arabs from the areas that became post-1948 Israel, one must look to a variety of related processes and causes.

What happened in Haifa is illustrative of the complexity of the exodus. The evacuation of Haifa's 70,000 Arabs (the city had about an equal number of Jews), as from the other main Palestinian centres, Jaffa and Jerusalem, began in December 1947 with the start of sporadic hostilities between neighbouring Jewish and Arab districts. The exodus slowly gained momentum during the following months as the British Mandate administration began to wind down and prepare for withdrawal from Palestine. The first to leave were the rich and the educated—the middle and upper classes with money to stay in hotels or with second homes on the Beirut seafront, in Nablus and in Amman, or with comfortably-off relatives abroad with large homes. The Palestinians' political and economic leadership disappeared. By mid-April, the bulk of the members of the National Committees of Haifa and Jaffa had left the country. By mid-May, only one member of the Arab Higher Committee (Dr Husayn Fakhri al Khalidi, of Jerusalem) was still in the country.

The gradual flight of the professionals, the civil servants, the businessmen, the traders and the shopkeepers, the doctors and lawyers and chemists, over December 1947–April 1948 had a cumulative, harsh impact on the Haifa Arab masses, who were at the same time demoralized by the incessant sniping and bomb attacks, by the interdiction of supply and reinforcement convoys, by price rises and unemployment, by the feeling that the Jews were stronger (and held the dominant, high ground), and by the sense that their own ragtag militia would fail when the test came (as, indeed, it did). The Arabs felt isolated and insecure, at the mercy of their neighbours up the Carmel and of the kibbutzim lying astride the city's approach roads. The impending British evacuation and the dissolution of British-led government bred an all-pervading fear of the future. Businesses, shops, and workshops closed, policemen shed their uniforms and left their posts, Arab workers could no longer commute to jobs in the Jewish districts, and agricultural produce was occasionally interdicted in ambushes on the approach roads. There was increasing unemployment and there were sharp price-increases. By mid-April, some 15,000–20,000 Arabs, apparently, had left the city.

Then came the Haganah assault on the Arab districts of 21–2 April. Several companies of Carmeli Brigade troops (supported by a company of Palmahniks), under cover of a constant mortar barrage, drove down the Carmel Mountain slopes into the Arab downtown areas. Arab militia resistance collapsed. Thousands of Arabs fled from the attacked outlying neighbourhoods (Wadi Rushmiya, Halissa) into the British-controlled port area, piled into boats, and fled northwards, to Acre. In their passage through the central Arab areas—Wadi Nisnas, Wadi Salib, the Suq—the refugees from the outlying neighbourhoods spread 'flight fever' among the downtown-district Arabs. The local leaders who remained sued for a ceasefire. Under British mediation, the Haganah agreed, offering what the British regarded as generous terms. But then, when faced with Moslem pressure, the largely Christian leadership got cold feet; a ceasefire meant surrender and implied readiness to live under Jewish rule. They would be open to charges of collaboration and treachery. So, to the astonishment of the British and the Jewish military and political leaders gathered on the afternoon of 22 April at the Haifa town hall, the Arab delegation announced that its community would evacuate the city.

The Jewish mayor, Shabtai Levy, and the British commander, Major-General Hugh Stockwell, pleaded with the Arabs to reconsider; the joint Jewish–Arab municipality had functioned amicably and efficiently for decades. The Haganah representative, Mordechai Makleff (whose parents had been butchered by Arab rioters in 1929), declined to voice an opinion. But the Arabs were unmoved, and the mass exodus, which had begun already during the morning under the impact of the Haganah mortars and ground assault, moved into top gear, with the British supplying boats (Z-craft) and an armoured-car escort to the departing Arab convoys. From 22 April to 1 May, almost all the Arab population departed the city. The rough treatment—temporary evictions, house-to-house searches, detentions of able-bodied males, and occasional beatings—meted out to the remaining population during that week by the Haganah and the Irgun Zva'i Leumi (IZL) troops who occupied the downtown areas led many of the undecided also to opt for evacuation. By early May, the city's Arab population had dwindled to three or four thousand.

In some respects, the experience of Arab Haifa was unrepresentative: Nowhere else in the country in April, or later, did Jewish leaders plead with their Arab neighbours to stay put; only in a few other places (Tiberias, Qumiya) did the British military assist the Arabs to evacuate; in few places was there an organized, considered decision by the local leadership to evacuate. But in most major respects, Haifa was typical: the middle-class flight months before the assault; the growing, general sense of insecurity; the expanding unemployment and the rising food prices; the cowardly disappearance before and during the battle of the local leaders; the mass flight under the impact and largely as a result of the Haganah assault.

The bulk of the Palestinian refugees—some 250,000–300,000— went into exile during those weeks between April and mid-June 1948, with the major precipitant being (Haganah / IDF or IZL) military attack or fears of such attack. In most cases, the Jewish commanders, who preferred to occupy empty villages (occupying populated villages meant necessarily leaving behind a garrison, which the units could ill afford to do), were hardly ever confronted with the decision whether or not to expel an overrun community: most villages and towns simply emptied at the first whiff of grapeshot.

In conformity with *Tochnit Dalet* (Plan D), the Haganah's master plan, formulated in March 1948, for securing the Jewish state areas in preparation for the expected declaration of statehood and the prospective Arab invasion, the Haganah cleared various areas completely of Arab villages—the Jerusalem corridor, the area around Mishmar Ha'emek, and the coastal plain. But in most cases, expulsion orders were unnecessary; the inhabitants had already fled, out of fear or as a result of Jewish attack. In several areas, Israeli commanders successfully used psychological warfare ploys to obtain Arab evacuation (as in the Hula Valley, in Upper Galilee, in May).

The basic structural weaknesses of Palestinian society led to the dissolution of the society when the test of battle came. Lack of administrative structures for self-rule, as well as weak leaders, poor or non-existent military organization beyond the single-village level, and faulty or non-existent taxation mechanisms, all caused the main towns to fall apart in April–May, as the British withdrew and the Haganah attacked. The fall of the towns and the exodus from them, in turn, caused fear and despondency in the rural hinterlands. Traditionally, the villages, though economically autarchic, had looked to the towns for political leadership and guidance. The evacuation by the urban middle classes and leaders (who often owned lands in the countryside and had rural origins), as well as the fall of the towns, provided the Palestinian villagers with an example to emulate. Safad's fall and evacuation on 10–11 May, for example, triggered an immediate evacuation of the surrounding Arab villages; so, earlier, did the fall of Haifa and the IZL assault on Jaffa.

Seen from the Jewish side, the spectacle of mass Arab evacuation certainly whetted appetites for more of the same. Everyone, at every level of military and political decision-making, understood that a Jewish state without a large Arab minority would be stronger and more viable both militarily and politically. The tendency of local military commanders to 'nudge' Palestinians into flight increased as the war went on. Jewish atrocities—far more widespread than the old histories have let on (there were massacres of Arabs at Ad Dawayima, Eilaboun, Jish, Safsaf, Majd al Kurum, Hule (in Lebanon), Saliha, and Sasa, besides Deir Yassin and Lydda and other places)—also contributed significantly to the exodus.

FAILED PEACE EFFORTS

The last major myth tackled incidentally or directly by the new historians concerns an Israel that in 1948 and 1949 was bent on making peace with its neighbours, and an Arab world that mono-lithically rejected all such peace efforts.

The evidence that Israel's leaders were not desperate to make peace and were unwilling to make the large concessions necessary to give peace a chance is overwhelming. In Tel Aviv there was a sense of triumph and drunkenness with victory—a feeling that the Arabs would 'soon' or 'eventually' sue for peace, that there was no need to rush things or offer concessions, that ultimately military victory and dominance would translate into diplomatic-political success (peace).

As Ben-Gurion told an American journalist in mid-July, 1949: 'I am prepared to get up in the middle of the night in order to sign a peace agreement—but I am not in a hurry and I can wait ten years. We are under no pressure whatsoever.'[16] Or, as Ben-Gurion records Abba Eban, Israel's ambassador to the UN, saying: '[Eban] sees no need to run after peace. The armistice is sufficient for us; if we run after peace, the Arabs will demand a price of us—borders [that is, in terms of territory] or refugees [that is, repatriation] or both. Let us wait a few years.'[17]

---

[16] Quoted in Shlaim, *Collusion*, p. 465.
[17] David Ben-Gurion, *Yoman Hamilhama-Tashah* [the war diary 1948–9], ed. Gershon Rivlin and Elhannan Orren (Tel Aviv, 1982) iii, 993.

As Pappe puts it:

Abdullah's eagerness [to make peace] was not reciprocated by the Israelis. The priorities of the state of Israel had changed during 1949. The armistice agreements brought relative calm to the borders, and peace was no longer the first priority. The government was preoccupied with absorbing new immigrants and overcoming economic difficulties.[18]

Israel's tergiversation or lack of urgency regarding peace was manifested most clearly in the protracted (1948–51) secret negotiations with Abdullah. Israeli Foreign Minister Moshe Sharett thus described his meeting with Transjordan's king at the palace in Shuneh on 5 May 1949: 'Transjordan said—we are ready for peace immediately. We said—certainly, we too want peace but one shouldn't rush, one should walk.'[19]

Israel and Transjordan eventually signed an armistice agreement, on 3 April 1949. But it had involved a great deal of brow-beating and arm-twisting by Israel (which, with unmerited exaggeration, British and American observers likened to Hitler's treatment of the Czechs in 1938–9). Abdullah took it realistically: 'If you meet a bear when crossing a rotten bridge, call her "Dear Auntie"', he said, quoting a Turkish adage. But the two countries never signed a peace treaty or a non-belligerency pact, as was suggested by Abdullah at one point.

Shlaim, who in *Collusion* considerably expands the description of the secret Israeli–Transjordanian negotiations first covered in Dan Shueftan's *Optziya Yardenit* (Jordanian Option), published in 1986, more or less lays the blame for the failed talks on Israel's shoulders. At one point, it is true, Shlaim writes: 'Two principal factors were responsible for the failure of the post-war negotiations: Israel's strength and Abdullah's weakness.'[20] But more often, Shlaim attributes more weight to the former and less to the latter, and the reader comes away with the clear impression of overwhelming Israeli responsibility for the failure. Israel refused to offer major concessions in terms of refugee repatriation or territory (Abdullah was particularly keen on getting back Lydda and Ramle)

[18] Pappe, *Britain and the Arab–Israeli Conflict*, 188.
[19] ISA, *Documents on the Foreign Policy of Israel, May–December 1949*, iv. 68, 'M. Sharett's Address at a Meeting of the Heads of Divisions in the Ministry of Foreign Affairs (Tel Aviv, 25 May 1949)'.
[20] Shlaim, *Collusion*, p. 621.

and was for too long unwilling to offer Jordan a sovereign corridor through its territory to the sea at Gaza (or Ashkelon). Throughout, says Shlaim, Israel was prodded if not guided by the 'blatant expansionism' of some of Ben-Gurion's aides, such as Moshe Dayan. As one of Dayan's colleagues, Yehoshafat Harkabi, later put it: 'The existential mission of the State of Israel led us to be demanding and acquisitive, and mindful of the value of every square metre of land.'[21] Ben-Gurion declined to meet with Abdullah and often the Hashemite monarch was spoken of in Tel Aviv with undeserved contempt.

Yet while all this was true, Shlaim fails sufficiently to acknowledge the importance of the 'Palestinization' of Jordan following the Hashemite annexation of the West Bank, which quickly resulted in the curtailment of Abdullah's decision-making autonomy and of his freedom of political movement both within Jordan and in the pan-Arab arena. The twin pressures exercised by his successive cabinets in Amman and by the Arab world outside successfully impeded Abdullah's ability to make a separate peace with Israel. He almost did so a number of times, but always he held back at the last moment and declined to take the plunge. It is possible, argues Shlaim, that more generous, up-front concessions by Tel Aviv at certain critical points in the negotiations would have given Abdullah greater motivation to pursue peace as well as the ammunition he needed to silence his anti-peace critics, but one will never know. What is certain is that Abdullah, though showing remarkable courage throughout, simply proved unable during his last years to go against the unanimous or near-unanimous wishes of his ministers and against the unanimous or near-unanimous anti-peace stance of the surrounding Arab world.

What happened with Abdullah occurred in miniature and more briefly with Egypt and Syria. During September–October 1948, Egypt's King Farouq, knowing that the war was lost, secretly sent a senior court official to Paris to sound out Israel on the possibility of reaching a peace based on Israeli cession of all or parts of the Negev and of recognition of Egyptian annexation of the Gaza Strip. Sharett and his senior Foreign Ministry advisers favoured continued negotiations, but Ben-Gurion flatly rejected the overtures. The

<hr>

[21] Shlaim, *Collusion*, pp. 444–5.

Cabinet on 6 October had voted for a renewed push against the Egyptians in the Negev and Ben-Gurion did not want possibly inconsequential peace talks to put a spoke in the wheels of the planned military offensive (Operation Yoav, which was launched on 15 October, and which resulted in the IDF punching a broad hole through the Egyptian-held Gaza–Faluja–Hebron line and relieving the Egyptian siege of Israel's two dozen Negev kibbutzim). It is possible that Farouq had ordered the peace feelers specifically in order to prevent Israel from launching the offensive rather than out of any real desire or intention to make a separate peace with the Jewish state.

Shlaim summarizes the episode thus: '[Ben-Gurion] may have been right in thinking that nothing of substance would come out of these talks. But he surely owed his cabinet colleagues at least a report on what had taken place so that they could review their decision [of 6 October] to go to war against Egypt on the basis of all the relevant information.'[22] New Egyptian peace feelers in November, in the middle of Operation Yoav, again came to nought as a result of Ben-Gurion's veto.

As for Syria, in May 1949 its new ruler, Colonel Husni Za'im, made major peace proposals which included recognition of Israel as well as Syrian readiness to absorb hundreds of thousands of Palestinian refugees. Za'im wanted Israel to concede a sliver of territory along the Jordan River (and perhaps half the Sea of Galilee). He asked to meet with Ben-Gurion. Ben-Gurion rejected the proposal, writing on 12 May:

'I am quite prepared to meet Colonel Za'im in order to promote peace . . . But I see no purpose in any such meeting so long as the representatives of Syria in the armistice negotiations do not declare in an unequivocal manner that their forces are prepared to withdraw to their pre-war territory' (that is, withdraw from the small Syrian-occupied Mishmar Ha'Yarden salient, west of the Jordan).[23]

Continued feelers, via the UN, by Za'im resulted again in Israeli stonewalling. As Sharett put it on 25 May: 'It is clear that we . . . won't agree that any bit of the Land of Israel be transferred to Syria,

---

[22] Shlaim, *Collusion*, p. 320.
[23] ISA, *Documents on the Foreign Policy of Israel*, iii. 563, R. Shiloah to R. Bunche, 12 May 1949.

because this is a question of control over the water sources [of the Jordan River].'[24] Za'im declined to meet Sharett and reiterated his wish to meet 'only [the] Prime Minister'.[25] Shabtai Rosenne, the legal adviser at the Israel Foreign Ministry, put it simply: 'I feel that the need for an agreement between Israel and Syria pressed more heavily on the Syrians.'[26] Therefore, why rush towards peace? A few weeks later Za'im was overthrown and executed; the Syrian peace initiative died with him. Whether the overture was serious or merely tactical—to obtain Israeli territorial concessions in the armistice agreement, or to obtain Western support and funds for his shaky regime—is unclear. What is certain is that Israel failed wholeheartedly or even half-heartedly to pursue it.

What was true of Israel's bilateral contacts with each of the main Arab states was true also of its negotiations with the Arab states under UN auspices at Lausanne in the spring and summer of 1949. There, the Arab states all too often exhibited obdurate, unconciliatory, and unrealistic positions, lining up, in a show of singular behaviour, behind the most extreme of their number. The Arabs spoke of a repatriation of all the refugees and a return to the 1947 partition borders, or worse; a few delegates—the Transjordanians, for example—in private spoke of a return of 'only' 400,000 refugees.

But Israel, too, proved ungenerous and unconciliatory. For months, UN and US officials pressed Tel Aviv to make a 'saving' gesture, a redemptive concession: to proclaim its willingness to take back 200,000–250,000 refugees; the Arabs would then be persuaded to take and resettle the rest. The months dragged on and neither side budged. When, under intense US–UN prodding, Israel at last offered to take back '100,000' (which, in reality was only 65,000, as Sharett explained to his colleagues), it was a clear case of 'too little, too late'. And Israel's more realistic offer, to accept the Gaza Strip

---

[24] ISA, *Documents on the Foreign Policy of Israel*, iv. 69, 'M. Sharett's Address at a Meeting of the Heads of Divisions in the Ministry of Foreign Affairs (Tel Aviv, 25 May 1949)'.
[25] ISA, *Documents on the Foreign Policy of Israel*, iii. 592, Shiloah to Sharett, 31 May 1949.
[26] ISA, *Documents on the Foreign Policy of Israel*, iii. 582, S. Rosenne to D. Ben-Gurion and M. Sharett, 18 May 1949. The most comprehensive review of the evidence concerning the Za'im peace initiative of 1949 is to be found in Arye Shalev, *Shituf Pe'ula Betzel Imut* [co-operation under the shadow of conflict] (Tel Aviv, 1989), 49–65. Shalev, like Shlaim, is critical of Israel's lack of eagerness in responding to the Za'im initiative.

along with its 200,000-odd refugees, was never seriously entertained by Egypt. So the prospect of a comprehensive Israeli–Arab peace was buried at Lausanne for at least forty years.[27]

There are people who use history to prove political points and buttress contemporary political positions; there are others who would brandish history in the service of present-day peacemaking. For myself, I am not sure that writing history serves any purpose or should serve any purpose that strays beyond the covers of each book and beyond the desire of practitioners and readers to penetrate the murk of the past. I am fairly confident that the new Israeli historiography—and I am not sure that it has a Palestinian counterpart—has succeeded, at least to some degree, in penetrating that murk and illuminating it to a degree never before attained, and that a more accurate and realistic understanding of the roots of the Israeli–Arab conflict is now emerging.

ADDENDA

October 1989

The publication of my *Birth of the Palestinian Refugee Problem, 1947–1949*, of Shlaim's *Collusion Across the Jordan*, and of the original version of this article on the New Historiography in the American Jewish bi-monthly *Tikkun* (issue of November–December 1988) triggered a major controversy in Israeli and Diaspora-Jewish academic circles. The New Historiography was roundly discussed in a two-day conference at Tel Aviv University in April 1989, and was comprehensively attacked in a series of articles (about 20,000 words *in toto*) by Ben-Gurion's biographer, Shabtai Teveth, in the Israeli daily *Ha'aretz* on 7, 14, and 21 April and 19 May 1989. My reply appeared in *Ha'aretz* on 9 May, with a short addendum in early June. Teveth subsequently published an abridged, amended version of the series in the American monthly, *Commentary*, in September 1989.

Several of the speakers at the TAU conference said that the historiography in question could not properly be referred to as New History (comparable, say, to the New History recently in vogue in France) as it did not offer a new outlook on history or new tools or areas of historical research but simply constituted a new interpretation within the bounds of traditional historiography. One generally sympathetic critic, Professor Yehoshua Porath of

---

[27] See Morris, *The Birth*, chap. 9, *passim*.

the Hebrew University, suggested that instead of contrasting New Historiography with Old Historiography, it would be more accurate to speak of
plain History versus Pre-History: what is currently being written in Israel is
History, said Porath, whereas in the 1950s, 1960s, and 1970s what was
written, by and large, was Pre-History. I have no objection to Porath's
suggested definitions or re-definitions.

Professor Itamar Rabinovich, of Tel Aviv University's Dayan Centre,
argued that peace agreements with the Arab states were not reached in the
immediate wake of the 1948 war not because of Israeli tergiversation or
intractability but essentially because of Arab 'rejectionism' and intransigence.
Rabinovich attacked Shlaim's claim that it was Israeli obduracy that
stymied the peace process with Abdullah during 1949–51 and that it was
Israeli indifference that frustrated Syrian President Za'im's pacific overtures in
mid-1949. Za'im, who only ruled Syria for four months, was a lightweight
who could not have carried through a peace process even had he been
serious—and his overtures do not appear to have been serious, argued
Rabinovich.

Shlaim responded that Israel had not been conciliatory enough or quick
enough with its concessions in the negotiations with Jordan and that this was a
key element in the failure of the talks before Abdullah's assassination. As
to Za'im, argued Shlaim, while it is not clear whether Za'im's overtures had
been serious, Israel should have vigorously pursued them if only to test the
Syrian leader's sincerity. Ben-Gurion and Sharett failed to do this, as they
had failed to pursue earlier peace feelers put out by Egypt in September and
November 1948.

To turn to Teveth's articles. Teveth attacks the New Historiography on
both political and historiographic grounds. He maintains that one of the
characteristics of the 'new historical club . . . is a sympathy somewhat
inclined to the side of the Palestinians'—or, to put it more simply, the new
historians are pro-Palestinian. Moreover, says Teveth, their aim is to
'deligitimise Zionism'. To demonstrate this, Teveth quotes from my original
Tikkun essay a passage stating that 'how one perceives 1948 bears heavily
on how one perceives the whole Zionist / Israeli experience . . . If Israel
was born tarnished, besmirched by original sin, then it was no more
deserving' of Western sympathy and aid than its Arab neighbours. Teveth
goes on to say that the 'original sin' Shlaim and Morris charge Israel with
consists of 'the denial to the Palestinian Arabs of a country' or state, and
'creating the refugee problem'. Both charges, says Teveth, 'are false'.

Later in the article Teveth quotes from a favourable reference to my book
by Professor Edward Said, the Columbia University English literature
teacher, PLO propagandist, and member of the Palestine National Council.
Damning by association. The new history, concludes Teveth, is bent on

'providing fresh sources of political sympathy for the Arabs and fresh sources of antipathy to the Jews'. Ultimately, what Teveth is saying is that the new Israeli historiography is unpatriotic or anti-patriotic and is serving Arab or Palestinian Arab political ends.

My response to this, in *Ha'aretz* and in a second article in *Tikkun*, 'The Eel and History: A Reply to Shabtai Teveth' (January–February 1990), was that the New Historiography, as far as I was concerned, had no political purposes whatsoever. The task and function of the historian, in my view, is to illuminate the past—to describe what happened and explain why things happened as they did, taking account of the motives and considerations of the various protagonists. In *The Birth of the Palestinian Refugee Problem, 1947–1949* I tried to describe and explain how the refugee problem was created. I evinced no sympathy for either side—indeed, the portrayal of the Palestinians, many Palestinians of my acquaintance have told me, is far from flattering—though I tried to explain why each side acted as it did during the prolonged process. If anything, most of my readers probably came away with the feeling that both Jews and Palestinian Arabs acted in an almost inevitable, understandable manner and, in the circumstances of 1948, could probably have acted no differently. I did not try or aim to delegitimize Zionism, which I regard as legitimate a national movement as the next one. Perhaps a world without nationalism would be a pleasanter place to live in; or perhaps not. In any event, Zionism's claim to legitimacy is as cogent as that of most national movements and, given the background of the Holocaust and the circumstances of 1948, was certainly more pressing and immediate than most.

In *The Birth* I rendered no moral or value judgements. I used the terms 'pure', 'innocent', and 'original sin' in the *Tikkun* article to explain not history or my own views but how others—specifically Israeli and Arab propagandists, who have over the decades viewed the conflict in black and white—have regarded the Arab–Israeli conflict and 1948. *The Birth*, one might say, occupies the grey, rather than the moral, high ground.

The possibility that his findings and conclusions might subsequently be used by propagandists and politicians of this or that ilk is surely no concern of the historian. If he begins to 'streamline' his descriptions, analyses, or conclusions according to this or that contemporary political calculation, sensibility, or interest, he will produce less, perhaps far less, than unbiased, impartial history. The historian must be judged according to the degree of accuracy and understanding he has achieved regarding the past—nothing else.

Teveth's 'political' objections and views seem to underlie his 'historio-graphic / professional' critique of the New Historiography in general and *The Birth* in particular.

The focus of Teveth's criticism of *The Birth* is on the causation of the Arab exodus from Palestine up until 15 May 1948. He writes in *Commentary*: 'before the invasion [of Palestine by the Arab armies on 15 May] the Palestinian Arabs were seen [by the Yishuv], for the most part, as citizens of a future Jewish state; after it, as declared enemies. Accordingly one may properly speak, in the former period, of an Arab flight, and in the latter of expulsion by Israel.'

To explain the flight up to 15 May Teveth quotes from a speech by Ben-Gurion in the Knesset on 11 October 1961:

> The Arabs' exit from Palestine . . . began immediately after the UN [partition] resolution . . . And we have explicit documents testifying that they left Palestine following instructions by the Arab leaders, with the Mufti at their head, under the assumption that the invasion of the Arab armies . . . would destroy the Jewish state and push all the Jews into the sea . . .

Teveth goes on to cite from the single piece of evidence he found—he refers to 'one [document] in particular', hinting that other, similar ones exist—that supports his (and Ben-Gurion's avowed) view that the Arabs of Palestine who fled their home, villages, and towns before 15 May (about half the total that left the country during the war) did so on instructions from their leaders. The document, the 'Haganah Intelligence Service Daily Report' of 24 April 1948, states: 'Rumours have it that the Arab Higher Committee in Jerusalem ordered the evacuation of Arabs from several localities in Palestine . . . Arab residents are advised to flee Palestine as soon as possible, and after its fall into the hands of the Arab governments, they will be returned as victors.'

Earlier, Teveth quotes from other Haganah intelligence reports that refer to specific orders by Arab leaders and commanders to a handful of villages to evacuate and to other orders to several local councils to evacuate women and children from combat zones or potential combat zones. (These documents are all cited and quoted from in *The Birth*.)

All this evidence, taken together, shows, according to Teveth (in *Commentary*) that 'the Arab exodus from Palestine . . . was all the work of instruction, whether by personal example, by word of mouth, or in writing, or even better, by the quickest telegraph of all, rumour.' (This formulation first appeared in Teveth's article in *Ha'aretz* of 14 April. Interestingly, after I had taken him to task for its relative obscurity and imprecision (which enabled Teveth to avow the 'Arab orders' explanation for the exodus without saying so clearly), Teveth abridged it somewhat, writing in *Ha'aretz* on 19 May that the Arab flight before 15 May had been precipitated by 'an order by personal example' (implying, apparently, that the Arab flight had been triggered by the exemplary flight of their local leaders and that this was tantamount to an order to flee by the Arab leadership).

In my rebuttal (in *Ha'aretz*, 9 May 1989, and in *Tikkun*, January–February 1990) of Teveth's explanation of the first half of the Arab exodus, I argued or, rather, reiterated that the exodus had been a complex, multi-staged phenomenon which had included, among its causes, the innate weaknesses of Palestinian Arab society (poor leadership and a lack of governmental structures, poor military organization and lack of self-confidence); material privations (rocketing prices and mass unemployment), in part stemming from the widening circle of hostilities; the gradual devolution of British rule and the spreading breakdown of law and order, especially in the towns and cities; a general fear of the future and a specific fear of Jewish conquest and rule; the earlier, demoralizing departure of the Arab middle class and the élite, including, in many cases, their local political and military leaders; actual and feared atrocities; Arab orders to specific communities to evacuate; specific Jewish expulsion orders; and Haganah / IDF assault and conquest or fears of imminent Jewish assault. I argued that this final cause—Jewish assault and conquest—was in most cases the main and final precipitant to flight.

In refuting Teveth's single-cause ('Arab orders') explanation of the exodus up to 15 May, I pointed out that there is simply no evidence to support it, and that the single document Teveth is able to cite, the Haganah report of 24 April, refers explicitly to 'rumours' and to an order to 'several localities' (rather than a blanket order to 'the Arabs of Palestine'). Moreover, neither these 'rumours' nor the purported order were referred to again in any subsequent Haganah intelligence reports (which surely would have been the case had these 'rumours' been confirmed and had an actual order been picked up). The fact is that the opposite occurred: Haganah intelligence and Western diplomatic missions in the Middle East at this time, around 5–6 May 1948, picked up, recorded, and quoted from Arab orders and appeals (by King Abdullah, Arab Liberation Army Commander Fawzi Qawuqji, and Damascus Radio) to the Arabs of Palestine to stay put in their homes or, if already in exile, to return to Palestine. Not evidence of 'Arab orders' to flee but of Arab orders to stay put during those crucial pre-invasion weeks are what one finds in Israeli and Western archives.

But Teveth's thesis is defective not merely because of a lack of evidence. It flies in the face of the chronology, which there is no getting around. There was an almost universal one-to-one correspondence between Jewish attacks in specific localities and on specific towns and Arab flight from these localities and towns. Tiberias was attacked by the Golani Brigade on 17 April; its Arab population evacuated on 18 April. Arab Haifa was attacked and defeated on 21–2 April; most of its 70,000 Arab inhabitants, evacuated the city over 22 April–1 May. Jaffa was assaulted by the Irgun Zva'i Leumi on 25–7 April; the bulk of its 70,000–80,000 population fled the city between

25 April and 13 May. Safad was attacked and conquered by the Palmah on 9–10 May; its Arab population of 10,000 fled the city on 10 May. Eastern Galilee was conquered by Palmah units between 2 May and 25 May; the villages in the area decamped during that period. And so on.

What this means is that Haganah / Irgun / IDF attack was usually the principal and final precipitant of Arab flight. Had, as Teveth argues, a general Arab order or series of orders been the cause and precipitant of flight, the flight would necessarily have occurred hard upon the issuance and publication of that order or series of orders. But the staggered, highly localized nature of the Arab flight from each area wreaks havoc with any such thesis. For if the Arab order / orders had been issued on 10 April, why did the inhabitants of Haifa wait a fortnight, and those of Safad or Eastern Galilee a month and more to depart? And if the order was issued, say, on 25 April, why did the inhabitants of Tiberias depart a week earlier, and those of Haifa begin to depart three days before; or those of Safad wait a further fortnight before leaving? And if the order was only issued on 5 May, why did the inhabitants of Tiberias, Jaffa, Haifa, and the Jerusalem Corridor depart or begin to depart weeks and days before and those of Safad only a week later? And so on.

Teveth could, theoretically, argue that the Arab order or orders to evacuate were issued at or around a specific date, but the Arab inhabitants in some localities pre-empted the order, and in others ignored the order and delayed their departure until the Jews attacked. But this would mean, simply, that the Arab flight was not caused or precipitated by the order / orders.

But the fact is that there was no order / series of orders and there was no co-ordinated, unified exodus from Palestine around a specific date: there was a cumulative process, there were interlocking causes, and there was a main precipitant, a *coup de grâce*, in the form of Haganah / Irgun / IDF assault in each locality.

Teveth, for some reason, dislikes my division of the exodus into four stages—Stage I, December 1947–March 1948; Stage II, April–June 1948; Stage III, July 1948; and Stage IV, October–November 1948. Unfortunately, the flight occurred in these stages, which were defined and circumscribed by the various stages of the war and, from April 1948, by the successive Haganah / IDF offensives, with periods of truce in between. Teveth also charges that I did not divine 'patterns' in the Arab flight—which is nonsense. Hundreds of pages of *The Birth* describe these patterns in great detail (the 'domino' phenomenon, of flight from one village precipitating flight from a neighbouring village; flight from central towns and cities provoking flight from satellite villages; the flight-inducing effects of atrocities; and so on).

Teveth in his articles also attacked my portrait of Ben-Gurion, as he emerges from the pages of *The Birth*. He would have the Yishuv's leader a benign father-figure, slow to anger, who was only propelled into animosity towards the Palestinian Arabs by the 15 May pan-Arab invasion. The truth is somewhat different. Early on Ben-Gurion understood that the prospective Arab minority represented the major, existential threat to a future Jewish state; and he understood, from at least the mid-1930s (as traced in Teveth's own *Ben-Gurion and the Palestinian Arabs*), that the Palestinians were implacably opposed to the emergence of a Jewish state in Palestine and would resist it to the hilt. So, already from 1937 we find Ben-Gurion (and most of the other Zionist leaders) supporting a 'transfer' solution to the 'Arab problem'. (This too is traced in Teveth's *Ben-Gurion and the Palestinian Arabs*, as well as in *The Birth*, pp. 23–8).

Come 1948, and the confusions and displacement of war, we see Ben-Gurion quickly grasp the opportunity for 'Judaizing' the emergent Jewish state. Certainly, he understood the requirements of statesmanship—continued lip service to the enlightened ideas of Western Democracy and Socialist Humanism and the necessity to hide traces of behaviour that others might construe as immoral or hard-hearted. But he also understood that one could not make an omelette without breaking eggs, Arab eggs. So he nudged his officers and officials in the right direction and, in the course of battle, most of the country emptied of its original Arab inhabitants.

Ben-Gurion was certainly a real-politician—devious, sly, and wise, resolute, single-minded, and ruthless: or what, in fact, history requires of successful nation-builders. No responsible Yishuv leader, in the dire straits of post-Holocaust 1948, would or could have acted otherwise. Teveth would have us believe in Ben-Gurion the lily-livered, soft-hearted liberal. But this wasn't Ben-Gurion; certainly not Ben-Gurion in 1948.

Teveth, in *Ha'aretz* and *Commentary*, charges that I portrayed Israel as 'a military "superpower", a juggernaut crushing the Palestinians and the Arab armies alike'—thus demolishing the myth of (the Jewish) David and (the Arab) Goliath. In *Commentary* he details the relative strength of the Arabs in artillery and the relative weakness in artillery of the Haganah / IDF in May–July 1948 in order to demonstrate the continued cogency of the (Jewish) David–(Arab) Goliath view of 1948.

I stand by my original thesis (to be found in *The Birth passim* and in my original article in *Tikkun*): that the Yishuv was vastly superior to the Palestinian Arabs in military strength, and that this superiority—in mobilization of manpower, command and control, numbers and training, and yes, most categories of weapons, together with the ability to concentrate units and weapons (partly due to short lines of communication and to superior organization)—enabled the Haganah, when it went over to

the offensive, to crush the Palestinian militias in a relatively short—
and bloodless—series of offensives over April–early May 1948. And the
Haganah / IDF was also, for much the same reasons, stronger than the
combined Arab expeditionary forces that invaded and fought in Palestine.
This superiority, again, was determined by superior command and control;
better trained and greater manpower (in mid-May the Haganah fielded
some 35,000 troops as opposed to the invading Arab armies' total of
25,000–30,000; in mid-July, the IDF had 65,000 troops; in November,
some 90,000, or twice as many as the combined Arab armies at the time);
short lines of communication (as opposed to very long ones for the Egyptian
and Iraqi expeditionary forces); and a superiority in most categories
of weaponry (except during the three critical weeks between 15 May and
11 June). By the offensives of October-November, the IDF's manpower
and weapons superiority (which was augmented by the *de jure* or *de facto*
British and American boycotts of weapons and ammunition to the Arabs)
over the Arab armies was stark and decisive.

Wars are almost invariably won by the stronger side, and 1948 was no
exception. This is not to belie the courage and self-sacrifice of the Jewish
troops. Courage and self-sacrifice, indeed, were crucial during the three
weeks in mid-1948 in which the invading Arab armies were stopped in their
tracks; and crucial in the battles of many kibbutzim, such as Yad Mordechai
and Negba, in repelling localized attacks. In all, the Yishuv suffered 6,000
dead or one person in every hundred. But the key to the victory of 1948 lay,
as always, in the traditional indices of strength—command and control,
manpower, and weaponry.

Lastly, Teveth charges that in *The Birth* I exaggerated the importance
and influence of Yosef Weitz, the director of the Jewish National Fund's
Lands Department, the chairman of the Negev Committee, and the head of
the first and second Transfer Committees. I refer the reader to Essay 4 in
the present volume, 'Yosef Weitz and the Transfer Committees, 1948–
1949'. The reader can then make up his own mind whether the first Transfer
Committee in fact existed (Teveth says it didn't) and what, if any, was
Weitz's contribution to the transfer of Palestine's Arabs.

May 1993

The publication of the original version of this volume in November 1990
and of the *Birth* in Hebrew in spring 1991 occasioned a new wave of
controversy, and fresh criticism of the New Historiography in certain
Palestinian (and pro-Palestinian) and Israeli academic circles.

What, above all and at base, seems to have pained both orders of critics
was the objectivity (or the attempt at objectivity) that suffused much if not

most of the New Histories. Still caught up in the political battle over the fate of Israel and the Palestinians, and having been nurtured on an essential pro-Zionist or pro-Palestinian diet, upheld and ornamented by the appropriate cache of literature, neither set of critics was able to fathom, recognize, or condone the presence of or effort at undiluted impartiality. Each set suspected, and sometimes charged, the New Historians with hidden or not-so-hidden bias and a political agenda. Indeed, the similarity between the charges levelled by Israeli and Arab critics of the New Historiography is quite remarkable though, in all fairness, it must be said that the Israelis have generally been subtler and softer on the pedal.

To turn first to some of the criticism that emerged from the Palestinian camp. The most extreme and sweeping example—relating to the work on the origins of the Palestinian refugee problem—was proffered by Professor Sharif Kanaana, of Bir Zeit University in the West Bank:

Benny Morris' book is thus, in my opinion, a piece of Israeli-Zionist propaganda despite all the dates, figures, quotes, footnotes and all the other elaborate scholarly paraphernalia . . . It is actually a lot more dangerous than the previous line of Israeli propaganda, because it is more sophisticated [and] articulate and deviously hides its thesis behind a facade of objective, scientific and academic sounding style and research methodology. (*Al Fajr* (English-language edition) (East Jerusalem), 5, 12, and 19 August 1991. The article originally appeared in Arabic in *Qadaya* (Jerusalem), August 1991)

Professor Kanaana (like Walid Khalidi before him) appears to have been upset by the failure of the *Birth* and *1948 and After* to uphold the traditional Arab explanation of the Palestinian exodus—that (in Kanaana's words) 'the Palestinian people were driven out of their homes and their country by [*sic*] the force of arms, within the frame [*sic*] of a pre-planned and well-orchestrated comprehensive Zionist plan to rid the country of its native population'. The assumption that this is the 'correct' explanation of the exodus underlies Kanaana's article.

But my failures as a historian are not merely ones of description and explanation; I have also failed, according to Kanaana, on the moral or judgemental plane. That is, I failed to 'blame'—the word recurs in Kanaana's article—the Israelis for what happened and, indeed, seemed to lay a large measure of the 'blame' for the exodus on the Palestinians themselves (they started the war; often they fled before being attacked by Zionist forces; in some cases, as in Lydda and Ramle, the townspeople had 'co-operated' with their Zionist expellers in the sense that they had probably wanted, on 12–13 July 1948, to go into exile as desperately as the IDF command had wanted them to depart; and so on).

Indeed, Kanaana goes one step further. Not only did I fail to 'blame' the Israelis but I had justified Haganah / IDF expulsions and, perhaps, massacres. Or as Kanaana put it, I 'was able to find justification for every' Israel expulsion in 1948. Let me quickly say that this is untrue. Kanaana has confused my *explanations* of why certain Israeli commanders and officials thought as they did and acted as they did with my own attitudes towards what was done in different places at different times. Kanaana failed—fails?—to understand that history consists not only of describing what happened—which I believe I did, and fairly accurately—but also of describing and trying to explain why people acted the way they did, for good or ill. This is by no means tantamount to justification.

In trying to prove Zionist pre-planning and premeditation (as well as savagery), Kanaana 'discovered' and rather confusedly described a set of 'patterns'—of attack, expulsion, massacre—which he implies were elements of the Master Plan. In other words, if Haganah units mortared Arab villages before moving in to attack and occupy them, and this resulted in the flight of their inhabitants, then *ergo* this was part of a systematic, predetermined plan of expulsion; if Jewish units—IZL, Haganah, or IDF—occasionally massacred Arab communities on the outskirts of a town, and the townspeople subsequently fled, then *ergo* the massacres were pre-planned and geared to engineering the evacuation of the towns' inhabitants. And so on.

It is not worth going into a detailed analysis and refutation of Kanaana's 'thesis'. All that needs to be said is that (*a*) there is no trace in any of the documentation of pre-planning of the massacres or, in most cases, of an intention to drive out the Arabs, and (*b*) under close scrutiny, the 'patterns' do not hold. Kanaana simply doesn't know the facts (which, fortunately or unfortunately, remain the basis of historiography and are likely to remain so for some time to come).

Let us look briefly at one of Kanaana's 'patterns'—that of massacre leading to urban flight. While it is true that there was a massacre in Lydda on 12 July before the expulsion of the town's inhabitants (and that the massacre certainly persuaded many of the survivors of the desirability of leaving) and there was a massacre in Deir Yassin, on the western outskirts of Jerusalem, before the flight of some of the city's Arab inhabitants (though many others had fled West Jerusalem before the massacre), it is also true that the expulsion of Ramle's inhabitants was preceded by no massacre, and that the flight of Jaffa's population was not preceded by a massacre (there was a *battle*, not a massacre, at Manshiya). Nor was the flight of Beisan's, Acre's, Beersheba's, or Majdal's Arab populations preceded or precipitated by a massacre of any sort. Moreover, no massacre directly preceded or precipitated the flight in the last week or so of April 1948 of the largest Arab urban concentration in Palestine, that of

Haifa. There had indeed been large-scale killing—one may describe it as a massacre—of Arab civilians at Balad ash Sheikh (see U. Milstein, *Toldot Milhemet Ha 'Atzma'ut, HaHodesh HaRishon* (The History of the War of Independence, The First Month) (Tel Aviv, 1989), 78–81), a large village just East of Haifa—but this had occurred some *five months before* the mass exodus from Haifa. And this exodus, which was pivotal to the whole Arab flight from Palestine, according to the documentation was triggered by things that happened—and didn't happen—in April (Jewish attack, flight of leaders, British non-intervention, panic, etc.) rather than the previous December. Too much is known about 1948, too much is well documented and detailed, for Kanaana to be able to contort and distort events to conform to a 'pattern' of his choosing. It simply won't wash.

That Kanaana's was not a voice in the wilderness but an authentic expression of mainstream Palestinian academic opinion became apparent when the *Journal of Palestine Studies* a few months later (21, 1 (autumn 1991), 66–97) published not one but two attacks on the *Birth* and *1948 and After*—'Myths, Old and New' by Norman Finkelstein and 'A Critique of Benny Morris' by Nur Masalha. The *JPS* kindly allowed me, in the same issue, a rebuttal ('Response to Finkelstein and Masalha', 98–114) and gave Finkelstein the last word—'Rejoinder to Benny Morris'—the following year (21, 2 (winter 1992), 61–71).

Both Finkelstein and Masalha tread familiar Palestinian territory: 'Palestine's Arabs were expelled systematically and with premeditation . . . Zionist policy throughout was one of expulsion' (Finkelstein). Masalha deduces from the fact that the Zionist leadership during the 1930s and early 1940s considered, and generally supported, a 'transfer' solution to the future Jewish state's 'Arab problem' a proof that a 'transfer policy' was indeed *ab initio* adopted and systematically carried out in 1948. Both Finkelstein and Masalha somehow avoid the rich world of nuance and deny multiple causation, and resist or ignore the variety and localism of which much of history, and certainly the 1948 war, is composed. Like Kanaana (and Teveth), they prefer their history simple; prefer a single-cause explanation of the Palestinian exodus, with the Zionists cast as systematic premeditating, expulsive devils. From the first, throughout, the Zionists were bent on transfer and expulsion; throughout, the Palestinians were hapless, innocent victims. For Finkelstein, it might be said, the only good Israeli is a bad Israeli (and, perhaps, all Arabs are good Arabs). As in Kanaana, so in Finkelstein: History is one large morality play, with the protagonists carefully separated into heroes and villains, good and bad. The historian is there not so much to describe and explain as to judge, hand out marks, and, in some cosmic-intellectual sense, punish. Perhaps it is worth noting that almost all the evidence

Finkelstein musters and deploys to prove his points is culled from *Birth* and *1948 and After*. But neither he nor Masalha are really able to get around or come to grips with four major obstacles: (*a*) the complete absence of documentary proof that there was a preconceived Israeli master plan and that an Israeli expulsion policy was in place from the start or, indeed, even in place through the spring, summer, and autumn of 1948; (*b*) the fact that a large part of the middle- and upper-class Palestinian families left Palestine on their own volition *months before* the Yishuv went over to the offensive, conquered Arab areas, or expelled Arab inhabitants; (*c*) the fact that, once the Haganah / IDF went over to the offensive, Jewish commanders acted differently in different places at different times, especially in July and October 1948; and (*d*) that a large number of Arab inhabitants were left in place, even in traditionally hostile, anti-Zionist villages, after Israeli attack and conquest.

The criticism of *Birth* and *1948 and After* by Palestinians and their supporters seems to reveal that they have learned little and forgotten a lot; or that, for them, historical truth (or its close approximations) must still bow before the needs, or presumed needs, of current political battle and propaganda.

Or perhaps there is a deeper, psychological truth at play here, pointing to the Palestinians' continuing need to pin the blame for their tragedy on someone else—Israelis ('they expelled us'), external Arab leaders ('they ordered us to leave'), or the British ('they advised us to leave, supported the Zionists, and failed, as was their Mandatory duty, to protect us'). In all three cases, the Palestinians of 1948, the fathers and forefathers of current Palestinian historians, are thus absolved of all responsibility ('guilt'?) for what happened—for the loss of land, self-respect, honour, the very source and basis of identity—and cleared of possible attendant charges of incompetence and cowardice. The Palestinian adult can thus with a clear conscience turn to his children and say: 'It was not we who lost you your birthright. It was their fault—the fault of the Arab potentates, the British mandarins, the powerful Zionist thugs. What could we, weak as we were, do?'

One last point in this connection. Perhaps Palestinian academic criticism of the *Birth* (as of Yehoshua Porath's two volumes on the origins of Palestinian nationalism, published in the 1970s) owes something to (understandable) displeasure arising from the fact that it is *Israeli* scholars who have produced well-received studies on central events and processes of *their* (Palestinian) history.

Adverse Palestinian academic opinion, let it quickly be said, has not been restricted to my own work. Other New Historians, including Shlaim, have been subjected to trenchant criticism in the pages of the *JPS*. If

Shlaim's original *Collusion* was by and large well received, indeed praised, by Palestinians and pro-Palestinian academics (see, for example, the review in *JPS* 19/2 (winter 1990), 108–10, by Ann M. Lesch), his subsequent, abridged, and revised version of the book, in paperback, retitled *The Politics of Partition: King Abdullah, the Zionists and Palestine 1921–1951* (New York, 1990), was accorded a serious tongue-lashing (*JPS* 21/1 (autumn 1991), 126–8, review by Kathleen Christison). Christison took Shlaim to task for dropping the pejorative term *Collusion* from the title; deleting from the revised version the assertions made in *Collusion* that 'violence was implicit in Zionism from the outset'; and that, for Moshe Dayan, 'expansionism was . . . a general world-view . . . a Zionist philosophy of life that measured achievements principally in territorial terms,' and so on. In general, implied the reviewer, whereas in *Collusion* Shlaim had given the Palestinians a sympathetic or at least fair hearing, in *Politics* the author, in the end, had blamed 'Palestinian intransigence' for the Israeli–Hashemite partition of Palestine and for the Palestinians' demise. The Jewish–Hashemite relationship, originally characterized by Shlaim as 'an unholy alliance', in *Politics* had become 'a pragmatic partnership'. The reviewer nowhere stops for a moment to reflect that perhaps Shlaim honestly felt that he had erred or shown bias in some of his earlier assertions and descriptions and, having realized this, had preferred to correct what he felt needed correction rather than let such descriptions and assertions continue their life in print. Is reconsideration and correction from one edition to the next illegitimate *per se*? Or is it illegitimate only when these conflict with the reviewer's political and/or historical views?

More serious, and somewhat surprising, has been the renewed onslaught on the New Historiography, and particularly on the *Birth* and *1948 and After*, from a particular quarter of Israeli academia, namely the orientalists or Middle East affairs experts.

In broad strokes, my description of the causes and character of the Arab exodus from Palestine has been generally accepted by the Israeli historiographic community; so, though perhaps to a lesser extent, has Shlaim's description of Yishuv–Hashemite relations down to 1951, including the premiss of tacit Israeli–Jordanian agreement during 1948. Many Israeli historians dealing with the period also now acknowledge that the Israeli leadership in 1948–51 did not do all it might have done to pursue and promote peace with Jordan, Syria, and Egypt, and that chances of peace were missed both because of Arab weakness, vengefulness, humiliation, and intransigence and because of Israel's drunkenness with victory, lack of flexibility, and unwillingness to compromise.

None the less, a new wave of scholars has emerged in Israel, whom one might justly dub 'New Old Historians'. Some of them have served, often as career officers, in the IDF Intelligence Branch, and have since done service in and for the Government in various ways. Most are connected to the Middle East Studies departments of the various universities. They include Dr Asher Susser, of Tel Aviv University's Dayan Centre; Professor Itamar Rabinovich, formerly head of the Dayan Centre and rector of Tel Aviv University, and currently Israel's ambassador to the US; Professor Immanuel Sivan, of the Hebrew University; and Dr Michael Oren, of Ben-Gurion University. These 'New Old Historians', like their forebears, the original 'Old Historians', seem to accept the basic premises of the Old Historiography—that Israel was always or almost always 'right', the Arabs always 'wrong'; the Jews were 'good', the Arabs 'bad'; the Jews wanted peace, the Arabs didn't; the Jews were weak, the Arabs strong, and so on. Like the Old Historians, the New Old Historians remain keenly aware of the ongoing political and propaganda battle between Israel and the Arabs and appear to be highly attuned to Israel's public relations and image needs. But unlike the Old Historians, the New Old Historians recognize that the old orthodoxy needs a little emendation, a facelift. Or as Itamar Rabinovich recently phrased it, there is a 'need to correct and refine the orthodox version' (Rabinovich, *The Road Not Taken* (New York, 1991), 219).

Indeed, *The Road Not Taken* contains the clearest advocacy of the 'New Old History'—and a concomitant frontal attack on the New Historiography. The book seems to have been written as a response to Shlaim's *Collusion* and other studies by New Historians, and sets out to describe and analyse the failed peace overtures and moves between Israel and Syria, Israel and Jordan, and Israel and Egypt in the years 1949–52. Rabinovich acknowledges that both Syria's Zaim and Jordan's King Abdullah wanted to make peace with Israel. (He is not so sure about Farouq's Egypt.) But neither, according to Rabinovich, was able to take the plunge: Abdullah was too weak, Zaim too vulnerable and untrustworthy. So, while it is true that Israel was unwilling to offer those substantial concessions that these leaders demanded as the price of peace (partial refugee repatriation, tracts of land, and half the waters of the Jordan and half the Sea of Galilee) and which might have enabled them to 'sell' a separate peace to their peoples and other Arab leaders, the blame for the 'missed' peace must really fall on their (Arab) shoulders. The facts that Ben-Gurion repeatedly refused to meet with Zaim and Abdullah and consistently rejected any concession of territory or water sources in exchange for a settlement are, in Rabinovich's eyes, irrelevant: What is important is that 'Abdullah . . . had lost control of his kingdom' and, so, was unable to parley with Israel and that 'it is difficult to believe that Zaim would have survived in power even if he had reached an agreement with Israel'. So, any agreement with the Syrian leader was doomed to failure and, hence, was not worth pursuing. Hence, Israel is absolved of any responsibility for missing peace with all or any of its neighbours in the aftermath of the 1948 war. A peace settlement was either completely beyond reach or, alternatively, it was the Arabs' fault that it was not achieved. The book suffers from a fatal dissonance between its narrative—which is relatively straightforward, if far from ground-breaking or comprehensive—and its conclusions, which are almost embarrassingly apologetic.

While thus defending Israel's record and actions, Rabinovich energetically strikes out at the 'New Historians'—and particularly Shlaim—who had taken Israel to task for being insufficiently flexible in the negotiations with Abdullah. The New Historians 'departed [i.e. started out] from an explicit contemporary political premise and sought to demolish an orthodox version of the past . . .', writes Rabinovich (*Road*, 216). In a subsequent, singular passage (*ibid.* 219), he adds:

The revisionist school, however, was hampered by several flaws—its point of departure was political and moralistic rather than academic; it relied almost exclusively on Israeli and Western rather than Arab sources, thereby presenting an imbalanced picture; and it introduced emotional issues that were not always the most important ones . . .

The imputation of political bias and intent is forthright. But Rabinovich never quite brings himself to elucidate: Are Shlaim, Morris, and Pappe anti-Israeli or pro-Palestinian and are these positions argued and promoted in their historical works? Have their politics, indeed, affected their historical research and findings? Rabinovich does not say—but clearly, as intended, leaves the unspoken charges dangling in the hollow of the reader's imagination.

The motif of political imputation and motive runs through most of the New Old Historians' criticism of the New Historiography. Almost always, it is through implication and innuendo rather than forthright; nowhere is this charge upheld by convincing or even partially persuasive evidence (an echo of Teveth's method). The concluding lines of Asher Susser's review (*The Jerusalem Report*, 18 April 1991) of *1948 and After* are typical: 'As for the political overtones in [Morris's] work, they are quite possibly unintended. Then again, maybe they are not.' Needless to say, the 'political overtones' are not spelt out and no effort is made to substantiate the intimated assertion. The passage (as perhaps the whole review) probably says more about Susser's politics and their connection to his academic work than about those of his subject's.

A similar political undertone reverberates through some of Sivan's criticism of the *Birth* (reviewed in *Yediot Aharonot*, 10 May 1991). Sivan writes:

> It would be difficult to know to what degree not only the panic following Deir Yassin but also the vengefulness adopted more than once by the Jewish forces, in response to Arab atrocities (atrocities that for some reason are mentioned in the book only cursorily and indirectly), contributed to the process [of Arab exodus].

Indeed it is difficult to quantify the 'atrocity factor' as one of the precipitants of the Palestinian exodus, but that is not the real purpose of Sivan's sentence, which is wilfully misleading, is based on a number of historically false assumptions, and is propagandistic. The *Birth*, as indicated by the title, deals with the factors that triggered the Arab exodus from Palestine. Jewish atrocities were one such (prominent) factor. Arab atrocities, on the other hand, while certainly appropriate to a study of Arab (or Arab and Jewish) fighting norms in 1948, were not directly responsible for Arab flight. Hence they do not figure prominently in the *Birth*. Sivan is well aware of this and his criticism is out of place. Moreover, the implication in the quoted passage is that it was Arab atrocities that provoked Jewish 'vengefulness' and atrocities. In fact, the opposite is the case: Two of the three major Arab massacres of Jews—of the Jewish workers in the Haifa Oil Refinery in December 1947 and of the doctors' and nurses' convoy on the way to Mount Scopus in Jerusalem in April 1948—were revenge attacks triggered by Jewish atrocities against Arabs. On the other hand, Jewish atrocities against Arabs (Deir Yassin in April, near 'Ein Zeitun in May, in Ad Dawayima, Safsaf, Saliha, Hule, Jish, etc. in October) were generally unconnected to or lacked any previous, direct Arab provocation.

Sivan's other major criticism of the *Birth*, which is echoed by Rabinovich, who applies it to the New Historiography in general, concerns the non-use or meagre use of Arab source-material. This charge (which was originally levelled by Teveth and was later also echoed by Avraham Sela (in *HaAretz*, 4 and 11 October 1991, in a review of the Hebrew edition of the *Birth*), and by Susser) is tainted by layers of misinformation and almost transparent hypocrisy.

To begin with, Sivan, Rabinovich, Susser, and co. *know* that there are almost no accessible Arab (or Arabic) primary sources regarding Arab–Israeli relations for the years 1947–52. The Arab states' archives are closed to all researchers, Jewish and Arab; the Palestinians produced no 'state' papers. Arab private and political party papers are also largely inaccessible or non-existent. There is simply no Arab *documentation* of the sort historians must rely on. By contrast, since the opening of the archives in Jerusalem, London, Washington, and New York, there is a profusion of first-rate, illuminating Israeli, Western, and UN documentation for these years, some of it about and from the Arab world. What exists in Arabic or translated from Arabic into Hebrew or English are some Arab political and military memoirs, newspaper clippings, chronicles, and histories. Much of this material, as Rabinovich and his fellow Middle East experts well know, is slight, unreliable, tendentious, imaginative, and occasionally fantastical. It can in no way bear comparison to the wealth, immediacy, and reliability of the available contemporary military, diplomatic, and political documentation available in the recently opened Israeli and Western archives. (I suspect that the fact that no Palestinian scholar managed to produce a general, comprehensive study of the exodus from Palestine—a major event in Palestinian history—in the four decades before the publication of the *Birth* can be chalked up, in large part, to the non-existence or non-availability of such Arab documentation. Interestingly, Arab reviewers of *Birth* and *1948 and After* did not generally comment on the sparsity of references to Arab sources in these works).

This said, there are a number of Arab (and Arabic) sources which are worth culling from—and the New Historians, myself included, have done so. For example, I made repeated use (Sivan's failure to notice this in the *Birth*'s footnotes notwithstanding) of Nafez Nazzal's *The Palestinian Exodus from Galilee, 1948* (Beirut, 1978), which was based on interviews conducted by the author among refugees from the Galilee living in and around Beirut in the early 1970s. I found Nazzal's descriptions and findings, after cross-checking against contemporary documentation, to be generally reliable. Similarly, the diaries of Khalil al Sakakini, a Jerusalem educator, are also useful. Arab political memoirs of the 1940s and 1950s tend to be unreliable, being self-serving, and inaccurate.

A blatant problem arises, in this connection, of stones and glass houses. Rabinovich's *The Road Not Taken*, which analyses Syrian–Israeli, Jordanian–Israeli, and Egyptian–Israeli relations between 1949 and 1952 and contains more than 250 footnotes, mentions Arab or Arabic sources in only half a dozen of them. Almost all Rabinovich's footnotes refer to Israeli, British, and American documents and publications. By contrast, Pappe's *Britain and the Arab–Israeli Conflict, 1948–1951* contains dozens of references to Arab sources; Shlaim's *Collusion* contains several dozen; and my own *Birth* contains more than a dozen. Yet Rabinovich charges the New Historians with relying 'almost exclusively' on Israeli and Western sources, 'thereby presenting an unbalanced picture'. Surely, by this yardstick, *The Road Not Taken* must be seen as fatally flawed!

But the whole question of the use or non-use of Arab (Arabic) sources, as brandished by Rabinovich, Sivan, Susser, and co., is something of a red herring. For, at least as regards the *Birth*, none of them argues that had I used the available Arab (or Arabic) 'sources', I would have emerged with a significantly different picture of the Arab exodus and its causes; none of them argues that had I used such and such Arab (Arabic) source, I would have avoided this or that error or misjudgement. Indeed, none showed or tried to show, by citing Arab (Arabic) chapter and verse, in what way a given unused Arab source would have cast significant fresh or corrective or supplemental light on this or that aspect of the problems and processes described and analysed in the *Birth*. (Indeed, Sivan at one point in his review criticizes my non-use of George Habash's memoirs—only to go on to say that these memoirs would merely have 'reinforced . . . [Morris's] version' of the events in Lydda and Ramle in July 1948. But if this is true, *why should I have used* Habash's memoirs, written decades after the event—when I had at my disposal *contemporary* Israeli and Western documents describing what happened in the two towns almost hour by hour, blow by tragic blow?)

In short, so long as these critics are unable to show exactly how a given Arab (Arabic) source could and would substantially and accurately alter, enhance, or correct the picture painted in the *Birth* and in *1948 and After*, the criticism regarding the (relative) non-use of Arab sources is irrelevant, a red herring designed, perhaps, to impress, mislead, and ultimately befuddle unsuspecting readers.

One last point. The emergence of the New Historiography, and the attendant bouts of controversy, have issued in a wave of essays on the historiography of early Israeli history, particularly of 1948. The original version of this article, as published in *Tikkun* (November–December 1988) may, perhaps, be seen as the first shot in the battle. It was shortly followed by 'Mabat Sheini LeAhor: Revizia BaHistoriographia shel Milhemet Tasha"h VeReishit HaMedina' (A Second Look Back: Revision of the Historioraphy of the 1948 War and the Early Years of the State) by Mordechai Bar-On (*Yahadut Zmaneinu*, 6 (1990), 89–115); 'A Historiographic Review of Literature on the Origins of the Arab–Israeli Conflict' by Kenneth Stein (*American Historical Review*, 97 (December 1991), 1450–65); 'Al HaHistoriographia shel Milhemet HaAtzma'ut' (On the Historiography of the War of Independence) by Yossi Ben-Artzi (*Cathedra*, 65 (September 1992), 159–67); and 'HaHistoriya HaHadasha shel Milhemet 1948' (The New History of the 1948 War) by Ilan Pappe (*Teioria U'Vikoret*, 3 (Winter 1993), 99–114).

Bar-On and Pappe both attempt to place Israel's New Historiography within the theoretical context of historical revisionism as manifested in other Western cultures and histories. Col. (Res.) Bar-On, a former IDF chief education officer and Knesset Member turned historian, goes on to analyse and categorize the stages and types of historiography of 1948, starting with the Old Historians and ending with the Revisionists. He analyses the reasons behind the emergence of the New Historiography— 'the change of generations', 'the decline of the [state-]founding establishment', the decline in the importance of historical issues as a tool of propaganda, and the opening of the archives. He then tries to categorize the types of revisionism according to motivation, i.e. those out to slaughter holy cows for the sake of iconoclasm *per se*; those out 'to close old accounts' with protagonists (such as disaffected generals and colonels, Herutniks who hate Mapai, Palmahniks who dislike Ben-Gurion, and so on); those out to rewrite history in order to promote current political agendas; and professional historians bent on trying to describe the past more accurately and fairly than was done by their predecessors. Bar-On relates only to the last category as serious historiography or 'historiography for its own sake'. He concludes with the caveat that the New Historians should beware of assuming the role of judges *vis-à-vis* their historical protagonists—an admonition unfortunately ignored recently by one of the New Historians, who at a conference at the Hebrew University of Jerusalem in April 1993 said that he willingly took up the offices of both 'judge and hangman'.

Stein, who teaches history at Emory University, took upon himself a more ambitious task—to review the successive generations of historiography not merely of 1948 and the years on either side of that watershed, but of the whole Arab–Israeli conflict, starting with the 1880s and ending in our time, and encompassing both Israeli and Arab chroniclers and historians, and assorted Western scholars. Almost unavoidably, the sixteen-page essay suffers from superficiality. He rejects most of what was written before the 1950s as 'ideologically orthodox, sycophantic, or self-centred' and then subdivides the subsequent historiography into three waves or 'periods'. I am not sure these categorizations are accurate or of much use, and he is far too generous in failing to point out that much written, especially by Israelis and Arabs, in the 1970s, 1980s, and 1990s suffers from various orders of 'ideological orthodoxy' and inhibition, and perhaps from political and career-bent sycophancy. His treatment of the New Historians (principally Shlaim and myself) is tendentious, and consciously belittling ('their conclusions are not new', 'neither Shlaim nor Morris amplify an old cause nor discover a new one', 'detailed explanations of previous postulations', and so on). Stein appears not to have discerned the (to me) crucial divide between the 'Old' and 'New'

Historiographies, and thus seems to have missed the whole point of the current controversy.

Not so Ben-Artzi, who teaches geography at Haifa University. The New Historians, he concedes, are professional 'historians'—unlike the Old Historians, who were at best chroniclers, at worst committed propagandists—but 'they commit the same sins as their predecessors: They are subservient to a conception they have formulated' and they (or their works) are driven by certain 'motives'. Ben-Artzi avoids explicitly defining these 'motives' but at one point seems to let the cat (or rat) out of the bag when he declares: 'these writers have a political and ideological position of their own, which influences their research and the version [of history] they try to present.' Ben-Artzi takes issue with Bar-On and asserts that he should have categorized Shlaim, Pappe, and myself among the historians trying to rewrite history in order to promote current political agendas. He winds up by accusing Bar-On himself, in his historiographic analysis, of having been swayed by his own political persuasions.

Ben-Artzi suggests that the *Birth* is an example of the 'pitfalls of overly narrow interpretation and of an analysis of some of the facts with the wisdom of hindsight . . . Morris failed to penetrate the period and to enter into the feelings of those who lived at the time, and to explain the period from within'. These are pitfalls 'that the historian [should] try to avoid whatever his [political] opinions.' Nowhere does Ben-Artzi attempt to prove his assertions or show whereby he arrived at these conclusions. On the other hand, he praises the works of Itamar Rabinovich and Avraham Sela (author, for example, of 'Transjordan, Israel and the 1948 War: Myth, Historiography and Reality,' *Middle Eastern Studies*, 28/4 (1992)), and implies that these are 'true' historians unmoved in their research and writing by political bias or motive. Again, Ben-Artzi nowhere attempts to substantiate this: Nowhere does he analyse Rabinovich's and Sela's writings or explain why the reader should assume that these two former career officers of IDF Inteligence Branch, one of them currently serving as Israel's ambassador to the US, are uninfluenced in their historiography by their political outlooks and allegiances.

If Ben-Artzi believes that political input and intention in historiography is to be deplored (as I certainly do) and that attribution to others of such input and intention is indeed a serious charge (as I do), then surely, in all fairness, he should have proved or at least made an effort to prove his assertions against those whose histories he finds questionable or unpalatable. Ben-Artzi's essay, to my mind at least, raises serious questions in the realms of intellectual integrity and motivation.

Ben-Artzi concludes his essay by calling for the emergence of 'a new generation of researchers, a generation that not only was not personally involved in the events [such as the Old Historians], but can also free itself from various [political, ideological] commitments to one or other side of the parties involved in the history of the period.' This certainly sounds good. But, in all logic, it would seem to be redundant in so far as Ben-Artzi has already asserted the existence of such an unbiased scholarly coterie (Rabinovich, Sela, and company).

But, all this said and done, Ben-Artzi has a point, albeit strictly circumscribed. The fly in the ointment of the New Historiography is Pappe. This becomes readily apparent in his historiographic essay. In it, Pappe clearly sets out his views on the historian's craft and argues that (*a*) historians have political attitudes and beliefs, and (*b*) should give them free rein in their works, even using these works to promote current political agendas. The historian, however, must remain honour-bound to gather and present his facts accurately and must 'warn' his readers that he has such-and-such beliefs and that they have influenced his work in such-and-such a manner. Pappe dismisses the assertion—made by me earlier in this chapter—that historiography can and should attempt to be objective and impartial: 'Israeli and Arab researchers dealing with the history of the conflict, whether or no they admit it, will never be able to free themselves from their [political] attitudes when they come to deal with the past.' He further suggests (and here I am in agreement with him) that the political views of the New Historians and current political concerns were among the factors that led these historians to research particular subjects (and, one might add, in the obverse, have led other Israeli historians to deliberately ignore certain subjects. At the Tel Aviv University conference on the New Historiography, back in 1989, one of the participants, over lunch, told me: 'I know far more about the IDF atrocities in 1948 than is described in the *Birth*. But I would never have written about them').

If Ben-Artzi attacks the New Historians from the right, Pappe, in his historiographic essay, as if waging guerrilla warfare from within his own camp, attacks historians such as Shlaim and myself not so much from the left as from above. His basic assertion is that we are (merely) 'critical' or 'positivist' historians, not true 'New Historians' at all. Pappe defines proper 'New Historiography' as necessarily judgemental, with the historian duty-bound to 'pass judgement on the events [and protagonists] of the past'; as characterized by the use of comparisons with other contemporary societies and cultures; the use of 'neutral' language to describe phenomena and events; and the necessary, large-scale use of social sciences' methodology, especially quantification. Shlaim and myself, he implies, have failed as 'New Historians' on at least two of these counts and perhaps on all four: We have not used social science methodologies and we have abjured comparisons of aspects of the Arab–Israeli conflict with other conflicts. What Israel and the Middle East conflict need, Pappe seems to be saying, is a new breed of New Historians, committed to and propounding certain political attitudes and programmes, unafraid of passing judgement, and utilizing various social science methods.

Pappe enunciated some of these views at the Hebrew University conference of April 1993. He came under attack from a number of directions. One attack—apparently directed generally against the New Historiography—was launched by Professor Ya'akov Shavit of Tel Aviv University. He took up the Old Historians' refrain, dressed up in modern sociological and historiosophic jargon, that historians must take account of the uses to which their works may be put by politicians and propagandists. The implication was that Israeli historians should streamline their research and conclusions with an eye to their possible use by Arab enemies.

A more Olympian view, seeminly removed from the immediate fray, was taken by Professor Uri Bialer, of the Hebrew University. Comparing the current controversy in Israel to the Revisionist–anti-Revisionist controversy in American historiography, Bialer seemed to argue that both the 'Old Historians' and the 'New Historians' were already old hat. Their argumentation, he suggested, should be viewed within the context of the traditional dialectic between Old and New, which must perforce issue in some form of post-Revisionist synthesis. Indeed, he suggested that such a post-Revisionist wave was already upon us.

But other conference participants felt that Bialer's prognosis was premature, perhaps by decades. Further ground-breaking, fact-laying studies—about the 1930s and 1940s; about the development of Arab–Jewish relations in the various localities, especially in 1946–8; about economic and social aspects of the development of the Yishuv and of the conflict: about the 1950s; about Israeli decision-making processes; about Israeli leaders such as Moshe Sharett and Pinhas Lavon—have first to be written and published before a post-Revisionist synthesis can be even contemplated. Indeed, some participants seemed to feel that, as the New Historiography was not really 'revisionist' (as the Old Historiography was not proper historiography at all), so a real 'revisionist' wave would necessarily have to follow the New Historiography rather than the Old Historiography, and the New Historiographic wave was itself far from over.

2

Mapai, Mapam, and the Arab Problem in 1948

The first Israeli–Arab war, in 1948, resulted in the creation of the Palestinian refugee problem. In great measure, that problem was a product of Jewish military and political actions. To facilitate understanding of these actions, and the attitudes and policies that underlay them, it is worth examining the evolution of attitudes to 'the Arab problem' and to the emerging refugee problem in the political parties of the Yishuv in the course of 1948.

The focus of such an examination must inevitably be on the only two parties that counted for much in the decision-making processes during that war—Mapai (*mifleget poalei eretz yisrael*, the Land of Israel Workers Party) and Mapam (*mifleget poalim meuhedet*, the United Workers Party).

The right-wing revisionists, perhaps representing 10–15 per cent of the electorate, were outside the decision-making process and were only of marginal military importance through their IZL formations. The General Zionists and Progressives, two liberal parties, though represented in the Cabinet, were small and ineffectual. The religious parties, also representing 10–15 per cent of the voters, were ideologically and institutionally completely removed from the mainstream of Yishuv life, especially in wartime.

The 1948 Cabinet, or Provisional Government of Israel as it was called then, had thirteen members. Four of these, holding, among others, the key posts of the Premiership and Defence Ministry (David Ben-Gurion), the Foreign Ministry (Moshe Shertok, later, Sharett) and the Finance Ministry (Eliezer Kaplan), were Mapai members. Two others—Agriculture Minister Aharon Zisling and Labour Minister Mordechai Bentov—were members of the sister socialist party, Mapam. Two other ministers, Police and Minority Affairs Minister Bechor Shitrit and Interior Minister Yitzhak Gruenbaum, who represented respectively the Sephardi (oriental Jewish) community, and a stream of dissident General Zionists, were for all intents and purposes allies or satellites of Mapai and almost invariably sided with the two socialist parties on major issues (when the vote was along party lines). These eight ministers together formed the core of the Provisional Government. The other members of the Cabinet were Pinhas Rosen (Felix Rosenbluett), the Progressive Party's Justice Minister; Peretz (Fritz) Bernstein, the General Zionists' Minister of Industry and Commerce; Yitzhak Meir Levine, the Social Affairs Minister from the ultra-orthodox Agudat Yisrael Party; Moshe Shapira, the Minister of Immigration and Health, from the Mapai-affiliated orthodox Hapoel Hamizrahi Party; and Yehuda Leib Maimon (Fischman), the Minister for Religious Affairs, of the orthodox Mizrahi Party.

The dominance of the two socialist parties, Mapai and Mapam, was fittingly reflected in the emergent state's main bureaucracies— in the Haganah and, afterwards, the IDF, in the Defence Ministry and its extensions (the military industries, the intelligence services, and so on), and in the other main ministries, the Foreign Ministry and the Treasury. Neither the religious nor the liberal parties enjoyed even a foothold in these main branches of government. Nor, save on certain economic issues, did they have much of a say in the policy- and decision-making, and policy implementation in the fields for which these bodies were responsible.

Among the minor parties, when it came to policy towards the Arabs, only the Revisionists spoke with a clear voice. The Revisionists continued through 1948 to lay claim to all Palestine west of the Jordan River, and to areas of Transjordan east of the Jordan, as the homeland of the Jewish people. They purported to believe that once the British left, Jew and Arab—under Jewish rule—could coexist in the homeland. In December 1947 they formally called on the Arabs to stay at peace. 'Only the British want war', argued the IZL.[1] The months of increasingly bitter warfare, however, persuaded the Revisionists that there could be no compromise over and coexistence in Palestine between Jew and Arab. As the breakaway Revisionist LHI group (*lohamei herut yisrael*, Freedom Fighters of Israel, called by the British the 'Stern Gang') put it in April, 'the Jewish Yishuv should not delude itself about good neighbourly relations and local peace agreements with the Arabs. All the

[1] JI, IZL Papers kaf—4/13/4, IZL poster 'To Our Arab Neighbours', 15 Dec. 1947.

agreements and treaties did not help the Hashomer Hatzair [Mapam] people in Mishmar Ha'emek . . . The front is throughout the country . . .'[2]

By April–early May 1948, with the life-and-death struggle at its height and an Arab invasion of Palestine imminent, a note of relief, satisfaction and even joy and gloating over the Arab exodus characterizes IZL broadcasts, though IZL commander Menachem Begin never openly espoused a policy of expulsion. But the IZL's goal with respect to the Arabs in Jewish territory was manifest in the attacks on Deir Yassin (9–10 April), Jaffa (late April) and in the Hills of Ephraim, southeast of Haifa (mid-May). LHI was franker. On 13 May, it declared:

A strong attack on the centres of the Arab population will intensify the movement of the refugees and all the roads in the direction of Transjordan and the neighbouring countries will be filled with panic-stricken masses and [this] will hamper the [enemy's] military movement, as happened during the collapse of France [in World War II] . . . A great opportunity has been given us, let us not waste it . . . The whole of this land will be ours . . .'[3]

The other parties, of the religious and liberal persuasions, whether out of a sense of weakness or out of a feeling that what was happening was for the best, adopted a 'policy of non-intervention', of leaving Mapai and Mapam to decide what to do about the Arabs, and of letting the two socialist parties get on with the job. A sense of the thinking in the Progressive Party on the Arab question is afforded by the following debate in its executive committee in

---

[2] JI, LHI Papers, kaf—5/5/2, LHI broadcast on *Herut Yerushalyaim*, undated. LHI was composed of far-left / Communist and Revisionist factions, with the Communists continuing to believe in the possibility of fraternity with the Arabs and the Revisionists usually denying the possibility.

[3] JI, LHI Papers, kaf—5/5/2, LHI broadcast on *Herut Yerushalayim*, 13 May 1948. While Begin and the IZL leadership were careful not to openly espouse a policy of expulsion, it is clear that the IZL's military operations were designed with the aim of clearing out the Arab inhabitants of the areas they conquered. Following the massacre at Deir Yassin, the IZL fighters trucked out the remaining villagers to East Jerusalem. In May in the Hills of Ephraim the IZL assault ended in the flight of the majority of the villagers; and those who remained in place were, within days, swiftly sent packing in the direction of Umm al Fahm (then in the Iraqi-held zone in the West Bank). In their post-operational reports, especially after the conquest of Jaffa's Manshiya district, the IZL commanders emphasized their satisfaction with the fact that the assaults ahd precipitated mass civilian-Arab flight. The same note of satisfaction and accomplishment is rung in Begin's subsequent memoirs, *The Revolt*.

December 1948, just before the country's first general elections, regarding the party's attitude to the possibility of a refugee return:

> *Executive Committee member Avraham Riftin*: The Arab question; why should we now give an answer . . . Why should we be the first and only ones [to do so? A refugee return] is something very unpopular among the [Jewish] masses. Expansionism also now has great popularity. Why then should we now speak out against it . . . ?
>
> *Moshe Kol.* . . . [our attitude should be] not to now promise specific things, we do not know what our situation will be [in the future], perhaps we will have to bring here the Jews from the Arab countries and then certainly there will be no room here for the Arab refugees.
>
> *Moshe Tomkevich.* . . . We have no need to add minorities. Every modern state is moving towards eliminating minorities.
>
> *Yitzhak Golan.* We should not worry about bringing back the Arabs, who will be a Fifth Column in our state.[4]

But in the end only Mapai and Mapam really counted when it came to policy towards the Arabs. Together, they had the backing of more than half the electorate (as was demonstrated in the country's first general Knesset elections on 25 January 1949); almost all the kibbutzim were affiliated to one of the two parties; the powerful trade-union federation, the Histadrut—which both represented the workers, and owned and controlled major parts of the economy (banks, industrial plants, agricultural produce, and marketing)—was dominated by Mapai; the two parties dominated the cabinet; and, perhaps most important in the circumstances, they controlled and almost completely officered the defence establishment, which was responsible for the implementation of policy towards the Arabs. Indeed, the Haganah and, later, the IDF were peculiarly politicized in the sense that most officers and, indeed, units, 'belonged' to one of the two socialist parties. The sense of 'belonging' was especially pronounced in the units identified with Mapam (which included the three Palmah brigades and their officers).

In wartime, political parties tend to lose some of their importance; and party-political differences tend to blur. But in the peculiar circumstances of the Yishuv in 1948, Mapai's leaders and the Mapam party institutions carried especial weight. In Mapai, decisions on major defence and foreign-policy issues were discussed and taken

---

[4] Massuah-Kibbutz Tel Yitzhak Archive, 10/5/Mem, protocol of the meeting of the Progressive Party Executive Committee, 26 Dec. 1948.

by the party leader, Ben-Gurion, and his small circle of aides (Kaplan, Shertok, Eshkol (Shkolnik)), while party institutions abnegated responsibility in deference to the will of the leader. In Mapam, a party split down the middle by its constituent components (see below), the party institutions—Political Committee, Centre, Secretariat—were where policy was determined; the party had no leader.

MAPAI

Perhaps the most striking thing about Mapai and the Arab question in 1948 was that the party almost never discussed it. The party leaders apparently felt that the war and policy towards the Arabs with which it was inextricably bound up were the rightful domain of Ben-Gurion and of the Cabinet, the high-ranking army officers, and the upper reaches of the civil service. As these were controlled largely by Mapai personnel, the party institutions took the attitude that they should and could be allowed to operate with a minimum of party interference. It is likely that Ben-Gurion instructed the party stalwarts to avoid these subjects; debate inevitably would give rise to expressions of dissent. The bulk of the party officials apparently were satisfied with what was happening and agreed to the policy or the mode of thinking which to some degree was shaping developments.

Before 1948 Mapai's platform had called for the establishment of a Jewish state in any part of Palestine, whenever possible. The party continued to regard the whole land of Israel as by right the Jewish people's but insisted that Jew and Arab could and should coexist in it peacefully. Above all, Mapai policy, steered by Ben-Gurion, during the post-World War II years was opportunistic and flexible: the Zionist movement must be realistic and extract from history as much as history would allow at any given moment. The UN Partition Resolution of 29 November 1947 awarded the Jews a small state in Palestine: Ben-Gurion took what was offered.

But the outbreak of war radically changed things: the Jews had accepted a 'mini-state' in a divided Palestine; the Arabs had not, and had initiated hostilities to block the establishment of the Jewish state. The war afforded the Yishuv a historic opportunity to enlarge the Jewish state's borders and, as things turned out, to create a state without a very large Arab minority. The war would solve the

Yishuv's problem of lack of land, which was necessary to properly
absorb and settle the expected influx of Jewish immigrants.

Ben-Gurion understood history, understood that war changed
everything; a different set of 'rules' had come to apply. Land could
and would be conquered and retained; there would be demographic
changes. This approach emerged explicitly in Ben-Gurion's address
at the meeting of the Mapai Council on 7 February: Western
Jerusalem's Arab districts had been evacuated and a similar,
permanent demographic change could be expected in much of the
country as the war spread.[5] At that meeting, the party stalwarts,
albeit briefly, for the first time touched on the Arab question,
highlighting the two 'philosophies' which were recurrently to clash
in the Yishuv during 1948. Eliahu Lulu (Hacarmeli), a Jerusalem
branch leader, asked: who could believe that the Arabs of Palestine
would long remain quiet and not rise up against the Yishuv? He,
Lulu, had lived among them all his life. He knew them. The Arabs
of Romema, a Jerusalem neighbourhood, were suing for peace. But
this was only to 'save their houses . . . and no more'. Talk of
possible Jewish–Arab fraternity was nonsense, he said.

By contrast, David Hacohen, from the Haifa branch, argued that
though now the Yishuv was at war with the Arabs, eventually, 'we
must not forget, we will also have to live with them. We talk with
them peace and we must abide by our declarations . . . There is
[Arab] terrorism and there is a Mufti . . . [But most of the Arabs]
want to live quietly.'[6]

But for months thereafter, as the hostilities turned into full-scale
war, Mapai's institutions refrained from discussing the war or the
Arab question. They talked of party finances, enlarging the branches,
relations with other parties, and preparations for setting up the civil
bureaucracies of the new state. But not of the war and not of the
Arabs. It was Golda Myerson (Meir) who broke the silence on 11
May, after a visit to the deserted quarters of Arab Haifa. Almost all
the city's Arabs had fled over 22 April–1 May. Myerson spoke of
the exodus, arguing that the party now had to face the issue,
especially in terms of a possible return of some of the (friendly)
villagers and preserving the abandoned villages for such a return.
She also said the party had to determine Israeli behaviour towards

[5] David Ben-Gurion *Behilahem Yisrael* [as Israel fought] (Tel Aviv, 1952), 68–9.
[6] LPA 22/35, protocol of the meeting of the Mapai Council, Tel Aviv, 7 Feb. 1948.

the Arabs who had remained in the state: should it be such as to encourage or deter the exiles from returning? More generally, she noted that the Yishuv had made no plans concerning what to do with the population of conquered Arab towns and villages. 'I confess', she said:

and this may have been naïveté . . . but I believed that our army [would behave] not as all the world's armies [have behaved] . . . This is a slightly delicate and slightly complex problem. I advise the party Centre to discuss the problem soon, seriously and frankly . . . and according [to the conclusions reached] to instruct the [labour] movement as a whole . . . If the party doesn't take the initiative, then things won't be put right.

But, at the same time, Myerson cautioned against turning the issue —of the Yishuv's (and particularly the Haganah's) treatment of the Arabs—into a bone of inter-party (Mapai–Mapam) controversy. She enjoined the party to launch an education campaign in the ranks against looting.[7] But no other participants related to the Arab question, which was not on the agenda. Nor did Myerson's call for a full-scale party debate on the question in fact prompt such a debate. It was as if a large stone had been thrown into a pool—but had caused no ripples at all.

During the following two months the party institutions ignored the Arab question. Shertok (Sharett) made only a passing reference to it at the meeting of the Mapai Council on 18 June. The 'weakness' of the Palestine-Arab community came 'as a complete surprise . . . this community rooted in the country for generations, for hundreds of years . . . Who hoped, who could have anticipated that come war, it would pull up roots and wander . . . While we, who only recently arrived . . . and [taken] root . . . have displayed such steadfastness.' Shertok compared the exodus to the Sudeten-German exodus after World War II, and asked whether it wasn't just deserts for a war the Arabs had unleashed.[8]

The silence in Mapai was broken, briefly, by the impact of the expulsion from Lydda and Ramle on 12–13 July. The veteran, liberal Mapai Secretary General of the Histadrut, Yosef Sprinzak, at a meeting of the Histadrut's Executive Committee, said:

---

[7] LPA 48/23 aleph, protocol of the meeting of the Mapai Centre, 11 May 1948.
[8] LPA 36/22, protocols of the meetings of the 36th Mapai Council, Tel Aviv, 18 June 1948.

During [the past] weeks and months . . . positions [that is, attitudes or policies] have come into being which cause dissent among all of us in this house [the Histadrut] . . . This applies to the robbery, the looting and the behaviour [in general] of the Jewish occupation forces . . . It is possible that these things result from a logical imperative . . . It is possible there are security reasons. But . . . [there] must be a limit . . . [*Sprinzak cited the alleged expulsion from the village of Abu Ghosh and the 'evacuation' from Ramle*]. This situation is impossible . . . and the responsibility here is on all [the political leadership].

Eliezer Bauer (Be'eri), a Mapam figure from Kibbutz Hazore'a, at this point commented that the looting, which was not planned or centrally inspired but was not being curtailed, and the expulsions, taken together, testified that 'there is an unannounced but very effective intention that Arabs will not be left in the State of Israel'.

Eliahu Lulu (Hacarmeli) commented: 'I have taken part more than once in the argument about looting . . . It was once said that looting was one of the characteristics of the oriental [Jews]. [But] the Ashkenazim [western Jews] have superseded us also in this. Even in this we have been discriminated against . . .'. Another Histadrut Executive member (Mapai), Zvi Yehuda, from the agricultural settlement of Nahalal, noted that the Arab neighbourhoods of Haifa, among others, had been looted by kibbutz members from Sha'ar Ha'amakim, Ramat Yohanan, and Yagur: 'This is apparently a primitive instinct of *homo sapiens*.'[9]

The Lydda–Ramle episode and the increasing international pressure for a refugee return at last prompted a full-scale debate on the Arab question in the Mapai Centre. It took place on 24 July and was to be the only such debate in the course of 1948 in any of the party's institutions.

Sprinzak said: 'There is a feeling that *faits accomplis* are being created . . . The question is not whether the Arabs will return or not return. The question is whether the Arabs are [being or have been] expelled or not . . . This is important to our moral future . . . I want to know, who is creating the facts? And the facts are being created on orders.' There appears to be 'a line of action . . . of expropriation

    [9] Histadrut Archive (Va'ad Hapoel Building, Tel Aviv), protocols of the meetings of the Executive Committee (*Ha'va'ad Hapoel*), 14 July 1948; and Yossi Amitai, *Ahvat Amim Bemivhan* (Brotherhood on Trial), (Cherikover, Tel Aviv, 1988), 38–9.

and of emptying the land of Arabs by force', said Sprinzak. If such was the policy, Sprinzak wanted to know, who had decided on it? He felt that the party institutions must first 'agree to it—I too have a right to a say in the matter', he said.

Sprinzak was supported only by Shmuel Yavnieli, one of the founders of Mapai and the Histadrut. Yavnieli described the question of a return as 'difficult'. In the past, he said, 'we resigned ourselves to the idea of a Jewish state with a large Arab minority'. Could Jews who 'for many generations were persecuted and expelled, slaughtered and destroyed', and were the butt of tyrants' contempt, now act like 'slaves who have become kings?' Mapai, he said, should declare that those Arabs who had not fought against the Yishuv could return. He cast doubt on the justice of previous transfers in history (Greeks and Turks), precedents cited by other Mapainiks in justification of the party line.

Ben-Gurion responded that one must pay attention to the chronology: 'The Arabs fled before the various places were conquered by the Jews.' Many of Haifa's, Jaffa's, and Jerusalem's Arabs fled before the Jews attacked. The same thing happened in Jenin. It was inexplicable, as if a 'dybbuk' had got into their souls. 'There was no necessity for them to flee', said Ben-Gurion. He added that when he had heard of the flight of Haifa's inhabitants, he had said: we will not run after them. 'If they flee—let them flee. We did not expel them.'

The two things that had surprised him during the war, said Ben-Gurion, were the Arab flight and the Jewish looting. 'It emerged that most of the Jews are thieves.' Everyone stole and looted, including 'the men of the [Jezreel] Valley, the cream of the pioneers, the parents of the Palmah [fighters]'.

Ben-Gurion, of course, had muddied the issue: he had implicitly denied that there had been expulsions by seemingly attributing the whole exodus to panic flight. Others at the meeting took a more forthright position. Shlomo Lavi, a veteran kibbutz movement and Mapai agricultural-sector leader, opposing a return, said: 'the . . . transfer of Arabs out of the country in my eyes is one of the most just, moral and correct things that can be done. I have thought this . . . for many years.' If a mass return were allowed, Lavi thought, the Arabs would 'stick a knife in [the nation's] back'. Lavi's views were endorsed by Avraham Katznelson. There is nothing 'more moral, from the viewpoint of universal human ethics, than the emptying of the Jewish State of the Arabs and their transfer elsewhere . . . This requires [the use of] force.' He, too cited the Sudeten precedent.

Lavi's statement had been in part a reaction to Shertok's political *tour d'horizon*. Shertok had said: 'It is desirable for us that the Arabs do not return, if it is at all possible . . . [This has] historical justification.' It is best for Israel and the Arab states in the long run that Israel should not have internal problems stemming from the existence of a large Arab minority, he implied. Shertok said, however, that he did not think the hour was ripe for this position 'to be formulated outwardly [that is, publicly]'.[10]

Sprinzak remained isolated. The matter was not raised again in the party's institutions for the duration of the war. Very few party members, if any, followed the example of Yitzhak Avira, a kibbutznik from Ashdot Ya'akov, in the Jordan Valley, who resigned his membership largely because of the party's stand on the Arab question. Not that he supported the return of the refugees, he wrote, but 'I do not agree with the party's way . . . I demand of our state that [we accord] elementary rights to the stranger living in our midst.'[11]

MAPAM

Mapam came into being in January 1948 when the Marxist Hashomer Hatza'ir and the socialist Hatnu'a Le'Ahdut Ha'avodah-Po'alei Zion parties united. Hashomer Hatza'ir, based largely on the kibbutzim of its Kibbutz Artzi Hashomer Hatza'ir kibbutz movement, had traditionally supported a bi-national Jewish–Arab state in Palestine, though gradually, after World War II, during the count-down to the 1947 UN partition resolution, it had come to accept the inevitability of partition, with the creation of a Jewish state in part of Palestine (albeit strongly linked by bonds of economy and 'anti-imperialism' to the other, Palestine-Arab state). Ahdut Ha'avodah, on the other hand, had traditionally supported the creation of a Jewish state in all of Palestine, with a Jewish majority coexisting with a well-treated Arab minority. Ahdut Ha'avodah, based largely

[10] LPA 48/23 aleph, protocol of the meeting of the Mapai Centre, 24 July 1948.
[11] LPA 1–48/3/4 aleph, Yitzhak Avira to the Mapai Centre, c.24 Oct. 1948.

on the kibbutzim of the Kibbut Me'uhad kibbutz movement, balked at Ben-Gurion's acceptance of the partition resolution and through the 1948 war pressed continuously for Haganah / IDF conquest of the whole of Mandate Palestine. The vision of what is today known as Greater Israel (*yisrael hashlema*, then known as *shlemut ha'aretz*) was the driving ideological force in Ahdut Ha'avodah and put it, perhaps, to the right of Mapai on foreign policy and defence issues (while it remained to Mapai's left in its economic and social outlook).

Against the backdrop of Jewish–Arab warfare in 1948, Mapam's leadership, equally drawn from the party's two component elements, was forced into an intricate and continuous juggling act to arrive at a succession of compromise formulas acceptable to their two (Hashomer Hatza'ir and Ahdut Ha'avodah) constituencies. Moreover, the realities of the conflict continuously and sorely tried the principles of the party members. As a Mapai kibbutz circular bitingly put it, not only was the 'distance' between the two Mapam components emerging starkly, but Hashomer Hatza'ir's behaviour was running contrary to its ideology. 'In practice, the kibbutzim of Hashomer Hatza'ir are participating in the acquisition of Arab property, harvest [Arab] fields, and more than this: [Hashomer Hatza'ir kibbutz] Mishmar Ha'emek was the first [kibbutz] to demand the destruction of the Arab villages around it . . .'. Meanwhile, stated the Mapai kibbutz circular, Mapam continued to blame Mapai for the Arab exodus.[12]

For Mapam's Hashomer Hatza'ir wing, the Jewish–Arab fighting was a large and continuing embarrassment. The party for years had hoped to turn the flank of Arab hostility and, making common cause with the 'peaceful, fraternal Arab workers', to achieve peaceful coexistence in a bi-national state. But national aspirations once again had overcome socialist premiss and vision. Hashomer Hatza'ir's left wing, led by the director of the party's Arab Department, Aharon Cohen, continued, however, to hope 'to build bridges to the Arab forces of progress . . .'.[13]

---

[12] Ihud Hakibbutzim ve'Hakvutzot Archive (Kibbutz Hulda) 111/2, *Igeret Gimel* (third circular), Gordonia-Maccabee Hatza'ir, the supreme leadership, Tel Aviv, 17 Sept. 1948.
[13] HHA-ACP 10.95.10 (6), Cohen to members of the Arab Department of Mapam, 17 Feb. 1948; and HHA 66.90 (1), protocols of the meeting of the Mapam Political Committee, 3 Mar. 1948.

But the war was destroying any chance of such fraternal bridge-building. In part, as Cohen saw things, it was a problem of Haganah policy—which appeared to him incapable of distinguishing between Arab foe and friend or potential friend: massive retaliation or 'aggressive defence' was killing any chance of peace. By March 1948, Cohen felt that there was a tragic lack of co-ordination between Haganah operations and the Yishuv's political purposes. He called for a full-scale debate in Mapam's Political Committee on policy towards the Arabs.[14] But no debate took place.

It took the shock of the exodus in late April of the Arabs of Haifa, a city where Jew and Arab had traditionally lived in peace, to stir Mapam's leaders sufficiently to agree to a full-scale debate.[15]

The internal Mapam debate on the Arab question began on 11 May and continued (in the Centre and in other party institutions) almost non-stop for the duration of the war. Marked by a deep and constant divide between the party's two wings, by less insistent disagreements within each wing, and by a comprehensive and often soul-searching treatment of the issues at stake, the protocols of the debate provide a major insight into the Zionist ethos and the Yishuv's views on the Palestine problem.

Preparatory to the start of the debate, Cohen wrote a memorandum entitled 'Our Arab Policy in the Midst of the War'. In his notes for the memorandum, penned on 6 May, Cohen wrote that 'a deliberate eviction [of the Arabs] is taking place . . . Others may rejoice—I , as a socialist, am ashamed and afraid . . . To win the war and lose the peace . . . the state [of Israel], when it arises, will live on its sword.'[16]

In the memorandum itself, Cohen lamented that during the first five months of the war, no basic discussion on policy towards the Arabs had taken place in the party. He cautioned that military victories should not go to the Yishuv's head. The Jewish state, once established, 'would have to fight for a long time for its existence. At best, our state will be an island in the large Arab sea.' Military successes had to pave the way for political accomplishments, or they

[14] HHA 66.90 (1), protocols of the meeting of the Political Committee of Mapam, 3 Mar. 1948; and HHA-ACP 10.95.11 (21), Cohen to Ya'acov Riftin and Leib Levite, 13 Mar. 1948.

[15] HHA 64.90 (1), protocol of the meeting of the Secretariat of the Mapam Centre, 27 Apr. 1948.

[16] HHA-ACP 10.95.10 (4), notes for memorandum, 6 May 1948.

were valueless. But, according to Cohen, 'out of certain political
goals and not only out of military necessity' the Arabs were being
driven out. 'In practice, a . . . "transfer" of the Arabs out of the
area of the Jewish state was being carried out', and this would
eventually redound against the Yishuv, both militarily (by increasing
pan-Arab anger) and politically.[17]

Cohen's memorandum was distributed to the members of the
Centre before the 11 May meeting. At the meeting, Mapam co-
leader Aharon Zisling (Ahdut Ha'avodah) berated the Yishuv for
the looting of Arab property but spoke rather vaguely on the
fundamental issues of expulsion, a possible return, and the treatment
of the Arabs. Co-leader Meir Ya'ari (Hashomer Hatza'ir) said he
was shocked that the party's Haifa branch had done so little to deter
the Arab exodus from the city; he too avoided the main issues. But
several second-rank Mapam figures then turned to what was to
become one of the foci of Mapam soul-searching—the role of the
party's Haganah officers in the formulation and implementation of
policy towards the Arabs. Yitzhak Yitzhaki called for a 'joint
meeting' between the party's Arab affairs workers and its 'people
[that is, officers] in the defence [establishment]', presumably to
hammer out guidelines of behaviour towards the Arab population.
Ze'ev Abramovich went further. The Secretariat of the Centre
should inform Mapam's members serving in the defence establishment 'that the party will hold them responsible for preventing
attacks on the Arab [civil] population . . .'.

Yitzhak Ben-Aharon, a leader of the Ahdut Ha'avodah wing,
whose kibbutzim furnished a large proportion of the Palmah brigades'
officers, was outraged.

They have loyally carried out their mission. No fact has been presented here
[which speaks against] our comrades . . . Our comrades were 'responsible'
in Mishmar Ha'emek, Haifa, Jerusalem, the South . . . [But] before the
Centre has to comment upon [that is, condemn] our comrades, it must first
discuss the facts, if there were any [cases of wrong-doing] . . . Anything else
would be a motion of no confidence in our comrades.

Ben-Aharon differentiated between 'looting and robbery' (which
he condemned) and expulsions out of military necessity.

[17] HHA-ACP 10.95.10 (4), 'Our Arab Policy in the Midst of the War', by Aharon
Cohen, 10 May 1948.

How can one free [Kibbutz] Mishmar Ha'emek from being a military objective without uprooting [the neighbouring Arab] villages. There was no doubt about [the necessity] for this. Or: Along the road to Jerusalem. Safad. Haifa. And the result: The Arab fellah, even if he is tranquil, becomes a refugee . . . This may increase the number of refugees, etc. but it also increases our security . . .

Cohen, taking a conciliatory tack, suggested that instead of issuing a caution as proposed by Abramovich, the Political Committee should 'bring to the knowledge of the [Mapam members in the] defence forces [the sense of] the discussion [in the Centre]'. Later, the Political Committee and the officers should meet and discuss the matter.

Ya'acov Hazan, a (Hashomer Hatza'ir) Kibbutz Artzi leader, mollified Ben-Aharon by saying that the proposal had not aimed at 'casting aspersion on the officers . . .'. Hazan proposed that the Centre 'charge all our comrades in the Haganah with meticulously keeping to the party's positions on this question'.

The meeting in the end empowered the Political Committee to hold a clarificatory talk (*beirur*) with the Mapam officers, 'and to transmit instructions to our comrades in positions of command regarding a standard [pattern of] behaviour'.[18]

Given the military situation, which included the Arab invasion of Palestine on 15 May, Mapam proved unable to organize a meeting of its political leaders with 'its' Haganah commanders. But Ya'ari (Hashomer Hatza'ir) continued to insist that the party 'should instruct people who can affect the process of exodus or halt it'. The party should 'demand' that its members in the defence establishment discuss the matter with the Political Committee and, afterwards, proclaim its stand. Party co-Political Secretary, Leib Levite (Ahdut Ha'avodah), however, said that most of the commanders in any case couldn't come and it was best that the party's position be hammered out now, in the committee.

'We did not want . . . to expropriate [Arab property] . . . or anarchy . . . But there is a war and it has a logic [of its own] which must be carried through', said Levite. He spoke against the 'ambivalence' of at once calling for the restriction of the Jewish state to the partition borders and calling for expulsions and settlement by

[18] HHA 68.9 (1), protocol of the meeting of the Mapam Centre, 11 May 1948.

Jews of the empty villages. Levite 'justified, supported, and endorsed
. . . every conquest and every eviction of every Arab settlement
necessitated by the war . . . Whoever wants peace, must win the
war . . .'. Looting, however, must be curbed with severity, he said.

The Hashomer Hatza'ir position at the 21 May meeting was
voiced by Aharon Cohen: 'What is being done today [is] that the
basis of existence of the Arabs who have left and will want to return
is being destroyed.' He implied that what was important was not so
much behaviour towards the conquered Arab communities as towards
the property and fields of those who had left: 'The crucial question is
the question of the return of the refugees', he said.[19]

The battle lines between the party's Hashomer Hatza'ir and
Ahdut Ha'avodah wings were being drawn. But they remained
blurred—mainly because all or almost all agreed that while the
Haganah had occasionally acted excessively and contrary to party
ideology, the Yishuv was fighting with its back to the wall; its
very existence was at stake. Now was not the time minutely and
rigorously to probe the ethics of every military action. But as the
immediate danger of Arab victory wore off, criticism of Haganah
treatment of Arab civilians mounted, inevitably highlighting the
Hashomer Hatza'ir–Ahdut Ha'avodah divide. The thrust of the
criticism was that Mapam's views appeared to have little or no effect
on the Yishuv's treatment of the overrun Arab communities, despite
the fact that Mapam's cadres made up much of the Haganah's
officer corps.

Eliezer Bauer (Be'eri) (Hashomer Hatza'ir) charged, at the
meeting on 26–7 May of Mapam's Political Committee, that under
the guise of military needs, things were being done for 'distinctly
political purposes, and without the party objecting and with party
members [carrying them out]'. Most of the Arabs who had left 'had
not been expelled. Many left before the [Haganah] conquests. The
conquests were a result of the flight.' But the Yishuv's attitude was
that almost every Arab who stayed 'had to be regarded as a spy or
potential saboteur'. At the same time, the economic infrastructure
of the Palestine Arabs was being destroyed, villages were being
razed, and new settlements on the abandoned sites were being
planned. The aim was 'to clear the State of Israel of Arabs . . .'.

[19] HHA 66.90 (1), protocols of the meeting of the Political Committee of Mapam,
21 May 1948.

No differentiation was being made between peaceful and hostile Arabs, and a policy of barring a return of the refugees was being implemented.

Moshe Erem said that the party had failed 'to educate the Haganah's units . . . Our comrades [if properly instructed] will serve as a brake on [expulsions] . . . We need commissars.' Erem thought that what was happening (Arab flight and the destruction of Arab villages) was happening without 'a directing hand'.

Hazan declared that a defeat in the war would mean 'the end of the Jewish people'. Hence, the war had to be fought with all necessary 'brutality and efficiency'. But, the fighting aside, what was happening was 'a political, moral, public and socialist scandal'. He specifically denounced the way the Haganah was treating the Arabs who had stayed put and the destruction of the villages. He spoke of Abu Shusha, a village near his home kibbutz, Mishmar Ha'emek. The Haganah had completely bulldozed the village instead of distinguishing between houses of enemies and houses of friends of the Yishuv. He spoke of Haganah 'killing, robbery, rape. I don't think our army should be like every army'. Hazan concluded by rejecting the establishment of a Jewish settlement on the lands of Abu Shusha. '[I] accept that next to us [that is, next to his kibbutz, Mishmar Ha'emek] there will always be an Arab village', he said.

Ya'acov Amit (Hashomer Hatza'ir), of Kibbutz Beit Zera, south of the Sea of Galilee, said that it was all very well to blame Ben-Gurion for everything. But why wasn't Mapam's dominant presence in the army being translated into political praxis? He asked, specifically, why Israel Galili, of the Haganah General Staff, was keeping quiet and why Hazan, on the board of directors of the JNF, was not curbing Yosef Weitz, the JNF Lands Department director, who was organizing the destruction of Arab villages. 'What are you sitting [on these bodies] for? Either intervene or don't sit there.'

Eliezer Pra'i (later, Peri) (Hashomer Hatza'ir), the editor of Mapam's daily, *Al Hamishmar*, questioned whether there was always a military reason for the razing of the Arab villages. He could understand, he said, the 'joy of the comrades who have been freed from the fear of the [neighbouring] Arab villages'. But what was happening was undermining 'the moral and political base on which our party was founded . . . Among the best of our comrades the thought has crept in that perhaps it is possible politically to achieve our ingathering in the Land of Israel by Hitlerite-Nazi means.'

But a number of committee members—Levi Kantor (Ahdut Ha'avodah) and Haim Darin-Drabkin—objected to what amounted to a wholesale condemnation of the Yishuv's policy towards the Arab population. Kantor said that if Mapam was to act as Pra'i was recommending, 'it would be seen as sabotaging our war effort'. Darin-Drabkin, a Tel Aviv party member, dismissed this facile condemnation of expulsions by pointing out that had Jaffa's population remained *in situ*, it would have 'posed a difficult problem' for the Haganah. The same applied to the Arab villages around Mishmar Ha'emek. 'Because of the desire to destroy [the Yishuv] on the part of the Arabs, there [cannot be] here Geneva conventions regarding civilian population.' Darin-Drabkin denied that there was any centrally organized policy of expulsion.[20]

Thinking critically and publicizing criticism of aspects of military operations while the war was in full swing was difficult. The commencement of the First Truce (11 June) opened the floodgates of dissent. Mapam co-leader Ya'ari let loose on 14 June, in an address to Kibbutz Artzi military men: 'There are those who say . . . "we did not expel them. They fled of their own accord . . . and so why should we not inherit after they expropriated themselves, as it were. Why should we not clear the area [of Arabs] and not snatch this unheard of opportunity?"' But these are 'barbarous growths', said Ya'ari; 'anti-imperialism and racism' cannot dwell together. 'In truth, thousands did flee, but not always of their own will. There were shameful episodes. . . . There was no necessity for all the villages to be emptied . . .'.

Ya'ari, however, opposed the return of the refugees during the hostilities.[21] So did Agriculture Minister Zisling (Ahdut Ha'avoda). But Zisling warned, at the Cabinet meeting of 16 June, that the Yishuv was on a course that would endanger any possibility of making peace. 'Hundreds of thousands of Arab dispossessed . . . are growing into haters who will promote war against us throughout

[20] HHA 66.90 (1), protocol of the meeting of the Political Committee of Mapam, 26–7 May 1948.
[21] HHA *Yediot Hakibbutz Ha'artzi-Hashomer Hatza'ir*, no. 274 (43), 8 Aug. 1948, 'If You Go to War', a speech by Meir Ya'ari to Kibbutz Artzi conscripts, 14 June 1948.

the Middle East . . . They will bear in their breasts the desire for revenge, compensation, and a return . . .'. The Arabs should be allowed to return to certain sites, such as Beisan, whose houses should not be destroyed. Zisling, joining Minority Affairs Minister Shitrit, sharply attacked Ben-Gurion for the destruction of the Arab villages. But when it cut close to the bone, Zisling spoke otherwise. 'I do not want the Arabs to return to Qumiya', he said, speaking of the abandoned village overlooking his own kibbutz, Ein Harod, in the Jezreel Valley.[22]

Zisling's criticism of Ben-Gurion was prompted by the sense of the meeting of Mapam's Political Committee of 15 June. Cohen had charged that 'it had depended on us whether the Arabs stayed or fled . . . [They had fled] and this was [the implementation of] Ben-Gurion's line in which our comrades are [also] active.' Ya'ari had pointed to the 'moral contradiction between [our ideology and the fact that] our comrades are implementing [Ben-Gurion's policy] . . . The comrades are doing things contrary to their conscience because they received orders from above. They also do things on their own initiative.' Ya'ari proposed that the party inform its officers in the IDF 'that they should carry out every order [even if it] runs against their conscience but should inform their superiors that they were acting against their conscience'. Ya'ari also proposed that the party probe the actions of several commanders. He was supported by Mordechai Bentov (Hashomer Hatza'ir), the Minister of Labour.

The Political Committee, in an eleven-point policy statement that summed up the prolonged party debate on the Arab question, ruled that 'the party opposes the objective of expelling the Arabs from the areas of the emergent Jewish state'; proposes that the government 'call on peace-minded Arabs to stay put . . .'; opposes 'the destruction of Arab settlements . . . not out of military necessity'; and proposes that the government call on 'the Arab citizens of the Jewish state, come peace, to return to a life of peace, respect and creativity', and that property be restored to the returnees.[23]

---

[22] KMA-AZP 9/9/3, transcript of Zisling's statements at the Cabinet meeting of 16 June 1948.

[23] HHA 66.90 (1), protocols of the meeting of the Mapam Political Committee, 15 June 1948; and HHA-ACP 10.95.11 (1), 'Our Policy towards the Arabs during the War, (decisions of the Political Committee from 15 June 1948)', the Secretariat of the Mapam Centre, Tel Aviv, 23 June 1948; a circular to party activists.

The Political Committee debate on the exact wording of the policy statement highlighted the growing Hashomer Hatza'ir–Ahdut Ha'avodah divide. The debate over the clause regarding the destruction of Arab villages was especially heated. Pra'i and Bauer sought a blanket prohibition of such destruction. Ben-Aharon demanded—and got—the qualification allowing for destruction 'out of military necessity'. The wording of the clause on a refugee return was also strongly debated. Zisling opposed the phrase in the original draft concerning the return of the refugees 'to their [original] places'—Qumiya, for example. The phrase was duly excised from the policy statement.[24]

Throughout June and July, Mapam spokesmen persistently criticized and condemned the continuing destruction of Arab villages.

The Israeli offensives of the 'Ten Days' (9–18 July) and the expulsion of the inhabitants of Lydda and Ramle substantially sharpened, indeed qualitatively transformed, the rumblings within Mapam to open, across-the-board dissent from Mapai over Arab policy. For the first time, the possibility surfaced of Mapam, even in mid-war, breaking with Mapai and bolting the coalition. On 15 July, Hazan said: 'The robbery, killing, expulsion, and rape of the Arabs could reach such proportions that we would [no longer] be able to stand it. But even then we would have to think [twice about bolting the coalition].' Hazan proposed, rather, that the party try to influence the course of events from within.[25] Zisling's criticism of Ben-Gurion and of the Lydda–Ramle expulsion in the Cabinet meeting of 21 July was bitter; Hazan, at the 14 July meeting of the Histadrut's Executive Committee, was only marginally less scathing about what he defined as the Mapai line.[26]

At the same time, the Lydda–Ramle expulsions dramatically conjured up and highlighted the divide within Mapam between its two component elements, inevitably renewing the full-scale debate on the party's Arab policy. The debate variously focused on ethical, political, and strategic considerations. The expulsions from the two towns were generally condemned by the Hashomer Hatza'ir stalwarts,

[24] HHA 66.90 (1), protocol of the meeting of the Mapam Political Committee, 15 June 1948.
[25] HHA 68.9 (1), protocol of the meeting of the Mapam Centre, 15 July 1948.
[26] KMA-AZP 9.9.3, transcripts of Zisling's statement in the Cabinet meeting of 21 July 1948; and Histadrut Archive (Va'ad Hapoel Building), protocol of the meeting of the Executive Committee, 14 July 1948.

as was the behaviour and judgement of the commanders involved, principally OC Operation Dani Yigal Allon (Ahdut Ha'avodah). The Ahdut Ha'avodah wing tended to support the generals, though eventually they acquiesced in a compromise formula which criticized the generals for expelling the inhabitants of Ramle but condoned the expulsion from Lydda (because, it was argued, the Lydda inhabitants had 'rebelled' against the IDF after conquest whereas Ramle's population had not). The compromise was reached after an informal 'investigation' of the generals by the party leaders, which included a 'guided tour', with explanations, by Allon of a handful of the leaders around the Operation Dani battlefields even before the operation had ended. While arguing strategic necessity, Allon pointed to Ben-Gurion as the origin of the expulsion order. The debate within Mapam about Lydda and Ramle sputtered on for months, the twin expulsion emerging as a general symbol of the alleged, continuing 'transfer policy' (orchestrated by Mapai) and, more particularly, of Mapam's involvement, through 'its' generals, in that policy.[27]

Ben-Aharon (Ahdut Ha'avodah) denied that there was a Hashomer Hatza'ir–Ahdut Ha'avodah divide over Arab policy. 'There is no argument over our attitude to the Arabs. There is no argument over our opposition in principle, fundamentally, to the expulsion of Arabs from the country . . . [and] against the destruction of [their] property . . .'. The argument, he said, was about 'what constitutes military necessity'. The problem lay in differentiating between expulsions out of military necessity and out of 'military convenience. We are against the expulsion of Arabs and the destruction of villages out of convenience . . .'. But there was no argument in the party over expulsions prompted by military necessity, said Ben-Aharon.[28]

Hashomer Hatza'ir agreed that there were cases of military necessity. The executive committee of the Kibbutz Artzi in August, in a bulletin to its members in the IDF, acknowledged that 'there are cases where the army is interested in evicting the Arabs after

---

[27] For further detail on the political debate within Mapam and between Mapam and Mapai on Lydda and Ramle, see Benny Morris 'Operation Dani and the Expulsion from Lydda and Ramle, July 1948', in *Middle East Journal*, Winter, 1986.

[28] HHA 10.18, transcripts of speeches delivered at the meeting of Mapam defence activists, 26 July 1948.

conquering an Arab site because we do not have enough forces to leave a garrison behind . . . The army cannot advance when to its rear villages or towns remain without effective supervision.'[29]

But, by and large, the Hashomer Hatza'ir leaders did not see the question as one of military necessity versus convenience: what was happening was 'political', in terms both of motivation and consequence. The expulsions and the razing of the villages were being carried out for political reasons and, often, by Ahdut Ha'avodah-affiliated officers (Yigal Allon, OC Palmah and OC Operation Dani; Yitzhak Rabin, Palmah OC Operations and Operation Dani OC Operations; and Moshe Carmel, OC Northern Front). As Hazan put it, concerning the destruction of the villages one had to distinguish between what occurred during battle and what occurred four months later. And 'there were many cases of expulsion that were not a necessity of war . . . If we adopt [Ahdut Ha'avodah Mapam Centre member Menahem] Durman's approach [that is, the fewer Arabs left in Israel, the better], it is possible to conclude that it is necessary to expel all the Arabs from the country', said Hazan. Expelling the Arabs will create enemies 'for at least two generations. There is no future for Zionism if one assumes frequent wars.'[30]

Ahdut Ha'avodah's stance was clarified by Yosef Tabenkin, the commander of the Palmah's Harel Brigade and the son of Yitzhak Tabenkin, Ahdut Ha'avodah's leader, at the meeting of Mapam defence figures on 26 July. The young Tabenkin did not agree to a transfer policy, he said. After the war the Arabs would return to the country and 'the land would not be clear of Arabs. In this country Arabs and Jews will live on foundations of equality.' But, and here was the crux, 'in war—do as in war'. Tabenkin defended the expulsion from Ramle by saying that he 'did not want the "just men" [that is, population] of Ramle [left] behind us, on the road to Jerusalem, now. The just men of Ramle . . . would have constituted a danger had they still been in Ramle . . .'.[31]

The Mapam (and Shitrit) attacks on Ben-Gurion, the Mapai 'line'

---

[29] HHA 11.18, 'Bulletin to the Mobilized [Members] no. 3', the executive committee of the Kibbutz Artzi, 25 Aug. 1948.

[30] HHA 68.9 (1), protocol of the meeting of the Mapam Centre, 15–16 July 1948.

[31] HHA 10.18, transcripts of the speeches at the meeting of the Mapam defence activists, 26 July 1948.

and the destructive activities of the Haganah / IDF and Weitz in May–July 1948 had had a major effect. It had resulted in the curtailment and cessation of the First Transfer Committee's operations and in the issuing of the order of 6 July by IDF Deputy Chief of Staff General Zvi Ayalon (in the name of the Chief of Staff) forbidding destruction of villages and expulsions without specific permission from Ben-Gurion. And it had induced Ben-Gurion and the generals to have to 'think twice' in the future when contemplating such acts and, if decided upon, to carry them out without fanfare or, usually, explicit, written orders. Aharon Cohen in July felt able to write that he discerned 'a certain measure of reward to [our] stubborn and occasionally desperate efforts'. He was speaking of the non-expulsion of the Arab inhabitants of Nazareth and its environs in mid-July, of the ministerial interventions that stopped the expulsion of the inhabitants of Al Fureidis and 'Arab al Ghawarina (Jisr Zarka) in the Coastal Plain and to the appointment of a string of Mapam officials to key Arab-affairs posts in the bureaucracies (Moshe Erem in the Minority Affairs Ministry, Eliezer Bauer in the Labour Ministry, Yitzhak Yitzhaki in the Histadrut's Arab Department, Yosef Vashitz in Haifa's Arab-Affairs Committee, and so on).[32]

But during the late summer and autumn of 1948, the Hashomer Hatza'ir–Ahdut Ha'avodah divide became somewhat blurred and irrelevant as many of the party's kibbutzim, of both wings, cast covetous eyes on the abandoned Arab lands. New settlements, affiliated to both the Kibbutz Me'uhad and Kibbutz Artzi movements, were set up on these lands.

A rearguard action was fought by some Hashomer Hatza'ir activists to halt the process. The protests focused not on stopping the establishment of new settlements or on stopping the cultivation of Arab fields (both of which would have been regarded as unpatriotic) but on halting the destruction of the empty villages (in the interest of a possible return and future Arab–Jewish fraternity). Letters denouncing the destruction reached the party leaders (and IDF and civil bodies) from a number of kibbutzim. These acted as 'constituency' grass-roots pressure on the leaders in internal party deliberations and in the set-tos with Mapai.[33]

---

[32] HHA-ACP 10.95.10 (4), Cohen (Kibbutz Sha'ar Ha'amakim) to Ya'acov Mayus (Prague), 30 July 1948.
[33] See e.g. HHA-ACP 10.95.10 (6), Peterzil to Erem, Bentov, Hazan, Zisling, 10

There were also some direct attacks on the take-over of Arab lands and the establishment on them of new settlements. Baruch Lin, of Kibbutz Mishmar Ha'emek (Hashomer Hatza'ir), a Kibbutz Artzi leader, denounced what most of his party comrades were beginning to call an 'agrarian reform' as nothing other than a 'transfer'. 'Transfer, not agrarian reform, is now in the air', he said. It was being argued that new settlements were being established on sites out of 'strategic need'. 'But every Arab village in the country [could be settled on the basis of] "strategic need"', he said. Most Mapam members, including men like Hazan and Erem, that autumn supported what they called 'agrarian reform', which meant the establishment of new Jewish settlements on half the abandoned Arab lands, with the other half (or less) to be set aside for the possible return of the refugees. It was argued that 'intensification' of cultivation would mean that half the lands could produce more than all of them had before 'intensification'. Even Hashomer Hatza'ir stalwarts such as Aharon Cohen, given the kibbutzim's avid desire for more land, refrained from coming out against the proposed agrarian reform. At meetings of the Political Committee, Ahdut Ha'avodah leaders Yitzhak Tabenkin and Ben-Aharon strongly supported the 'reform' but resisted setting aside lands for returnees near new Jewish settlements. 'Otherwise', argued Ben-Aharon, 'we will establish a settlement with a defect, which will constantly struggle with the [neighbouring] Arab settlements over every dunam of land.' Ben-Aharon demanded the establishment of new settlements—'as a strategic-settlement necessity'—in the Jerusalem corridor. The corridor's original inhabitants should be 'settled elswhere'. Tabenkin, for his part, said: 'It is necessary to settle . . . if we don't settle on the [abandoned] land, we will endanger our existence . . . we must not exhibit a guilty conscience in this matter . . . We must cultivate every [piece of land] without determining in advance what will be the fate of this settlement [drive] when the Arabs return.'[34]

The Mapam kibbutz members' desire for new lands was such that it touched not only those tracts abandoned by fleeing Arabs but

Aug. 1948; and HHA-ACP 10.95.10 (5), Kibbutz Sha'ar Ha'amakim to Golani Brigade HQ, 8 Aug. 1948.

[34] HHA 66.90 (1), protocol of the meeting of the Mapam Political Committee, 19 Aug. 1948.

also fields belonging to Arabs still in the country. Yagur member
Noah Prover, who served as an inspector of abandoned property in
the Haifa area, complained that kibbutz members 'are expelling
. . . Arabs who have legal rights or rental contracts regarding lands
near old and new kibbutzim . . .'.[35]

During August–October 1948 the debate between Mapam's constituent factions, and within Hashomer Hatza'ir itself, regarding the
need to set aside lands for possible returnees increased in volume.[36]
A yawning gap developed between Mapam's political professions
and its members' actions. The party—and more vehemently, the
Kibbutz Artzi—supported a refugee return. But the kibbutzim
coveted the abandoned lands. The kibbutzim took over fields, and
some kibbutzim egged on expulsions and helped to destroy villages.[37]

In September, Yitzhak Tabenkin, the Ahdut Ha'avodah and
Kibbutz Me'uhad leader, presented what amounted to his credo on
the Arab question, the refugees, and the lands issue. It is worth
quoting at length:

We are on the eve of [the renewal of] the hostilities . . . Among us there was
an argument whether to expel or not. [But] the Arabs did not even ask our
people whom they caught and killed barbarically . . . Every expulsion is
difficult. But if we are confronted by the choice [:] the expulsion [of Arabs]
or the murder [of Jews] everyone will choose expulsion . . . Though [the
expulsion from] Ramle does not weigh on my conscience, one might say
that most of the Arabs [in the town] were not expelled but were tricked
[into leaving]. There are some 300,000 Arab refugees and had they known
that the result of the war would have been their expulsion it is possible that
they would not have chosen [this course] . . . Are our [Jewish] refugees
worse than Arab refugees? . . . I am not indifferent towards the Arab
refugees, but we are a people of refugees . . . And *aliya* [that is, Jewish
immigration to Israel] is inconceivable without land . . . I accept the Arab's

[35] Amitai, *Ahvat Amim Bemivhan*, p. 43.
[36] See e.g. HHA 5.10.5 (2), protocol of the meeting of the executive committee of
the Kibbutz Artzi, 9 Sept. 1948; HHA 66.90 (1), protocol of the meeting of the
Political Committee of Mapam, 25 Nov. 1948; and KMA 12–3, protocols of the
meeting of the Kibbutz Me'uhad Council, statement by Reuven Cohen, 6 Nov. 1948.
[37] See e.g. CZA A246–13, p. 2,354, entry for 14 Apr. 1948, p. 2,364, entry for 23
Apr. 1948, p. 2,367, entry for 26 Apr. 1948, for the case of Kibbutz Kfar Masaryk
and the Ghawarina beduins of Haifa Bay; HHA-ACP 10.95.10 (6), Nahum
Horowitz to Aharon Cohen or Mapam's Political Committee, Sept. 1948, requesting
the destruction of a string of Lower Galilee villages; and HHA-ACP 10.95.10 (5),
Peterzil to Erem, Bentov, Hazan, and Zisling, 10 Aug. 1948, on destruction by
Kibbutz Ma'ayan Baruch of a neighbouring Arab village.

right to live here, a right equal to our own. But we need not announce this now . . . He who fights against us now endangers his rights . . . Our war is defensive . . . I do not regard the Ramle affair as embarrassing to us . . . The Arab will be happiest [living] among [fellow] Arabs . . . Ramle was not a failure for our party . . . The failure of our party is that we did not know how to resist one man's [Ben-Gurion's] assumption of control over the army and the war effort . . .[38]

The renewed fighting in October in the Galilee and the Negev was swiftly followed by reports and rumours of IDF atrocities. Mapam commanders and soldiers were implicated, directly and indirectly. Months before, Ya'ari had lamented what he saw as the failure of the Kibbutz Artzi's education system: it had produced, when it came to fighting, a 'wonderful generation, brave and courageous'. But, on the moral plane, the citizen-soldiers had not stood the test of the war.

The youth we nurtured in the Palmah, including kibbutz members, have [occasionally] turned Arabs into slaves; they shoot defenceless Arab men and women, not in battle . . . Is it permissible to kill prisoners of war? I hoped that there would be some who would rebel and disobey [orders] to kill and would stand trial—and not one appeared . . . They are not against transfer. What does it mean . . . to empty all the villages? . . . What did we labour for . . .?

Ya'ari asked the kibbutz educators.[39]

The atrocities of late October in Operation Hiram (in the Galilee) and Operation Yoav (in the south) confronted Mapam with the practical problem of persuading 'its' officers and soldiers to give evidence before the ministerial commission of inquiry (in the end carried out by Attorney-General Ya'acov Shimshon Shapira alone) that had come into being partly because of Mapam's pressure on Ben-Gurion. The atrocities, and Mapam's part in them, were debated in the party's Political Committee on 11 November. The Hashomer Hatza'ir–Ahdut Ha'avodah divide again surfaced. Aharon

[38] HHA 68.9 (1), protocol of the meeting of the Mapam Centre, 16 Sept. 1948.
[39] HHA-Meir Ya'ari Papers 7.95.3—aleph (2), text of speech by Ya'ari at a meeting of teachers in Kibbutz Mizra, August 1948. Ya'ari was misinformed. There had been a number of cases of soldiers refusing to carry out barbaric orders. At least two cases—of soldiers of the Palmah's Third Battalion outside 'Ein az Zeitun and soldiers of the 89th Battalion, 8th Brigade at Ad Dawayima—are recorded in Benny Morris, *The Birth of the Palestinian Refugee Problem, 1947–1949* (Cambridge, 1988).

Cohen, speaking of the divorce in Mapam between theory and praxis, called for a full-scale, internal party investigation. Galili (Ahdut Ha'avodah) said that the Mapam leaders should not rush to accuse party members without proof. Bentov (Hashomer Hatza'ir), the Labour Minister, said that the ministerial probe was encountering difficulties as the troops were refusing to testify. Benny Maharshak (Ahdut Ha'avodah), a senior Palmah officer, said that Mapam members should not use phrases like 'Nazi acts' to describe IDF actions. Ya'acov Riftin, a Hashomer Hatza'ir hardliner, said that there was no need to 'mix up' the subject of expulsions with atrocities; he implied that there was no connection between the two. But he called for 'death sentences' for the perpetrators of atrocities. The committee decided that it should hold an investigatory meeting (*beirur*) with the relevant Mapam commanders.[40] At the same time, the executive committee of the Kibbutz Artzi instructed the movement's soldiers to come forward and testify on IDF maltreatment of Arabs in the recent campaigns.[41]

During October–November, various Kibbutz Artzi–Hashomer Hatza'ir members began publicly to criticize Abba Kovner, of Kibbutz Ein Ha'Horesh, a well-known poet and World War II partisan and Holocaust survivor. Kovner served as the cultural officer in the Givati Brigade and composed the brigade HQ's circulars to the troops. During the July fighting, addressing himself to the brigade's armoured-vehicle drivers, Kovner had written: 'Don't be deterred, sons: dogs of murder—their sentence must be blood! And the better you run over these dogs of blood the better will you love the beautiful, the good, and freedom . . .'.

On 20 October, Kovner wrote: 'The bayonet is just and the blood is free, because the vision of retribution says: Vengeance. Vengeance. Vengeance!'

Kovner was personally assailed in various kibbutz gatherings and in Mapam party meetings. In a letter to the Mapam leadership, Kovner denounced his critics and even charged that one of them, a senior party figure, had called him 'a Fascist propagandist'. Kovner demanded that the charges against him be publicly aired in a

[40] HHA 66.90 (1), protocol of the meeting of the Mapam Political Committee, 11 Nov. 1948.

[41] HHA 5.18 (1), 'Bulletin no. 76', the executive committee of the Kibbutz Artzi, 12 Nov. 1948.

meeting of the party institutions.[42] It seems that such a meeting did not take place.

The Kibbutz Artzi's annual council, held in Nahariya over 10–12 December and gathering together representatives from all the movement's kibbutzim and the Hashomer Hatza'ir leadership, turned into a full-fledged and painful debate on Mapam's policies during the war. Everything was reviewed—the Haganah's initial retaliatory strategy, the offensives of April, Haifa, expulsions, the destruction of the villages, Lydda–Ramle, relations within Mapam, relations with Mapai, the takeover of lands, the establishment of new settlements. It was a prolonged stock-taking and a summation.

Many of the kibbutzim held preparatory general meetings of members before the council convened. Often, the focus was the refugee problem. 'In every kibbutz the Arab question gives no rest', one leading Kibbutz Artzi member reported.[43]

At Ma'anit (Narbata), east of Hadera, the members met in early December.

There are contradictions between the declared positions of the Kibbutz Artzi and the feeling of some of the [kibbutz] comrades . . . We have comrades who are close to Mapai's positions on the Arab question. This is a serious danger as one cannot long be a revolutionary socialist outside and a reactionary at home. It is difficult to withstand the waves of chauvinism which arise during times of victory . . . And those comrades who think that it is possible to develop a democratic, free state while badly treating the Arabs are mistaken,

said Yosef Menahem, one of the kibbutz leaders.

Binyamin Winter, the *mukhtar* (headman) of Ma'anit, said that during thirty years of struggle, 'we failed' to persuade the Arabs that 'they could live with us in peace'. The British, on the other hand, succeeded in convincing the Arabs of the 'slaughter' the Jews would unleash against the Arabs if the Jews took control. So the Arabs fled, fearing 'retribution'. Now, the 'transfer' was a *fait accompli*, and there would be no return. Winter asserted that 'our efforts' had been responsible for the fact that the inhabitants of Al

---

[42] Avraham Eilon, *Hativat Givati Mul Hapolesh Hamitzri* (The Givati Brigade Opposite the Egyptian Invader) (IDF Press-Ma'arachot, 1963), 298–9, 524; and Amitai, *Ahvat Amim Bemivhan*, 43–4.

[43] HHA 5.20.5 (4), protocols of the Kibbutz Artzi council, statement by Zvi Lubliner, 12 Dec. 1948.

Fureidis and 'Arab al Ghawarina had not fled. 'Elswhere we did not manage to hold the Arabs. Now, the Right also regrets the expulsion of the Arabs—as it lacks unorganized labourers. But the matter was primarily strategic. Had we left the villages intact and made do only with evicting the young men, we would have endangered our security.' Winter dismissed the notion that Mapai was responsible: true, 'Ben-Gurion got his way'. But 'the commanders were ours [that is, Mapam's]'.

Another kibbutz member, 'Lucy', said that even had Mapam controlled the Yishuv, 'things would not have been different. We would have demolished like the others. One can do no other [in wartime] . . . For us every Arab is now a hater or potential hater . . . He who wishes to kill you, rise up first and kill him.'

Pinhas Ger took a contrary tack. Zionism had never intended 'to settle the Jewish immigrant in the expelled Arab's house'. He upheld the Arabs' right to return and thought that Jewish housing problems should not be solved at the expense of the Arabs. But other kibbutz members opposed a return: 'In Transjordan and Iran [Iraq?] there are wastelands [where the refugees could be resettled]', said Yardena Avner.[44] This was to be a microcosm of the following, wider Kibbutz Artzi council debate.

In advance of that debate, Ya'ari wrote that the Yishuv had failed to exploit the opportunity offered by the IDF victories. 'We could have stopped the confused flight and ended the panic that took hold of the whole Arab population . . . We could have nurtured among them allies . . . Instead . . . we reinforced the panic. Through our behaviour we turned the Arab flight into an almost complete exodus.'[45]

The debate of 10–12 December was frank and comprehensive. Eliezer Hacohen, of Kibbutz Beit Alfa, summarized the year that had passed by saying that, on the Arab question, Mapam had in effect been 'paralysed' and its platform ignored. The fault lay with the 'party's' Haganah / IDF officers, who had carried out operations which ran counter to the party line. He seemed to imply that the party had not disciplined the commanders because of the Hashomer

[44] Ma'anit Archive 4/ayin, *Benirbata* (the kibbutz's internal bulletin), 8 Dec. 1948.

[45] HHA 5.20.5 (3), Meir Ya'ari, 'The Kibbutz Artzi after the [Mapam] Unification and after the Establishment of the State', Nov.–Dec. 1948.

Hatza'ir–Ahdut Ha'avodah divide, which could have turned into a schism had the issue been strongly pressed by the Left.

Ya'ari went so far as to accuse his Hashomer Hatza'ir colleague Riftin of taking the side of the Ahdut Ha'avodah generals, specifically over the expulsion from Ramle, 'in order to maintain party unity'. So, while the party officially repudiated a policy of expulsion, 'its' generals had helped implement it, and Ahdut Ha'avodah's leaders and some Hashomer Hatza'ir figures had sanctioned it.

Ya'ari said that in the early months of the war, when the Yishuv fought with 'Stens [that is, sub-machine-guns] against cannon . . . it was possible to understand' what had happened. But later, from Lydda–Ramle onwards, and despite party decisions to the contrary, the generals had done things with which Mapam could not agree. But the party leaders had also been remiss—in having failed to punish the miscreants.

As to the present and future, interest focused on the issue of a refugee return. In principle, all the Council participants favoured a return. But the party was 'afraid to speak up', said Zvi Lubliner. General elections (eventually held on 25 January 1949) were at hand and the party's opponents, it was feared, would argue that Mapam 'wanted to bring back Arabs' at the expense of new Jewish immigrants. Allowing refugees back was unpopular; advocating it would cost Mapam votes. None the less, Hazan spoke up in favour of a return. If there was no return, Israel would be encircled by 'a whole generation [seething with] hatred . . . ready at any moment for a war of revenge, a generation that will view us as robbers and murderers, who stole from it everything—its homeland and its property'. Riftin, too, backed a return, but not necessarily to the original abandoned sites, and 'within the framework of a development plan'. But party member Hemda Gilrovitz suspected that conditioning a return on a 'development plan' would result in no return. Weitz, she said, also spoke originally of a return within the framework of such a plan. She added that the party didn't seem to be 'exerting itself' too much on behalf of a return. David Kna'ani, of Kibbutz Merhavia, supporting a return, said that 'the Land of Israel is [the Arabs'] home as it is ours'.

Outright opponents of a return were rather mute at the council meeting. A member of Kibbutz Sha'ar Hagolan, identified in the protocols only as 'Shmuel', was probably the most forthright:

For us, the question of the refugees is not abstract. We see the long line of huts of the refugees [across the Jordan River] from our observation posts. There are many dangers in allowing back the refugees. I am not happy with the idea of having a large Arab minority. Our treatment of the Arabs is not so bad. We were told here of an example of transfer from Greece [to Turkey]. This transfer brought Greece thirty years of peace . . .

The Kibbutz Artzi council concluded its meeting on 12 December by adopting a number of resolutions, which included allowing the return of 'the peace-minded refugees', and their absorption within a 'development plan' framework. The council also called on the Mapam Centre to reconsider the party's policies on expulsions not prompted by military necessity and treatment of Arabs in general with a view to curbing such things as 'racial discrimination . . . and robbery'.[46]

Taken all in all, the Yishuv's political parties had little influence on the shaping of the Yishuv's policy towards the Palestine Arab communities. The religious and liberal centre parties were weak and ineffectual. The Revisionists, considered by the majority as 'outside the fold', had a limited effect through IZL and LHI operations and through the (limited) influence of their views on sections of public opinion.

Mapai was something else. In many senses, the party was all-powerful. In 1948 its leaders became Israel's leaders. Led by Ben-Gurion, they decided on and carried out policy. But the *party institutions* consciously abdicated interest in and influence over defence and foreign policy; the unspoken feeling and motive was: 'Let our / the country's leaders get on with the job.' And the stalwarts by and large (Sprinzak was an exception) were happy with the policies and performance of the leaders—Ben-Gurion, Shertok (Sharett), Kaplan, David Remez, Golda Myerson (Meir), Levi Shkolnik (Eshkol). So there was virtually no debate within the party on policy towards the Arabs.

Not so in Mapam, where the party institutions from May 1948 onwards frankly and exhaustively discussed 'the Arab question'. The

---

[46] HHA 5.20.5 (4), protocols of the meeting of the Kibbutz Artzi Council, Nahariya, 10–12 Dec. 1948; and in HHA *Yediot Hakkibutz Ha'artzi* (Kibbutz Artzi Bulletin) of Jan. and Feb. 1949, which contain edited excerpts from the council deliberations.

party held two of the thirteen Cabinet posts and had disproportionately strong representation among the Haganah / IDF (especially Palmah) high-ranking officers. But Mapam proved unable to bring its full weight to bear on national, military, and political decision-making and operations. In large measure, this was due to the congenital split in the party between 'soft-liners' and 'hard-liners', roughly running along the Hashomer Hatza'ir–Ahdut Ha'avodah divide. The clash between the Marxist and defence-'activist' philosophies of the two groups sapped the party's resoluteness, and substantially softened or disembowelled decisions taken by party bodies on the Arab question.

This connected with the party's second major problem, the application or implementation of the party line in the field, by the 'party's' commanders in the Haganah / IDF. Ahdut Ha'avodah's general, if rarely openly enunciated, support of the 'transfer' approach to the Arab problem from the start rendered the idea of the party disciplining 'its' colonels and generals essentially absurd.

To this must be added the third paralysing factor—the common interest of all the party's kibbutzim and its two kibbutz movements in laying hands on the abandoned Arab lands in order to expand and to establish new settlements. Nor did the kibbutzim want hostile Arab communities in their vicinity.

The 'compromise' struck, as it were, was the continued enunciation of fraternal Jewish–Arab principles while in practice doing little or nothing to curb 'transfer' activities in the field. The party bodies and leaders raged or murmured against expulsions and the destruction of villages while, in the field, the party's kibbutzim and generals played a prominent part in these activities. Moreover, both kibbutz movements went ahead with the harvesting of the Arab fields, the take-over of the abandoned lands, and the establishment of new settlements. Professing support for a refugee return and for setting aside 'surplus' tracts for returnees was, in the context, as Ahdut Ha'avodah saw things, innocuous and meaningless. But a handful of Hashomer Hatza'ir activists throughout 1948 kept up the criticism of the state's behaviour towards the Palestinians, and of their party's compromises. And a number of party stalwarts concretely assisted certain Arab communities and prevented their displacement.

By the end of 1948, even the limited, ambivalent dissent of Mapam had become largely irrelevant. Following the Kibbutz Artzi council, Mapam emerged from Israel's first general elections in January 1949 with nineteen Knesset members to Mapai's forty-six. Ben-Gurion formed a Mapai-led coalition with centre and religious parties, without Mapam. Mapai's policies towards the Arab minority (Military Government), towards the refugees (no return), and towards the Arab states (no territorial concessions) were among the reasons Mapam remained outside the coalition.

FIG. 2.   The Palestinian Arab Exodus, 1948–1950
(rough numbers: the total of Palestinian Arab refugees in 1948–50 was
600,000–760,000)

3

The Causes and Character of the Arab Exodus from Palestine: the Israel Defence Forces Intelligence Service Analysis of June 1948

Since 1948, two contradictory explanations have dominated the historical debate about the causes of the Palestinian Arab exodus. The 'traditional' Arab explanation was that the Yishuv had mounted a pre-planned, systematic campaign of expulsion already unleashed in the first months of the first Israel–Arab war. The official Jewish explanation was that the exodus had been part of a 'plot' in which the Arab leaders, inside and outside Palestine, had asked or ordered the Palestinian masses to flee their homes in Jewish-controlled territory in order to embarrass the emergent Jewish state, to justify the subsequent Arab invasion of 15 May, and to clear the ground physically, as it were, for the advance of the invading Arab armies.

The events in Palestine in 1948–9, which resulted in the Arab mass exodus, were far more complex and confused than either coherent explanation indicates. A great deal of fresh light is shed on the multiple and variegated causation of the Arab exodus in a document which has recently surfaced, entitled 'The Emigration of the Arabs of Palestine in the Period 1/12/1947–1/6/1948 (*t'nu'at ha'hagira shel arvi'yei eretz yisrael ba't'kufa 1/12/1947–1/6/1948*)'.[1]

I would like to thank the warm and efficient archivists at the Hashomer Hatza'ir Archive for helping me find material and for giving me access to the Aharon Cohen Papers before they had been finally organized and made generally available.

[1] The document is be found in the newly organized and released private papers of Aharon Cohen, the long-standing director of the Mapam (United Workers Party) Arab Department and a leading Middle East affairs expert, in the Hashomer Hatza'ir Archive (Givat Haviva, Israel), 10.95.13 (1). A notation in Cohen's hand on the cover page of the document says: 'Sent—8/7/48—Received 11/7/48'. Apparently it was sent to him by a contact in the IDF Intelligence Service or in the General Staff.

All quotations in this article are from the Intelligence Service report unless otherwise stated.

Using the term 'IDF Intelligence Service' in this context is something of a misnomer. The Haganah's Intelligence Service (the Shai), founded in the mid-1930s,

Dated 30 June 1948, it was produced by the Israel Defence Forces
Intelligence Service during the first weeks of the First Truce (11
June–9 July) of the 1948 war. The report was written by Moshe
Sasson, who was the assistant to the director of the Service's Arab
Department, Shmuel Divon. (Sasson, the son of Eliahu Sasson,
the Jewish Agency Arab affairs expert, subsequently shifted to the
Foreign Ministry, where he served as Israel's ambassador to
Rome, head of legation in Ankara, and ambassador to Egypt.)
The document consists of two parts, typewritten in stencil foolscap
pages: a nine-page text and a fifteen-page appendix. The text
analyses the number of refugees, the stages of the exodus, its
causes, the destinations of the refugee communities, and the
problem of their initial absorption in the host areas. The appendix,
proceeding district by district, traces—village by village—the
dates, causes, and destinations of the emigration, and the numbers
involved. The details in the appendix serve in large measure as the
basis for the statistical breakdown in the text. The report does not
state who ordered the Intelligence Service to produce the analysis
and why. It is possible that the analysis was produced at the behest
of Defence Minister and Prime Minister David Ben-Gurion or
acting IDF chief of staff and OC Operations, General Yigael
Yadin. These men, like other members of the newly formed IDF
General Staff, no doubt wanted to understand the Palestinian
exodus, which had at first surprised, indeed astonished, the Yishuv
leaders.[2]

continued to function as the Yishuv's main intelligence service down to the summer
of 1948. At the end of May 1948 the Haganah itself became the Israel Defence
Forces, the army of the new State of Israel. But the underground army's Intelligence
Service, for bureaucratic reasons, in fact continued to exist through June, and was
only reorganized and renamed the IDF Intelligence Service at the beginning of July.
But the fact that officially the Haganah ceased to exist by the start of June makes it
incongruous to speak of a report produced by the Haganah Intelligence Service at the
end of June. (The IDF Intelligence Service, incidentally, in 1949, after a shake-up
involving the dismissal of its head, Lieutenant-Colonel Isser Be'eri, and its merger
with the already-existing IDF Operations / Intelligence Department, was renamed
the IDF Intelligence Department which, in turn, became IDF Intelligence Branch or
Division (Aman)—its current name—in 1953).

[2] For the Yishuv's astonishment at the exodus, see, for example, the memorandum
by Israeli Foreign Minister-designate Moshe Shertok (Sharett) on his meeting in
Washington with US Secretary of State George Marshall, Dean Rusk, and other State
Department officials on 8 May 1948, in Gedalia Yogev (ed.), *Documents on the
Foreign Policy of the State of Israel, May–September 1948*, I (ISA, Government Press,

The weeks of the First Truce gave the Intelligence Service officers their first prolonged respite in more than six months from the demands of daily, battle-geared operations. The major waves of Palestinian emigration (before June 1948) had occurred in the preceding weeks, during the second half of April and in May, making an analysis of the phenomenon topical and relevant. Added urgency was perhaps provided by the political context. Internally, elements in the left-wing Mapam Party (The United Workers Party), a mainstay of the Israeli coalition government, began during May and June to berate Ben-Gurion and his dominant Mapai Party (Land of Israel Labour Party) openly for waging a 'war of expulsion' against the Palestinians. In the international arena, the Palestinian refugee problem moved in June to centre stage. Instrumental in pushing the refugee problem to the fore was the newly appointed UN Mediator for Palestine, Count Folke Bernadotte, who that month began his peace shuttles around the Middle East.

But, to judge from its conclusions, the Intelligence Service analysis of the exodus was hardly produced with an eye to easing the situation of the Israeli negotiators in their dealings with the Mediator, the UN in general, or the US. Rather than suggesting Israeli blamelessness in the creation of the refugee problem, the Intelligence Service assessment is written in blunt factual and analytical terms and, if anything, contains more than a hint of 'advice' as to how to precipitate further Palestinian flight by indirect methods, without having recourse to direct politically and morally embarrassing expulsion orders. 'The factor of surprise, prolonged [artillery] barrages making loud explosive sounds, [use of] loudspeakers in Arabic [to spread frightening 'black propaganda' messages], proved their great efficacy when used properly (as in Haifa particularly)', states the report. And, under the heading of 'general comments', the report adds: 'Incidentally, no attempt was made to attach fearful-sounding sirens to the wings of aircraft bombing enemy points—their effect could be great.' The comment is included in a discussion of means which might precipitate civilian flight.

This detour into advice is the only departure in the document from straightforward analysis, whose aims, as explained in the

1981), 758, 760. At the meeting, Shertok referred to 'the astounding phenomenon' of the Palestinian exodus, and said 'something quite unprecedented and unforeseen was going on'.

'general introduction', are 'to measure the dimensions of the emigration and its various stages of development, to elucidate the various factors which directly bore upon [caused] the movement of population and to indicate the destinations of the exodus'.

The Intelligence Service then gives an assessment of the number of refugees involved, allowing for a 10–15 per cent margin of error regarding the refugee population from areas inside the Jewish state as defined by the 1947 UN Partition Plan Resolution. A greater measure of inaccuracy, states the report, must be allowed for in its estimates of refugee numbers from areas lying outside the 1947 Jewish state boundaries. The facts and figures cited below, it must be emphasized, are for the period up to 1 June 1948 (except for the Jenin area, also included in the analysis, whose population fled in the last week of May and during the first week of June).

On the eve of the UN Partition Plan Resolution of 29 November 1947, according to the report, there were 219 Arab villages and four Arab, or partly Arab, towns in the areas earmarked for Jewish statehood—with a total Arab population of 342,000. By 1 June, 180 of these villages and towns had been evacuated, with 239,000 Arabs fleeing the areas of the Jewish state. A further 152,000 Arabs, from 70 villages and three towns (Jaffa, Jenin, and Acre), had fled their homes in the areas earmarked for Palestinian Arab statehood in the Partition Resolution, and from the Jerusalem area. By 1 June, therefore, according to the report, the refugee total was 391,000, give or take about 10–15 per cent. Another 103,000 Arabs (60,000 of them Negev beduin and 5,000 Haifa residents) had remained in their homes in the areas originally earmarked for Jewish statehood. (This figure excludes the Arabs who stayed on in Jaffa and Acre, towns occupied by Jewish forces but lying outside the 1947 partition boundaries of the Jewish state.)

The Intelligence Service identified four stages in the Palestinian exodus up to 1 June. Stage one, December 1947–February 1948, affected only a small number of places and involved a relatively small number of refugees, mainly from the coastal plain. The reference in the report is to the flight of much of the Arab middle class from the towns of Haifa and Jaffa.

Stage two, covering March, involved only a small number of emigrants. Emigration in general that month was in decline, but the report registers an increase in the exodus from the Jaffa and the Sea of Galilee areas.

In stage three, during April 1948, there was a 'moderate increase' on almost all fronts in the rate of emigration, according to the report. The Intelligence Service ascribes the increase to the Arab evacuation of Tiberias (18–19 April), Haifa (22 April–1 May) and the Tel-Hai (Galilee Panhandle) districts, which were a result of major Haganah offensives in those areas in the second half of April.

Stage four, in May 1948, is defined as 'the main and decisive stage in the emigration movement of the Arabs of Palestine. A psychosis of emigration began to develop, a crisis of confidence in Arab strength.' As a result, says the Intelligence Service, there was a great increase in the rate of emigration from the Tel-Hai, Gilboa, Jaffa, and Western Galilee districts, and evacuation began of the Arab villages in the Negev. May was the 'record month' of the Arab exodus, according to the report. In the predominantly Jewish coastal plain, May marked 'the final chapter', meaning that all the area's Arab inhabitants fled, except for only a few villages. It was 'the end of the job (*siyum hamelacha*)'.

Two comments are perhaps worth making about the report's analysis of the stages of the Arab exodus: (*a*) The Intelligence Service does not provide any statistical breakdown of the numbers involved in each stage, and (*b*) the description of the rate of emigration in April as 'moderate' appears questionable, in the light of the large numbers of refugees caused by the Haganah conquest of Haifa, and the major Haganah offensives in the Galilee and along the approaches to Jerusalem.

Looking to the causes of the Palestinian exodus, the core of the report, the Intelligence Service first clears the ground by dismissing the relevance of a number of factors. The report states:

One can assume that this emigration did not come as a result of economic factors—be it a serious lack of employment, food or any other economic hardship. The Arab economy [during the period up to June 1948], so long as the inhabitants stayed in their places, was not damaged in a manner which destroyed the population's capacity to subsist. The economic factor was a motive force [for emigration] only in the very earliest stages of the exodus, when the rich Arabs sought to safeguard their property and firms by getting out quickly.

According to the report, there were 'fluctuations' in the state of the Palestine-Arab economy in the cities, 'which was a factor accelerating emigration for some social strata'. But, taking the broad view, the economic factor was not 'a serious factor when speaking of the mass emigration of the Arabs of Palestine'.

The report then goes on to dismiss as precipitants of the exodus what it defines as 'pure political factors'. Political decisions and developments, in the narrow sense of the word, had 'no effect on the exodus', states the report. The Intelligence Service went on to reject specifically any linkage between the major political developments of May—the British withdrawal, the establishment of the state of Israel, the Arab declarations of intent to destroy the Jewish state and to go to war—and the mass emigration of that month. 'It must be noted here that if there were places where the political factor was a motive force in the exodus, then it was limited to the cities and, there, to a very limited social class.'

What the Intelligence Service is saying here is that Arabs did not leave the areas of the Jewish state because of opposition to the establishment of the state or political opposition to the prospect of life under Jewish rule. According to the detailed survey in the appendix, only one Arab village or community, Arab Jallad (?), in the coastal plain, fled on 15 May, because of 'the influence of the declaration of establishment of the Jewish state'.

The report then outlines what the IDF Intelligence Service regards, in June 1948, as the factors which precipitated the exodus, citing them 'in order of importance':

1. Direct, hostile Jewish [Haganah / IDF] operations against Arab settlements.
2. The effect of our [Haganah / IDF] hostile operations on nearby [Arab] settlements ... (... especially—the fall of large neighbouring centres).
3. Operations of the [Jewish] dissidents [the Irgun Z'va'i Leumi and Lohamei Herut Yisrael].
4. Orders and decrees by Arab institutions and gangs [irregulars].
5. Jewish whispering operations [psychological warfare], aimed at frightening away Arab inhabitants.
6. Ultimative expulsion orders [by Jewish forces].
7. Fear of Jewish [retaliatory] reponse [following] major Arab attack on Jews.
8. The appearance of gangs [irregular Arab forces] and non-local fighters in the vicinity of a village.
9. Fear of Arab invasion and its consequences [mainly near the borders].
10. Isolated Arab villages in purely [predominantly] Jewish areas.
11. Various local factors and general fear of the future.

The Intelligence Service then gives a detailed breakdown and explanation of these factors, stressing that 'without doubt, hostile [Haganah / IDF] operations were the main cause of the movement of population'.

The wave of emigration in each district, explains the report, followed hard upon 'the increase and expansion of our [Haganah / IDF] operations in that district'. May brought a major increase in large-scale Jewish operations; so it also witnessed the widespread mass emigration of Arabs. 'The departure of the British . . . of course helped the [Arab] evacuation, but it appears that the British withdrawal freed our hands for action more than it influenced the [Arab] emigration directly.'

The Intelligence Service notes that it was not always the dimensions of a Jewish attack which counted: it was 'mainly the psychological' factors which affected the rate of emigration. The report cites 'surprise', protracted mortar barrages, and use of loudspeakers broadcasting threatening message as factors which had a strong influence in precipitating flight.

An attack on one village or town often affected its neighbours. 'The evacuation of a certain village because of an attack by us prompted in its wake many neighbouring villages [to flee]', states the report. This was especially true of the fall of large villages or towns. 'The fall of Tiberias, Safad, Samakh, Jaffa, Haifa and Acre engendered in their wake many waves of emigrants.' The psychological motive force in operation here was '*im ba'arazim nafla shalhevet*' ('If the cedars caught fire . . .', a paraphrase of 1 Kings 5: 13).

The report concludes: 'It is possible to say that at least 55 per cent of the total of the exodus was caused by our [Haganah / IDF] operations and by their influence'. To this the Intelligence Service adds the effects of the operations of the dissident Jewish organizations, 'who directly [caused] some 15 per cent . . . of the emigration'. The Intelligence Service notes that the activities of the dissidents were of especial importance in the Jaffa–Tel Aviv area, in the coastal plain to the north, and around Jerusalem. 'Elsewhere, they had no direct effect on the [Arab] evacuation.'

The Intelligence Service cites the 'special effect' of the dissident operation in Deir Yassin and of the 'abduction [at the end of March, 1948] of the five [Arab] notables at Sheikh Muwannis [north of Tel Aviv]'.

The action at Deir Yassin, especially, greatly affected the thinking of the Arab; not a little of the immediate flight during our [Haganah / IDF] attacks, especially in the central and southern areas . . . was due to this factor, which can be described as a decisive accelerating factor (*gorem mezarez mach'ri'a*).

Regarding the coastal plain, 'many of the villagers . . . began fleeing following the abduction of the notables of Sheikh Muwannis. The Arab learned that it was not enough to reach an agreement with the Haganah and that there were "other Jews" of whom to beware, and possibly to beware of more than of the Haganah, which had no control over them [that is, over the dissidents]'. The dissident organizations also played a decisive role in the evacuation of Jaffa and the villages around it, states the report. Altogether, the report states, Jewish—meaning Haganah / IDF, IZL, and LHI—military operations (comprising categories 1, 2, and 3) accounted for 70 per cent of the Arab exodus from Palestine.

Category 4: orders and commands by local Arab commanders and leaders, the Arab Higher Committee, and the Transjordan govern-ment—accounted for some '5 per cent of the villages' evacuated, according to the Intelligence Service. These orders to evacuate were given for 'strategic reasons . . . out of a desire to turn the village into a base for attack on the Jews or out of an awareness that there was no possibility of defending the village or out of a fear that the village could turn into an [anti-Arab] Fifth Column, especially if it reached an agreement with the Jews'. The latter cause was especially important in the Gilboa area (threats by the Arabs to leave directed at the Zu'abiya beduin), in the Sea of Galilee area ('Circassian villages'), in the Tel-Hai district along the Syrian border, and 'in the Jerusalem area (Arab Legion orders to evacuate a string of villages to set up bases in northern Jerusalem, and the order of the Arab Higher Committee to Issawiya [to evacuate])'.

Category 5: Jewish 'whispering' (psychological warfare) operations, usually involving 'friendly advice' by Jewish liaison officers to Arabs to quit their villages—according to the IDF Intelligence Service (which ran the liaison officers), accounted for only some 2 per cent of the exodus nation-wide. But in a number of regions, states the report, 'whispering' campaigns were of considerable importance. In the Tel-Hai district, for instance, such a campaign in April–May accounted for 18 per cent of the Arab exodus, and in the coastal plain villages, for 6 per cent. In the coastal plain and in the

Gilboa district, whispering operations were disorganized and unsystematic. But in the Tel-Hai district 'the operation was carried out with predetermination, with relatively wide scope and organization'—and so led to greater results. The operation itself was carried out, explains the report, in the form of 'friendly advice' by Jews to their neighbouring Arab friends.

Category 6: orders of expulsion by Jewish forces to Arab villages —accounted (up to the start of June 1948) for some 2 per cent of the total of villages evacuated, said the report. Such orders were especially 'prominent' in the coastal plain, less common in the Gilboa district, and still less in the Negev. 'Of course, the effect of [such an] ultimatum, like the effect of "friendly advice", came after a certain laying of the groundwork through hostile [Jewish] operations in area. Therefore, such [expulsion] orders are more [in the nature nature of] a final motivation and propellent, than a decisive factor.'

Another 1 per cent of the emigration was caused, according to the report, by category 7—Arab fear of Jewish retailiation after an Arab attack on Jews. This occurred in the Western Galilee (following the Arab attack on the Yehiam convoy), and after the attacks in April on Kibbutz Mishmar Ha'emek (western Jezreel Valley), and Kibbutz Gesher (Jordan Valley). According to the report, less than 2 per cent of the exodus was caused by categories 8, 9, and 10 combined. The arrival of Arab irregular forces in a village, villagers' fears that the impending Arab invasion would turn their homes into a battleground, and the fact of being an isolated village in a predominantly Jewish area all had little effect on the villagers.

The report names two further direct causes of flight: 'general fear' and 'local factors'. General fear, which 'had a great influence and role in the exodus', accounted for some 10 per cent of the refugees. In this context the report mentions the initial waves of emigration at the start of the hostilities, caused 'at first glance, by no special reason'. These were rooted in a 'general fear' resulting primarily from 'the crisis in confidence in Arab strength'.

The Intelligence Service thus places this 'crisis of confidence' in the Arab power to fight and withstand or defeat Jewish arms as 'the third most important factor, after our own [i.e., Haganah / IDF] operations and those of the dissidents', in the Arab exodus. The report states that 8–9 per cent of the exodus was caused by 'local factors', such as the breakdown in specific localities of Arab–Jewish peace negotiations and the Arabs' 'inability to adjust to certain real situations'.

Following this statistical breakdown, the report offers some 'general comments' identifying some direct and indirect contributory factors which hastened, precipitated, or increased waves of emigration in various areas at different times. First and foremost, the report refers to a 'psychosis of evacuation' which gripped some Arab communities during the hostilities, 'increasing the rate of evacuation'. It appeared, stated the report, 'like a contagious disease'. As an example, the Intelligence Service cites the case of Acre, which fell to Haganah forces on 17 May. There 'it is possible to assume . . . that the massive arrival on the scene [a fortnight before] of the refugees from Haifa, who planted in the hearts of Acre's inhabitants a psychosis of evacuation . . . had a decisive influence'. Thus, 'light attacks' and 'nudges' by the Jewish forces around Haifa had the effect of precipitating flight in a population already affected by 'evacuation psychosis'. The appearance of typhus also prompted flight. 'More than the disease itself', states the report, 'the panic created by the rumours of the spread of the epidemic was a factor prompting evacuation.' The report points out that where there was a 'strong Arab military force' the villagers did not evacuate 'readily', and 'only a direct and serious operation [by the Jewish forces] brought about the destruction of this [military] force, bringing flight [of the civilian population] in its wake'.

At the start of the evacuation 'the Arab institutions attempted to struggle against the phenomenon of flight and evacuation, and to curb the waves of emigration'. The Arab Higher Committee decided to impose restrictions, and issued threats, punishments, and propaganda in the radio and press to curb emigration. The committee also tried to mobilize the governments in the neighbouring Arab states to assist in this; there was a coincidence of interests. 'Especially, they tried to prevent the exodus of youngsters of military age', states the report. 'But all these actions completely failed because no positive action was taken which could have curbed the factors pushing towards emigration.' The sole upshot of these efforts was corruption and bribery, whereby officials began selling permits to would-be emigrants wishing to leave Palestine or to enter other countries. But this arrangement, states the report, broke down once emigration turned into a mass movement.

The penultimate section of the report deals with the destinations of the refugee communities. The authors note certain patterns. For instance, city-dwellers of rural origin often returned to their ancestral villages, as did Jaffa residents who had originated in Faluja, for example. Similarly, according to the Intelligence Service, city-dwellers who had come, or whose fathers had come, from neighbouring countries tended during the hostilities to return to those countries. Thus many Haifa residents fled directly to Lebanon and Syria. In general, the report points out, urban dwellers, including the rich, had fled directly to their final destinations whereas rural refugees tended to 'hop' through a number of way-stations before reaching their final point of rest.

Often, villagers fled at first from isolated rural sites to neighbouring Arab towns or cities. Then, when the town fell to Jewish forces, they moved on. The report cites the case of the inhabitants of Beit Sussin, in the south, who first fled to Mughar, then Yibna, and then Isdud, before coming to rest in Gaza. By and large, the refugees from the villages in the first instance moved only to nearby sites. This, according to the report, caused the Haganah problems; the Jewish units, which did not have sufficient troops to garrison every captured village, faced the prospect that the villagers might attempt to return to their homes. 'More than once,' states the report, '[Haganah / IDF units were forced] to expel inhabitants [after they had returned to their homes].'

Without giving a numerical breakdown, the report states that the wealthier Arabs mainly emigrated directly to Arab states (meaning, primarily, to Beirut and Cairo); the poorer Arabs of the northern border areas fled to Syria and Lebanon: and the inhabitants of the south and Jaffa, and some Jerusalemites and Haifa residents, moved to Egyptian-held territory (meaning mainly the Gaza strip). Most of the emigrants to Transjordanian-held territory came from the Sea of Galilee area, the Jezreel Valley, the Gilboa area, Acre, Jaffa, and the Jerusalem area.

The report ends with a look at the manner in which the refugees (by June 1948) had been absorbed in the host countries or areas. The wealthier Arabs, by and large, had no absorption problems. But most of the emigrants were poor, most had left without the bulk of their belongings, and this had led to 'severe absorption problems', says the report. This had prompted the governments of the host countries to try to persuade the refugees to go back and to put pressure, especially on able-bodied males, 'to return to the front'.

Transjordanian radio from Jerusalem, for example, in May broadcast lectures to the Palestinians to go back and lend a hand in the war effort, maintaining that 'there was no danger to the lives of those returning'.

Some Israelis feared that the embittered refugees might be turned into soldiers who would return to fight against Israel. The Intelligence Service analysis dismissed this danger: 'The Arab emigrant did not turn into a fighter, his only interest now is in collecting money [philanthropy]. He has resigned himself to the lowest form of life, preferring it to mobilizing for battle.' In conclusion, the report states that the refugees were a burden which would continue to grow and weigh upon the Arab states, especially as 'no serious and comprehensive organized step was being taken by the Arab states in order to solve the problem'.

How accurate is the information conveyed in this document? How sound is its analysis of the causes of the Palestinian exodus up to June 1948? What is its significance in relation to the traditional perceptions of the character and causes of that exodus?

In theory at least, the IDF Intelligence Service—Israel's main intelligence service in June 1948—was very well placed to collect and analyse data about the Palestinian exodus. The officer or officers who produced this report had access to the reports of Israeli agents and Arab informants in the various Arab localities, to the signals and reports of the Haganah / IDF unit intelligence officers (one at least was attached to every battalion and brigade) and, probably, to signal traffic and reports of the various unit commanders and front commanders around the country.

It is also possible that the authors of the report were supplied, at their request, with special reports by units' intelligence officers and perhaps unit commanders as well detailing each unit's history of conquest and treatment of Arab settlements. The respite provided by the first weeks of the First Truce would have made possible the writing of such reports. An indirect indication that such reports were indeed produced and, at least in part, served as the basis of this analysis is afforded by the absence of one of the two appendices which, according to the table of contents printed on the covering page of the document, were to have accompanied the text—'appendix 1' giving 'regional surveys analysing the problems of emigration in each and every district'. Presumably, these surveys were to have been written by unit, front (*hazit*), or district (*nafa*) intelligence officers. Either some of them were not delivered or those delivered were regarded as inadequate for reproduction along with the text and the originally entitled 'appendix 2', which details the exodus from each village, by district, around the country. (Appendix 2, in fact, was included, retitled 'appendix 1'.)

In the end, the authors apparently decided that the analysis, buttressed by the village-by-village appendix, was sufficient, and the regional analyses at first contemplated were left out (though sallies into regional analysis are to be found interspersed unsystematically throughout the text).

Real-time signal traffic and post-operational reporting by and large were accurate in the Haganah / IDF in 1948. But until mid-May—covering almost the whole period dealt with in the report—the Haganah was an underground force, and did not produce or store the kind of comprehensive documentation about its operations that a good regular army would have done. Much of the reporting up the chain of command and orders handed down the chain of command in the first months of 1948 were necessarily oral, and much of the signal traffic was never recorded or was subsequently lost. Hence, in producing this analysis of the exodus, the Intelligence Service perforce had to rely to some extent on the memories of commanders and local intelligence officers rather than on contemporaneous chronicling.

Moreover, the dissident organizations—the IZL and LHI, to whose operations the report attributes some 15 per cent of the exodus—produced even less written material than the Haganah and, if it existed in June, this was never made available to the Haganah and IDF. (The Haganah regarded the IZL and LHI as hostile organizations; June, indeed, marked the high point of the conflict between the groups, with the IDF killing a number of IZL combatants and sinking off Tel Aviv a ship bearing arms for the dissident force.)

Lastly, a number of operations by local Haganah units and by Jewish settlements against neighbouring Arab communities were carried out with Haganah National Staff command, authorization, or approval, and were never accurately reported upon to the National Staff *ex post facto*.

The reservations about sourcing aside, there is no reason to cast doubt on the integrity of the IDF Intelligence Service in the production of this analysis. The analysis was produced almost certainly only for internal, IDF top brass consumption. (No copy of it has surfaced in any collection of private papers of the 1948 Israeli Cabinet ministers; nor, save for the copy used in this paper, in any civilian archive. Nor was its existence or content ever referred to in any recorded political party debate.)[3] The authors of the report would have certainly been conscious of their 'consumer public', and aware that many of the consumers were highly familiar with parts of the subject matter of the analysis. On the other hand, the authors will not always have been familiar enough with given incidents to catch all errors or distortions in the reports of local commanders and intelligence officers. So, while the details of the report and its analysis by and large conform with the facts as recorded in other sources from the period, a degree of analytical inaccuracy and factual imprecision and error is none the less evident. This point is worth elucidating before going on to weigh up the significance of the document.

The village-by-village survey in the appendix lists 14 villages evacuated as a result of Haganah or IDF orders or ultimatums.[4] In peacetime these villages together had a population of some 20,000.

[3] The report was received by Cohen, a member of the Mapam Centre and of the party's Political Committee, on 11 July 1948. These party institutions, through the summer, very frankly and thoroughly debated the Yishuv's policy towards the Palestinian Arabs, covering such subjects as expulsions, the possibility of a refugee return, etc. Yet neither Cohen nor anyone else ever referred in these recorded debates to the IDF Intelligence Service analysis. One possible explanation is that the report, being contemporary and on a sensitive subject, was regarded by Cohen as something too 'hot' to use or refer to openly. Mapam, Cohen, and his contact might have been in deep trouble. Ironically, only a few years later Cohen landed in prison after being convicted of unauthorized contacts with Soviet agents.

[4] The villages named are Ad Dumeira (population 620—evacuated 10 Apr. 1948); Miska (population 650—evacuated 15 Apr. 1948); Khirbet as Sarkas (evacuated 15 Apr. 1948); Arab an Nufei'at (population 910—evacuated 10 Apr. 1948); Khirbet Azzun (population 994—evacuated 3 Apr. 1948); and Arab al Foqara (population 340—evacuated 10 Apr. 1948), all in the coastal plain; Dana (population 400—evacuated 28 May 1948), in the Gilboa district; and Zarnuga (population 2,600—evacuated 27 May 1948); Yibna (population 5,920—evacuated 4 June 1948); Huj (population 800—evacuated 28 May 1948); Arab Rubin (population 1,550—evacuated 1 June 1948); Kaukaba (population 1,870—evacuated 17 May 1948); Sumsum (population 1,200—evacuated 12 May 1948); and Najd (population 600—evacuated 12 May 1948), all in the south. It is worth noting that the expulsions detailed in the appendix are almost all part of two 'series'—one in the northern coastal plain on 10–15 April 1948 and the other in the northern Negev approaches on 27–8 May 1948.

Yet in the analysis of the causes of the exodus, the report speaks of only 2 per cent 'of the villages' (out of a total of 250 evacuated) as leaving because of Haganah / IDF expulsion orders. Fourteen out of 250 represents more like 5 per cent.

Moreover, the report leaves a large, poorly demarcated grey area between outright expulsion by Jewish order and evacuation of Arab villages in the course of Haganah / IDF 'military operations' (which are said to account for 55 per cent of the exodus).

Some of the villages said to have been evacuated because of 'military operations' (and presumably included in that 55 per cent), are seen in the detailed breakdown in the appendix to have been de-populated in a somewhat less straightforward manner. For example, the 710-strong population of Khirbet Lid (al-Awadim), near Afula, in the Jezreel Valley, is said in the appendix to have left because of 'the influence of [the nearby battle of] Mishmar Ha'emek' in April 1948. But in the subsequent 'comment', the appendix also states: 'They tried to return. And were expelled.' Khirbet Lid was presumably not included under the expulsion category.

Nor was Fajja, a large village next to Petah Tikva. Part of the population left after the IZL attack on 17 March. The final evacuation on 15 May took place, according to the appendix, because of 'pressure by us [and] a whispering [that is, psychological warfare] campaign'. Presumably Fajja was listed among the 2 per cent of evacuations caused by psychological warfare; but, given the reference to 'pressure' by the Haganah, it could also have been included perhaps in the expulsion category (which it presumably was not).

Nor was Al Khalisa, the site of present-day Kiryat Shmona, in the Galilee Panhandle. The village, with a population of 1,840, is said to have been evacuated on 11 May because of 'the fall of Safad', a major Arab centre to the south. But according to the appendix, that was not all. 'They wanted [to reach] an agreement with us. They were turned down. [So] they fled', states the report. Presumably, Khalisa was included under the 'local factors' category rather than under the expulsion category. As in Al Khalisa, so in As Salihiya, a village of 1,520 a few kilometres to the south. 'They wanted to negotiate—we did not show up', states the report. The villgers fled Palestine on 25 May.

In general, the situation on the ground made it impossible in many cases to draw a clear distinction between a Haganah / IDF or

IZL 'military operation' which ended in villagers fleeing their homes and 'expulsion orders', which had the same effect. In some 'military operations', such as the Haganah conquest of the Arab parts of Haifa, the Jewish troops by and large had no clear intention of provoking an Arab exodus and their military strategy was not calculated to produce such an outcome. In other military operations, such as the IZL attack on Jaffa, and probably the Haganah offensive in Western Galilee in May 1948, the flight of the Arab inhabitants was clearly desired and deliberately provoked by the attacking troops. The IZL / LHI attack on Deir Yassin near Jerusalem on 9 April ended not only in a massacre but also in the expulsion by the conquering unit of the surviving Arab villagers. (The Intelligence Service report catagorizes the flight of the Deir Yassin inhabitants as a result of a dissident operation rather than under the heading of expulsion.)

While the report was not produced with any propagandizing intention in mind, its authors seem to have exhibited a perhaps understandable tendency to minimize the role direct expulsion orders played in bringing about part of the Palestinian exodus. The proportion of villages expelled is computed incorrectly and a large grey area of 'semi-expulsions' is included under the category of flight due to 'military operations' or some other 'non-expulsion' category.

Moreover, the report also includes a number of factual errors and omissions in this context; presumably these were the result of misinformation in the reports by local unit commanders and field intelligence officers. For instance, part of the population of the Arab town of Beisan (Beit Shean) is said to have fled on 1 May because of 'fear and the influence of [the fall of Arab] Haifa'. The remainder of the population, according to the appendix, is said to have left on 12 May as a result of the Haganah 'conquest [of the town]. Fear. The influence of Haifa.' But this is not completely accurate. Hundreds of the town's residents stayed on after the conquest, and were expelled only days later—some to Nazareth, others across the Jordan River—at Haganah command.[5]

[5] See Binyamin Etzioni (ed.), *Ilan Va'shelah*, an account of the Golani Brigade's operations in 1948 produced by the unit's soldiers, (IDF Publications (Ma'arachot), Tel Aviv, 1950?), 146, See also Central Zionist Archives S53–437 (the Eliezer Granovsky Papers), Yosef Weitz to Eliezer Granovsky, 25 May 1948; and Yosef Weitz, *Diaries* (Massada, Tel Aviv, 1965) iii. 301–2, entry for 13 June 1948.

The small village of 140 tenant farmers of Qira wa Qamun near Yoqne'am, on the western edge of the Jezreel Valley, was evacuated in March by its inhabitants after they received 'friendly advice' from the local Haganah intelligence officer at Yoqne'am, Yehuda Burstein.[6] But the report gives the reason for the Qira evacuation as 'fear and the influence of the attacks in the area'—not really the same thing.

More inexplicable is the omission altogether from the appendix of the fate of a string of Western Galilee villages—Az Zib, Manshiya, As Sumeiriya, Al Bassa and others—all evacuated during or before the Haganah's Operation Ben-Ami in mid-May. It is quite possible that the Haganah commander in Western Galilee or the relevant intelligence officers simply failed to submit to the Intelligence Service a report on the Arab exodus from their area.

The report's treatment of villages evacuated as a result of edicts or orders by Arab authorities, political or military, is also worth examining. Altogether, 21 villages out of the 250 are listed in the appendix as having been evacuated or partially evacuated as a result of Arab command, be it by the Arab Legion, the Arab Higher Committee, or other Arab bodies.[7] The figure is higher than the '5 per cent' cited in the report's analysis as having fled because of Arab commands. Here too the report omitted or ignored material instancing Arab advice or orders to communities to partially or completely evacuate their settlements. For example, the 'defence and security section' of the (Arab) National Committee in Jerusalem, basing itself on instructions from the Arab Higher Committee issued on 8 March, in mid-April ordered the national committees in the Sheikh Jarrah, Wadi Joz, Sa'ad wa Sa'id, Musrara, and Katamon

---

[6] Interview with Eliezer Be'eri (Bauer), Kibbutz Hazore'a., April 1984.

[7] The report lists the following villages as evacuated, or partly evacuated, at higher Arab command: Shu'fat, Beit Hanina, Al Jib, Judeira, Beit Nabala, and Rafat (total population 4,000–5,000—all on Arab Legion orders) all on 13 May 1948; Issawiya (population 780—evacuated at Arab Higher Committee command on 30 Mar. 1948); Ar Ruweis, on 24 Apr. 1948; Ad Dahi, Nein, Tamra, Kafr Misr, At Tira, Taiyiba, and Na'ura, all in the Gilboa district and evacuated on 20 May 1948, after threats from Arab irregulars; and, in the Sea of Galilee area, Adasiya (evacuated on 15 May 1948 at Transjordanian command); and Sirin, Ulam, Hadatha, and Ma'dhar (all in the Galilee, evacuated at the command of the Arab Higher Committee on 6 Apr. 1948). Within months, the populations of Shu'fat, Beit Hanina, Al Jib, Judeira, Issawiya, and Tamra had returned to their homes.

quarters of Jerusalem to order the women, children, and the old in their areas to leave their homes and move to areas 'far away from the dangers. Any opposition to this order . . . is an obstacle to the holy war . . . and will hamper the operations of the fighters in these districts.'[8]

In early May, units of the Arab Legion entered the town of Beisan and reportedly ordered the evacuation of all women and children.[9] At about the same time, the Arab Liberation Army was reported to have ordered the villagers in Fureidis, south of Haifa, to 'evacuate the women and children from the village and to make ready to evacuate the village completely'.[10] In general, the IDF Intelligence Service report fails to stress the importance in the Arab exodus of the early departure in many cases from the villages of the women and children. This tended to sap the morale of the menfolk who were left behind to guard the homes and fields, contributing to the final evacuation of villages. Such two-tier evacuations—women and children first, the men following weeks later—occurred in Qumiya in the Jezreel Valley, among the Ghawarina beduin in Haifa Bay, and in various other places.

What then is the significance of the IDF Intelligence Service report in understanding the Palestinian exodus of 1948? To begin with, it thoroughly undermines the traditional official Israeli 'explanation' of a mass flight ordered or 'invited' by the Arab leadership for political–strategic reasons. Quite clearly, according to the report, Arab orders to evacuate villages were restricted to a number of areas, were guided by local strategic considerations, and affected no more than 10 per cent of the Palestinian refugee population. (About half of the villages evacuated because of Arab command, those in the Jerusalem and lower Galilee areas, were in fact subsequently repopulated by their original inhabitants once circumstances had changed.)

The report makes no mention of any blanket order issued over Arab radio stations or through other means, to the Palestinians to evacuate their homes and villages. Had such an order been issued, it

[8] ISA, FM 2570/11, announcement by the National Committee of Jerusalem, 22 Apr. 1948.
[9] CZA, A246–13 (the manuscript of the Weitz Diaries), entry for 4 May 1948.
[10] Private information.

would without doubt have been mentioned or cited in this document; the Haganah Intelligence Service and it successsor, the IDF Intelligence Service closely monitored Arab radio transmissions and the Arabic press.

Indeed, the Intelligence Service report in its main thrust seems to go still further in undermining the official Israeli historiography. For not only is the 'Arab orders' explanation seen to be limited in the numbers it affected and extremely restricted geographically; but the report goes out of its way to stress that the exodus was contrary to the political–strategic desires of both the Arab Higher Committee and the governments of the neighbouring Arab states. These, according to the report, struggled against the exodus—threatening, cajoling, imposing punishments, all to no avail. There was no stemming the panic-borne tide. (To this, a caveat must be attached. The report does not record or analyse the *dates* of the official Arab efforts to stem the exodus. The dates may be significant. Whereas there is evidence of a large number of Arab attempts to stop the exodus during December 1947 and during the first months of 1948 and in early May 1948, there is far less material of this sort relating to April and mid- and late May 1948, when the flight reached its peak.) But neither does the Intelligence Service report uphold the traditional Arab explanation of the exodus—that the Jews with premeditation, in centralized fashion, and systematically had waged a campaign aimed at the wholesale expulsion of the native Palestinian population.

The exodus was certainly viewed favourably by the bulk of the Yishuv's leadership; it had solved the embryonic Jewish state's chief and agonizing political–strategic problem, the existence in it of a very large actively or potentially hostile Arab minority. A tone of satisfaction with the exodus does indeed pervade the report; but from it emerges a very definite impression that the depopulation of the villages and towns was an unexpected outcome of operations the purpose of which was wholly or primarily the conquest of military positions and strategic sites in the course of a life-and-death struggle. Jewish military operations indeed accounted for 70 per cent of the Arab exodus; but the depopulation of the villages in most cases was an incidental, if favourably regarded, side-effect of these operations, not their aim. Had the population of the villages and towns remained *in situ* during and after the Jewish attack and conquest, the Haganah

/IDF and IZL would have been faced at each site with the successive dilemma: to expel or not to expel. As it was, the population, by taking to its heels at the first whiff of grapeshot, usually solved this possible problem. The report's estimate of the proportion of villages depopulated by calculated, direct Jewish expulsion orders is none the less somewhat low. For the period up to 1 June 1948, something around 5 per cent seems closer to the mark than the 2 per cent cited. Even after adding to this the villagers 'nudged' into flight by deliberate military pressures and psychological assault, one is still left with only a small proportion of the exodus accounted for in this manner.

One must again emphasize that the report and its significance pertain only up to 1 June 1948, by which time some 300,000–400,000 Palestinians had left their homes. A similar number was to leave the Jewish-held areas in the remaining months of the war. The circumstances of the second half of the exodus—during the IDF conquest of Lydda and Ramle, and the central Galilee in July, the northern Negev in October–November, and the northern Galilee in October—are a different story. But for an understanding of the Palestinian exodus until 1 June, one must, according to IDF Intelligence, reach mainly for the vast middle ground between pre-planned, outright IDF expulsion and Arab-engineered, Machiavellian flight. There, amid the frightening, threatening boom of guns, the loss of confidence in Arab might, the flight of relatives and friends, the abandonment of nearby towns, and a general, vast fear of the uncharted future, one will find the bulk of the pre-June Palestinian refugees.

4

Yosef Weitz and the Transfer Committees, 1948–1949

I met Ben-Gurion . . . [He said:] 'The Arabs of the Land of Israel, they have but one function left—to run away'. With that he got up and ended the conversation.

(Ezra Danin, special adviser on Arab affairs at the Foreign Ministry (Tel Aviv), to Elias Sasson (Paris), director of the Middle East Affairs Department, Foreign Ministry, 24 October 1948.)[1]

There is reason to assume, that what is being done . . . [is being done] out of certain political aims and not only out of military necessity . . . In fact, what is called a 'transfer' of the Arabs out of the area of the Jewish state is what is being carried out . . .

(From 'Our Arab Policy During the War', a memorandum to the Political Committee of Mapam by Aharon Cohen, director of Mapam's Arab Department, 10 May 1948.)[2]

The migration of the Arabs of the Land of Israel was not caused by persecution, violence, expulsion . . . [it was] a tactic of war on the part of the Arabs . . .

(The Weitz Committee Report, November 1948).[3]

As the Yishuv welcomed the 29 November 1947 UN General Assembly Partition Resolution on Palestine, its leaders grimly pondered the future prospect of war and the emergent Jewish state's major problem: of the 1.1 million or so people included in the

---

[1] ISA, FM 2570/11, E. Danin (Tel Aviv) to E. Sasson (Paris), 24 Oct. 1948.
[2] HHA-ACP, 10.95.10 (4).
[3] ISA, FM 2445/3, the report of the Transfer Committee (Yosef Weitz, Ezra Danin, Zalman Lifshitz), entitled 'Regarding the Solution to the Arab Refugees', Nov. 1948.

areas earmarked for Jewish independence, close to 45 per cent were Arabs. Was there a solution to 'the Arab problem', as it was commonly referred to in Yishuv leadership circles?

Within weeks, hostilities between Arab and Jew engulfed large areas of the country; within two to three months, tens of thousands of the land's Arab inhabitants, mostly from the urban middle class of Jerusalem, Jaffa, and Haifa, departed for Beirut, Cairo, and the Hebron Hills and the area then known as the 'Triangle' (encompassing Nablus, Jenin, and Tulkarm).

The steady Arab exodus took the Yishuv's leaders by surprise; for most, a pleasant surprise. With his eye for history, the Yishuv's leader, Jewish Agency chairman David Ben-Gurion, quickly recognized the exodus as the possible start of a thoroughgoing demographic-political-economic revolution which could solve the 'Arab problem'. Perhaps most or all the country's Arabs would go. 'What happened in Jerusalem and . . . in Haifa, could happen in large parts of the country if we stand fast . . . It is possible that there will be very great changes in the country in the [coming] six or eight or ten months of this war . . . Certainly there will be great changes in the composition of the population of the country . . .' Ben-Gurion told the Mapai (Land of Israel Labour Party) Council on 7 February 1948. He was speaking after a brief visit to western Jerusalem, which had become '100 per cent Jewish . . . In many Arab districts in the west one sees not a single Arab. I do not believe this will change', he said.[4]

A similar feeling that a giant, historic transformation was under way also gripped Yosef Weitz (1890–1972), director of the Jewish National Fund's Lands Department who, since the 1930s, was responsible for land acquisition (mostly from Arabs) by the Yishuv. The departing Arabs, he was convinced, would not return, and events were leading to 'a complete territorial revolution . . . The State [of Israel] is destined to expropriate . . . their land.'[5]

---

[4] Labour Party Archives (Beit Berl), 22/35, protocol of the Mapai Council meeting 7 Feb. 1948. A slightly different version is given in David Ben-Gurion, *Yoman Hamilhama-Tashah* [the war diaries, 1948–9] (Tel Aviv, 1982) i. 210–11, entry for 6–7 Feb. 1948. (The Ben-Gurion diaries henceforward will be referred to as DBG.)

[5] Yosef Weitz, *Diaries*, 5 vols., iii, (Tel Aviv, 1965), 288, entry for 20 May 1948. (The Weitz Diaries will henceforth be referred to as Weitz.)

Weitz early on realized that the state of anarchy created by the hostilities and the steady breakdown of British Mandate rule could and should be exploited if the 'Arab problem' was to be solved and the Jewish state established on solid foundations. He was excellently placed to do this exploiting and to egg others on to do the same.

By 1949, the Yishuv's main pre-state 'National Institutions'—the Jewish Agency, the JNF, the National Committee (*ha-Va'ad ha-leumi*) and so forth—had lost many or all of their powers, giving way to the new institutions of state, primarily the government ministries, the Cabinet, and the Knesset. But through 1948, while the ministries were still being established, the National Institutions retained major powers. As one of the National Institutions' chief executives, Weitz in 1948 still sat astride the crossroads of power in the new state.

As the JNF executive in charge of land acquisition and its allocation to Jewish settlements, as the JNF representative on the Committee of Directorates of the National Institutions (*Va'ad ha-Hanhalot shel Hamosdot ha-Leumim*) and on the Settlement Committee of the National Institutions, as chairman of the Negev Committee (the civilian government of the Jewish settlements in the southern desert region) and as a member of the three-man Arab Affairs Committee of the National Institutions, Weitz was well placed to shape and influence decision-making regarding the Arab population on the national level and to oversee the implementation of policy on the local level. The JNF's branches and personnel around the country were at his disposal.

To old and new Jewish settlements, Weitz was a powerful patron figure, the dispenser of much-needed tracts of land. For the Yishuv's political leaders, he was an expert on territorial, settlement, and Arab matters. Through 1948 he had ready access to key cabinet ministers, such as Foreign Minister Moshe Shertok (later Sharrett) and Finance Minister Eliezer Kaplan—and often, he met with Ben-Gurion, who from mid-May was Prime Minister and Defence Minister. Weitz's connections also encompassed the Yishuv's military brass, especially on the level of district, area, and battalion commanders, most of whom came from the kibbutzim with which Weitz had continuous dealings. His expertise on land matters and Arabs—stemming from years of organizing land deals and regional development projects—was the basis of his standing among the

Yishuv's intelligence apparatus, the Haganah's Sherut Yediot (the Shai), and its successor organization, the IDF Intelligence Service.

EVICTING TENANT-FARMERS AND BEDUIN

Following the start of Arab–Jewish hostilities at the end of 1947, Weitz was among the first to apppreciate and act upon the potential for land acquisition inherent in the state of anarchy which had descended upon Palestine as rival militias traded blows under the eyes of British regiments preoccupied with organizing their own safe withdrawal from a land that had become ungovernable. His attention in early 1948 initially focused on the Arab tenant-farmer communities which 'squatted' on JNF-owned land. Absentee Arab landowners had previously sold the land to the JNF but the tenants in some areas had refused JNF compensation offers and refused to move off, or accepted compensation and then stayed put. In some cases during the 1940s, the JNF, assisted by local Haganah forces, had destroyed such squatters' houses and fields in an effort to drive them off. In the hilly Ramot–Menashe area, south-east of Haifa, three such tenant communities—Ju'ara (with 14 families), Daliyat ar Ruha (with 53 families) and Qira wa Qamun (with 42 families)— had been compensated and in the main evicted in the mid-1940s. But some of the tenant families had stayed on and others had returned to Daliyat ar Ruha and Qira, rebuilding their houses and renewing cultivation of the fields. The British Mandate authorities barred the Yishuv from using force to evict them.[6]

In early 1948 Weitz saw his chance. Travelling north on 11 January, Weitz met in Haifa with officials of the JNF's Northern District office to discuss the situation in Ramot–Menashe, an area strategically, economically, and politically vital to the Yishuv as it linked the Jewish population centre in the coastal plain with the Haganah and kibbutz centre in the Jezreel Valley. Despite its predominantly Arab population, the area was included by the November 1947 UN Partition Plan in the territory of the prospective Jewish state. 'Was not now the time to be rid [of the tenant-farmers]? Why continue to leave in our midst these thorns which represent a

[6] Central Zionist Archives, (CZA) S-25/10682, a memorandum: 'On the Question of Eviction of Arabs' by Yosef Weitz, 20 Mar. 1946.

potential danger . . .'? Our people are [now] weighing up . . . the matter,' Weitz noted in his diary after the meeting.[7]

The following day Weitz journeyed to Yoqne'am, where he met the local Haganah intelligence officer, Yehuda Burstein. The two 'discussed . . . the question of the eviction of tenant-farmers from Yoqne'am and Daliyat [ar Ruha] with the methods now acceptable. The matter has been left in the hands of the defence people [that is, the Haganah] and during the afternoon I talked with the [Haganah] deputy commander in the district.'[8] But the Haganah as yet had formulated no policy regarding the Arab population of Palestine; local commanders had no authority to evict Arabs. The matter hung fire. But Weitz persisted. On 22 February he participated in what he defined as 'a final discussion' about 'the evacuation of our lands in Yoqne'am, Daliyat and [Qira wa] Qamun, and the means that must be employed [to achieve this]'.[9] A few weeks later, Burstein ordered the tenant-farmers of Qira wa Qamun off the land, on pain of attack by the Haganah. They left. So did those living in Arab Yoqne'am and most of those at Daliyat ar Ruha, possibly after similar intimidation by Burstein or in a domino reaction, based on fear, following the exodus from Qira wa Qamun.[10]

In late March, Weitz, on another visit to Haifa, noted that the tenant-farmers at Yoqne'am had departed. The 'problem' of what to do with their fields and shacks remained. It was decided, in a discussion with JNF officials, 'to take everything into our possession . . . to dismantle the shacks . . . and to pay the tenant-farmers compensation . . . .'.[11]

Daliyat, however, remained a problem. Some 12 families had remained *in situ*. It was decided to pay them 'what was due in compensation, on condition they leave the site. If they don't agree [to go]—we will force them to do so. They cannot be left in our midst because of the danger that alien gangs [of Arab irregulars] will

---

[7] Weitz, iii, p. 226, entry for 11 Jan. 1948.

[8] CZA, A-246/12, p. 2290, entry for 12 Jan. 1948. Yosef Weitz's diaries were published in a somewhat abridged and edited form by Weitz in 1965. The originals of the diaries, in manuscript notebooks are deposited in the CZA, in file A-246. The differences between the original manuscripts and the published diaries are important especially with regard to the subject dealt with in this essay.

[9] CZA, A-246/13, pp. 2,315–16, entry for 22 Feb. 1948.

[10] Interview with Eliezer Be'eri, Kibbutz Hazore'a, Apr. 1984, for information on Burstein and the intimidation of Qira.

[11] Weitz, iii, pp. 256–7, entry for 26 Mar. 1948.

infiltrate into their midst and attack our settlements.'[12] The problem of Daliyat ar Ruha remained unresolved. On 2 April Weitz raised the matter with one of Ben-Gurion's senior aides, Levi Shkolnik (later Eshkol, who became Ben-Gurion's successor as Prime Minister in 1963). Weitz complained that the Haganah 'did not want to act there'. The discussion more generally covered 'the eviction of Arabs' from Jewish-owned lands. Shkolnik said that he knew nothing about the Daliyat problem, and Weitz concluded: 'It appears that I will personally have to deal with all [matters] pertaining to JNF tracts.'[13] In mid-April, the last tenant farmers left Daliyat ar Ruha, and on 29 July 1948 a new Israeli settlement, Kibbutz Ramot-Menashe, was established near the site.

While in Haifa in the early months of 1948, Weitz also took a keen interest in another problem area, the Beit Shean (Beisan) Valley, where the JNF had long sought to buy out Arab landholdings to set up new Jewish settlements and to establish a continuous concentration of Jewish habitation and cultivation where full-scale regional planning would be possible. (Under the Mandate, Jewish rural regional planning, in which Weitz figured largely, was almost impossible because of the intermixed populations and landholdings in every district.) In late February Weitz noted that the semi-nomadic beduins of the valley—Al Bawati, Al Ghazawiya, As Safa, Az Zarraa, Al Khuneizir, Al Hamra, Al Arida, Umm Ajra, and As Sakhina—were beginning to decamp and move across the Jordan River to Transjordan. 'Possibly now is the time to activate our original plan and to transfer them there', Weitz wrote.[14]

But the situation in the valley, part of the future Jewish state according to the partition plan, was complex. Arab cultivators and roving beduins lived on Jewish-owned land, on Arab lands, and on state-owned lands, which until the British evacuation in May were the property of the Mandate Government. Some of the state lands were formally leased to Arabs until long after the termination of the Mandate. At Al Ashrafiya, some Arab residents had pulled out. The question, for Weitz and his Haifa JNF staff, was whether 'to seize [the Ashrafiya land] now. My opinion was negative', wrote Weitz. 'We have no interest in entering into conflict with the

[12] Weitz, iii, p. 257, entry for 26 Mar. 1948.
[13] Ibid., p. 261, entry for 2 Apr. 1948.
[14] Ibid., pp. 239–40, entry for 20 Feb. 1948.

[British] government over the land. What must be done: To make sure the beduins don't occupy the tracts and to be ready, come May . . . to take over the land ourselves.'[15]

But the beduins began to trickle back into the valley at the end of March and beginning of April. Weitz took up the matter with his Haifa staff and the local Beit Shean Haganah commanders on 26 March. Moshe ('Musa') Goldenberg, Haganah area commander (*maaz*) of Kibbutz Beit Alfa, and a representative of Kibbutz Maoz, 'demanded' the immediate establishment of another Jewish settlement near Kibbutz Kfar Ruppin 'as a means of liberating our land and preventing the return of the beduins who had fled to Transjordan . . . At my insistence', wrote Weitz, 'it was agreed that the [Jewish] settlements in [the] Beit Shean [Valley] would begin to receive the lands and cultivate them. As to defence [matters], our activities must be directed towards the evacuation [of the Arabs] from the whole Beit Shean Valley apart from the town [that is, Beisan]. Now is the time. We shall [later] pay the owners the price of the land.'[16] At Daliyat ar Ruha and Qira wa Qamun, Weitz had dealt with the eviction of Arab tenant-farmers squatting on Jewish-owned lands; in the Beit Shean Valley, he was dealing with the expulsion of Arabs from Arab-owned lands (as well as from Jewish lands) to Transjordan.

At the 26 March meeting with Goldenberg, Weitz also raised the problem of the villages of Tira and Qumiya, near Kibbutz Ein Harod, in the Jezreel Valley. 'These villages are also planted in our midst and their inhabitants do not accept the responsibility of preventing the infiltration' of Arab irregulars. 'They must be forced to leave their villages until peace comes. If they do not agree [to go] they must be forced to do it.'[17] Two days later, Weitz reported that David Baum, the Haganah area commander in Kfar Yehezkeel, near Ein Harod, had told him that the bulk of Qumiya's inhabitants had departed, the British authorities having provided transport. The villagers had left behind 'less than 20 men to look after the village and its fields. However, this cannot be allowed', commented Weitz and 'it is clear that our people will have to take over [the village]'. As to Tira, Weitz wrote, it was still 'an obstacle. There is

[15] CZA, A-246/13, p. 2,315, entry for 20 Feb. 1948.
[16] Weitz p. 257, entry for 26 Mar. 1948.
[17] Ibid., p. 257, entry for 26 Mar. 1948.

still no decision to transfer its inhabitants, but we shall have to do this. We must . . . We must plug the holes in our midst, even against our will', he wrote.[18] Tira was evacuated by its inhabitants on 15 April after receiving 'friendly Jewish advice'.[19] Weitz presented the Qumiya incident in a somewhat different light to his boss, JNF chairman Dr Avraham Granovsky (later Granott). On 31 March Weitz wrote him that 'there is a tendency among our Arab neighbours . . . to abandon their villages. Last Saturday all the inhabitants of Qumiya . . . left and went to [the town of] Beit Shean [Beisan]. This will force our people to enter the village. More such [events] are imminent. And this poses for us very interesting and very grave problems'.[20]

By mid-April the Beit Shean Valley problem had not been solved. Weitz raised the matter on 13 April with the chief of the Haganah National Staff, Yisrael Galili, citing pressure by Goldenberg. According to Weitz, Goldenberg was demanding Haganah National Staff permission to take over the village of Al Ashrafiya. Galili, according to Weitz, promised to reply the following day, but failed to do so.[21] The Haganah did not occupy the village and on 26 April Goldenberg, meeting Weitz in Haifa, reported that the Arabs were busy reaping the crops in the Ashrafiya fields 'under British-army guard'. No word had reached him from Galili and 'the beduins are beginning to return. King Abdullah [of Transjordan] is pressing them to go back [to the Beit Shean Valley]'.[22] Weitz responded that 'we must employ counter-pressure so that also those who have remained in the valley will leave it'.[23]

The situation was apparently no better on 4 May, when a delegation of Beit Shean and Jezreel Valley settlement leaders came to see Weitz in Tel Aviv. They said that units of the Transjordanian army, the Arab Legion (then formally under British control) had returned to the town of Beisan. They asked 'me to influence the [Haganah] staff here [to launch an attack]'. Weitz for his part, was angry with the settlement leaders that 'the [Beit Shean] Valley was still seething with enemies'. He told them: 'The eviction [of the Arabs from]

[18] Weitz p. 257, entry for 28 Mar. 1948.   [19] Private information.
[20] CZA, Eliezer Granovsky Papers, A-202/217, Y. Weitz to E. Granovsky, 31 Mar. 1948.
[21] CZA, A-246/13, p. 2,353, entry for 13 Apr.
[22] CZA, A-246/13, p. 2,366, entry for 26 Apr. 1948.
[23] Weitz, iii, p. 273, entry for 26 Apr. 1948.

the valley is the order of the day . . .' That evening, Weitz went to Ben-Gurion's aide, Shkolnik, and spoke about Beit Shean. 'He agreed with me', Weitz recorded. Shkolnik told him to go and talk to Ben-Gurion and the Haganah brass. Whether Weitz subsequently pressed the matter with Ben-Gurion and the Haganah staff in Tel Aviv is unclear.[24] But during the following weeks, 'counter pressure' was effectively applied and the valley was completely cleared of its Arab inhabitants; the town of Beit Shean fell to Haganah attack on 12 May and most of its inhabitants fled or were expelled across the Jordan River to Transjordan.[25] The remaining inhabitants were expelled a few weeks later. On 10 June, two kibbutzim—later named Reshafim and Sheluhot—were established on Ashrafiya lands. On 25 May, Weitz reported to Granovsky that 'we control all the Beit Shean Valley [and] that most of the Arab population has left, and the town [of Beisan] is almost completely empty: Only some 300 souls are left in it for now'.[26] On 13 June Weitz recorded that no Arabs were left in the town.[27]

The extent of Weitz's influence on events in the Beit Shean Valley in the spring and summer of 1948 is unclear, though it does not seem to have been negligible. His intervention in developments in western Galilee seems to have been even more effective. During his visit to Haifa in late March, Weitz instructed the JNF office officials, regarding the Ghawarina or Al Awarna beduins of the Haifa Bay area: 'They must be evicted from there so that they too will not join our enemies.'[28] The officials apparently discussed the matter with the Haifa area Haganah commanders, but by mid-April nothing had happened.

On 14 April a representative of Kibbutz Kfar Masaryk in the bay came to see Weitz in Tel Aviv and raised the question of 'the eviction of the beduins from the bay. [He] was astonished', recorded Weitz, 'that [it] had not been done yet. I [then] wrote a letter to the Haganah [commander] there and to [Mordechai] Shachevitz [a Haganah intelligence officer and JNF land-purchasing agent in

[24] CZA, A-246/13, p. 2,373, entry for 4 May 1948.
[25] *Ilan Va-shelah*, ed. Binyamin Etzioni, IDF publications Maarachot (Tel Aviv, ?1950), 146.
[26] CZA, S-53/437, Y. Weitz to E. Granovsky, 25 May 1948.
[27] Weitz, iii, pp. 310–12, entry for 13 June 1948.
[28] Ibid., p. 257, entry for 27 Mar. 1948.

Haifa] to move quickly in this matter.'[29] A week later, Shachevitz informed Weitz that 'most of the beduins in the bay [area] had gone, [but] some 15–20 men had stayed behind to guard [the abandoned property]. I [Weitz] demanded that these also be evicted and that the [beduin] fields be ploughed over so that no trace of them remains.'[30]

On 26 April Weitz recorded that the northern part of the bay was completely clear of beduins, their shacks destroyed, and their fields ploughed over. But in the southern end, 'the operation must still be completed . . . we must be rid of the parasites'. But there were pangs of conscience, for Weitz added: 'In war—[act] as befits war.'[31] Meeting the following day with representatives of the two bay kibbutzim, Kfar Masaryk and Ein Hamifratz, Weitz 'ordered them to finish the job within five days'.[32] On 25 May Weitz was able to inform Granovsky that 'our Haifa Bay has been completely evacuated [by the Arabs] and there is almost no trace of those who had trespassed on our lands'.[33]

SETTING UP THE FIRST TRANSFER COMMITTEE

Through his contacts in the Haganah, the JNF offices, and the settlements around Palestine, Weitz through the spring of 1948 helped facilitate the exodus of Arab communities from various localities. But the problem—'the Arab problem'—was a national one, and required a comprehensive solution on a national level. During the spring Weitz began lobbying among the political leadership of the Yishuv for the appointment of an authority or committee which would co-ordinate and oversee what he called 'the Transfer Policy'.

Through March Weitz pressed for an appointment with Haganah national chief Galili 'to discuss the problem of new Jewish settlements and the question of the Arab villages'. But Gailili kept calling off scheduled meetings.[34] The two at last met on 31 March, with Weitz,

[29] CZA, A-246/13, p. 2,354, entry for 14 Apr. 1948.
[30] CZA, A-246/13, p. 2,364, entry for 23 Apr. 1948.
[31] CZA, A-246/13, p. 2,367, entry for 26 Apr. 1948.
[32] CZA, A-246/13, p. 2,368, entry for 27 Apr. 1948.
[33] CZA, S-53/437, Y. Weitz to E. Granovsky, 25 May 1948.
[34] CZA, A-246/13, p. 2,338, entry for 18 Mar. 1948.

as he put it, 'raising the question of the evacuation / eviction[35] of the Arabs from our [that is, November 1947 Partition Plan Jewish] areas, which has begun of its own accord in certain places'. Weitz 'demanded' that a policy be decided upon and 'the appointment of a committee with authority to act'. Galili, recorded Weitz, reacted 'positively' and said that he would bring up the matter with the relevant officials.[36]

That evening Weitz met in Tel Aviv with the members of the newly formed Committee for Abandoned Arab Property, which was composed of senior Arab affairs and intelligence experts, including Gad and Moshe Machnes, two prominent Tel Aviv citrus-grove owners, Ezra Danin, a senior Haganah intelligence officer and leading Hadera businessman, and Yoav Zuckerman, the Gedera-based JNF land-purchasing agent. The question discussed was: should the Yishuv 'help create conditions that will bring about an [Arab] evacuation or the contrary: To influence to avoid evacuation . . .? I myself adopted the first line. Ezra [Danin] agreed with my approach . . . The others hadn't a clear stand. They maintained that they had not been appointed to decide on a policy of eviction but to look after [abandoned Arab] property. Let those empowered to do so deal with my proposal', was the general attitude, Weitz recorded.[37]

Weitz, however, felt the matter too important to let drop; the opportunity must not be allowed to slip away. On 2 April he went to see Shkolnik, who was soon to be named Deputy Minister of Defence. They discussed 'the question of the eviction / evacuation of the Arabs from various [Jewish] areas. He knows nothing at all about it.' Weitz concluded that he would have to deal personally with whatever pertained to JNF lands.[38] Weitz pressed Shkolnik to arrange a meeting for him with Ben-Gurion to discuss 'the problem of the eviction / evacuation of the Arabs'.[39] Ben-Gurion, directing the Yishuv's life-and-death struggle, was apparently too busy.

Weitz persisted in his efforts to obtain a national-level decision. On the evening of 14 April, after spending part of the day dealing with the Haifa Bay beduin problem, Weitz again met with members

[35] The Hebrew word *pinui* means both voluntary evacuation and eviction or expulsion. It is used by Weitz repeatedly. I have translated it in accordance with the context in which it appears, though occasionally there is ambivalence.
[36] Weitz, iii, p. 260, entry for 31 Mar. 1948.
[37] Ibid.   [38] Ibid., p. 261, entry for 2 Apr. 1948.
[39] Ibid., pp. 261-2, entry for 4 Apr. 1948.

of the Committee for Abandoned Arab Property—Danin, Gad
Machnes, and Yitzhak Gvirtz, a member of Kibbutz Shefayim and
a Haganah intelligence officer. According to Weitz's account, the
committee members wanted to know his attitude to their work.
Weitz said he was 'dissatisfied'; they dealt with the safeguarding of
Arab property, not 'political military' decision-making. What was
needed, said Weitz, was a body which 'would direct the Yishuv's
war with the aim of evicting as many Arabs as possible from our
[that is, November 1947 Partition Plan] areas. The preservation of
their property after the eviction is a secondary question in which
one could act with great fairness.' The meeting ended, Weitz
recorded, with the committee members asking him to prepare 'an
eviction proposal'.[40]

Weitz quickly got to work. Four days later he presented his
proposal to the committee. 'I drew up a list of the Arab villages
which I think must be cleared [of Arabs] in order to round out
Jewish areas. I also made a summary of the places which . . . need
to be settled [by Jews] . . .'.[41] Weitz set out his thinking on the
matter in his diary entry for 22 April, when referring to the Haganah
conquest that day of Haifa. The Arab population had begun to flee:
'I think that this state of mind should be exploited . . . and [we
must] hound the rest of the inhabitants so that they should not
surrender [and then stay put]. We must set up our state.'[42]

The next day Weitz went up to Haifa, and on 24 April the
adjutant of the city's Haganah commander came to see him. The
officer told Weitz that that day, two Arab suburbs of Haifa, Balad
esh Sheikh and Yajur, were 'being evacuated', adding that perhaps
'in the coming days the road to the north beyond Acre would be
opened and the [Arab] villages [along the way] will have been
shaken [by Haganah actions]. I was happy to hear from him that this
policy was being implemented by the [Haganah] headquarters [in
Haifa]. To frighten the Arabs [into flight] so long as the flight-
inducing fear was upon them.'[43] The Haganah victories and the
mass Arab exodus of April–May reinforced Weitz's conviction that

[40] CZA, A-246/13, p. 2,354, entry for 14 Apr. 1948.
[41] CZA, A-246/13, p. 2,358, entry for 18 Apr. 1948. In the published version of
the diaries, Weitz altered the phrase 'villages which I think must be cleared [of
Arabs]', to 'Arab villages which have been evacuated'. See Weitz, iii, p. 268.
[42] CZA, A-246/13, p. 2,364, entry for 22 Apr. 1948.
[43] CZA, A-246/13, p. 2,365, entry for 24 Apr. 1948.

a fundamental change was taking place in Palestine, 'a complete territorial revolution'.[44] But the transformation had to be controlled, speeded up, and augmented. New life was breathed into Weitz's efforts to obtain a national policy decision from the Yishuv's leaders with Ezra Danin's resignation in mid-May from the Committee for Abandoned Arab Property, which had proved almost completely ineffective in stemming the looting of Arab properties by Haganah, IZL, and Lehi units, and by individuals, in the wake of each conquest.

On 18 May, Danin, home and unemployed in Hadera, wrote Weitz that he was now free and willing to join the type of body Weitz was proposing should be established. Danin explained that he had left the property committee because 'it had not been my purpose to cover up individual acts of robbery'. In any case, he agreed, this was all a relatively irrelevant sideshow. What was now needed was 'an institution whose role will be . . . to seek ways to carry out the transfer of the Arab population at this opportunity when it has left its normal place of residence'. Danin thought that 'Christian interests' could perhaps be found who, acting under the banner of 'saving the refugees', could be persuaded to help resettle them permanently in Arab countries. 'Let us not waste the fact that a large Arab population has moved from its home, and achieving such a thing again would be very difficult in normal times', Danin wrote. He offered some concrete proposals, including buying up Arab land, for which 'the time is ripe'. He wrote: 'If we do not seek to encourage the return of the Arabs to the villages or towns they inhabited—then they must be confronted by *faits accomplis*.' Danin outlined the types of *faits accomplis* he had in mind: 'One possibility is the destruction of the buildings (this needs a central decision, and you promised to deal with this, and nothing substantial has been done in this area). Another [means] is settling Jews in all the area evacuated and to find legal means which will give the new [Jewish] inhabitants certain rights [over the abandoned property] . . . .'.[45]

Danin's joining Weitz seems to have added important momentum to Weitz's efforts to persuade the Yishuv leadership to pursue an organized 'Transfer Policy' *vis-à-vis* the Palestinian Arabs. That

[44] Weitz, iii, p. 288, entry for 20 May 1948.
[45] Institute for Study of Settlement (Rehovot), Weitz Papers, E. Danin (Hadera) to Y. Weitz (Tel Aviv), 18 May 1948.

1948 and After

policy was the focus of the meeting between Weitz and the newly appointed Foreign Minister of Israel, Moshe Shertok (later Sharrett) on 28 May. Should the Yishuv 'take action to transform the flight of the Arabs from the country and the prohibition of their return into an accomplished fact? If so, is it not necessary to empower a person or two to three people to deal with this according to a preconceived plan?' Weitz asked Shertok. Weitz then proposed that the Cabinet appoint himself, Elias Sasson, the newly appointed head of the Foreign Ministry's Middle East Affairs Department, and Danin 'to hammer out a plan of action designed [to achieve] the goal of transfer'.

According to Weitz, Shertok 'congratulated' him on his initiative. Shertok's 'view also is that this momentum [of Arab flight] must be exploited and turned into an accomplished fact,' but the Foreign Minister wanted first to consult with Ben-Gurion and Finance Minister Eliezer Kaplan. For the moment, Shertok cautiously endorsed Weitz's proposal that the Yishuv buy land from 'departing Arabs'.[46] Shertok's own notes from the 28 May conversation, while somewhat cryptic, conform with the drift of Weitz's diary entry. Shertok headed his note: 'To discuss with B[en-]G[urion]'. Referring to 'transfer', the Foreign Minister wrote that 'after the fact of evacuation / eviction, exchange of population [Jews from Arab lands would come to Israel as Palestinians departed for Arab lands], appointment of a committee'. Shertok mentions Weitz, Danin, and Sasson as the first three candidates for the proposed committee. According to Shertok, Weitz also proposed the immediate establishment of Jewish settlements in areas evacuated by the Arabs—specific mention is made of western Galilee and the Jerusalem corridor—as well as purchase of land from departing Arabs. Shertok does not mention destroying Arab villages or exacerbating the ongoing Arab exodus as among the measures discussed.[47]

THE FIRST 'SELF-APPOINTED' TRANSFER COMMITTEE

Two days later, Weitz, Danin, and Sasson met to outline the committee's prospective work. 'From now on, I shall call it the

---

[46] CZA, A-246/13, p. 2,403, entry for 28 May 1948.
[47] ISA, FM 2564/20, memorandum entitled '[Talk] with Yosef Weitz' (in pencil, by hand), 28 May 1948.

"Transfer Committee"', Weitz records in his diary. The official Cabinet appointment of the committee was imminent, he felt. That evening, 30 May, Weitz discussed the matter with Finance Minister Kaplan, who, according to Weitz, agreed 'that the fact of the transfer must be consolidated and that the Arabs not be allowed to return'.[48] On 1 June, a number of senior ministers and officials, including Foreign Minister Shertok, Minority Affairs Minister Shitrit and Cabinet Secretary Ze'ev Sharef, met in Tel Aviv and, according to Ben-Gurion's diary, decided that 'the Arabs were not to be helped to return', and that IDF commanders 'were to be issued orders in the matter'.[49] Weitz, who apparently had not heard from Shertok for about a week, felt ignored and put out. On 3 June he wrote a strong letter of complaint to the Foreign Minister: '. . . You promised me a speedy answer on the question of "retroactive transfer".' Weitz related that he had met with Danin and Sasson, with Shitrit and Kaplan, and had 'prepared an outline scheme. But from this point on we cannot take a single step forward without getting your consent.'[50] The next day, 'the committee that had appointed itself', as Weitz referred to it, met in Tel Aviv to discuss 'the miracle' of the Arab exodus 'and how to make it permanent'. The committee concluded that 'first of all, the return of the Arabs must be prevented'. Money was needed, 'and I agreed to allocate I£5,000 to Ezra [Danin] in order to begin destruction and renovation activities in the Beit Shean Valley, near Ein Hashofet [Ramot-Menashe] and in the Sharon [the Coastal Plain]'. Destruction of the abandoned villages meant that the refugees would have nowhere to return to; renovation meant readying the sites for Jewish settlement.[51]

The next day, 5 June, Weitz at last saw Ben-Gurion. Weitz came armed with a comprehensive, three-page memorandum, entitled 'Retroactive Transfer, A Scheme for the Solution of the Arab

[48] Weitz, iii, p. 294, entry for 30 May 1948.
[49] DBG, ii, p. 477, entry for 1 June 1948.
[50] ISA, FM 2564/20, Y. Weitz to M. Shertok, 3 June 1948.
[51] CZA, A-246/13, p. 2,410, entry for 4 June 1948. In the published version of the diaries, Weitz wrote not that he had allocated I£5,000 (about $20,000 at the time, a not insignificant sum) from JNF funds but that 'we have obtained the sum of I£5,000 . . . .'. Presumably, Weitz in 1965 was loath to reveal that in early June 1948, without JNF directorate authorization, he had allocated JNF funds for the destruction of villages. Subsequently, on 10 June, the directorate voted I£10,000 for Weitz to use 'to cover eviction expenses'. See Weitz, iii, p. 301, entry for 10 June 1948.

Question in the State of Israel', and signed by Weitz, Danin, and Sasson. In the memorandum, the committee stated that the war had brought about an 'unexpected phenomenon': 'the uprooting of masses [of Arabs] from their towns and villages and their flight out of the area of Israel to neighbouring countries . . .'. By 2 June, the committee estimated, some 190 villages and seven towns had been evacuated, encompassing some 335,000 Arabs. 'This process may continue as the war continues and our army advances', the memorandum went on. The flight and its consequences—the destruction and takeover of Arab property—would no doubt deepen Arab enmity for Israel, the committee warned, creating an enmity so strong 'as perhaps to make impossible the existence of hundreds of thousands of Arabs in the State of Israel and the existence of the state with hundreds of thousands of inhabitants who bear that hatred'. Left in place, such a minority would cause Israel no end of problems.

Two months later, Danin was to set down clearly his feelings in this matter in a letter to a critic of the government's hard-line policy towards the Arabs:

I believe with complete faith that the good of both peoples lies in complete separation. Here will remain a deposit of bitterness which will encourage endless conflict. Therefore, I would do everything possible to reduce the number of this minority. . . .[52]

According to Weitz, Danin, and Sasson, the conclusions to be drawn from these assumptions were, first, that 'fair neighbourly' relations, long sought by the Yishuv with the Arabs, 'have been undermined, not through our will . . . Israel must be inhabited largely by Jews, so that there will be in it very few non-Jews.' And second, 'the uprooting of the Arabs should be seen as a solution to the Arab question in the State of Israel and, in line with this, it must from now on be directed according to a calculated plan geared towards the goal of "retroactive transfer" . . .'. The committee then outlined its proposals for 'action' to consolidate and amplify the transformation which was taking place:

(1) Preventing the Arabs from returning to their places.
(2) [Extending] help to the Arabs to be absorbed in other places.

[52] ISA, FM 2570/11, E. Danin (Tel Aviv) to Yitzhak Avira, a member of Kibbutz Ashdot Ya'akov in the Jordan Valley, 16 Aug. 1948.

The first activity subdivides into a number of aspects:

(1) Destruction of villages as much as possible during military operations.

(2) Prevention of any cultivation of land by them, including reaping, collection [of crops], picking [olives] and so on, also during times of ceasefire.

(3) Settlement of Jews in a number of villages and towns so that no 'vacuum' is created.

(4) Enacting legislation [geared to barring a return] . . .

(5) [Making] propaganda aimed at non-return.

The committee also proposed purchasing land from Arabs leaving the country, negotiating with the Arab countries about a planned resettlement of the refugees, and assessing the value of the property left behind by the refugees. To implement the plan, the committee —which still had no official standing—proposed the establishment of a 'non-governmental three-man committee, invested with clear and defined cabinet authority'. The committee would set up a labour battalion to 'destroy and / or renovate Arab villages . . ., co-ordinate Jewish settlement in the empty sites, prepare legislation to legalize the transformation and to negotiate with Arab representatives the resettlement of the refugees'. The committee estimated that a budget of 'I£150,000' would be needed to cover 'destruction and renovation in village and town', 'I£2,250,000' for setting up some ninety new Jewish settlements and 'I£100,000' to bankroll the committee's apparatus at home and abroad. No mention is made of a budget for funding the refugees' resettlement abroad—though presumably the abandoned property to be expropriated by the Yishuv would be used to cover that.[53]

How did Ben-Gurion react? According to Weitz, 'he agreed to the whole line [that is, policy]', but thought there was an order of priority. According to Weitz, Ben-Gurion wanted 'the actions in the country done first'—destruction of villages, settlement on abandoned sites, prevention of Arab cultivation. Planning the refugees' resettlement abroad could be done later. Ben-Gurion favoured the idea of a supervisory committee but 'he did not agree to our temporary committee'. Nevertheless, Weitz then told the

[53] ISA, FM 2564/19, Memorandum entitled 'Retroactive Transfer, A Scheme for the Solution of the Arab Question in the State of Israel', undated, signed Y. Weitz, E. Sasson, E. Danin.

Prime Minister that he had 'already given orders to begin here and there destroying villages and [Ben-Gurion] approved this. I left it at that', Weitz records.[54] According to Ben-Gurion, who devoted two paragraphs in his diary to the meeting, he proposed that a committee of three—composed of representatives of the JNF (Weitz), the Jewish Agency settlement department, and the Agency's treasury department—be set up, its job being to oversee 'the cleaning up of the [Arab] settlements, cultivation of their [fields] and their settlement [by Jews], and the creation of a labour battalion to carry out this work'. Ben-Gurion, like Weitz, stressed that it would not be the government carrying out these activities, but they would be carried out 'with its knowledge, by the National Institutions'. Nowhere in these paragraphs does Ben-Gurion refer clearly to the destruction of Arab villages, the prevention of a return of the refugees, amplifying the Arab exodus, or buying up Arab land as having been broached during the discussion; nor does he refer anywhere, even obliquely, to the Weitz committee memorandum.[55]

The next day, 6 June, Weitz sent Ben-Gurion a detailed list of the abandoned villages and towns, with the appropriate population figures, and a covering note stating, 'I . . . allow myself to set down your answer [yesterday 5 June] to the scheme-proposal I submitted to you, that: (A) You will call a meeting immediately to discuss [the scheme] and to appoint a committee and [outline] its plan of work; (B) You agree that the actions marked in clauses 1, 2 . . . will begin immediately [that is, the destruction of Arab villages and prevention of cultivation of Arab fields].' Weitz continued: 'In line with this, I have given an order to begin [these operations] in different parts of the Galilee, in the Beit Shean Valley, in the Hills of Ephraim and in Samaria [meaning the Hefer Valley].'[56] Weitz was covering himself. Aware of Ben-Gurion's *modus operandi* in this sensitive matter— nothing in writing, nothing traceable directly to himself or the Cabinet—Weitz was trying not to leave himself open to charges that he had acted on his own. Perhaps he also hoped that a written response would be forthcoming from the Prime Minister, as is implied by his diary entry for 7 June: 'Have heard nothing from

[54] CZA, A-246/13, p. 2,411, entry for 5 June 1948.
[55] DBG, ii, p. 487, entry for 5 June 1948.
[56] ISA, FM 2564/19, Y. Weitz to D. Ben-Gurion, 6 June 1948. (Also dated 'Year One to the Freedom of Israel.')

D[avid] B[en] G[urion] and M[oshe] S[hertok]. I am acting in this matter, therefore, on my own. Is it right?'

But, at this stage, Weitz was not to be deterred by the lack of a formal, written permit for his activities. He spent the day talking with Danin about how to go about destroying the abandoned villages— where would the money come from, the tractors, the dynamite, the manpower? And where was it best to begin? 'Preparations are under way for action in the villages. We have brought in [Yoav] Zuckerman, who will act in his area [that is, around Gedera, southeast of Tel Aviv]. The questions are many: The town of Beit Shean, to leave it alone completely, or part of it . . . and Acre and Jaffa? and Qaqun? And what shall we work with? We are looking for tools of destruction.'[57]

With most able-bodied men in the Yishuv conscripted into the IDF, with most equipment, such as tractors and tracked caterpillars, in use by the army or in agriculture, and with dynamite in perennially short supply, Weitz had a job of it organizing what amounted to an enormous project of destruction. Added to this was Weitz's unease, from the start, because of the absence of formal, explicit endorsement of his operations by Ben-Gurion, the Prime Minister's oral declarations notwithstanding. Ben-Gurion wanted Weitz to implement the 'Transfer Committee' scheme, but without his name being involved or cited as the source of the committee's authority. It were best that 'things' happened as if of their own—villages razed, cultivators barred from their fields, refugees barred from returning and, indeed, villagers expelled—without his personal imprimatur. Ben-Gurion in this was probably as sensitive to the reputation of the new Jewish state as to his own standing in future histories.

But there is no doubt that Ben-Gurion agreed to Weitz's scheme. Finance Minister Eliezer Kaplan said as much to Weitz when they met on 8 June, adding his own endorsement of the plan. Kaplan added that he had concluded with Ben-Gurion that a committee to oversee the plan's implementation be set up, composed of representatives of the JNF, the Jewish Agency, and the Ministry of Defence. (The inclusion of a Defence Ministry man was an innovation and ran counter to both Ben-Gurion's and Weitz's initial desire that the government not be directly involved, and tarnished in so doing. But

[57] CZA, A-246/13, entry for 7 June 1948.

technically the activities of the committee were better carried out in co-ordination with the IDF—clearly requiring a Defence Ministry official to liaise.) Weitz proposed to Kaplan that Danin, who belonged to none of these bodies, also be included, and Kaplan agreed, Weitz recorded.[58]

Weitz seemed to have made some progress in early June in establishing 'his' committee. But an omen appeared a few days later, when the 'natural' Defence Ministry candidate for the committee, Levi Shkolnik, on 10 June informed Weitz that he was not joining. Weitz sadly recorded this as a symptom of the 'complete chaos which reigns in thinking, or lack of thinking, about this grave subject, as about other subjects', in the political leadership of the Yishuv.[59]

Meanwhile, Weitz's temporary Transfer Committee continued functioning. Weitz sent two settlement officials, Asher Bobritzky and Moshe Berger, to tour the coastal plain 'to determine in which villages we will be able to settle our people, and which should be destroyed'.[60] At the same time, Zuckerman informed him that he had 'arranged the destruction [of the village] of Al Mughar [near Gedera], which will begin tomorrow morning'. That same day the JNF directorate allocated I£10,000 to Weitz to carry out the work of destruction.[61]

On 13 June, Weitz travelled north to the Beit Shean and Jezreel valleys, where he saw 'our people . . . reaping in the fields of [the Arab village of] Zir'in'. In Kibbutz Beit Hashita, Weitz met Goldenberg, David Baum from Kfar Yehezkeel, and the commander of the IDF's (Golani Brigade) battalion in the Jezreel, Avraham Yoffe. 'From the start of our talk', Weitz recorded, 'it became clear that there is agreement among us on the question of the abandoned villages: Destruction, renovation and settlement [by Jews].' Another participant in the meeting, representing Kibbutz Nir David, urged the immediate settlement of 'Zir'in, Sandala and Faqqu'a' and barring a return of the refugees to the Beit Shean Valley 'so long as no peace treaty was signed'. Weitz concluded: 'There is a consensus

---

[58] Weitz, iii, p. 300, entry for 8 June 1948.
[59] CZA, A-246/13, p. 2,415, entry for 10 June 1948.
[60] Weitz, iii, p. 301, entry for 10 June 1948 and CZA, A-246/13, p. 2,415, entry for 10 June 1948.
[61] Weitz, iii, p. 301, entry for 10 June 1948.

everywhere: "No" to a return of Arabs, on no account. They must be prevented from returning and at the same time the "vacuum" must be filled [with new Jewish settlements].'[62]

On his way back to Tel Aviv the following day, Weitz met Danin, who reported on a conversation he had had (apparently on 13 June) with Foreign Minister Shertok about the Transfer Committee's work. 'It appears that he [that is, Shertok] has not yet taken a [formal, open] position', wrote Weitz. Shertok reportedly asked Danin: 'Are you doing [things]?' Danin replied: 'Yes'. Shertok said: 'Continue to do [things].' Danin then asked the Foreign Minister what he would say when asked abroad about the committee's activities. Shertok 'remained silent', Danin reportedly told Weitz.[63] During their meeting, Danin also told Weitz about the progress made in the destruction of the village of Fajja, near Petah Tikva.[64] Zuckerman that day gave Weitz a progress report on the destruction of Al Mughar.[65] The next day, Weitz went to see for himself. At Al Mughar

three tractors are completing its destruction. I was surprised [as] nothing moved in me at the sight . . . Not regret and not hatred, as this is the way of the world. Yes, we [the Jews, now] want to enjoy life in this world and not in the next. We simply want to live, and the dwellers of these mud-houses did not want us to exist here. They sought not only to rule over us but also to destroy us . . . And, interestingly, this is the opinion of all our boys, from one end [of the political spectrum] to the other. If there are doubts about this work, then they are among certain political party leaders who have not forgotten to employ their dialectics . . . [The reference is to the Marxist Hashomer Hatza'ir element in Mapam].[66]

On 16 June, probably on the basis of a progress report from Weitz, Ben-Gurion summarized the destruction of some of the Arab villages to date:

[Al] Mughar near Gedera, Fajja, Biyar Adas (near Magdiel) have been destroyed. [Destruction is proceeding in] Miska (near Ramat Hakovesh), Beit Dajan (east of Tel Aviv), in [the] Hula [Valley], [in] Khawassa near Haifa, As Sumeiriya near Acre and Ja'tun [? perhaps Khirbet Ja'tun] near

[62] Ibid., entry for 13 June 1948.
[63] Ibid., p. 302, entry for 14 June 1948.
[64] CZA, A-246/13, p. 2,418, entry for 14 June 1948.
[65] Ibid.
[66] Weitz, iii, p. 303, entry for 15 June 1948.

Nahariya, Manshiya . . . near Acre. Daliyat ar Ruha has been destroyed and work is about to begin at [Al] Buteimat and Sabbarin [both in the Ramot-Menashe area].[67]

Meanwhile, Bobritzky, flanked by Moshe Berger and another of Weitz's Haganah Intelligence Service and JNF land-purchasing contacts, Yaakov Barazani, spent mid-June touring the coastal plain to determine which sites were suitable for Jewish settlement and which should be levelled. Bobritzky consulted with, and was assisted on his tours by, local IDF commanders. Berger was apparently named to oversee the destruction in the area (as Zuckerman was responsible for operations in the area south of Tel Aviv).

On 11 June, a senior officer in the IDF unit responsible for the coastal plain (from Tel Aviv northwards to Tantura, south of Haifa), the Alexandroni Brigade, informed IDF General Staff / Operations that 'according to the directive by the Arab Department [*sic*], all the Arab villages in the [area of the] brigade must be destroyed after consulting with the Agricultural Centre and the [Jewish] settlement [bodies]. Motta [Moshe] Berger has been appointed to the post [of overseeing the destruction of these villages]. The destruction of these villages will be carried out after permission [is given] by the settlement bodies and by you [that is, IDF General Staff / Operations], from a security viewpoint.'

What General Staff / Operations thought of this letter, and how it responded to it, is unknown. But it highlighted the mechanics of Weitz's operation during June. While attempting to obtain national-level authorization and sanction for his activities, he proceeded to carry out his 'mission' with the tools and personnel at hand, and this included co-ordination with and a measure of instructions to, the local, middle-level IDF authorities.

Bobritzky, who submitted a progress report on his activities on 21 June to Weitz and the other relevant Jewish authorities (the Agricultural Centre and the Jewish Agency Settlement Department), named both Berger and Barazani as being 'charged with destroying the Arab villages'. Bobritzky listed 20 villages which he thought were of no use for Jewish settlement and could be destroyed— including Qannir, Kafr Qari, Bureika, Khirbet as Sarkas, Wadi Ara, the dwelling places of Arab al Foqara and of ad Dumeira, near

---

[67] DBG, ii, pp. 523–4, entry for 16 June 1948.

Hadera, and Umm Khalid (which Bobritzky misnames as Umm Walid), near Netanya.

He listed seven village sites as suitable for Jewish settlement—including Fajja, which he found was being destroyed and where he asked that '10–11 rooms' be left intact for Jewish settlers, Tantura, Khirbet Beit Lid, An Nusseirat, Sabbarin, and two smaller sites. Four sites, according to Bobritzky, required 'special clarification'. Another eleven—including Miska, Beit Dajan, Arab Abu Kishk, Al Kheiriya, Jalil, and Khirbet Azzun (Tabsar)—he had not yet visited.

In his concluding remarks, Bobritzky thought it worth mentioning that Berger and Barazani 'had orders' to speed up the destruction of the villages and that the IDF district OCs (*mefakdei nafot* or *mafanim*), concurred with this approach. Bobritzky, for his part, asked the two officials and the district OCs to hold off on the destruction of the sites he regarded as appropriate for Jewish settlement. Here, perhaps for the first time, surfaced the inherent contradiction between the settlement officials' desire to preserve buildings and space for the settlement of Jewish immigrants and the political desire, seen by its proponents as a need, to destroy as many habitable sites as possible to prevent an Arab refugee return.[68]

[68] ISA, MAM 307 gimel/33, Bechor Shitrit to David Ben-Gurion, 23 June 1948. Shitrit's letter quotes verbatim the full text of the letter of 11 June 1948 from 'Oded', Alexandroni Brigade to General Staff / Operations. I would like to thank Dr Charles Kamen for letting me see a copy of this document. For Bobritzky's report, see LA 235 IV/2060 aleph, A. Bobritzky to Settlement Department, 21 June 1948. All three letters, from Minority Affairs Minister Shitrit, from the Alexandroni Brigade officer 'Oded' and from the settlement official Bobritzky, reflect the bureaucratic decision-making confusion of the time as well as the semi-clandestine nature of Weitz's Transfer Committee activities. The State of Israel had only just come into being, and under the worst of circumstances. Large areas remained in which authority was unclear or disputed. The Ministry for Minority Affairs was only donning skin and bone; the Arab Affairs Committee of the National Institutions (of which Weitz, Danin, and Sasson were members) and Gad Machnes's Abandoned Property Committee were becoming powerless, empty hulks. Weitz's Transfer Committee, operating in the shadows, still lacked official sanction and public recognition. The Ministry of Agriculture was only beginning to flex its muscles and usurp some of the authority traditionally vested in the Settlement Department of the Jewish Agency, the Agricultural Centre, and the JNF Lands Department. In general, the line demarcating the IDF's authority from the various civil agencies—in all that concerned the Arab minority and the abandoned Arab villages and property—during the summer of 1948 remained unclear, with all concerned jockeying for positions of authority. It was, all in all, a boom-time for private, semi-official, and official initiatives by single-minded, dogged executives—such as Weitz.

OPPOSING THE TRANSFER COMMITTEE

Ben-Gurion may have been content, indeed happy, with the situation; the Transfer Committee was operational though without formal government authorization. But Weitz was growing increasingly frustrated and perturbed. Months of lobbying had failed to secure for the Transfer Committee the coveted letter of appointment. On 15 June he again met with Shertok and 'demanded . . . that the committee be set up at long last with the clear authority to carry out its complete programme'. According to Weitz, Shertok again promised to bring up the matter with Ben-Gurion and 'to speed up the appointment of the committee'.[69] But Ben-Gurion procrastinated. Since mid-May, the Prime Minister has been busy fending off embarrassing questions and charges in Cabinet concerning the destruction of Arab villages. Strong hints were repeatedly thrown out, especially by Mapam ministers, that this destruction was part of an unannounced general policy of expulsion against Israel's Arab population being carried out by Ben-Gurion, his emissaries, and the IDF behind the Cabinet's back.

During May and the first half of June, Mapam's main political bodies, the Political Committee and the Centre [*Merkaz Mapam*], debated policy towards the Palestinian Arabs. On 15 June the Political Committee summarized the debate with a list of conclusions, broadcast a week later by the party centre in a circular to all 'party activists'. In forthright language, the statement declared the party's opposition to the expulsion of Arabs, proposed that the government issue an appeal to 'peace-loving Arabs' to stay put, and opposed 'the destruction of Arab villages . . . not out of direct military necessity'. The statement supported the return of the refugees to Israel at the end of the war.[70]

Once this position was reached and publicized by Mapam, any open endorsement by Ben-Gurion or the Cabinet majority of a policy of 'transfer' would have led to a breakdown of the government coalition, in which, for all their differences, Ben-Gurion's Mapai and Mapam were the chief and generally aligned components. The

---

[69] CZA, A-246/13, p. 2,419, entry for 15 June 1948.

[70] HHA-ACP 10.95.11 (1), 'From the Log-Book of the Secretariat, No. 4'. 'Our Policy Towards the Arab During the War' (The Decisions of the Political Committee of 15 June 1948), 23 June 1948, Tel Aviv.

appointment by Ben-Gurion or the Cabinet of a committee with terms of reference as proposed by Weitz would have placed Mapam's leaders in an impossible position; the party, whose rank and file in the Kibbutz Artzi and Kibbutz Meuhad settlement movements and urban branches provided much of the IDF's officer corps, most of the country's farmers, and many senior civil servants, would most probably have bolted the coalition.

Ben-Gurion, busy directing a life-and-death struggle against the Arab states, faced with dissension which bordered on revolt from the Right and an open rift with the IDF brass, and under heavy pressure from the UN and the Western powers on a variety of crucial issues, could hardly contemplate a cabinet breakup in mid-1948. Moreover, it ran against Ben-Gurion's grain openly to endorse and put his name to a policy which contemporary and future critics might brand as morally questionable.

It is worth tracing specifically the emergence of awareness among Mapam's leaders of Weitz's essentially covert activities and how this awareness was translated into the criticism and opposition in Cabinet which ultimately frustrated Weitz's hopes of winning official endorsement for the Transfer Committee's activities. At the 26 May meeting of Mapam's Political Committee, Eliezer Prai, a member of Kibbutz Merhavia and the editor of the party's daily newspaper, *Al Hamishmar* (On Guard), charged that there were elements in the Yishuv carrying out a 'transfer policy', by 'blood and fire', aimed at emptying the Jewish state of its Arab inhabitants. 'It has already been said that Weitz gave an order to expel the Arabs from Western Galilee', said Prai, probably referring to Weitz's instructions to the (Mapam-affiliated) kibbutzim Kfar Masaryk and Ein Hamifratz, and possibly also to his 'advice' to the Haganah brass in Haifa, regarding the Arabs in the areas north of Haifa. 'This is the policy and thinking behind [the destruction of the Arab villages in the area]', he said. Another participant at the meeting referred critically, in passing, to Weitz's trips around the country, dispensing 'instructions' regarding the disposition of Arabs and Arab villages.[71]

There was also criticism of a more personal order. In July, Haim Cafri, of Kibbutz Maanit, near Hadera, and a leading Mapam

[71] HHA 66.90 (1), protocol of the meeting of the Mapam Political Committee, 26 May 1948.

defence figure, at a closed meeting of Mapam defence personnel, charged—but without openly naming him—that Ezra Danin had profited personally from the Arab exodus, and that Arab friends of Transfer Committee members were receiving preferential treatment from the Yishuv's executive bodies. Cafri named Danin and (mistakenly) Gad Machnes (who was by then the Director General of the Minority Affairs Ministry) as the men responsible for 'overseeing the glorious department of "landscape improvement", as it is called in their language'.[72] Mapam's Cabinet ministers, Agriculture Minister Aharon Zisling and Labour Minister Mordechai Bentov, participated in these deliberations, and subsequently raised Mapam's concerns at Cabinet meetings. While previously they had somewhat loosely criticized the destruction of Arab villages, at the Cabinet meeting of 16 June Bentov asked the Prime Minister directly whether there existed a committee, composed of 'E. Danin, Y. Weitz and [*sic*] M. Nahmani . . . empowered to damage Arab property'.

Ben-Gurion parried, promising 'to investigate and respond'. How, if at all, Ben-Gurion answered the question at a later date is unknown; events during the summer of 1948 came thick and fast, one concern quickly replacing others in ministers' minds. The ministers grew accustomed to Ben-Gurion's failure to answer Cabinet questions.[73]

But Zisling was not to be put off this time. Later in the day, he wrote an angry note to Ben-Gurion, with copies to all Cabinet members, denouncing the depredations against Arab property. 'There is increasing information', he hinted darkly if vaguely,

that [these are] activities which according to their nature and scope cannot be done except by [permission of higher] authority. I would like to know: Who gave the order to demolish houses and destroy settlements—in Beit Shean, in the villages around it and in other parts of the country?

Is there a basis for the rumours that on various occasions responsible persons were heard to give 'suggestions' which were understood by the hearers to be tantamount to an order, giving an assessment of the number of Arabs who were to be left in future in settlements being evacuated

---

[72] HHA 10.18, protocol of meeting of Mapam defence activists, 26 July 1948.
[73] KMA-AZP 9.9.1, 'Decisions of the Provisional Government', meeting of 16 June 1948.

(Haifa and elsewhere)? [The reference is to a report then circulating in Mapam leadership circles that Ben-Gurion had told his aides that he wanted no more than 15,000 Arabs left in Haifa]. If there is a foundation for the information reaching me, [continued Zisling,] then the responsibility stems from government sources, and it is inconceivable that . . . actions of this sort continue contrary to what is heard in cabinet deliberations.[74]

Such criticism helped to stop Ben-Gurion from issuing the letter of appointment sought by Weitz. But it failed to prompt the Prime Minister to issue hard and fast instruction that the Transfer Committee halt its work of destruction immediately. On 14 July Zisling returned to the fray, charging that some IDF officers were blowing up villages 'on the basis of unauthorized orders'. The minister explained that he had heard that 'civilians' were dispensing such orders, citing such an order issued to the IDF commander in the town of Beit Shean. Ben-Gurion interjected: 'A [military] commander cannot receive an order from any committee but only from his [military] superior.' As if paying no attention to the interruption, Zisling went on to recount that he himself had seen Arab villages in the Hadera area being destroyed after the fighting in the area had long died down. Those responsible should be disciplined, Zisling said and, turning to Ben-Gurion, added: 'And I don't accept your answer that you don't know who destroyed them.'

Ben-Gurion challenged Zisling to name such destroyed villages. Zisling replied: '[Khirbet as] Sarkas', a village in the Hadera area whose inhabitants had been expelled by the Haganah on 15 April.[75] Zisling added: 'In an earlier [Cabinet] meeting I mentioned [Moshe] Goldenberg, who spoke of [Weitz's] order to destroy villages and mentioned your [that is, Ben-Gurion's] name, and I said that I did not believe that [Weitz's order] was given in your name.' The implication of Zisling's statement was that whereas in the past he had not believed that Weitz had been acting with Ben-Gurion's authorization, he now suspected that this was the case. Still, he

[74] ISA, FM 2401/21, A. Zisling to D. Ben-Gurion, 16 June 1948.
[75] KMA-AZP 9.9.3, transcript of Zisling's statements in the Cabinet meeting of 14 July 1948, being verbatim extracts of the Cabinet minutes. Zisling's reference appears to have been to the meeting on 13 June at Kibbutz Beit Hashita, Jezreel Valley, between Weitz and regional IDF commanders, including Goldenberg, the Beit Alpha area commander, on policy towards the Arabs.

held back from saying so openly, because, possibly, to do so—to recognize openly that transfer policy stemmed from the Prime Minister—would leave the Mapam ministers little choice but to declare an open rift with Mapai and perhaps bolt from the government.

Weitz and his circle clearly recognized Mapam as the chief opponents in the Yishuv of a policy of transfer. But Weitz does not seem to have been aware of the major influence the party and its representatives in the Cabinet succeeded in exerting on Ben-Gurion, repeatedly frustrating official endorsement of the Transfer Committee. Weitz seems not to have known that his committee's activities were a subject of open Cabinet debate. Mapam's criticisms of what they regarded as the transfer policy were usually delivered in closed, or very limited forums, and were never publicly enunciated, for fear of handing Israel's Arab enemies political ammunition. Weitz heard Mapam's views chiefly from Kibbutz Artzi movement leader Yaakov Hazan, who sat with Weitz on the JNF board of directors. On 9 June, for example, Hazan told Weitz that he opposed 'transferring all the Arabs to neighbouring countries'. But, according to Weitz, Hazan agreed to JNF allocation of funds 'for expenses for destroying villages . . . located on [JNF-owned] land or on land owned by effendis [that is, usually absentee, large landowners] which would in the end be sold to the JNF'.[76]

On 17 June Weitz angrily noted a speech by Mapam leader Meir Yaari to the Zionist Executive, in which Yaari condemned 'the eviction of Arab villagers'. Weitz commented in his diary: '. . . as if he does not know that all his friends in the kibbutzim are doing it with complete devotion. That is the power of an abstract ideology [that is, Marxism].'[77]

Weitz's opponents were not restricted to Mapam. His boss in the JNF, its chairman Avraham Granovsky, a founder of the centrist Progressive Party, repeatedly attacked at meetings of the JNF directorate and in private conversations with Weitz, the general policy of destroying Arab villages as 'a negative and dangerous

---

[76] Weitz, iii, p. 300, entry for 9 June 1948.
[77] CZA, A-246/13, p. 2,420, entry for 17 June 1948 and Weitz, iii, p. 309, entry for 28 June 1948.

phenomenon'.[78] But Granovsky' opposition seems to have had only a limited effect on Weitz's freedom of action and on his use of JNF funds and facilities for Transfer Committee operations; the majority of members of the JNF board of directors supported Weitz's Mapai-backed policy.

Much more dangerous to his activities was the opposition of Minority Affairs Minister Bechor Shitrit, who saw himself as an oriental-type patron and benefactor of those whose affairs and interests he was charged with overseeing. Weitz met him on 16 June, apparently after the day's Cabinet meeting, and recorded: 'There is no stability in his opinions. They [Shitrit and his ministry director general, Gad Machnes] support me to my face, but I am not sure they don't speak differently behind my back.'

On 23 June[79] Shitrit complained directly to the Prime Minister about the activities of the Weitz committee (though it is unclear whether, at this time, he was fully aware of their extent and of Ben-Gurion's complicity in them). Enclosing a copy of the letter from 'Oded', Alexandroni Brigade, to IDF General Staff / Operations of 11 June (see note 68), Shitrit complained that the instruction to destroy the Coastal Plain villages had not come from 'the Arab Department', which he took to refer to the Minority Affairs Ministry. 'The Arab Department never issued this order or a similar order or even [issued] a hint to destroy Arab villages.' Shitrit bristled at the assertion that the Agricultural Centre and the settlements should be consulted about such destruction. And he demanded that Berger, charged with overseeing the destruction, according to the Alexandroni Brigade letter, be ordered 'not to interfere in matters pertaining to the Arab Department [that is, the Ministry for Minority Affairs]'. Shitrit demanded that Ben-Gurion find out on what basis Alexandroni's 'Oded' had written the letter. Lastly, he asked that

---

[78] Weitz, iii, p. 310, entry for 1 July 1948. Weitz apparently had problems, albeit ephemeral, with his own staff. Yosef Nahmani, the JNF land office head in the Galilee, on 6 May complained to Weitz about 'the brutal behaviour of our people towards all the Arabs'. Weitz, after persuading Nahmani of the justice of the Zionist cause and the lack of any alternative course of action, jotted down in his diary: 'He apparently finds it difficult to cut himself off from the concepts that we became accustomed to during the period of enslavement under the British Mandate.' CZA, A-246/13, p. 2,377, entry for 6 May 1948.

[79] CZA, A-246/13, pp. 2,419–20, entry for 16 June 1948, and ISA, MAM 307 gimel/33, B. Shitrit to D. Ben-Gurion, 23 June 1948.

everyone else be barred from all activity relating to his ministry's areas of jurisdiction.

By the end of June, the momentum of the first, 'self-appointed Transfer Committee' had fizzled out. 'There are no tools and no materials' with which to continue the destruction of the villages, Weitz recorded.[80] Lack of official recognition entailed lack of funds.

But it went deeper than that. How could Weitz and his committee take upon themselves such politically momentous actions without clear-cut endorsement from the Yishuv's political leaders? Weitz got cold feet. He understood Ben-Gurion's dilemma, and the Prime Minister's tactics, of having others (Weitz, Jewish settlements, local IDF units) carry out the razing of the villages without himself being directly involved in these activities. Weitz saw this as indicating lack of determination and strength on the Prime Minister's part. On 30 June Weitz briefly met Ben-Gurion, who asked about 'the state of the [Transfer Committee] activities'. But the Prime Minister failed to keep his appointment for the following day with Weitz, when Weitz had hoped to settle Transfer Committee matters with the Prime Minister once and for all. Angry and frustrated, Weitz 'instructed [his officials] to cease work'.[81]

Under pressure from the soft-liners, Ben-Gurion had thus brought about a halt to the Transfer Committee's operations, effectively ending the first chapter in its history. Subsequently he informed Foreign Minister Shertok, the committee's main patron in the Cabinet, of the new situation. But neither Prime Minister nor Foreign Minister regarded the situation as final. In mid-July, Shertok issued a 'letter of appointment' to Ezra Danin, naming the Arabist a special adviser to the ministry's Middle East Affairs Department and the ministry's representative 'to the body which will deal with the problem of the transfer of Arabs out of the area of Israel and their resettlement in the neighbouring countries. This body has not yet been set up because the policy of transfer has not yet received the required endorsement. From my conversation with the Prime Minister on this matter', the letter of appointment continued, 'it became clear that the previous directive [that is, instructing Weitz to destroy the villages] has been rescinded and one must now await

[80] CZA, A-246/13, p. 2,425, entry for 25 June 1948.
[81] Weitz, iii, p. 310, entry for 1 July 1948.

new directives.'[82] Because of the mounting political pressures, which included a shuttle around the Middle East by UN Mediator for Palestine Count Folke Bernadotte (who was attempting to persuade Israel to allow the refugees back), the IDF's parallel razing of Arab villages was also temporarily curtailed.[83]

But the thrust of the Prime Minister's thinking, Mapam's and Bernadotte's importunings notwithstanding, remained firm and clear. As the second truce in the hostilities approached, Ben-Gurion jotted down his priorities for the weeks ahead. They included strengthening the army, expanding Israel's arms-production capacity, and drawing up 'a list . . . of abandoned villages standing on dangerous, strategic sites, in order to destroy them, and settlement [by Jews] of abandoned places . . . must be taken in hand'.[84] At Mapam's urging, responsibility for the fate of the abandoned villages —destruction, renovation, resettlement—in mid-July devolved upon the newly constituted Ministerial (or Cabinet) Committee for Abandoned Property, which apparently met for the first time on 13 July and was formally empowered by the full Cabinet on 21 July to decide the fate of the villages. The committee was composed of Defence Minister Ben-Gurion, Foreign Minister Shertok, Finance Minister Kaplan, Justice Minister Felix Rosenblueth (later Pinchas Rosen), Minority Affairs Minister Shitrit, and Agriculture Minister Zisling. The *modus operandi* of the ministerial committee was outlined to Weitz on the evening of 21 July by Kaplan: 'The military staff brings its proposals, to destroy or occupy a village, to establish a permanent hold on land, to the committee . . .'. The committee's decision, if unanimous, becomes policy. If there is dissent, the matter is resolved in the full Cabinet.

Authority for destroying the villages had thus been taken out of Weitz's hands. Now the Cabinet meant to abrogate the powers of the various settlement bodies as well. Until mid-July 1948, the Jewish Agency, the JNF, and the Agricultural Centre of the Histadrut, in consultation with the defence forces, had determined settlement policy and had overseen its implementation. 'According to the [new

[82] ISA, FM 2.570/1, M. Shertok to E. Danin, 16 July 1948.
[83] KMA-AZP 9.9.1. for the IDF General Staff / Operations order of 6 July 1948 prohibiting 'destruction of towns and villages . . . without special permission or explicit order from the Minister of Defence . . .'.
[84] DBG, ii, p. 603, entry for 21 July 1948.

decision], we can no longer decide on our own . . .', Weitz complained, 'We may as well pack up', Weitz told Kaplan, blaming the Mapam ministers, 'the "just men" in our camp, Zisling and Bentov, who "worry about" the neighbours living in our house'.[85]

BUYING UP ARAB LAND

During July, various kibbutzim continued to turn to Weitz for advice and help in matters concerning the abandoned villages. Representatives from Degania Aleph and Kinneret, for example, came to Tel Aviv to inform him that the regional Jewish settlements committee had decided against allowing the Arabs to return. The representatives came to work out 'a settlement plan for the [abandoned] lands' along the banks of the Jordan River and the Sea of Galilee. Weitz promised to do what he could.[86] But Weitz's main attention, diverted from his initial preoccupation with increasing the Arab exodus and preventing the refugees' return by destroying their villages, now focused on another aspect of his original transfer scheme—the purchase of land from the refugees and the financial inducement of other Arabs to leave their areas and settle outside Israel.

The day after his angry meeting with Kaplan, Weitz began planning a trip by Danin and the lawyer Yosef Strumza to France or Switzerland 'to meet Arabs . . . to buy land (and to investigate the possibility of [accomplishing] the transfer, I add to myself)'. That day, Weitz spoke to Zuckerman and Yosef Nahmani, the head of the JNF land office in the Galilee, about renewing land purchases from Arabs.[87] On 26 July Weitz wrote a comprehensive survey of lands the JNF had its eye on for future Jewish settlement and regional development.[88] The following day, Weitz heard from one of his purchasing agents about efforts to buy land from the villagers of Al Hamidiya (on the northern edge of the Beit Shean Valley), who would then 'move to settle in Transjordan'. 'The question is', wrote Weitz, 'should we enter into [such a] partial transfer activity or should this be postponed until the transfer question is solved in its

[85] CZA, A-246/13, p. 2,444, entry for 19 July 1948.
[86] CZA, A-246/13, p. 2,452, entry for 28 July 1948.
[87] CZA, A-246/13, p. 2,445, entry for 22 July 1948.
[88] CZA, A-246/13, p. 2,449, entry for 26 July 1948.

entirety? And if [we should go in for] partial [solutions]—[should we do so] now, when the Arabs who are leaving are still standing on their own two feet, or should we wait until they collapse [and are willing to take lower prices for their land]?'[89] Weitz encountered some unexpected opposition to the Hamidiya land purchase. JNF chairman Granovsky asked: 'Has it already been decided that [the] Beit Shean [Valley] will be clear of Arabs?' But if the purchase was to be made, he added, then certainly the Arabs' prices should be lowered. 'I chuckled to myself', Weitz recorded.[90] Weitz raised the larger issue when the two continued their discussion the following day: the JNF must not wait for instructions from others, even from the Cabinet, in carrying out its historic mission, 'redeeming' the Land of Israel: 'We must act as we have always acted: gain possession of land in all ways, and not formulate new theories which will delay us . . .'. Granovsky apparently agreed.[91]

But purchasing land from Arabs in the circumstances of late summer 1948 was not easy. Nahmani thought that the Arabs in the Galilee and the refugees now in Lebanon would not dare sell their land to Jews; in the circumstances, it was tantamount to high treason. Moreover, the Palestinians in the north in mid-1948 had not yet grasped that the situation had radically altered, and that the refugees would not be returning. The Arabs, complained Weitz, continued to conduct land negotiations along pre-1948 lines, with 'wearying talks, high prices and other conditions'. The Arabs, he thought, must be made to understand that there would be no return and that only by selling to the Jews would they be assured of 'saving their property' and obtaining the means for resettling comfortably elsewhere.[92]

Weitz and his purchasing agents pressed on. After knocking down the Arabs' prices, deals were concluded in September in Hamidiya (140 dunams—a dunam is approximately a quarter of an acre) and Yafia (200 dunams), and in the Hula Valley in Northern Galilee (200 dunams).[93] But Weitz realized that this was chicken-feed. It was 'quite sad', he recorded. 'Among the Arabs there is not even a

[89] CZA, A-246/13, p. 2,451, entry for 27 July 1948.
[90] CZA, A-246/13, p. 2,452, entry for 29 July 1948.
[91] CZA, A-246/13, p. 2,453, entry for 30 July 1948.
[92] Weitz, iii, pp. 323–4, entry for 3 Aug. 1948.
[93] CZA, A-246/13, p. 2,478, entry for 8 Sept. 1948.

sign of panic movement towards selling land. They are apparently
sure that everything will return to its former state . . .'[94]
The matter continued to vex Weitz.

The Arabs do not see their situation as it really is . . . A refugee Arab
dwelling for months now in a sack-tent is not ready to sell his land [near
Nazareth], except for a small amount [of land] in order to maintain his
family and himself. He hopes that soon he will return to cultivate his
holdings as before. He does not consider the other possibility that perhaps
he will not be able to return [to his village], and that it is better for him to get
rid of his property while its value has not completely depreciated.

Scouting around for an explanation for the refugees' stubbornness,
Weitz conjectured: 'Maybe . . . it lies in his rootedness. After all,
he and his kind have been bound to the soil . . . for generations, and
it is not easy to dissolve these ties.'[95]

The publication in September of the 'Bernadotte Plan', the UN
mediator's testament, as it were, to the warring tribes of Palestine
(he was assassinated that month in Jerusalem by Jewish terrorists),
only added to Weitz's difficulties. According to JNF officials in the
north, the plan's provision for the refugees' return promoted a
feeling among the Arabs 'that they were about to return . . . and
[now] felt no compulsion to sell'.[96]

But there were countervailing factors: the political uncertainty,
the continuing expansion of the Jewish state, so clearly stronger
than its Arab enemies, and the Israeli authorities' attitude and
policy towards the Arabs who had remained within the state. At
Yafia, for example, the villagers were willing to sell another 500
dunams but were demanding what Weitz regarded as an excessive
I£25 per dunam. He advised his officials to wait, reasoning that the
Arabs were not being allowed to cultivate their fields; eventually
they would 'be forced to sell'.[97] At the same time, Weitz formulated
plans to buy land from absentee and refugee landowners living in
Cairo, Beirut, and Europe. Foreign Minister Shertok supported
Weitz's scheme to send land-purchasing agents to Paris. But Weitz
wondered out loud whether some of the money paid for land might
not be used by the Arabs to finance their war effort. Shertok

---

[94] Weitz, iii, p. 339, entry for 9 Sept. 1948.
[95] Ibid., p. 341, Weitz to Rema, 11 Sept. 1948.
[96] CZA, A-246/14, p. 2,497, entry for 29 Sept. 1948.
[97] CZA, A-246/14, pp. 2,537–8, entry for 2 Dec. 1948.

replied: 'The reasons for buying [Arab land] outweigh [the reasons against].'[98]

After much deliberation and delay, Zuckerman and Gad Machnes were eventually shipped off to Paris to seek out Arab landowners and conclude deals. But no sooner were they in Europe than the Cabinet ordered the JNF to stop all land purchases from refugee and local Arabs. Ben-Gurion told Weitz and Danin at a meeting in Tiberias on 18 December: 'The JNF [henceforward] would buy land only from the State. There was no need to buy land from Arabs.' According to his diaries, the Prime Minister argued that Israel's problem was not an absence of land on which to settle Jews but an absence of Jews willing to settle on the land.[99] According to Weitz, Ben-Gurion said that 'the Cabinet was resolved to forbid [the JNF] from buying land from Arabs'.[100] Weitz then ordered the JNF men in the north to suspend purchases 'for the time being'.[101]

Weitz explained the opposition to buying land from Arabs thus: '. . . the politicians . . . say: There is no need to buy land; after all, it was redeemed with the sword and the blood of our sons, and it is [now] all in our hands . . .'.[102] Ben-Gurion preferred to act as did most nations at war—what nation paid for territory after conquering it? Besides, Israel was poor. Weitz cabled Zuckerman and Machnes —who reported that they were on the verge of success—to fly home.[103]

The government's ban on land-purchasing from Arabs threatened the JNF's *raison d'être*. The JNF directors debated the matter on 4 January 1949. The directorate expressed 'understanding' for the Cabinet's opposition to purchases from refugees 'but does not agree to the government's stand' prohibiting also purchase from Arabs living inside Israel. In defiance of the Cabinet, the directorate instructed Weitz to go ahead with purchases of some 55,000 dunams which the JNF had been interested in before the war 'in Shfar-am' [Shafa Amr], Isfiya, Daliyat [al] Karmil, Ijzim, [Al] Birwa, Ilut, Yafia, [Al] Mujeidil, Umm al Kannem [?], Kislut [? Islut], Indur

[98] Weitz, iii, p. 338, entry for 6 Sept. 1948.
[99] DBG, iii, p. 885, entry for 18 Dec. 1948.
[100] Weitz, iii, p. 366, entry for 18 Dec. 1948.
[101] Ibid., and CZA, A-246/14, p. 2,553, entry for 18 Dec. 1948.
[102] Weitz, iii, p. 362, Weitz to Rema, 9 Dec. 1948.
[103] Weitz, iii, p. 373, entry for 28 Dec. 1948, and Weitz iv, p. 3, entry for 6 Jan. 1949.

(Ein Dor), Tamra, [Al] Manara, Beit Shean [Beisan], Kafr Misr, Sirin, Dabburiya, . . . Lubiya, Madhar, Maghar Durruz, Turan, Arraba, Sakhnin, Deir Hanna and Bueina'.[104]

SETTLING THE ABANDONED LANDS

Weitz resumed his land-purchasing campaign, though it was to remain his secondary activity during the latter months of 1948. First and foremost, his energies were spent on the establishment of new Jewish settlements in the areas emptied of Arabs. Weitz saw in the settlement effort, before and during 1948, the primary tool for entrenching and consolidating the Jewish people's hold on the Land of Israel and of determining its borders. As well, settlement would finalize the Palestinian exodus, assuring as nothing else could that the refugees could never return. He wrote:

The abandoned villages, whether destroyed or standing whole, are a vacuum . . . which threatens to become a major obstacle to solving the Arab refugee problem [by way of resettling them abroad]. So long as [the vacuum] exists, there will also exist pressure to fill it up by a return of [the original Arab] inhabitants . . . The danger of this vacuum must be removed by settling Jews [in it].[105]

Weitz's settlement plans and efforts followed hard on the heels of the IDF's conquering columns. In May, he pressed for the swift expansion of Jewish settlement in Western Galilee, an area left out of the Jewish state by the UN Partition Plan of November 1947 and conquered by the Haganah in the days following the declaration of independence of the State of Israel. Weitz's attachment to this fertile strip along the Mediterranean was deep and anguished: in 1946 his eldest son, Yehiam, was shot dead by Arabs near the Az-Zib (Achziv) bridge there during a Palmah raid. Kibbutz Yehiam, named in his memory, was set up in the area. The kibbutzim of Western Galilee, and especially Yehiam, were under Arab siege from March until the Haganah conquest of the area; their stand as embattled islands in an Arab sea riveted the Yishuv's attention.

Within weeks of the conquest, the Western Galilee's Arab villages had been levelled and preparations were well advanced to establish

[104] CZA, KKL 10, protocols of the JNF board of directors meeting of 4 Jan. 1949.
[105] Weitz, iii, pp. 339–40, entry for 11 Sept. 1948.

new settlements: Kibbutz Sa'ar was set up in July 1948; Kibbutz Ga'aton in October. In July, a day after its conquest, Weitz toured the Lydda (Lod) airport area, mentally establishing settlements here and there on the rich 'brown-black-red' soil.[106] The following month, three settlements went up on the abandoned lands of Wilhelma—Nehalim, Atarot (later renamed Bnei Atarot), and Be'erot Yitzhak.

Weitz fluctuated between joy and despair as periods of inactivity seemingly followed each conquest and as the nation's leaders debated a succession of vast settlements plans. 'No movement, the engine is too heavy and the drivers are many', he lamented. It was not enough that the executives of the settlement bodies—Weitz himself, Hartzfeld of the Agricultural Centre, and Yehuda Horin, director of the Jewish Agency's settlement department—wanted new settlements. 'It is necessary that Ben-Gurion will truly want, and that [Finance Minister] Kaplan will want . . . I am in bad spirits', he wrote in June.[107]

Towards the end of the month, at Weitz's urging, the JNF directorate approved a settlement plan involving nineteen new settlements to be set up immediately in the Jerusalem corridor, the Beit Shean valley, and the lower Galilee.[108]

At a meeting with Ben-Gurion in Tel Aviv, attended also by Shkolnik, Weitz, on 23 July, urged that conquests be succeeded immediately by new settlements so that the 'military victories should be translated into political achivements'. But should new settlements also be established outside the areas earmarked in the 1947 partition resolution for the Jewish state and / or on Arab-owned lands?

On the first point, it was agreed that new settlements should go up in the Ramle–Lydda and Jerusalem corridor areas (both lying outside the partition boundaries and strategically straddling the road to Jerusalem). But Weitz noted that Ben-Gurion and Shkolnik, who spoke of '10–12' new settlements beyond the partition boundaries, carefully avoided responding to the question of settling on Arab-owned lands—though plans to settle the Jerusalem corridor implied

[106] Ibid., pp. 314–15, entry for 13 July 1948.
[107] Ibid., p. 302, entry for 14 June 1948.
[108] CZA, KKL 10, protocols of the JNF board of directors meeting, 24 June 1948.

as much, as little of the land there was Jewish-owned.[109] Through August and September, Weitz pressed doggedly for immediate settlement of western Galilee, the central Galilee, and the corridor, slowly overcoming resistance from the Mapam ministers and Granovsky, who initially opposed Jewish settlement on Arab-owned lands. Weitz in this was strongly supported by the defence establishment. The Defence Ministry in August proposed establishing sixty-one settlements, mostly along the new borders. The settlement institutions—the JNF, Jewish Agency, and Agriculture Centre settlement departments—preferred a more modest plan, involving thirty-two settlements, only five of which were to be within the 1947 partition borders and about half on Arab-owned land.

Speaking before the Ministerial Committee for Abandoned Property, Weitz stressed that the Arab-owned lands proposed for Jewish settlement were empty of Arabs. But Agriculture Minister Zisling, from Mapam, persuaded the committee to accept the caveat that some of the lands of each abandoned village to be settled by Jews should be set aside for the possible return of the original inhabitants, political developments permitting.[110] The Mapam caveat was to remain a formality, and a short-lived one at that. Hundreds of new settlements had to be established 'on the Arab lands which were being depopulated', Weitz told the JNF directorate in September.[111] By December, the idea of setting aside land for returning Arabs was dead. On 18 December Weitz asked Ben-Gurion, who was on vacation in Tiberias, whether such land still had to be set aside. Ben-Gurion replied: 'Not [in sites] along the border, and in each village we'll take all [the land], in accordance with our settlement needs, and the Arab will not return.'[112] In any case, the concept of 'surpluses' had been a fiction from the start. Each new settlement during the second half of 1948 was allocated by the settlement bodies as much land as it needed and could handle without attention being paid to the Mapam-initiated caveat.

[109] Weitz, iii, p. 319, entry for 23 July 1948.
[110] ISA, FM 2564/13, protocol of Meeting of the Cabinet Committee for Abandoned Property, 20 Aug. 1948.
[111] Weitz, iii, p. 343, entry for 20 Sept. 1948.
[112] Ibid., p. 366, entry for 18 Dec. 1948.

THE SECOND TRANSFER COMMITTEE

While dealing with renewed land purchase from Arabs and the settlement by Jews of successive abandoned sites, Weitz had never lost sight of his original goal—the appointment of an executive body, preferably with himself at its head, to oversee a policy of transfer. The appointment of Danin in mid-July to be the Foreign Ministry's representative in such a body, once established, reinforced Weitz's hopes that it would yet come into being. Weitz met Ben-Gurion and Shertok on 25 July to press for a decision on transfer policy. He achieved what appeared to be movement. Ben-Gurion empowered Shertok to supervise the implementation of the 'Transfer Policy', once again displaying both his desire that the matter be expedited and his wish that he himself not be directly involved. Ben-Gurion failed to record the meeting in his diary.[113]

But Shertok, perhaps busy with other matters (Bernadotte), perhaps waiting for a formal letter of authorization from Ben-Gurion, dragged his feet. Weitz lamented: 'Though the Foreign Ministry has set a line . . . it has not yet [begun] to act on it. A special apparatus is needed which will act and activate [others].'[114] The following day Weitz wrote to Shertok to remind the Foreign Minister of the decisions taken at the 25 July meeting with Ben-Gurion: 'You told me that from now on the initiative in the matter of the 'transfer' would be in your hands and that you would immediately call for consultations and action . . . If I am not mistaken, the consultation has not yet been called and the concrete, practical implementation has not yet been arranged.' Weitz warned that, meanwhile, the whole matter was up in the air, with everybody doing in his own domain as he saw fit. Weitz called for setting up the special apparatus, which would also act to convince the Arabs through propaganda that there would be no return. He asked Shertok not to be angry with his importuning, explaining that he regarded 'the realization of the transfer' as 'the crown of our victory' in the war.[115]

Shertok called in his two chief Middle East advisers, Danin and

---

[113] The existence and upshot of this meeting are referred to in a letter from Y. Weitz to M. Shertok on 4 Aug. 1948, ISA, FM 2564/20.
[114] CZA, A-246/13, p. 2,456, entry for 3 Aug. 1948.
[115] ISA, FM 2564/20, Y. Weitz to M. Shertok, 4 Aug. 1948.

Ya'akov Shimoni, caretaker director of the ministry's Middle East Affairs Department, and within a day the two formulated a one-page memorandum entitled 'Proposals for Immediate Actions Connected with the Prevention of the Return of the Arab Refugees to Israel Before A Definitive Policy Regarding the Problem is Determined'. It was submitted to Shertok on 5 August. The eight-point document proposed: the collection of data about the present whereabouts of the refugees and their numbers; listing their abandoned property; 'A fresh examination of the military and defence considerations necessitating the destruction of Arab buildings and assistance, in advice and funding, in implementing this destruction'; collection of information about 'the wandering, flight or expulsion' of other populations around the world ('Greece–Turkey . . . Pakistan–Hindustan . . .'); formulating plans for the resettlement of the refugees in the Arab states; and the appointment of a 'team of workers' to carry out 'the aforementioned work'. The document notes that some JNF employees can be mobilized for this purpose and proposes; 'For the organization of the operation and its implementation [we] propose the engineer Zalman Lifshitz and Mr. Hiram Danin.'[116]

That day, Ezra Danin informed Weitz that Shertok had agreed 'that we begin work aimed at the solution of the Arab problem in line with our our policy: prevention of their return and formulation of plans to settle them in Arab countries.' Weitz then wrote to Zuckerman and Nahmani to begin collecting data on the Arab exodus,[117] and the following day asked Lifshitz to join the still 'unofficial committee for matters of transfer'. Lifshitz agreed.[118]

Weitz spent the following fortnight amassing details about the movement of Arabs out of Palestine. On 18 August Ben-Gurion summoned the country's leading Arab affairs and defence experts for a full-scale consultation on the refugee problem, the possibility of a return, and policy towards Israel's Arab minority. The meeting, in Ben-Gurion's office, was attended by Shertok, Kaplan, Shitrit, the Directors-General of the Treasury and the Minority Affairs Ministry, Weitz, Danin and Lifshitz, Shimoni and Reuven Shiloah,

---

[116] ISA, FM 2566/13, memorandum entitled 'Proposals for Immediate Actions . . .', 5 Aug. 1948.
[117] Weitz, iii, p. 324, entry for 5 Aug. 1948.
[118] Ibid., entry for 6 Aug. 1948.

the Foreign Ministry's liaison with the defence and intelligence forces, Major-General Elimelech Avner, head of the Military Government in the Occupied Territories, and others.[119]

Apart from the Cabinet ministers, Weitz and Lifshitz were the chief speakers in the debate, which eventually focused on the necessity for barring a refugee return, a policy on which there was complete unanimity. Weitz outlined the dimensions of the refugee problem: 286 villages had been 'evacuated', 179 of these within the Jewish state's partition plan borders. In all, some three million dunams of land had been abandoned by the Arabs. He explained what must be done, closely following the outline-scheme the Transfer Committee had submitted to Ben-Gurion in early June. Some villages had to be destroyed, others settled. What could be bought, should be. Abandoned fields should be cultivated and propaganda begun among the Arabs explaining that the exile was final; there would be no return. He urged that a body be appointed to study the possibilities of resettling the refugees permanently abroad and to prepare 'a plan for the transfer of the Arabs and their resettlement [abroad]'.

When Minority Affairs Minister Shitrit commented that the decision whether to allow a return was not entirely in Israeli hands, Ben-Gurion cut him short with: 'We are proceeding from the assumption of how to assist those who will not return—as many as they will be (and for us it is preferable that they are as many as possible)—to settle abroad.' Shimoni supported Weitz's call for 'an apparatus to investigate, and settle refugees abroad' and subsequently saw in the 'advisory gathering' in Ben-Gurion's office a major step towards getting a transfer committee at last officially endorsed and appointed. The participants, Shimoni wrote the next day to the Paris-based director of his department, Elias Sasson, were unanimous in opposing a return and about doing everything possible to prevent it. Finance Minister Kaplan and his Director-General, David Horowitz, however, 'were more conservative and careful about the means' to be employed 'with regard to Arab property', Shimoni noted.

[119] An abbreviated, four-page protocol of the meeting, written by Ya'akov Shimoni, is in FM 2444/19. It is the best record kept of the meeting. Long entries on the discussion are also to be found in DBG, ii, pp. 652–4 and Weitz, iii, p. 331. In his letter to E. Sasson of 19 Aug. 1948, Shimoni evaluated the previous day's meeting (in ISA, FM 2570/11).

The Cabinet formally approved the appointment of the Transfer Committee during the last week of August, and on 29 August the Cabinet Secretariat informed Weitz that Ben-Gurion had appointed him, Danin, and Lifshitz 'as a committee which must submit to him a proposal about possibilities of settling the Arabs of the Land of Israel in the Arab states'.[120] These terms of reference represented a considerable constriction of Weitz's original conception of the body he had hoped to head. The whole sphere of praxis within the borders of the state, aimed at precipitating further Arab flight and preventing a return, was apparently left outside the committee's purview.

On 31 August the committee met with Cabinet Secretary Ze'ev Sharef to discuss terms of reference for the letter of appointment. That evening, Weitz and his wife Ruhama went to the theatre for the first time 'since [their son] Yehiam's death'. They saw *He Fell in the Fields*, a play by Moshe Shamir about the life and death of a Palmah soldier. 'We wanted to see moments from the life of Yehiam and his death near the [Az-Zib] bridge.'[121] About a fortnight after the committee began work, committee member Lifshitz went to Ben-Gurion to unburden himself of a grave concern: only a minority of the refugees, he related, were living in the neighbouring states proper—'75,000 in Transjordan, 5,000 in Iraq, 12–15,000 in Lebanon and 20,000 in Syria.' The bulk of the *fellahs* 'were encamped [in the Gaza Strip, the West Bank, and Upper Galilee] along the front lines and hope to return'. Lifshitz proposed that these refugees be 'intimidated' into moving away from Israel's borders.[122]

The problem of the refugee concentrations within Palestine along the front lines preoccupied the committee through September, especially against the backdrop of the 18 September publication of the Bernadotte Plan, which proposed the inclusion of western Galilee in Israel with the Negev going to Transjordan, and allowing the refugees to return to their homes. After reading the plan, Weitz became deeply troubled. The plan threatened to bring back 'almost all the Arab refugees through the back door', he commented.[123] Weitz was especially worried by the large refugee concentrations

[120] Weitz, iii, p. 336, entry for 29–30 Aug. 1948.
[121] CZA, A-246/14, p. 2,473, entry for 31 Aug. 1948.
[122] DBG, iii, p. 683, entry for 13 Sept. 1948.
[123] Weitz, iii, p. 344, entry for 22 Sept. 1948.

along the Majdal (Ashkelon)–Faluja–Hebron Hills line in the northern Negev approaches and in the upper central Galilee. The committee formally discussed the problem on 23 September, Weitz expressing the fear that 'the solution of the Arab problem . . . might soon come and not in a manner we had desired'. Danin, according to Weitz, said that a solution to the problem of the refugee concentrations lay in intimidation (*hatrada*) which would force those in the Galilee to move off northwards. Alternatively, Danin suggested, Israel could open talks with the Lebanese and Syrian authorities to persuade them to allow the refugees to move into and settle permanently in their countries. He implied that Israel could grease Arab palms to this purpose. The committee resolved to bring the matter to Ben-Gurion.[124]

Weitz first discussed the technicalities of intimidation with one of his field-men and then, on 26 September, went to see Ben-Gurion. What was to be done about the refugee concentrations? the Prime Minister asked. 'Intimidation', was Weitz's response, 'intimidation using all means.'[125] There were some 100,000 refugees in the central Galilee, Weitz said. They would return to their homes in Israel—in line with the Bernadotte Plan—unless intimidated into moving away.

According to Ben-Gurion, who also recorded the conversation in his diaries, Weitz proposed that the intimidation operation in the Galilee be carried out by Israeli Arabs, Syrians, and Lebanese gendarmes. In the south, the refugees should be intimidated 'without end' (*bli sof*), Ben-Gurion recorded Weitz as saying (but without naming him). Weitz proposed that Shiloah—the Foreign Ministry liaison with the IDF—be placed in charge of the operation, assisted by the Weitz–Danin–Lifshitz committee. 'Weitz asked that I issue orders to Shiloah', Ben-Gurion recorded, not saying how he acted in the matter subsequently.[126]

With the renewal of hostilities in mid-October, almost all the Arabs—locals and refugees—in the south fled or were pushed out of Israeli territory into the Egyptian-held Gaza Strip or the Hebron

---

[124] CZA, A-246/14, p. 2,492, entry for 23 Sept. 1948.

[125] CZA, A-246/14, p. 2,493, entry for 25 Sept. 1948 and Weitz, iii, p. 344, entry for 26 Sept. 1948.

[126] Weitz, iii, p. 344, entry for 26 Sept. 1948 and DBG, iii, p. 721, entry for 26 Sept. 1948.

Hills, held by the Transjordanian Arab Legion. But in the north, in Operation Hiram, the IDF acted in haphazard fashion, here and there expelling and razing villages, in most places leaving the Arab population, including many refugees from areas conquered by the IDF earlier, *in situ*. Weitz was informed by JNF official Moshe Berger on 29 October that the advance into the Arab pocket in upper central Galilee had begun. Weitz commented: 'There is need to arrange that the refugees will flow from there outwards. I wrote a note about this to Yig[ael] Yadin [IDF chief of operations]'.[127]

But Yadin failed to act on Weitz's advice. Following Operation Hiram, Danin toured the newly conquered area and reported: 'There was no plan about [what to do with] them. The different commanders each acted according to their own judgement. At the same time, reprehensible acts were committed here and there by our side.' Danin thought it was essential to plan in advance Israeli behaviour towards the population of the 'Triangle' (the Jenin–Nablus–Tulkarm sector of the area today known as the West Bank) and the Hebron Hills, which seemed to be next on the agenda of conquest, 'We decided to do this at our next meeting', Weitz recorded.[128] The same lack of a predetermined, unified approach, according to Weitz, seemed to misguide Israeli policy towards the Negev's beduins, some of whom the government was allowing to stay on Israeli territory, over Weitz's strong objections.[129]

The committee's terms of appointment at the end of August had been restricted to theoretical evaluation, investigation, and recommendations concerning the fate of Arabs who had already moved out of Israel. But during the autumn of 1948 the committee as a body and its members individually remained active as consultants and lobbyists regarding the possible fate of various Arab communities. The committee acted as a pressure group, albeit of experts, urging the IDF brass and the country's political leadership to expel Arabs and move refugees away from the new, expanding borders. In effect, this marked a reversion by Weitz to his role in the spring and summer of that year. At the same time, the committee took an active part in promoting and advising about 'unofficial' propaganda

---

[127] CZA, A-246/14, p. 2,511, entry for 29 Oct. 1948.
[128] CZA, A-246/14, p. 2,522, entry for 9 Nov. 1948, and A-246/14, p. 2,526, entry for 18 Nov. 1948.
[129] CZA, A-246/14, p. 2,526, entry for 18 Nov. 1948.

aimed at convincing the Arab states and the refugees that the exodus was a *fait accompli* and that the refugees would not be allowed by Israel to return. (The public official line was that while the refugees would not be allowed to return during the hostilities, the matter was open for negotiation after the war.)[130]

Danin himself defined the committee's tasks as gathering information about various transfers of population in the recent past (Armenians, Greeks, Kurds, Turks, and so on)—'If we succeed in this amassing [of information], let us hope that we will be able to give every respectable nation its list of crimes in this sphere, in order that they may restrain themselves in their criticism of what is being done in this field in Israel', he wrote—listing and evaluating the abandoned property, and formulating development and resettlement plans for the refugees in the Arab states. Danin was writing the first chapter (historic parallels), Lifshitz the second (abandoned property), and Weitz the third (resettlement schemes), with Hiram Danin acting as committee secretary. However, as if by the way, Danin added that the committee from time to time did deal with practical questions as well, such as 'the problem of infiltration [of refugees back to Israel]; the problem of the large [refugee] concentrations near Israel's borders; and the problem of organized counterpropaganda . . .'.[131] The counter-propaganda campaign involved planting reports in Israel's Arabic newspapers and among foreign correspondents that Israel had no intention of allowing the refugees back.[132]

The 'Transfer Committee' laboured over its report through September and most of October. On 21 October Danin went to Ben-Gurion and informed him that the committee's work was almost done. The two discussed possible Israeli actions *vis-à-vis* the 'Triangle' and the Hebron hills, and Ben-Gurion according to Danin said that he expected the Arabs to flee, which Danin took as encouragement from the Prime Minister for the Transfer Committee's practical activities.[133]

[130] FM 2564/1, Y. Shimoni to M. Shertok, 13 Sept. 1948, and ISA, FM 2570/11, E. Danin (Tel Aviv) to E. Sasson (Paris), 22 Sept. 1948.
[131] ISA, FM 2570/11, E. Danin (Tel Aviv) to E. Sasson (Paris), 22 Sept. 1948.
[132] ISA, FM 2570/11, Y. Shimoni (Tel Aviv) to E. Sasson (Paris), 19 Aug. 1948, and Weitz, iii, p. 346, entry for 3 Oct. 1948.
[133] ISA, FM 2570/11, E. Danin (Tel Aviv) to E. Sasson (Paris), 24 Oct. 1948. Danin mistakenly says that his meeting with Ben-Gurion took place on 22 Oct. 1948.

The committee reported on its major findings and recommendations to Ben-Gurion at his office in Tel Aviv on 26 October. The Prime Minister summarized the committee's eight points as follows:

(A) The Arabs themselves are guilty of their flight.

(B) They should not [be allowed to] return, because they will constitute a Fifth Column, they will hold a grudge [against us] in their hearts, their economy [that is, economic infrastructure] has been destroyed and repatriation [of the refugees] will require giant sums, beyond the state's capacity.

(C) The Arabs who remained inside the state should be treated as equal citizens. . .

(D) The Arabs who fled—will be resettled by the Arab governments in Syria, Iraq and Transjordan . . . [and] Lebanon . . .

(E) The resettlement [costs should come out of] the value of the immovable goods [that is, lands, houses abandoned] in the country (after reparations [for war damage to the Yishuv] are deducted), the Arab states will give land, the rest [will come]—[from] the UN and international institutions.

(F) The extrication of the Jews of Iraq and Syria.

(G) What to do if the Arab states refuse to resettle the refugees?

(H) [What to do] if a return [of refugees] will be forced on us? On no account will we accept a return to the border villages, [and] to the cities only a certain percentage (15 per cent of the Jews [that is, of the Jewish population of each city]), only craftsmen and others who can support themselves. . .[134]

According to Weitz, Ben-Gurion endorsed all eight points.[135] The committee recommended that 235 of the 300 abandoned sites be settled. Ben-Gurion, for his part, suggested that the Jewish communities in the Arab countries be excluded from consideration in the report. He also recommended that all the refugees be settled in one country, preferably Iraq, rather than be dispersed among the neighbouring states. He was set against resettlement in Transjordan.[136]

The core of the report was submitted to Foreign Minister Shertok on 5 November. He approved it 'as a first stage' and said that the committee should continue 'to function as a permanent body affiliated

[134] DBG, iii, pp. 776–7, entry for 26 Oct. 1948.
[135] Weitz, iii, p. 349, entry for 26 Oct. 1948.
[136] DBG, iii, pp. 776–7, entry for 26 Oct. 1948.

with the Foreign Ministry' to be consulted on refugee matters.[137] The completed version of the report, entitled 'Regarding the Solution for the Arab Refugees', and covering several hundred pages, was signed by its authors on 25 November and submitted by Lifshitz to Ben-Gurion on 3 December.[138] The report covered the causes of the flight of the Palestine Arabs, the scope and dimensions of the exodus, and the migration of peoples around the world in recent times.

Unlike other recent migrations, wrote the authors, 'the migration of the Arabs of the Land of Israel was not caused by persecution, violence, expulsion. . .'. Indeed, wrote the authors, the Yishuv tried to persuade its Arab neighbours to stay put. Explicit mention is made of the Arabs of Sheikh Muwannis and Abu Kishk, just north of Tel Aviv, who left despite Jewish entreaties that they 'not leave . . . and [the Jews] promised them defence and protection . . . and mutual cooperation . . . if only they refrained from taking part in the war'.[139] Why then did the Arabs leave? It was

a tactic of war on the part of the Arabs who directed the war against the Jews, whose aim was to remove the Arabs from the neighbourhood of the Jews so that they, the attacking Arabs, would have freedom of action in the war, meaning: To attack, bomb and bombard [the Jews] and the Arabs would not be harmed not by [the attacking Arabs] and not by the Jews by way of retaliation.

Weitz–Danin–Lifshitz wrote that the Arabs expected that their exile would last only a few weeks, after which time they would 'return not only to their own homes but also to the houses of the Jews, and [the Arabs] would inherit the possessions'. In order to make the Arab flight comprehensive, its instigators, reinforced by British Mandate officials, highlighted alleged Jewish atrocities committed against occupied Arab communities. 'The Arabs of the Land of Israel obeyed the order of their leaders in the country and in [the Arab] League, and the Arabs became affected by panic' and fled the country.[140]

---

[137] Weitz, iii, p. 352, entry for 5 Nov. 1948.
[138] Ibid., p. 357, entry for 25 Nov. 1948 and p. 363, entry for 3 December 1948. Also DBG, iii, p. 863, entry for 3 Dec. 1948.
[139] ISA, FM 2445/3, the committee's memorandum entitled 'Regarding the Solution for the Arab Refugees', p. 2.
[140] Ibid., p. 3.

Explaining the destruction of the Arab villages which followed, the authors wrote: 'When the battles developed . . . whole areas became battlefields, many Arab villages were damaged in the actual military actions.' Moreover, the Israeli forces carried out 'retribution' against some hostile villages. The fear of retribution 'hastened the flight and abandonment . . . though in most cases there was no compulsion behind this flight . . . because the Arabs could have lifted a white flag . . . and remained in their places . . .'. Neither Israel's citizens nor its army nor its government 'generally resorted to acts of violence, apart from those [customary] in war, against the Arab citizens to force them to abandon their homes and possessions . . .'. In a special appendix, devoted to unravelling the causes of the exodus, the authors add that the flight was 'deliberately organized' by the Arab leaders 'in order to arouse Arab [feeling] of revenge, to artificially create an Arab refugee problem . . . and to prepare the ground for the invasion [of Palestine] by the Arab states who could then appear as saviours of their brother Arabs'.

The authors specifically link the exodus of the Arabs from the coastal plain at the end of March, beginning of April 'to the end of the citrus-picking season . . . At the end of the season, the Arab Higher Committee gave orders to evacuate the Sharon [that is, coastal plain].' The authors bring this information, they emphasize, to negate charges that the exodus was sparked by the Irgun–Lehi massacre at Deir Yassin, west of Jerusalem, which occurred subsequently, on 10 April. The authors add that at least some of the refugees were Arabs who only years or decades before had immigrated to Palestine from neighbouring Arab states and who, in 1948, because of the compulsions of war and through fear, simply took the opportunity to 'return home'.[141]

The report went on to review the state of the refugees, whose total, according to Weitz–Danin–Lifshitz at the end of November 1948, reached some 460,000. Theirs was a miserable existence, 'encamped under trees . . . or in streets in towns'. It was 'no wonder' they wished to return, wrote the committee. But they had nothing to return to—their houses had been destroyed by war or had been filled with 'Israeli refugees', and their herds no longer existed. 'The only asset the Arab refugees can perhaps take into

[141] ISA, FM 2445/3, the committee's memorandum entitled 'Regarding the Solution for the Arab Refugees', 'Appendix 3'.

consideration is the land. The world *perhaps* needs emphasizing as there is room for the government of Israel to expropriate [the land] as the property of the enemy who fought us. So Czechoslovakia did with all the property of the Sudeten Germans.'

On the practical front, the chief question addressed by the report was whether the refugees should be allowed to return. The authors were unanimous and unequivocal: 'By bringing back the refugees . . . a large Fifth Column would be introduced which would act in [the Arab states'] interests.' Among the Jews, in Israel and the Diaspora, 'opinions are divided', states the report. 'The majority stresses that the refugees should not be brought back . . . under any conditions, and a minority thinks that some of them should be allowed back.' This minority, humanitarian arguments aside, wrote the committee, believed that the continued existence of the refugees along Israel's borders would provoke 'continuous warfare . . . especially as the refugees would breed hatred in the Arab countries for Israel'.

But having considered the pros and cons, the committee ruled flatly against a return. The cardinal fact was that the refugees had already 'transferred' out of the country, a solution always regarded as ideal to the Arab problem in the Jewish state. Allowing them back would be an enormous economic burden; would carry the threat of a 'knife in the back' from the returnees; and would cripple Israel's ability to absorb Jewish refugees wishing to come to the Jewish state —'and when we pose one against the other . . . it is clear that [Jewish] refugees take precedence'. The report went on to recommend that the refugees be settled in three 'thinly-populated' Arab countries—Iraq, Syria, and Transjordan—with stress being laid on the first country, the one with no border with Israel. The report went into great detail about the absorptive capacity of each country and recommended precise areas where the refugees could and should be relocated.[142]

SOLVING THE REFUGEE PROBLEM

The Transfer Committee recommendations regarding Israeli initiatives and help in resettling the refugees in Arab countries were

[142] Ibid. The full Weitz–Danin–Lifshitz memorandum is not on file, but its key 'Introduction' and 'Appendix 3' are available.

never implemented. Rather, Israel and the Arab states in the first half of 1949 focused their diplomatic endeavours on the politics of military disengagement; armistice negotiations and agreements between Israel and each Arab state preoccupied the parties. During the spring, a full-scale peace conference, under the auspices of the UN-appointed Palestine Conciliation Commission, convened at Lausanne. The refugee issue was quickly pushed to the fore by the Arab states, who demanded that Israel agree to a general return as a precondition to reaching any general political resolution of the conflict.

The Arab states were uninterested in vast resettlement schemes, despite the assurance of large-scale US aid; the Palestinians were not eager—they still hoped to return to their former homes; and Israel was interested in promoting and assisting such schemes only within the framework of a general settlement of the Israel–Arab conflict. There was also a growing tendency in the Israeli leadership to link the fate of the Palestinian refugees to that of the Jewish communities in the Arab states, who starting in late 1948 began to immigrate to Israel in large numbers, usually leaving most of their property behind. The dispossession of Palestine's Arabs was equated with and nullified by the dispossession of the Arab world's departing Jews. The problem of compensating the Arabs for the abandoned property, already whittled down by analyses, such as that of the Transfer Committee, of what had befallen Palestinian houses, chattels, and even fields, was ultimately narrowed down to a vague need to compensate only for Arab landholdings. Help in resettling refugees hung fire, pending progress in the political negotiation.

The political deadlock during the spring and summer of 1949 epitomized by Lausanne left the Transfer Committee members deeply perturbed. In March 1949 Danin travelled to London to try to promote resettlement schemes for the refugees, especially in Transjordan. 'I see it as a sacred duty to finish what we began regarding the settlement of the refugee problem', he wrote to Weitz from London at the end of April. While humanitarian considerations may have figured in Danin's thinking, his chief motive was that 'so long as the problem of their [re-]settlement abroad is not solved, your fears . . . will be well-anchored in reality', he wrote to Weitz.[143]

[143] Institute for Study of Settlement, Weitz Papers, E. Danin (London) to Y. Weitz (Tel Aviv), 26 Apr. 1949.

Weitz's 'fears' were clear, set down in a letter to Foreign Minister Sharett in late May 1949: 'The chain of bitter refugees surrounding us from all sides with hatred and [feelings of] revenge will not give us rest for many years, and it will stand as an obstacle to reaching real peace between us and our neighbours.'[144]

Danin proposed that Teddy Kollek, an aide of Ben-Gurion's, join him in London, together to seek 'partners' in solving the refugee problem by constructively settling them in Arab countries. Danin believed that there existed 'Frenchmen. . . Britishers and oil people, especially Americans', who could be roped in for such an enterprise. 'Money will solve everything', Danin concluded, adding that Sharett had approved his efforts. Sharett's only fear was that resettling the refugees in Transjordan might in the long term prove harmful to 'the bearded one [that is, King Abdullah]'.[145]

The thrust of Weitz's letter to Sharett in late May was an appeal to pay the refugees the compensation owing for their lands, which would ease the refugees' bitterness, enable them to settle properly in the Arab countries, and salve Israel's conscience to boot: 'If we were ready to purchase peace with the blood of beloved sacrifices, shall we avoid purchasing it with money?' he wrote. Weitz urged the government to issue a clear statement confirming Israel's willingness to contribute its share towards resettling the refugees. Such a statement, he proposed, should be coupled with a firm declaration that Israel would not take back any of the refugees. This would serve to extinguish any hope among the refugees of an ultimate return and undermine the ability of the Arab leaders to stoke the fires of a return in the refugees' hearts.[146]

Through April, May, and June 1949, Danin, sometimes assisted by Kollek, laboured to put together a resettlement package for the refugees. At the start of June he wrote to Weitz that British companies —airlines, construction firms, and others—were showing a keen interest in employing the refugees in the Middle East. Employment would mean earnings, and earnings, said Danin, would mean the growth of a new market for British products. The key problem, according to Danin, was whether Israel would 'allot a substantial

[144] ISA, FM 2444/19, Y. Weitz (Haifa) to M. Sharett (Tel Aviv), 27 May 1949.
[145] Institute for Study of Settlement, Weitz Papers, E. Danin (London) to Y. Weitz (Tel Aviv), 26 Apr. 1949.
[146] ISA, FM 2444/19, Y. Weitz (Haifa) to M. Sharett (Tel Aviv), 27 May 1949.

sum' which would set the ball rolling. Danin had written to Tel Aviv requesting that such a sum be allocated.

But if we receive a negative answer, we shall have to return [to Israel] having achieved nothing, and then he [that is, Sharett] will continue his project of resettling the Palestinian Arab refugees in brilliant speeches [and in the speeches of] Abba Eban [Israel's head of mission to the UN], Sasson, Eytan [the Foreign Ministry Director General] and Zalman [Lifshitz], and the Lord will have mercy on His flock [that is, Israel], which is in need of mercy.[147]

In a letter to Sharett, Danin explained how he was going about finding 'partners' for the refugee resettlement scheme. Marcus Sieff, the British businessman, was approaching British firms on his behalf, wrote Danin, asking that they offer the refugees work in the Middle East. Danin wrote that he had told Sieff that Israel, for its part, would give I£10–15 million towards the resettlement project. This sum, Danin said, was 'the final compensation for the . . . assets' left behind by the refugees. Sieff asked Danin to obtain an official statement from the Israeli government stating how much it was willing to contribute before he would make the rounds of his fellow businessmen. Aware of Sieff's strategy and needs, Danin endorsed Sieff's request.[148] To his letter, Danin attached a memorandum 'redrafted by Mr. Marcus Sieff' on 'The Resettlement and Employment of Palestine Arab Refugees in Middle East Development Schemes'. The memorandum asserted that only a small proportion of the refugees would return to Israel. Their upkeep in refugee camps had so far cost £8 million sterling. Some £30–£40 million sterling were needed properly to resettle '400,000' refugees, who could be integrated into existing or planned regional development schemes. The Arab states sorely lacked manpower, and the Arab governments would come to see the refugees as a boon.

The Sieff–Danin memorandum saw the refugees being integrated into irrigation, industrial, and oil projects in the Arab countries. Specific mention was made of the Ghab Valley reclamation scheme in Syria, the Orontes River dam, Euphrates River irrigation schemes (Iraq), and the construction of the Beirut–Damascus highway.[149]

[147] Institute for Study of Settlement, Weitz Papers, E. Danin (London) to Y. Weitz (Tel Aviv), 5 June 1949.
[148] ISA, FM 2444/19 E. Danin (London) to M. Sharett (Tel Aviv), 3 June 1949.
[149] ISA, FM 2444/19, for text of Sieff–Danin memorandum.

No concrete Israeli compensation offer was forthcoming, however, and Sieff wrote to Ben-Gurion in early July that while both Shell and Iraq Petroleum executives had expressed a positive interest in his ideas, implementation of the scheme 'entails the admission of some Arabs to Israel and some payment for Arab property . . .'. Sieff also complained that Israel's public relations regarding the refugees could be improved; all that one read in the British press, he wrote, was of Israel turning back or imprisoning refugees trying to infiltrate back to their homes.[150] No movement on compensation was forthcoming from Tel Aviv, and Danin returned dispirited to Israel at the end of summer. Talk of compensation and planned refugee resettlement schemes coupled with regional Middle East development projects came to naught. The foundering of the PCC talks at Lausanne in August at the same time marked the end of any serious Israeli effort to help solve the refugee problem which, as predicted by Weitz and Danin, was to remain at the core of the Middle East conflict in the following decades.

The activities of Yosef Weitz and his two 'transfer committees', one 'self-appointed' and semi-official, active in late May and June 1948, and the other, official and active from late August to November, form a major and instructive chapter in the story of the Palestinian refugees. The exodus was a tale both of 'voluntary' flights and expulsion, and many fine gradations between; Weitz's activities, more or less covert, cast light on the causation and unfolding of the exodus among the rural Arab communities and on the evolution of Yishuv policy which, in part, brought it about. As the powerful, energetic head of the JNF Lands Department and a member of key inter-departmental committees, Weitz in 1948 played a major role as executive, adviser, and lobbyist in the emigration of Palestine's Arabs, in the takeover of Arab lands and villages, and in the crystallization of opinion and policy in the Yishuv against allowing a return of the refugees.

In the early spring of 1948, Weitz initiated or prompted the expulsion of a number of Arab tenant-farmer communities from JNF-owned land. Subsequently, his focus shifted to large areas, such as the Beit Shean Valley, Western Galilee, and Ramot–

[150] ISA, FM 2444/19, M. Sieff (London) to D. Ben-Gurion (Tel Aviv), 5 July 1949.

Menashe, in which the JNF had long had an 'interest' in terms of eventual intensive Jewish settlement and regional development. Using both his executive powers (and in June, at least, claiming authority from Ben-Gurion), and his wide range of well-placed contacts in the civilian bureaucracies, the settlements, and the IDF, Weitz was instrumental in emptying these areas of their Arab populations before or just after 14 May.

Weitz was a man of integrity, vision, and action. To the settlements, old and newly established, Weitz was the respected voice of the government and the National Institutions; for the government, Weitz was the spokesman of the landed interests and the settlement bodies of the National Institutions.

While immediately active on the local, *ad hoc* level, Weitz quickly saw the need for decision-making and policy implementation on a national level in order to accomplish the 'transfer' which alone could solve the new Jewish state's 'Arab problem'. Towards the end of May, Weitz organized the self-appointed Transfer Committee. As its head until 1 July, when it suspended operations, Weitz was to show the Yishuv the way in translating the Arab exodus into an irreversible *fait accompli*. After gaining the hesitant oral consent of Ben-Gurion and Shertok, Weitz was to oversee a small but systematic and important operation involving the destruction of abandoned Arab villages with the primary aim of barring a return, ever, of the refugees to their homes. At the same time, he pressed for and organized new Jewish settlements on the abandoned lands, rendering their return to Arab possession all but impossible while creating an ever-expanding, powerful, vested-interest group firmly opposed to a return. The allocation of abandoned fields to established Jewish settlements long in need of additional cultivable land, served the same purpose. Lack of formal, public authorization of his committee's operations compelled Weitz at the end of June to suspend its activities, whereupon he turned to other means of assuring Arab departure and non-return, focusing on efforts to buy out Arab landholders. Weitz was to be frustrated in his efforts to become the chief executive of what he called the 'Transfer policy'. Ben-Gurion preferred that what happened should happen away from the full glare of public appointment and endorsement, and was best carried out on the local level by Jewish settlements and IDF units, especially under the cloak of an enveloping fog of battle. When at last official sanction did materialize, it was for a transfer committee of far smaller, more theoretical scope than originally envisaged by Weitz, with a focus on planning the resettlement of the refugees in the Arab countries rather than overseeing their continued departure from Israel or the conversion of their abandoned villages to rubble or into new Jewish settlements.

But quasi-officially, Weitz and his fellow committee members, Ezra Danin and Zalman Lifshitz, continued to dabble in the praxis of population transfer, mostly in a consultative, lobbying capacity. IDF policy in October–November 1948 towards at least some of the newly conquered areas may have owed something to the advice and lobbying of the committee members.

The Transfer Committee in its report of November 1948 formulated the main line and arguments of Israeli propaganda in the following decades. It denied any Israeli culpability or responsibility for the Arab exodus—denied in fact, its own members' roles in various areas and contexts. It also strongly advised against the return of the refugees and proposed that the government play a major role in promoting refugee resettlement in the Arab host countries.

The Weitz committee recommendations on Israeli compensation and promotion of resettlement schemes abroad proved stillborn. On the other hand, its stand on the question of a refugee return was a powerful prop to those in the Cabinet who in any case were opposed to a return, something almost no one in Israel by the start of 1949 was willing to contemplate.

The political deadlock over the refugee problem effectively frustrated all efforts, even by those so inclined, such as Weitz and Danin, to have the Israeli government pay compensation and promote refugee resettlement abroad. The Arabs' insistence on a full-scale return rather than on resettlement among them played into the hands of those in Israel who were in any case unenthusiastic about paying compensation and regarded the refugee problem, henceforward, as an Arab problem to whose solution Israel, impoverished by war, need contribute nothing. By the summer of 1949, the Weitz committee's positive recommendations were dead. But the refugee problem had become, as Teddy Kollek wrote to Foreign Minister Sharett, 'in many ways . . . the central problem of our foreign affairs'.[151] This was also the opinion of Weitz and Danin.

It is difficult to quantify the effects of Weitz's activities in 1948, when the Transfer Committee was only one of a large number of local and national Yishuv bodies dealing with policy towards the Arabs. In terms of organizing, or prompting others to organize, the expulsion of Arabs, Weitz's direct role may have encompassed only a handful of villages. Similarly, his organization and supervision of the destruction of abandoned villages may have accounted for no more than one or two dozen sites. But indirectly, his personal efforts and those of the Transfer Committee, in both its mutations, probably had a powerful influence on the course of events. On the local level, the settlements and IDF units learned from Weitz and his agents what needed to be done and how to do it. On the national level, Weitz and Danin proved persuasive lobbyists for the transfer cause. On both levels, Weitz provided clarity and guidance in a sphere engulfed by confusion and divided counsels; in the anarchy of the times, in a country undergoing revolution, Weitz attempted to point out the direction and fashion a uniformity of purpose. Weitz's standing in the Yishuv gave legitimacy to the course he was promoting.

The Transfer Committee's consistent and inflexible position from May 1948 onwards against allowing a return of refugees carried a great deal of weight in the decision-making councils of the Yishuv. The committee's codification of its opposition to the return and its reasoning in this context certainly helped to crystallize official and, by a process of osmosis, public opposition to a return. But the committee's 'positive' recommendations, regarding compensation and resettlement of the refugees abroad, for a variety of reasons were ignored. Events and policies in 1949 evolved in such a way as to bar Israeli involvement in compensation or resettlement schemes.

---

[151] ISA, FM 2444/19, Teddy Kollek (London) to M. Sharett (Tel Aviv), 10 June 1949 and Y. Weitz (Haifa) to M. Sharett (Tel Aviv), 27 May 1949.

5

Yosef Nahmani and the Arab Question in 1948

For close on forty years, Yosef Nahmani (né Agronovsky) was at the cutting edge of the Zionist enterprise in Palestine—as a member of the pre-World War I HaShomer, the Yishuv's first self-defence force; then as a Haganah activist in Eastern Galilee; and, lastly, as the director of the Jewish National Fund's branch office in Tiberias, responsible for land purchases and infrastructure development for new Jewish settlements. Land-acquisition and defence matters, the twin pillars of the whole Zionist endeavour, were the core of his life's work. As we shall see, additional tasks devolved upon him in the course of the 1948 war. And, as we shall also see, Nahmani, in his attitudes and actions, came to embody some of the deep, painful contradictions at the heart of socialist Zionim and of the Zionist enterprise itself, which was guided by this ideology towards statehood and beyond.

Yosef Nahmani was born in the town of Aleksandriya, in the southern Ukraine in 1891. He grew up in an observant, but Zionist household. Against the backdrop of the major pogroms that swept Russia in 1903–6, in which hundreds of Jews were slaughtered by Russian mobs, and trouble with the local police, Yosef and his brother Moshe decided on emigration to Ottoman-ruled Palestine.

I would like to thank the archivists of the HaShomer Archive, in Kfar Gil'adi, Israel, and particularly Yehudit Orkabi, for finding and making available to me Nahmani's Diary, referred to in the notes as ND, for the years 1947–9. Nahmani used annual desk diaries, of different sizes, but instead of jotting down appointments, he wrote about each day's events, his conversations and impressions, and so on. The twenty or so consecutive annual diaries, including those for 1947 and 1949, are kept in the archive in a large carton; the vol. for 1948 is, unaccountably, missing. Fortunately, the diaries for the 1940s, including 1948, were at some point transcribed by typewriter, possibly by Nahmani himself, perhaps with a view to future publication. A comparison of the transcription of the earlier years with the original desk diaries shows that the work was done accurately, save for some minor typos. The typed version of the diary for 1948, which runs to forty-four tightly packed folio pages, can be assumed to be an accurate rendering of the original.

They reached Palestine at the end of 1907 or at the start of 1908, when Yosef was 16–17.

Within months, Nahmani was on the central committee of Po'alei Zion (or, in full, *Mifleget HaPo'alim HaYehudit HaSozial Demokratit — Po'alei Zion*), the minuscule Marxist-Zionist party established in 1906 by others who had come on the 'Second Aliya' (the second wave of Zionist immigration to Palestine), that included Ben-Gurion, the future founding prime minister of Israel; Yitzhak Ben-Zvi, the future second president of Israel; and Yitzhak Tabenkin, the future head of the Kibbutz Meuhad kibbutz association.

In 1911 Nahmani moved to the Galilee, where he was to live for the rest of his life, and joined HaShomer, the semi-clandestine organization which guarded the new Jewish settlements that had begun to spring up in the middle of the clusters of Arab villages. He worked as a guard at Merhavia, then at Sejera, Yavniel, and Beit-Gan, and eventually became HaShomer's secretary and treasurer. Like other members of that organization, he learnt fluent Arabic and Arab ways, including horse riding. He came to be known in HaShomer as *'Yusuf Awantaji'* (Yosef the sly one), a trait that was to serve him well in the often complex bargaining and wheeling-dealing that land-purchasing from Arabs entailed.

With the official disbandment of HaShomer in 1920, following the institution of the British Mandate in Palestine, Nahmani joined the newly organized Palestine Police and, clandestinely, served in the Haganah, where he became a local organizer, weapons-purchaser, and fund-raiser. Between 1922 and 1935, utilizing his good contacts with Arab villagers and landowners, Nahmani served as a land-purchaser on behalf of the Palestine Jewish Colonisation Association. In 1935 he moved from PICA to the JNF, serving as its head of office in the Galilee for the next thirty years. Between 1937 and 1947, the JNF—meaning Nahmani—purchased all told some 90,000 dunams (about 23,000 acres) in eastern Upper Galilee.[1] Nahmani, who had married in 1914, settled with his family in Tiberias in 1921. He served on the

---

[1] Y. Weitz (ed.), *Yosef Nahmani* (Ramat-Gan, 1969), 33. The volume, in effect an anthology, consists of letters by Nahmani, excerpts from his diaries, and articles by and on Nahmani, all selected, edited, and, often, abridged by Weitz, who was head of the JNF's Lands Department and Nahmani's boss.

municipal council of this (until 1948) mixed Jewish–Arab town from 1927 until October 1950, and died in Tiberias in 1965.

The purpose of this chapter is twofold: To try to trace Nahmani's major activities in the course of the 1948 war in the belief that this will contribute to an understanding of the Yishuv's attitudes, policies, and activities *vis-à-vis* the Palestinian Arabs; and, more broadly, to tap the relevant documentation, especially that unique, hitherto unexploited resource, Nahmani's diary for the years 1947–9, to help shed additional light on various aspects of the war, especially as it unfolded on Nahmani's turf, the Galilee.

Nahmani well understood the roots of Arab antagonism towards the Zionist enterprise in Palestine. But the successive waves of Arab attack (1920–1, 1929, and 1936–9) left him with a feeling that the Zionist establishment, too, was somehow at fault. In his view, the Zionist politicians devoted insufficient time and thought to 'the Arab–Jewish question'.[2] But it wasn't really or only a matter of time and thought: 'We have no Arab policy,' he wrote in June 1936, shortly after the eruption of the Arab Rebellion.

Those who stand at the head of our [Zionist] movement do not know Arabic and [Arab] culture is alien to them, and they are afraid . . . to hand over responsibility for [Jewish–Arab relations] to the Jews of this country who know Arabic . . .

Perhaps Nahmani was thinking of people like himself. He recommended establishing a newspaper in Arabic 'to explain the truth and give the Arabs a correct idea about Zionism, to dissipate the fears, [to explain] that we have no intention of dispossessing or subjugating the Arabs; to combat the lying propaganda and the unbridled [anti-Zionist] agitation . . .'.[3]

But if in mid-1936 Nahmani still denied that Zionism's aim was to dispossess Palestine's Arabs or, at least, that its ultimate result would necessarily be such dispossession, the Arab Rebellion (1936–9) against the Mandatory Government, with its concomitant protracted assault on the Yishuv, seems to have wrought a radical change in Nahmani's thinking. Or, perhaps, he merely

[2] Ibid., 82, letter Nahmani to Y. Ben-Zvi, 21 Mar. 1932.
[3] Ibid., 85, 88, Nahmani to Ben-Zvi, 26 June 1936.

realized and acknowledged what had been dormant in his thinking all along: He began openly to advocate 'transfer' as the solution to the problem posed by the prospective large Arab minority in the Jewish state-to-be. It is probable, over the years, that Nahmani's land-purchasing activities also propelled him in this direction: After all, each land-purchase represented, in microcosm, an effort at dispossession and 'transfer'; the point of each acquisition was the expansion of Jewish holdings and the diminution of Arab holdings, meaning the dispossession of Arab landowners and tenant-farmers (*arisim*). And, throughout, the Zionist purchasers tried to make sure that the dispossessed moved as far away from their former lands as possible, preferably out of Palestine altogether.

Perhaps Nahmani's ability to think in 'transfer' terms was facilitated by his evolving attitude towards Arabs in general. He spoke their language and, over the decades, came to know them well (or so he felt). Familiarity did not breed admiration—far from it, to judge from Nahmani's diary entries:

18 May 1939: I travelled to Dafna. They had begun destroying the [Arab tenant-farmers'] houses. We spoke about the tenants who did not want to leave the site. I found Moshe [Aliovitz] weak and infirm. In Dafna and the Hula [Valley] we must act firmly. The Arabs are cowards and given to submissiveness, and if they meet a man who speaks gently, they will become uppity and insubordinate . . .[4]

12 March 1941: . . . Kamil [Hassan] could become dangerous for us and could easily change his stripes. He is without gratitude . . . Like all Arabs he is ready to kick [us] at the first opportunity.[5]

30 March 1943: . . . The Arabs, when you move near to them and try to show that you are not superior but their equal, lose their civility towards you. They are used to treating with respect only those who show that they are above them, so they must always be held at a certain distance.[6]

Contempt clearly helped Nahmani to contemplate a transfer solution to the Arab Question. On 13 February 1939 Nahmani travelled to Safad and met the British deputy district commissioner. Nahmani spoke of turning the Hula Valley into an agricultural 'paradise', in which Jewish settlers and 'those Arabs who would not want to leave' would prosper. Meanwhile, he,

[4] ND, 18 May 1939.   [5] ND, 12 Mar. 1941.   [6] ND, 30 Mar. 1943.

Nahmani, was busy trying to 'arrange' for the tenant-farmers who had to be evicted:

The homeland of the Arabs is not confined to the borders of Palestine. And their transfer to other land in Syria or Transjordan . . . does not [therefore mean] compelling them to leave their homeland. On the other hand, the only homeland of the persecuted Jews is Palestine . . .[7]

In December 1942, Nahmani showed Y. L. Magnes, a leading proponent of binationalism and Jewish–Arab conciliation, around the Galilee Panhandle:

Magnes agreed with my premiss that the radical solution to our problem was the transfer [*ha'avara*] of the [Arab] population to the empty Arab states. But since the [Palestine] Arabs will oppose this, he opposed the use of force [in implementing a transfer], because it is immoral, and would spark the opposition of the Moslem world, [and] would create hatred of the Jews[8]

But Magnes failed to convince Nahmani: 'One must support the transfer idea and once and for all solve our problem', he stated bluntly in 1944.[9]

LAND-PURCHASE

Nahmani, like most Zionists, always viewed the success of the whole enterprise in terms of two categories, land and people or demography. He himself, through almost all his adult life, had been involved, in one way or another, in what he (and other Zionists) called 'the Redemption of the Land' (*ge'ulat karka* or *ge'ulat ha'aretz*). 'The consolidation and success of our National Home are dependent on the amount of land which will be in the possession of our people,' he wrote to Weitz in 1938[10]. Indeed, the very contours of the Jewish state-to-be would be determined by the tracts of land Zionism would manage to 'redeem'.[11]

As the Mandate drew to its close, the Jewish authorities possessed about one million dunams of Palestine's land (about 7 per cent of the country's mass). Of this, the JNF, in September

---

[7] ND, 13 Feb. 1939.   [8] ND, 8 Dec. 1942.   [9] ND, 10 July 1944.
[10] *Nahmani*, 96, Nahmani to Weitz, 4 Nov. 1938.
[11] Ibid., 98, Nahmani to Weitz, 16 Apr. 1943; and 99, Nahmani to Weitz, 15 Sept. 1944; and CZA, KKL 9/31, Nahmani to Weitz, 5 Jan. 1948.

1947, owned 928,000. Yosef Weitz, the head of the Fund's Lands Department and Nahmani's superior, noted that the JNF had managed to buy during September 1946–September 1947 some 42,000 dunams from non-Jews (mainly Arabs); he wanted to round out the Fund's holding to one million dunams during the following year: 'It is a sacred duty, and it must be done,' he wrote to Nahmani.[12]

The problem was that, as the Arab–Jewish conflict neared a climax, the Zionist agencies found it more and more difficult to purchase land. Part of the problem, according to Nahmani, was that the Zionist leadership in Jerusalem seemed to be insufficiently aware of the importance of the land-acquisition campaign—which, like the Zionist leaders, he was wont to call 'the war of conquest' (*milhemet ha'kibush*).[13] The movement, unfortunately, was led by 'weak-spirited, weak-willed' people, who were not up to the exactions of history and were failing to accord to land-acquisition efforts the priority they deserved.

But there were other, more severe, obstacles on the road to the Redemption of the Land. One was the Mandatory Government's efforts to halt or interfere with Arab land-sales to Jews, in conformity with the provisions of the 1939 White Paper. Even more serious was the Arab nationalists' increasingly determined and violent campaign to thwart such sales. Arab political activists and gunmen were intimidating potential land-sellers and were preventing, by threat and terrorism, Arab tenant-farmers living on lands already purchased by Jews from evacuating. The increasing difficulty of purchasing land from Arabs and the increasing Arab nationalist intimidation of potential land-sellers can be traced in Nahmani's correspondence with Weitz and in his diary during the last years of the Mandate.[14]

In late 1946 Nahmani pointed out that his office had failed to meet the land-purchasing projections for the previous twelvemonth. The potential for land-purchases had been there; the Arab

[12] CZA, KKL 9/416, Weitz to JNF Office, Tiberias, 26 Sept. 1947.

[13] *Nahmani*, 98, Nahmani to Weitz, 16 Apr. 1943; 96, Nahmani to Weitz, 4 Nov. 1938; and 99, Nahmani to Weitz, 15 Sept. 1944.

[14] See e.g. CZA, KKL 9/416: Nahmani to the JNF Head Office, Lands Department, Jerusalem, 24 Oct. 1946; Weitz to JNF Office, Tiberias, 26 Sept. 1947; Nahmani to JNF Head Office, Jerusalem, 8 Oct. 1947. *Nahmani*, 237, entry for 2 Sept. 1946; 238, entry for 5 Nov. 1946; 240, entry for 2 Dec. 1946, etc.

owners were economically hard-pressed and willing; but 'the terrorism and threats on the part of the [Arab] nationalists' deterred sales. 'The nationalists had succeeded in gaining control over the Arab public and in making it obedient,' reflected Nahmani. The problem was not restricted to Palestinian Arab nationalists; the governments of Syria and Lebanon were also making sure that their nationals, who owned land in the Galilee, did not sell to Jews.[15] Nahmani called for the intervention of the Haganah to protect potential Arab land-sellers and other Arabs co-operating with the Yishuv and to retaliate against Arab militiamen and terrorists working to prevent the transfer of land to Jewish hands.[16] But the task was beyond the Yishuv's powers, and in the months before the outbreak of the 1948 war Jewish land-purchases in the Galilee ground to a halt.

Yet Nahmani, perhaps driven by wishful thinking, perhaps by fears of redundancy, was far from convinced that the JNF's mission was over: The Fund must continue to exist and carry out its chief task—purchasing Arab land—whatever the hostilities might bring. So, at least, was his constant refrain to Weitz in the first months of the war.[17]

THE OUTBREAK OF WAR

The passage in November 1947 of the UN General Assembly Partition Resolution on Palestine—providing for the emergence in the country of two states, one Jewish, the other Palestinian Arab—sparked consternation and anger among the Palestinians, especially in the towns. Almost immediately, there was anti-Jewish rioting, stone-throwing, ambushes, and a general strike—though Nahmani seemed to feel that in rural Upper Galilee, the Arab villagers were by and large 'indifferent', and perhaps not averse to being included in the Jewish state. But, within forty-eight hours there was a series of incidents, with one Arab assailant, from

[15] CZA, KKL 9/416: Nahmani to JNF Head Office, Lands Department, Jerusalem, 24 Oct. 1946; and Nahmani to JNF Head Office, Jerusalem, 8 Oct. 1947.
[16] *Nahmani*, 105, 107–8, Nahmani to Weitz, 19 Oct. 1946.
[17] Nahmani Papers, HaShomer Archive Dalet–7–52, Nahmani to Weitz, 16 Dec. 1947; and CZA, KKL 9/31, Nahmani to JNF Head Office, Lands Department, Jerusalem, 5 Jan. 1948.

the Galilee Panhandle village of Khisas, being shot dead by a Jewish watchman.[18]

In the Yishuv, the UN Resolution was greeted with rejoicing and celebrations. In Tiberias, as in the other centres of Jewish population, the young danced in the streets as the old looked on, teary-eyed and happy. Nahmani, that veteran embodiment of militant Zionism, was himself carried aloft by the crowds. But 'in my heart there was joy mixed with sadness,' he jotted down in his diary. 'Joy that the peoples [of the world] had at last acknowledged that we were a nation with a state, and sadness that we lost half the country, Judea and Samaria, and, in addition, that we have 400,000 Arabs . . .'.[19]

Nahmani in the past may have been convinced that massive 'transfer' was, at least theoretically, the ideal or the only solution to the future Jewish state's Arab minority problem; he may have toyed, in the late 1930s and early 1940s, with the idea of British-engineered or voluntary 'transfer' schemes. But after the eruption at the end of 1947, his thinking underwent substantial, sobering change. The British were going, the Yishuv was about to turn into a state, and it was a completely new ball game. Nahmani, to judge from his diary and internal correspondence, put aside all notion of a blanket, general 'transfer' policy: For good or ill, the new State of Israel was to be born with a large Arab minority, of 400,000, and it was going to have to learn to live with at least most of them as best it could. Transfer, so ran Nahmani's thinking and wishes, was to be the fate of only a minority of this number, according to clearly limited, defined categories.

Nahmani methodically set out his thoughts in a programmatic three-page letter to Weitz in January 1948, five weeks after the start of the hostilities: The emergent Jewish state's problem was that

most of the arable land, cultivated and worthy of cultivation, is owned by the large Arab minority. The Jewish Goverment . . . would not be able or willing to use discriminatory laws to dispossess land for Jewish settlement alone. Its position would force it to care equally for all farmers without differentiation according to religion . . . As a result, there will be no change in the future in the JNF's land policy. The role and importance of

[18] ND, 1–2 Dec. 1947.　　　[19] ND, 30 Nov. 1947.

redemption of land will increase. We will have to continue to purchase land in the way we have done until now, using new methods adjusted to the new circumstances, and to carry it out energetically and at an increased tempo . . .

Nahmani went on to detail the amounts of land owned by Jews, Arabs, and others (state, Wakf, churches) in the two districts he was responsible for, Tiberias and Safad, and to outline the possibilities of purchase that would open up once the state was established and the Arab owners were 'freed of the pressure of Arab terrorism in all its forms'. Of the million or so dunams of land in the two districts, about half was Arab-owned. Of these about 100,000 dunams were owned by non-resident effendis, of whom half lived outside Palestine. Nahmani believed that the effendis 'would agree to sell their holdings'. As to the Arab tenant-farmers who lived on the effendis' lands, these would have to be cared for by Israel—and not, as in the past, by 'merely paying them compensation' but by arranging for their orderly transfer and resettlement in Syria or Transjordan. 'This method [of eviction] is of especial importance as it reduces the number of Arabs in the country and saves [us] the worry about finding them alternative employment.'

Nahmani was also optimistic about being able to buy out and move to Syria those Arab villagers whose ancestors had come from Morocco and settled in Eastern Galilee (Maghrebis). 'There is a good chance of transferring them if we know how to prepare the way and create the appropriate conducive conditions,' wrote Nahmani. He was also hopeful that he could similarly engineer the departure of the Circassians who lived in Reihaniya, 'in poor conditions'. Similarly, Nahmani felt that the Shiite villagers of Nabi Yusha and Al Malikiya could be induced to move to Lebanon if land was found for them on the Lebanese side of the border. Taken together, these purchases and voluntary transfers would gain the JNF 55,219 dunams of land, predicted Nahmani.

As to the remaining 350,000-odd dunams of land in Arab hands, owned by smallholding villagers (*fellahin*), Nahmani felt that perhaps 58,000 were available for purchase. He argued that 'there was a considerable number of *fellahin* who owned more land than they could efficiently cultivate.' If they wished to make their cultivation more efficient, they would require capital—which they could obtain by selling part of their holdings to the JNF. 'Knowing the situation among the villagers, we estimate that we will be able to buy from them lands totalling about 57,906 dunams . . .', concluded Nahmani.

In other words, Nahmani was saying (and proposing) that the revolutionary circumstance of Jewish statehood would, in his area of responsibility, enable the JNF to purchase a little over 200,000 dunams of Arab-owned land, purchases that had previously been rendered impossible by Arab pressure, terrorism, or recalcitrance. Moreover, a large number of Arabs owning or living on these lands could, as part of the purchase agreements, be induced to leave the territory of Israel and resettle in Lebanon, Syria, or Transjordan. Nahmani was not advocating a mass, compulsory transfer, with attendant uncompensated dispossession. Rather, he was proposing a selective but large-scale transfer, of specific, defined categories of Arabs—tenant-farmers, Maghrebis, Circassians, and Shiites—with due payment and compensation. Implicit in Nahmani's projected scheme of things was that most of Eastern Galilee's Arab villagers would remain *in situ* in the Jewish state, albeit with their landholdings somewhat reduced by Jewish purchase.[20]

As late as the end of March 1948, with Arab–Jewish hostilities moving into their fifth month, Nahmani was still able to write in his diary: 'we have no intention to destroy or harass or rule over the Arabs. Our [only] aim is to live and work together in one country.'[21]

Such were Nahmani's views at the start of the 1948 war about the future of Israel's Arab minority. We shall return to this subject later, as the war unfolded and as Nahmani's views changed. But let us turn to Nahmani and the war itself, and particularly to the question of Jewish–Arab relations during the war.

The 1948 war, which began in December 1947 as a civil and guerrilla war between two highly intermixed populations and in May 1948 changed into a conventional war between states, unfolded only gradually, by fits and starts, taking weeks and even months to spread from Jerusalem and the Tel Aviv–Jaffa area to

[20] CZA, KKL 9/31, Nahmani to Weitz, Jan. 1948.
[21] ND, 31 Mar. 1948.

the outlying districts of the country. At first, neither Jews nor Arabs understood that they were embarked on a *war*; rather, it seemed that here was merely a replay of the events of 1936–9, which the Arabs called a 'Rebellion' (or 'the Great Rebellion') but the Jews termed only 'the disturbances' (*HaMe'ora'ot*).

Nahmani, from his perch in the mixed city of Tiberias, which had about 6,000 Jews and 2,000 Arabs, in the first months of the hostilities was above all concerned that they should not spread to his district and town. Above all, his thinking dominated by a sense of Jewish weakness and Arab numbers and militancy, Nahmani was afraid that a full-scale conflict would result in Jewish defeat, or, at least, in the massacre of Tiberias's Jewish community. He repeatedly spoke of impending 'annihilation'[22] and 'catastrophe and disaster'.[23] 'We must realize,' he wrote at the outset of the conflict, 'that we face a large force and it must not be provoked needlessly . . . '. Moreover the Jewish community 'would have to live with the Arabs in the future in one state'.[24] In other words, there were two good reasons for Jewish restraint: The Arabs were very strong and might, if provoked, destroy the Jews; and, in any event, whatever the outcome of the struggle, Jews and Arabs would have to live together, so it was best to avoid conflict, which would sour future relations.

It was these two calculations (as well as moral misgivings) that underlay Nahmani's bitter criticism of the Palmah raid on Khisas, at the northern end of the Galilee Panhandle, on 18 December 1947, in which ten Arab civilians, including five children, were killed. The attack was launched, over the opposition of local Jewish civil leaders and Arab affairs experts, in retaliation for the killing of a Jew.[25]

'This matter causes horror and nausea,' wrote Nahmani.

Such acts . . . will only increase the number of those who hate us. How were the children to blame? . . . If [we] want to punish, the guilty must be punished . . . Such acts persuade the Arabs that we hate them . . . [and] help the extremists among them to throw the whole country into a bloody maelstrom . . . The Khisas affair depressed me greatly . . . The situation in the Galilee had been tense but this was not expressed in

[22] ND, 14 Dec. 1947.   [23] ND, 22 Dec. 1947.   [24] ND, 11 Dec. 1947.
[25] See B. Morris, *The Birth of the Palestinian Refugee Problem, 1947–1949*, (Cambridge, 1988), 33–4, and 306 n. 12.

attacks on the Jews and [Khisas] is [will be?] the cause of untimely eruptions.[26]

Acts such as Khisas could drive the Arab 'moderates' into the hands of the extremists (or 'gangs', in Nahmani's and the Yishuv's parlance).[27]

Khisas pointed to an emerging problem within the Yishuv: The existence of a civilian–military dissonance—the military commanders paid no heed to the views of the local civilian leadership 'and acted against its will'.[28] The civilian leaders wanted peace and non-belligerence; the local military sought to provoke conflict. What was needed, wrote Nahmani, was 'war management [guided by] tact and understanding'.[29] (He bemoaned the fact that the Jewish military authorities were making no use of his skills[30] and recommended, for example, that Yishuv agents try to sow dissension in Arab ranks, for example by prompting the Druse minority in Syria to rebel against the government in Damascus.)[31]

Four months after the outbreak of hostilities, Nahmani reported on a conversation with Hillel Landsman, of Kibbutz Ayelet HaShahar, of the Second Aliya, and one of the local leaders in Eastern Galilee. Landsman reinforced Nahmani's fears. The 'unemployed security men' (i.e. Palmah units) were not heeding the advice of the Galilee civilian leaders:

Heading the security [forces] were young men who had contempt for death and had in their heads only military thoughts and plans but do not take into consideration all the [peripheral] matters such as supplies and economics [i.e. logistics] without which no army can fight. Similarly, they laugh at the need to maintain [good] relations with Arab neighbours. They do not think it important. They believe simply that there is a need to win using all means and then matters will sort themselves out. The interesting thing is that it is particularly the [left-wing] HaShomer HaTza'ir people, who advocate good neighbourly policies, who are the most extreme in this respect.[32]

A fortnight after Khisas, Nahmani had been even more critical of the Jewish dissidents' (IZL) terrorist attack against an Arab crowd outside the Haifa Oil Refinery. In spontaneous retaliation,

---

[26] ND, 19 Dec. 1947.   [27] ND, 25 Dec. 1947.   [28] ND, 22 Dec. 1947.
[29] ND, 24 Jan. 1948.   [30] DBG–YH i. 187.   [31] ND, 25 Jan. 1948.
[32] ND, 22 Mar. 1948.

the Arab workers at the refinery massacred more than forty of their Jewish co-workers. Nahmani jotted down in his diary:

[I was] told about the bomb that the Jews threw at a crowd of [Arab] workers . . . and there are dead. The Arabs [then] attacked the Jewish clerks . . . and killed some . . . This incident depressed me greatly. After all, the Arabs had announced a cease-fire, and why should [we] cause the death of innocents and again anger the Arabs, so that they have no choice but to resort to all means in order to respond to the Jews, and the matter [i.e. the cycle of violence] will be without end . . .

Nahmani went on to condemn such 'unrestrained and irresponsible acts' which would bring about a 'disaster' and turn against us 'those [Arabs] who had supported our enterprise'.[33] Throughout the first months of the war, Nahmani registered his condemnation of Haganah and IZL attacks on 'innocent' Arab civilians as immoral and counterproductive.[34]

As Nahmani (and other critics of the Khisas raid) had predicted, the conflagration quickly spread to Eastern Galilee, and Arab and Jewish ambushes on the roads and sniping in the fields became frequent. Nahmani lamented the lack, on the Yishuv's side, of central guidance and organization in defence matters and bemoaned his own forced uninvolvement in this sphere.[35] In general, he felt that those responsible for Jewish defence in the district, and especially in Tiberias, were incompetent and woefully 'inexperienced'. Guards did not show up for shifts; fortifications had not been built. 'Tiberias faces a difficult and bitter fate,' he feared.[36] As to the district in general, 'there was no unity of command. Every group has its commander. There is no one hand

[33] ND, 30 Dec. 1947. It is worth noting that Weitz, in editing *Nahmani*, seriously perverted Nahmani's views and meaning by showing only the diary entry for 31 Dec. 1947 and omitting altogether the passage quoted above, from 30 Dec. The start of the entry for 31 Dec., as transcribed by Weitz, reads: 'The disaster that struck the [Jewish] workers in the Haifa Oil Refinery depressed me greatly.' But, when this entry is read together with the full entry for the previous day, it is clear that Nahmani's depression was triggered principally by the Jewish provocation and, secondarily, by the cycle of Jewish–Arab violence that it had unleashed. Weitz omits all mention of the IZL bomb attack that had provoked the refinery massacre. Similar omissions and excisions mar Weitz's editing of other parts of the diary as they appear in *Nahmani*.
[34] See e.g. ND, 12 Feb., 13 Feb., 18 Feb. 1948, etc.
[35] ND, 14 Jan. 1948.   [36] ND, 23 Jan. and 3 Mar. 1948.

controlling and organizing war matters . . . [Meanwhile] Arab strength grows apace.'[37] He feared an Arab surprise attack.[38]

With no possibility of initiating or concluding land-deals with Arabs, Nahmani spent his days trying to organize the construction of access roads to a number of outlying, strategically important Jewish settlements (Misgav-'Am, Manara). Lack of equipment and manpower—mobilized or otherwise diverted to the war effort—bedevilled his activities.

In Tiberias itself matters gradually deteriorated. In January and February 1948, there were occasional exchanges of shots along the seams between the two communities. By and large, 'the Arabs want peace'; but Jewish actions, deliberate or incidental, usually carried out by Haganah troops, repeatedly resulted in clashes.[39] 'Our people continue [to carry out] irresponsible actions that will result in a bloody explosion,' he wrote on 10 March. The Jewish militiamen 'exaggerate their own strength' and 'are always intent' on 'humiliating' the Arabs.[40] This feeling of Jewish weakness and Arab strength was to dog Nahmani until July.

The Jewish civil leaders, including Nahmani, repeatedly organized peacemaking meetings with their Arab counterparts in the city. On 4 February, the two groups of notables met at the house of Shihadeh Khouri,

in friendly fashion, as if there were no incidents or tension. The Arabs showed great maturity and apparently still control the street [i.e. the populace] and if strangers [i.e. foreign Arab gunmen] do not arrive and there will not be special reasons [i.e. provocations] from the Jewish side, peace will reign in the town, which is very important. Our people in responsible positions [i.e. the Haganah commanders] do not understand the seriousness of the situation. The desire to fight and false honour guides their activities and they do not control our street [i.e. populace] and I fear that it will be the Jews who will cause an explosion in Tiberias.[41]

Two days later Nahmani returned to the theme:

The Arab leaders are making all efforts to stop [the hostilities] and to get through this period in peace . . . but I have the feeling that the Jews will precipitate the explosion without any cause. The aggressive spirit in

[37] ND, 9 Feb. 1948.   [38] ND, 12 Feb. 1948.   [39] ND, 4 Feb. 1948.
[40] ND, 10–11 Mar. 1948.   [41] ND, 4 Feb. 1948.

Jewish circles in Tiberias will bring about a disaster if they are not stopped.[42]

But in meetings with British officials, Nahmani continued to put a good Zionist face on things. On 17 February he told the British District Commissioner in the Galilee, D. J. Evans, that

there was a will on both sides to reach a [peace] agreement . . . but if the Arab . . . is the aggressor . . . and [the British] encourage him to [attack] and he is certain that might will prevail and that the Jews will be easily beaten [then there is no chance]. [Only] after a war in which it is proven that . . . it will not be easy, and perhaps it will be impossible, to defeat the Jews will [the Arab] begin to think about an agreement. And then both sides will prefer peace to war which will bring destruction to both sides.[43]

Mid-March saw repeated, serious outbreaks of shooting in downtown Tiberias. Again, Nahmani registered fears that the fighting was premature and that the Jews were not yet strong enough to beat the Arabs.[44] And, again, Nahmani led the effort to re-instate the cease-fire. He bewailed the fact that the 'lives of thousands' were in the hands of such incompetent Haganah commanders,[45] and believed that the provocative Jewish behaviour was not in line with 'Ben-Gurion's policy'.[46] On 14 March Tiberias's Jewish and Arab civil leaders met again in the city hall. 'The Arabs presented proof that . . . the Jews' irresponsible behaviour had brought about the outbreak of fighting. In my heart I endorsed the Arabs' charges.'[47]

The bout of shooting, which had resulted in eleven Arab and four Jewish dead, and many wounded, had demoralized the Jewish community in the (mixed) downtown Old City area, and the Jews began to leave the quarter for the wholly Jewish neighbourhoods to the West. The Jews, 'particularly from the Sephardi communities', were filled with 'aggressiveness'. Nahmani felt that he was 'beginning to lose his influence [in the community] as I am moderate and among those trying to seek peace.'[48]

Nahmani was not optimistic. One problem was that the Sephardi Jews (whose 'language is Arabic') went about 'boasting', within earshot of the Arabs, about the coming day of reckoning:

---

[42] ND, 6 Feb. 1948.   [43] ND, 17 Feb. 1948.   [44] ND, 11 Mar. 1948.
[45] ND, 12 Mar. 1948.   [46] ND, 13 Mar. 1948.
[47] ND, 14 Mar. 1948.   [48] ND, 15 Mar. 1948.

All their talk . . . badly hurts the Arabs. What is needed is to explain to these primitive [Jewish] elements . . . that we don't intend war with the Arabs or [the Arabs'] destruction. . . . And as the Arabs of Tiberias only want peace and do not intend to attack us, we must not act in a manner that will push them . . . to call for [outside] help . . . Our struggle, which is difficult, must be moral. If we want to establish a state, we must prove our tolerance and we must adopt an attitude of understanding [towards the Arabs] and to prevent as far as possible unjustified acts of revenge that will make us hated . . .[49]

The problem of Jewish aggressiveness, as Nahmani put it, was not restricted to downtown Tiberias. The countryside was also affected. On 22 March Nahmani met Hillel Landsman, the regional council leader from Kibbutz Ayelet HaShahar, who told him about the Palmah raid on Al Huseiniya, on the night of 16/17 March, in which dozens of Arab villagers were killed.[50] The raid had been triggered by repeated Arab attacks on Jewish transport in the Hula Valley. The Palmah mounted a massive retaliatory strike. 'The story, in its brutality, made a harsh impression on me,' recorded Nahmani. Landsman had related how the raiders had entered the house of 'Othman, the village mukhtar, who traditionally had been friendly. 'Othman had 'pleaded for his life: "Twenty-eight years I have been your friend and have friendly relations with you and we have helped one another . . ." Don't worry, they told him, [just] come out, and when he was at the door they murdered him.' This act 'shook me to the foundations', wrote Nahmani. 'How did the Jews come by such cruelty? . . . This does not augur well.'[51]

Arabs from the countryside, with whom Nahmani had for years been doing business, in March 1948 began to turn to Nahmani to help them straighten out relations and keep the peace with neighbouring Jewish settlements. One problem which loomed— and necessitated local cease-fires—was the impending harvest; the Arabs (and the Jews) wanted to harvest their summer crops without hindrance. The villagers of Majdal, just north of Tiberias, on the north-western shores of the Sea of Galilee, sought to harvest their crops unhindered by the Jewish settlers of neighbouring Migdal. Majdal's relations with Migdal traditionally had been

[49] ND, 17 Mar. 1948.   [50] See Morris, *Birth*, 157.
[51] ND, 22 Mar. 1948.

pacific. But the villagers no longer trusted the assurances of the Jewish settlers after men from Migdal had shot dead an Arab boy (and a horse) from Ghuweir Abu Shusha, a village just north of Migdal. Apparently a settler named Pinhas Jino, an LHI member, was responsible, and the Haganah leaders in Migdal were unable to control him. The Majdal villagers turned to Nahmani. Nahmani duly talked to the Haganah commanders in Tiberias, but was unable to obtain any assurances; no one, it seemed, could control anyone in Migdal. Nahmani couldn't help. A passage in Nahmani's diary provides a pointer to what was about to happen:

The Arabs [in the area] are beginning to become deeply afraid. The[ir] faith in the Jews' goodwill is being undermined. The Arabs in the area are weak and traditionally there prevailed good relations between them and the Jews. Now, after undisciplined actions by Jews that, without cause, put their lives and property in danger, they see and fear that they will not be able in future to live among the Jews as the aggressiveness of the Jews proves that whenever they want to, [the Jews] will be able to destroy them.[52]

Three weeks later, on 18 April, in the wake of the Jewish conquest of Tiberias and the Arab evacuation of the town, Nahmani added: 'Sheikh Mutlak of Majdal and all the village's inhabitants are filled with fear of the Jews . . . [They] are taking care to do nothing against the Jews but the inefficient [Haganah] Intelligence Service . . . may involve the village [in the hostilities] and [it] could become the objective of [Jewish] retaliatory actions.' Nahmani wrote that he was 'fighting for the village's [continued] existence'.[53] It was a fight he was to lose. The villagers of Majdal fled four days later, followed within a week by the last inhabitants of neighbouring Ghuweir Abu Shusha.

THE FALL OF ARAB TIBERIAS

For Nahmani, the war reached a certain climax in mid-April, with the Jewish capture of Arab Tiberias and the flight of its population. The final battle was preceded, on 28 March, by one last attempt by the notables of the two communities to consolidate a lasting cease-fire. The Arabs did not demand, as Nahmani had

[52] ND, 31 Mar. 1948.   [53] ND, 18 Apr. 1948.

expected, the withdrawal of the small Haganah contingent from the Old City, whose Jewish population had fled to the town's western neighbourhoods during the previous weeks. Rather, the Arab representatives 'again emphasized the need for peace and [said] that the leaders of both communities must employ every means to prolong the calm.' One of the Arab notables, Sheikh Tabari, who had just returned from a visit to Damascus, said that 'Tiberias lay outside the Arab attack plans.' But should hostilities erupt, Tiberias would then be included in Arab war-planning—'something that is not desirable to both communities'. 'Perhaps we shall succeed' in maintaining the peace, opined Nahmani. 'This conversation again persuaded us that the local Arabs do not want disturbances,' he concluded. 'It all depends on the Jews.'[54]

Less than a fortnight later, on 8 April, matters began rapidly to deteriorate. Shooting broke out—apparently initiated by bellicose or panicky Arabs—in the downtown area, with six Jews killed and a dozen or so wounded. The Arab notable Kamil Tabari called for a cease-fire and asked for a meeting to sort out what had happened. The town's Haganah commander, Pinhas Optikman, rejected the offer. Nahamani tried to reason with the local Haganah brass and their supporters. He said that national Yishuv policy was

not to attack Arabs unless first attacked. We want quiet in Tiberias, firstly for ourselves, so that we may amass supplies, [build] fortifications and strengthen our postions, [and also to assure the safety] of traffic to Upper Galilee . . . [We shouldn't] reject a possibility of a cease-fire.

Other participants at the meeting attacked Nahmani, but he refused to budge. As he put it, an outbreak of serious hostilities 'would draw [in] foreign Arab forces'. However, the local Haganah had orders—from Haganah HQ in Tel Aviv—not to reach any formal peace agreement and to cease fire only if the Arabs stopped first.[55]

The following day the Arabs—in the person of Sudqi Tabari— renewed the cease-fire offer but the Jewish mayor, Shim'on Dahan, said he 'could not respond, as the [Haganah's] line was to reject any negotiation'. Nahmani was at a loss to understand Haganah policy. He attributed it to 'poor information', fed the

[54] ND, 28 Mar. 1948.   [55] ND, 8 Apr. 1948.

high command by 'Sha"i [Haganah Intelligence Service] . . . men, most of whom don't know Arabic and, more important, don't know the Arabs and their psychology. And everythging is being done with an aggressive spirit.' Nahmani was afraid that an attack by an Arab force from outside the town would overwhelm its Haganah defenders. In the event, no Arab attack materialized, and the shooting was halted that afternoon by intervention by the city's British garrison, which fired off a few artillery rounds.[56] A tense quiet descended on the town. Renewed Arab–Jewish exchanges were again halted by British fire on 11 April. The British commanders tried to negotiate a formal Arab–Jewish cease-fire. The Haganah again avoided committing itself to an agreement, arguing that the Arabs could not be trusted to keep it. Nahmani debated the point with the Jewish commanders—'the Arabs are even more interested than us [in quiet]', 'we must look to the near future . . . [when] mutual [Arab–Jewish] relations will be very important', the Arabs will be forced to call in outside help—but to no avail.[57]

But, unknown to Nahmani, the Haganah command had apparently decided, on 9–11 April, to launch a major offensive with the aim of conquering Arab Tiberias as well as opening the vital South–North road running through the town. A multi-staged plan was hammered out.[58] The following day, 12 April, the Haganah raided the Arab village of Khirbet Nasir ad Din, just West of Tiberias. The village, and the neighbouring Sheikh Qaddumi hill, overlooked and dominated the new Jewish districts of Tiberias to the East. At the same time, the village's capture cut off Arab Tiberias from Arab centres, and possible help, from the West.[59] Nahmani reported that the attack, which lasted eight hours, could be seen from Tiberias. The British refused to intervene and about 'twenty' Arabs, including children, were reportedly killed:

---

[56] ND, 9 Apr. 1948.   [57] ND, 11 Apr. 1948.

[58] Nahum 'Av, *HaMa'avak 'al Tveriya, HaRishona LeShihrur BeMilhemet Ha'Atzma'ut* (The Struggle for Tiberias, the First [City] Liberated in the War of Independence) (Tel Aviv, 1991), 185–6. 'Av's book, while unfootnoted and largely based on oral testimony and recollection, is the most comprehensive work on the struggle for Tiberias.

[59] See Morris, *Birth*, 71–2.

I cannot justify this action by the Haganah. I don't know whether there was justification for the assault and the killing of so many Arabs. The flight of the women and children of the village in panic [towards Tiberias] made a harsh impression on me. I saw it all from [my] window . . . I don't think such acts are justified . . .[60]

The attack and its results, including the reports of atrocities brought by the survivors, were to help unnerve the Arab inhabitants of Tiberias. The unsettling impression left by the attack on Nasir ad Din was reinforced, in Nahmani's mind, by the news of the IZL attack and slaughter at Deir Yassin two days earlier. Commenting on the IZL massacre (and perhaps also influenced by the action at Nasir ad Din), Nahmani wrote: 'Atrocities Jews are [apparently] able to commit undermine all our morality; I wouldn't want our state to be founded on the blood of innocent women and children . . . I am very depressed.' Nahmani jotted down in his diary that he would have liked to leave Tiberias for a few days, for 'a change of air'. But, as a city councillor with responsibilities, he stayed put.

The British[61] demanded that the Haganah withdraw its units from the empty Jewish Quarter in the Old City or else face a British artillery attack—but then extended the ultimatum. Life in the mixed town had largely come to a standstill; all shops were closed, most traffic halted. Arab snipers dominated the main South–North road through the town, severing the Jewish settlements in the Galilee Panhandle from the Jewish centres to the South; Arab strong points in the Old City cut off the main Jewish neighbourhoods (Kiryat-Shmuel, etc.) on the slope to the West from the small Haganah contingent, now virtually besieged, in the old Jewish Quarter. Arab snipers that day killed one Jewish child and wounded another. Nahmani was in 'no doubt that the Arabs were planning to conquer the town'. But the Haganah defenders were in high spirits.[62]

The following day the Haganah attacked and neutralized some

[60] ND, 12 Apr. 1948; and 'Av, *HaMa'avak*, 187.
[61] Like Ben-Gurion, Nahmani throughout the war (mistakenly) believed that the British were backing the Arabs to the hilt and were bent on the Yishuv's 'destruction'. Nahmani was repeatedly to confide in his diary that the British had lost all moral values and direction in their foreign policy in the region (see, for example, ND, 26 Jan., 31 Jan., 16 Apr. 1948, etc.).
[62] ND, 13 Apr. 1948.

Arab snipers. The British imposed a curfew in the town. Nahmani was (apparently incorrectly) informed that, 'at the Arabs' request, the army was moving the Arab women and children out of the town.'[63] On 15 April, the British lifted the curfew on pedestrians but left it in force for vehicles. Nahmani suspected the British of anti-Zionist designs; the British had just handed over to Arab control the police forts at Nabi Yusha and Al Khalisa, in the Galilee Panhandle.[64] The following day Nahmani walked about the town and reported that British soldiers were looting the abandoned, shuttered Jewish shops in the Old City: 'During the past few days the [British] army has emphasized its hatred for us . . . They want [the Arabs] to slaughter [the Jews]. They want to take revenge against the Jews for the [anti-British] deeds of the IZL and LHI.'[65]

That night, 16/17 April, the Haganah struck. The immediate impulse was provided by the severing of the vital South–North artery through the Old City and the growing isolation of the Haganah contingent in the Jewish Quarter. Nahmani, all along, had expected an outside Arab force to intervene in the battle for the city; in the event, Haganah units managed to cut off Arab Tiberias from outside help, and it was Haganah troops from outside, units of the Golani Brigade and the Palmah's 3rd Battalion, who entered the town and decided the issue as the British garrison looked on. The battle was over in twenty-four hours.

About two companies of fresh Golani and Palmah troops moved into town and under cover of mortar and machinegun fire, advanced into the Old City. Using dynamite, they blew up Mahfuza House, a key Arab position, and several neighbouring houses. Their aim was to crack open the Arab defence lines, silence the snipers, and open the South–North through-road. The loud explosions, the successful Jewish attack, British non-intervention, and the non-arrival of Arab reinforcement and supplies from outside, thoroughly demoralized the town's Arab inhabitants. The following day, 17 April, the leading Arab notable family, the Tabaris, repeatedly asked their Jewish counterparts for a meeting 'to clarify city matters and relations between the two communities'. No meeting took place; apparently there was a Haganah veto. 'The principle question', according to Nahmani, was 'whether the Tabari family and other [Arab] leaders could guarantee peace and prevent outbreaks [of violence] such as had occurred.' In other words, if—as the Haganah assumed or at least argued—they couldn't, as extremists were in control of the Arab camp, then what was the point of a meeting? But Nahmani, apparently, wasn't persuaded. Unable to get through to Tel Aviv, he called the Mapai leader in Haifa, Abba Khoushi, who in turn called Ben-Gurion, to ask what to do. Nahmani apparently hoped to get Ben-Gurion to reverse the Haganah veto. He was unsuccessful. He was told to come to Tel Aviv as 'such matters could not be discussed on the telephone'. Nahmani met the Haganah commanders, including Optikman and Yosef Fein (a Sha"i man from neighbouring Kibbutz Degania Aleph), but apparently was unable to persuade them and refrained from telling them of his decision to go to Tel Aviv.[66]

But events were to outstrip Nahmani's feeble efforts at conciliation. He never got to Tel Aviv. The Jewish military successes the previous night had stunned the Arab community. These were followed, that night, 17/18 April, by renewed Jewish attack and the Palmah's conquest of the key Tiberias Hotel, at last clearing the road to the North. Already during the day, on 17 April, according to Nahmani, Arabs in large numbers began to leave the town, under British protection. The local notables, after seeking and failing to obtain British intervention to halt the Haganah advances, became desperate. The following morning, 18 April, Colonel Anderson, the senior British officer in the town, met with the remaining Arab notables (many, perhaps most, had already fled). He apparently suggested the idea of a complete evacuation of the Arab populace to Nazareth and Jordan, under British protection, with the British also taking care of logistical arrangements. The notables agreed. The Jewish leaders with whom Anderson next met, Moshe Tzahar and Yitzhak Tajar, according to Tzahar's later testimony, said that they opposed the Arab evacuation and asked to meet Arab representatives. Anderson repeatedly replied that no authoritative Arab representatives were left and that he was going ahead with the evacuation. The matter had been settled.[67] The bulk of the exodus took place that afternoon, after dozens of trucks and buses were brought in from Nazareth. A curfew was briefly reimposed by the British to facilitate the Arab evacuation. The Jews looked on, from windows and balconies, as their former neighbours departed the town westwards, up the winding road to Lubiya and Nazareth. The last Arab was out of Tiberias by evening. 'They say the city has [completely] emptied of Arabs,' Nahmani noted in his diary. 'I saw the [Arab] procession [leaving town] and it left me feeling depressed.' Even at this late hour, sometime on 18 April, Nahmani made one last effort at conciliation and negotiation:

I tried, without success, to persuade the security men [i.e. the Haganah commanders] to heed the Arab request to meet them. I explained to them that we must take the future into account, when we shall have to work together with the Arabs, and we must not burn the bridges, but, alas, they have no understanding and have no opinion in these matters . . . We are making ourselves hateful to Arabs without cause or justification.

Just how thoroughly the bridges were being burnt became apparent to Nahmani within hours: 'The Jewish mob descended upon [the evacuated Arab area] and began to pillage the shops that the Arabs had left. The looting was halted by the armed intervention of the Jewish police . . . How shameful . . . What a moral decline . . .'.[68] The military and civil authorities in the town issued proclamations forbidding looting and vandalism of Arab property, including mosques and churches.

Preserving the property of the Arabs who left is a good thing. After all, most of them are peaceful people . . . and good and, from the political point of view, for the future, it is very important for us that the [Arab]

---

[67] Morris, *Birth*, 71–2; 'Av, *HaMa'avak*, 207. Tzahar's testimony, that he and Tajar had opposed the Arab exodus and that they had asked Anderson to arrange a meeting with Arab notables to persuade them to stay, is uncorroborated by any other source.
[68] ND, 18 Apr. 1948; 'Av, *HaMa'avak*, 211–12; and Morris, *Birth*, 70–3. Needless to say, in Weitz's *Nahmani*, all reference to Tiberias Arab peace overtures and Jewish looting after the Arab exodus is deleted from the diary excerpts.

property be preserved and that when they return they will find it whole. It will also make a good impression on the rest of the world. In the streets there is [Jewish] rejoicing . . . but in [my] heart there is not joy but sadness. The Arab departure, that was encouraged by the British, makes a harsh impression. I believe that a way must be found for them to return, albeit while assuring [our] security.

Nahmani that day, 19 April, at last travelled to Tel Aviv, where he met Weitz; Ezra Danin, one of the founders of the Haganah Intelligence Service; and Gad Machnes, an Arab affairs expert who was about to be named director general of the Ministry for Minority Affairs in the new Israeli government. 'All agreed', according to Nahmani, 'that the exodus of the Arabs of Tiberias is not [in accord with] our official policy and the matter needs to be discussed.'[69]

Nahmani was struck by the relative tranquillity in the Jewish city, while war was raging around the country. 'Life in Tel Aviv is flowing normally, the streets, the coffee shops, the cinema are all packed as if no danger lurks.' He added, explaining the 'danger', that the Arab governments, including Transjordan's Abdullah, were threatening to invade the country—'but I am not afraid . . . We can and shall beat them.' His optimism stemmed, at least in part, from what he had seen of the Jewish troops' morale and courage in Tiberias.[70]

On 21 April, Nahmani met Reuven Shiloah (Zaslani), a senior Jewish Agency official and Arab affairs expert who was to become the founding director of Israel's foreign intelligence service, the Mossad. They discussed the future of Tiberias and 'the return of the permanent Arab residents'. Nahmani encountered 'full under-standing' and 'an identity' of views—meaning that (as far as Nahmani understood) Shiloah also supported the return of Tiberias's Arabs. Shiloah promised 'to bring the matters before Ben-Gurion'.[71]

But Nahmani returned to Tiberias on 22 April, only to find that the civil and military injunction against looting had completely broken down. The situation was

wild. Groups of dozens of Jews walked about pillaging from the [abandoned] Arab houses and shops . . . How ugly. This tarnishes our flag

[69] ND, 19 Apr. 1948.   [70] ND, 20 Apr. 1948.
[71] ND, 21 Apr. 1948.

... The Haganah people hadn't the strength to control the mob after they themselves had given a bad example and participated in the robbery. [It was as if] there was a contest between the different Haganah platoons stationed in Migdal, Genossar, Yavniel, 'Ein Gev, who came in cars and boats and loaded all sorts of goods [such as] refrigerators, beds, etc. . . . Quite naturally, the Jewish masses in Tiberias wanted to do likewise. The special police appointed to protect the [Arab] property turned a blind eye and reportedly took bribes . . .

The looting [*reported Nahmani the following day*] in the Arab houses continues. The old and women, regardless of age . . . religious [and non-religious], all are busy with robbery . . . Shame covers my face and [I] would like to spit on the city and leave it . . . This will rebound upon us and upon the education of [our] youth and children.[72]

In Haifa, which fell to the Haganah on 21–2 April and which Nahmani visited on the 25th, there had also been 'a lot of looting and contempt for the Arab leaders', but there the Jewish authorities had quickly reined in the Jewish looters and vandals. The Haganah was protecting the Arabs who had remained 'and facilitating the return of Arabs'. Peace-minded Arabs were being allowed to stay, observed Nahmani. 'In this way Arab nationalist propaganda that the Jews wanted to expel the Arabs was being confounded.'[73]

The problem of the abandoned and looted Arab property was to exercise Nahmani for days. On 2 May Nahmani was appointed a member of the new Tiberias municipal committee set up 'to protect the absentee Arabs' property'. 'When [the Arabs] return,' he wrote two days later, '[it is to be hoped that] they will be able to get back [their property]. The important question is how do we retrieve the looted property.' The committee debated the matter for days, but to no useful effect.[74] The attitude to the abandoned Arab property was at this time something of a touchstone in understanding general attitudes towards the wider questions of Arab flight, expulsions, and a possible return.

Nahmani still felt that 'Arab inhabitants who do not fight should be treated with civility and not as an enemy.' He (briefly) reported favourably about the Haganah's 'clearing' operation *vis-à-vis* the Arabs inhabitants between Ghuweir Abu Shusha and Rosh Pina—

[72] ND, 22–3 Apr. 1948.   [73] ND, 25–6 Apr. 1948.
[74] ND, 2, 4 May 1948.

but it is quite possible that he was not aware of the exact details of what was (accurately) called 'Operation Broom (*Mivtza Matate*)'.[75]

Be that as it may, on 6 May, Nahmani, again in Tel Aviv, complained to Weitz about the marginalization of the JNF office in the Galilee. He also complained of 'the brutal behaviour of our people towards all the Arabs'. Weitz countered by explaining and justifying Jewish behaviour on the basis of the justice of the Zionist cause and the lack of alternatives. Nahmani may not have been completely persuaded. Weitz jotted down in his diary: 'He apparently finds it difficult to cut himself off from the concepts that we became accustomed to during the period of enslavement under the British Mandate.'[76]

But Nahmani, at this time, was no bleeding-heart liberal. Indeed, he was already moving towards a harder line. His position, in those mid-May days, in so far as the evidence suggests, may have been similar to that prevalent in much of the Yishuv: There were 'good Arabs' and 'bad Arabs'. Peace-minded Arabs should be left in peace; belligerent Arabs could justifiably be expelled. At least this seems to be the sense of Nahmani's diary entries for 9 and 13 May, which deal, in part, with the Haganah conquest of Arab Safad. The town's Arabs had traditionally been anti-Zionist. On 9 May Nahmani wrote that he was 'afraid' that the Haganah would prove unable to 'cleanse [*le'taher*] Safad and so, inciting Safad, that bastion of inciters, will remain in place'.[77] But the town fell to Palmah assault the following day, and its 10,000 Arabs fled Palestine. Nahmani visited Safad three days later and walked around the abandoned Arab quarters. The Haganah was preventing looting and 'getting ready to level the houses of the important inciters. This must be done quickly before a spoiling party interferes.' Nahmani wondered why the 'well-fortified' Arab townspeople had fled. But he was far from sorry: 'Safad, the nest of inciters, has been abandoned, and all means must be used [to make sure that] the inciters do not return to it.'[78]

[75] ND, 3 May 1948. Operation Broom is described in Morris, *Birth*, 121–2.
[76] CZA, A–246/13 (Yosef Weitz's diary notebooks), p. 2,377, entry for 6 May 1948. Interestingly, Nahmani's own diary records the meeting, and other matters discussed, but makes no mention of this part of the conversation.
[77] ND, 9 May 1948.   [78] ND, 13 May 1948.

He seemed to be speaking of the whole Arab population rather than of particular miscreants.

The first half of the war, for Nahmani as for the rest of the Yishuv, was crowned on 14 May by the declaration of the establishment of the State of Israel, 'one of the greatest days of my life'. But joy was mixed with sadness as he contemplated the loss of 'an important part of our country', that is Judaea and Samaria (somewhat more than the area of the present-day West Bank), which had been earmarked for Palestinian Arab statehood. 'It is difficult to agree to such surgery but there was no other way to save the patient,' was how Nahmani put it. Meanwhile, the neighbouring Arab states were preparing to invade Palestine—but Nahmani had 'great faith' in the Jewish army, which, though untrained, had a powerful fighting spirit.[79]

NAHMANI AND THE ABANDONED ARAB LANDS IN THE NEW STATE

Already in the weeks before the establishment of the state, Nahmani had been involved in the JNF's main activity that spring and summer—planning and clearing the ground for new Jewish settlements. Between December 1947 and April 1948, Eastern Galilee had been in tumult, hostilities preventing normal life, let alone the establishment of settlements. The Haganah conquest of most of the area in April–May and the war-induced flight and expulsion of most of the area's Arab inhabitants cleared the way for new settlement ventures. Already in mid-April, Weitz had written to Nahmani asking his advice about how the JNF could, in the new, changed circumstances, lay its hands on Galilee lands that it had already purchased but had never actually taken possession of—at Qadas, Al Malikiya, Al Zawiya, Shauqa at Tahta, Al Madahil, Al 'Abisiya, Hunin, Biriya, and As Samra.[80] The lands must be 'freed' of the tenant-farmers who still lived on them and settlements established, wrote Weitz, specifically of As Samra and 'Arab Bashatiwa, South of Kibbutz Gesher.[81] Weitz was especially interested in a number of tracts of land along the

[79] ND, 14 May 1948.
[80] CZA, KKL 5/15931, Weitz to Nahmani, 18 Apr. 1948.
[81] CZA, KKL 5/15931, Weitz to JNF office, Tiberias, 6 May 1948.

northern shore of the Sea of Galilee (Tabigha, the lands of 'Arab Shamalina, etc.).[82]

Nahmani spent part of his visit to Tel Aviv on 6–8 May discussing new settlements with Weitz and Avraham Hartzfeld, the head of the Histadrut's Agricultural Centre. On 11 May he met local officials and some of the prospective settlers earmarked for As Samra, on the south-eastern tip of the Sea of Galilee. New settlements at nearby Khirbet ad Duweir and at Qasir (later Beit Katzir or Tel Katzir) were also discussed. The kibbutzim Ma'agan, Ha'on, and Beit (later Tel) Katzir were soon established at the sites.[83] The establishment of other new settlements—near Blida (later Kibbutz Yiftah), at Mansurat al Kheit (Kibbutz Kfar HaNassi), near Qadas (Ramot-Naftali), and at Al Malikiya (Malkiya)—were discussed, and in principle, approved, at a meeting of departmental heads in Tel Aviv on 16 May, attended by Nahmani.[84]

The settlement institutions, for military and political reasons as well as because of a lack of manpower, equipment, and funds, were not in a position, around 15 May, to exploit the mass Arab exodus from Eastern Galilee and immediately to set up a string of new settlements. The first priority, in most cases, was to take physical 'possession' of the lands, meaning, in the circumstances, to reap the summer crop and, later, sow the winter crops. Nahmani attended some of the decision-making meetings in Tel Aviv in whch the share-out of these lands for harvest among the kibbutzim was approved in principle.[85] Nahmani himself was instrumental in deciding on the exact share-out of the various tracts to the different kibbutzim in the Panhandle; he was intimately knowledgeable about the needs and capabilities of the different settlements.[86] These temporary allocations of abandoned Arab land for harvest were to form the basis of the permanent

---

[82] HaShomer Archive, Nahmani Papers Dalet–7–52, Weitz to Nahmani, 11 May 1948.

[83] ND, 6, 8, 11, and 12 May 1948.

[84] ND, 16 May 1948.

[85] ND, 16–17 May 1948. See also CZA, KKL 9/31, Ra'anan Weitz to JNF offices Tiberias, Haifa, etc., 17 May 1948, detailing the distribution of the abandoned Galilee Panhandle lands for cultivation to the various kibbutzim.

[86] See e.g. CZA, KKL 9/31, Nahmani to Weitz, 19 July 1948.

distribution of the tracts among old and new kibbutzim in the months that followed.[87]

The invasion of Palestine by the armies of Egypt, Jordan, Iraq, Syria, and Lebanon, on 15–16 May, once again had placed Tiberias near the firing line. The Syrian thrust through Samakh towards Degania, South of Tiberias, for a few days left Nahmani 'very tense'. Most of the town's able-bodied male residents spent 18–20 May digging trenches and fortifications just South of the city, in preparation for the expected onslaught. The overflight of Arab aircraft added to the tension. The city elders decided on the evacuation of the town's women and children. But the Haganah district commander reprimanded them: 'Nobody is allowed to leave Tiberias,' and assured the elders that the Arabs would be stopped.[88] In the event, he was right: The Haganah halted the Syrian advance, in one courageous action using Molotov Cocktails against tanks at the gates of Degania. A day or so later, a battery of ancient light mountain artillery pieces was brought up and deployed on the ridge to the west of the Sea of Galilee. Its barrages clinched the battle. The Syrians, apparently, were surprised and dismayed by the appearance of the Jewish artillery. Nahmani, using binoculars, watched the panicky Arab retreat eastwards.[89]

However, for weeks Nahmani was on tenterhooks, anticipating a renewal of Syrian (and perhaps Iraqi) attacks in the direction of Tiberias. He also feared an attack from the west, by Qawuqji's forces in Nazareth and Lubiya—'and Tiberias is unfortified'. He even travelled to Tel Aviv to discuss the problem with Ben-Gurion.[90] With the renewal of fighting ('the Ten Days') on 8–9 July, tensions reached a fever pitch. According to Nahmani, many women and children had left Tiberias during the weeks of the First Truce (11 June–8 July). The townspeople were again busy building trenches and bunkers. But as things turned out, the IDF (the Haganah's successor organization) pushed the Arab armies back on all fronts, except at Mishmar HaYarden, on the Syrian

---

[87] CZA, KKL 9/31, The Committee for Distribution of Land in the Hula (i.e. H. Gvati, Y. Schutzberg, and R. Weitz) to the JNF, etc., 3 Sept. 1948. See also Ch. 7, below, *passim*.

[88] ND, 18–19 May 1948.

[89] ND, 20 May 1948.

[90] ND, 1, 4, 5 July 1948, etc.

border, to the North of Tiberias, and conquered fresh territory in Western and Central Galilee, including the town of Nazareth. This 'will enable us to set up new settlements', reflected Nahmani.[91] With the institution of the Second Truce, on 18–19 July, the threat of renewed Arab attack in the Tiberias area finally disappeared.

Meanwhile, Nahmani concentrated on pushing ahead with the new settlements, especially at Blida, Al Malikiya, Qadas, and Mansurat al Kheit. He feared that if settlements were not established quickly, a UN-imposed cease-fire or renewed conquest by the Arabs would mean the loss for ever of these border areas. The problem was that the major decision-making roles were in the hands of the head offices of the various settlement agencies in Tel Aviv and 'I have ceased to be influential,' he lamented.[92] Nothing seemed to move, or, at least, movement was painfully slow. On 2 June Nahmani accompanied Weitz, Hartzfeld, and Yehuda Horin, director of the Jewish Agency Settlement Department, on a tour of the potential settlement sites near Blida, Qadas, and Al Malikiya.[93] His anxiety was such that he even dreamt about Al Malikiya.[94] Nahmani's fears, in fact, proved not without foundation. The Jewish garrison retreated from Al Malikiya–Qadas under Arab attack on 6 June—and the area only reverted to Jewish control in Operation Hiram, at the end of October 1948.

Nahmani henceforth focused on the rapid settlement of the Blida lands and Mansurat al Kheit,[95] and of the areas abandoned by the tenant-farmers in the Hula Valley. 'When the [absentee] landowners return to claim the lands, we must cut a deal with them and pay them compensation.' He also favoured paying compensation to the former tenants. Nahmani suggested—to Weitz and the director of the JNF, Avraham Granovsky (Granott)—contacting the landowning effendis in Transjordan, Syria, and Lebanon and making offers to buy them out before they returned to Palestine.

The effendis, who were ready [in the past] to sell their lands and only the threat by the [Arab] nationalists prevented them [from selling], will now be happy to receive the payments and invest them in profit-making businesses, and the tenant-farmers will be able, with the compensation

---

[91] ND, 9–10, 17 July 1948.   [92] ND, 29, 31 May 1948.
[93] ND, 2 June 1948.   [94] ND, 4 June 1948.
[95] ND, 17, 26, 29 June 1948; and CZA, KKL 9/62, Nahmani to Weitz, 16 July 1948.

they receive, to settle properly [i.e. comfortably] in the neighbouring countries.[96]

On 2 July, Nahmani at last attended the dedication ceremony at Mansurat al Kheit, marking the establishment of 'HaBonim' (later renamed Kfar Hanassi) at the site.[97] He continued in the following weeks to push for more settlements. But the process of confiscation of Arab lands, which included the physical destruction of many of the abandoned villages, was encountering opposition within the government. At a meeting on 22 July, Weitz explained his problems to Nahmani. 'There is great opposition by HaShomer HaTza'ir [i.e. Mapam] people to the destruction of the villages and the expropriation of the abandoned lands . . . The Cabinet ministers believe that one must deal carefully with the problem of the [abandoned] property and the relations with the Arabs.' In any event, said Weitz, the JNF was sending agents to Europe to make contact with Arab landowners living abroad to clinch land deals[98] and 'in order to prepare the ground for transferring the Arab refugees to the neighbouring states [of] Iraq, Transjordan and Syria. I [i.e. Nahmani] had spoken with Weitz about this idea a while back . . .'.[99]

Nahmani indeed was troubled by the (growing) Palestinian refugee problem:

It is very serious and if we don't find a way, before it reaches the negotiating table, to act resolutely and energetically to solve it, we may find ourselves confronting a difficult situation which will weigh heavily upon the State [of Israel] and the Government. The public [unfortunately] regards the matter with levity and is certain that this problem is no problem at all [and] need not be dealt with.[100]

In August, Weitz asked Nahmani to urgently supply him with details about the Arab exodus from the Safad and Tiberias districts—numbers, origins, and destinations. It was part of Weitz's effort to amass information about the refugee problem,

---

[96] ND, 19 and 27 June 1948.   [97] ND, 2 July 1948.

[98] Nahmani, like Weitz, appreciated that many Arab landowners had been hard hit by the disaster in Palestine and hoped that they were now amenable to selling off their assets. At the same time, Nahmani understood that so long as there were hostilities, it would be very difficult if not impossible for Arabs to sell land to their enemies, the Jews (see ND, 22 and 29 July, and 18 Aug. 1948).

[99] ND, 22 July 1948.   [100] ND, 23 July 1948.

information that was to serve as the basis of the Transfer Committee's report that was completed that winter.[101] Presumably,
Nahmani supplied Weitz with the required details.

While Nahmani himself was caught up on a day-to-day basis
with the problems of distributing the formerly Arab-cultivated
lands, and of establishing settlements on them, he frowned upon
the growing Jewish avarice in this respect. He linked the settlers'
territorial-agricultural acquisiteveness with what he regarded as
general Yishuv 'aggressiveness' on the political-military plane. On
26 July Nahmani was visited by two settlement representatives,
from the veteran kibbutzim of Ashdot Ya'akov and Kinneret, who
had come to ask for more land:

They are members of a Jordan Valley settlements committee concerned
with the Arab lands. The appetite grows with the eating. Aggressiveness
[*tokfanut*] is a contagious disease and destroys the framework of morality.
Material and national interests know no boundaries. And there is no
difference between a cultured man, who speaks [i.e. who claims that he is
acting] in the name of morality, and a primitive person who is far from
such considerations.[102]

Nahmani bemoaned the rivalry, which was to go on for many
months, in different areas of the country, between various
settlements for choice tracts of land.[103]

But clearly Nahmani himself was affected by the war-induced
winds of change. In April and early May he had spoken favourably
of the return of Tiberias's Arab inhabitants; by the end of July,
like most Israelis, he firmly opposed the idea of a return.

In the newspapers . . . they have begun to talk of bringing back the
refugees, concentrated in Nazareth, to Tiberias, etc. Such things [i.e.
ideas] are inconceivable, that during wartime Arabs should return to
Tiberias or to other places and to allow, in such a way, the undermining of
security.

At the same time, Nahmani expressed full approval of the fair
treatment, by Israel's military authorities, meted out to the Arabs

[101] For details, see Ch. 4, above.
[102] ND, 26 July 1948.
[103] ND, 29 Aug. 1948. See e.g. CZA, KKL 9/27, secretary of Ramot Naftali to
Nahmani, 19 July 1949, for arguments over land between Ramot-Naftali and
Malkiya.

still living in Israeli territory, in and around Nazareth.[104] Yet in September he wrote that new settlements needed to be established—in the area East of Rosh Pinna—in order to help bar an Arab refugee return.[105] One reason for opposing a refugee return was the need to find accommodation for the masses of Jewish immigrants now arriving in the country. In August, Nahmani was involved in bringing some of these immigrants to Tiberias—and settling them in abandoned Arab houses.[106]

On 19 August, a new settlement (eventually called Kibbutz Yiftah) was at last dedicated on the lands of Blida, on the Lebanese border. It was an army operation. Nahmani was mortally offended: He and his office were not informed, and he had not been invited to the ceremony. Nahmani attributed this sequence of events to the general 'decline' in the status of the JNF.[107] Often, he felt that 'instead of dealing with land projects, we have become road-builders'.[108] Nahmani was referring to his continuing efforts to organize access roads to a number of isolated Eastern Galilee settlements (such as HaBonim and Kfar (later Ma'ayan) Baruch), efforts which seemed to be taking up a great deal of his time. 'In future', he wrote, 'I will not agree that our office take upon itself such tasks. Our office should be concerned with land matters, its preparation [for settlement], its afforestation, and overall supervision of road-building, etc.'[109]

The last act of the 1948 war in the Galilee was Operation Hiram, in which in a three-day blitz, during 29–31 October, the IDF conquered North-Central Galilee and a string of Lebanese border villages besides. The operation was marked by a succession of

---

[104] ND, 30 July 1948. It is worth noting that Nahmani was here opposing not a return of anonymous Arab refugees from abroad but fellow townspeople, with whom, in general, he had had good relations for decades, still resident inside Israel—in Nazareth—to another site in Israel, his home town.

[105] ND, 21 Sept. 1948.

[106] ND, 16 Aug. 1948.

[107] ND, 20 Aug. 1948; and CZA, KKL 9/62, Nahmani to JNF Head Office, Jerusalem, 26 Aug. 1948, Nahmani, of course, was right. The JNF, like the Jewish Agency, had been a main pillar of the Jewish state-to-be during the British Mandate. But following the establishment of the state, the old so-called 'National Institutions' (*HaMosdot HaLeumi'im*) lost their primary importance, conceding the field to the new institutions of state, such as the various ministries.

[108] ND, 7 Nov. 1948.

[109] ND, 9 Nov. 1948.

atrocities against the conquered Arab civilian population, a large part of which was driven into exile.[110]

Nahmani visited the area a week later. In one Lebanese village, El Aadeisse, 'hundreds' of villagers approached him and asked that the IDF remain and not give the area back to Lebanon. But he was shocked to hear, from a number of sources, including Immanuel ('Mano') Friedman, the Minority Affairs Ministry representative in Eastern Galilee, details about

the cruel acts of our soldiers. In Safsaf, after they had entered the village and the inhabitants raised a white flag, they had collected and separated the men and women, tied the hands of fifty–sixty fellahin and shot and killed them and buried them in a pit/well. And also, they had raped several of the village women. Next to the wood, [Friedman said he] had seen several dead women, including a woman holding in her arms her dead child. At Eilaboun and Farradiya the [Israeli] soldiers had been greeted with white flags and rich food, and afterwards had ordered the villagers to leave, with their children and women. When the [villagers] had begun to argue that this was contrary to the flyers and promises [distributed by Israel], [the soldiers] had opened fire and after some thirty people were killed, had begun to lead the rest by foot to [Mount] Meiron. One woman had left her baby by a tree as she hadn't had the strength to [continue to] carry him . . . In Saliha, where a white flag had been raised, they had carried out a real slaughter. They had killed about sixty–seventy men and women. Where did they come by such a measure of cruelty, like Nazis? They [i.e. the Jewish troops] had learnt from them [i.e. the Nazis]. One officer told me that those who had 'excelled' had come from [the Nazi concentration/extermination] camps. The reports of the atrocities made a difficult impression on [Minority Affairs Minister Bechor] Shitrit, Machnes, and others. Is there no more humane way of expelling the inhabitants than by such methods and afterwards to rob their property[?][111]

The October massacres in the Galilee triggered an interesting, sad exchange between Nahmani and Zionism's elder statesman, Dr Chaim Weizmann (1874–1952), soon to be sworn in as Israel's first president. In mid-November, Weizmann and his wife were

[110] The operation and the atrocities are described in Morris, *Birth*, 224–34.
[111] ND, 6 Nov. 1948. In general, Nahmani's diary description of the Oct. atrocities conforms with the descriptions in the *Birth*, which were based on documents from Israeli and UN archives. But there are discrepancies—as, for example, in the details about the Eilaboun massacre. Moreover, Nahmani tells about only three or four of the atrocities.

holidaying in Tiberias's Galei Kinneret Hotel (where Ben-Gurion
also normally spent his holidays). Weizmann invited Nahmani
over, and opened by saying that it was 'a great miracle that we
have won a state in our lifetime'. He then said: 'I have heard that
we are not treating the Arab inhabitants who stayed nicely. I have
heard of acts of robbery, rape, and pressure/attacks . . . This
will redound on us. We will be judged by our behaviour and
morality . . . Where did our children learn such cruelty? How did it
happen? Don't they ask you [i.e. Nahmani] how to behave with
the Arabs?' Nahmani: 'They don't ask [me].' And he asked:
'Do they ask you, as president of the state?' 'No,' answered
Weizmann, speaking 'quietly, with a despondent, depressed
voice—no, you are right, they don't ask.' Weizmann, according to
Nahmani, then added: 'I am worried, [for] if we behave like all the
other peoples [*kemo kol ha'goyim*], we will be unimportant. Our
power, if not based on moral values, will be without value.'
'Weizmann was very depressed,' concluded Nahmani.[112]

The two men met again the following day. 'All night I couldn't
calm down [sleep?] because of the acts of our lads against the
Arabs,' Weizmann told Nahmani. 'What could be done to prevent
such acts?' he asked. Nahmani: 'Only the Government has the
power to curb the outburst of such instincts among our boys.'
'That is true', Weizmann responded, 'as his eyes expressed that
special "Weizmannish" sorrow.' And he had added: 'Unfortunately
. . . I have no influence. They [Ben-Gurion and company?] make
sure that I have no influence.'[113]

Nahmani seemed to assume that the Operation Hiram massacres
were part of a general policy or campaign of expulsion, a means of
prodding the villagers on to the road to Lebanon. He castigated
the means—but seemed not to take issue with their assumed
objective, of expulsion.

In any event, now that much of the population had fled, it was
up to the settlement institutions to make sure that there was no
Arab return, through 'infiltration' or otherwise, 'by settling and
populating' the area with Jews. 'It is necessary, in my opinion, to
put new immigrants in all the [abandoned] villages . . . [and] to
give each family a cow and a small chicken coop . . .'. If 'we don't

---

[112] ND, 13 Nov. 1948.   [113] ND, 14 Nov. 1948.

hurry and populate [the Galilee with Jews], the Galilee will face a
danger [of return to Arab sovereignty as] it is impossible to retain
it empty [i.e. unless populated by Jews].'[114]

It was possible that the international community might force
Israel to allow back the refugees. 'But if all or most [are not
allowed to] return, then the JNF will still have a lot to do,'
concluded Nahmani, responding, perhaps, to those who had
begun to intimate that the JNF's work was done and that it no
longer had a useful function.[115]

Nahmani spent November and December organizing road-
building projects, but also trying to seek out potential Arab land-
sellers. Weitz at first appeared 'unenthusiastic' about purchasing
land from Arabs who had remained in Israel, but he eventually
agreed.[116] Ben-Gurion, according to Weitz, opposed purchasing
any land from the Arabs who had left the country. The IDF had
conquered their land and Ben-Gurion intended to sell the land
(some 'one million dunams') to the JNF. Nahmani wasn't sure the
Cabinet would agree to the scheme but, eventually, the 'deal' went
through (see Chapter 4).[117]

Otherwise, Nahmani's main concern during these weeks was
organizing new settlement ventures in the areas conquered in
October. On 16 December he toured the mostly depopulated sites
just south of the Lebanese border—Iqrit, Tarbikha, Mansura,
Sasa, Sukhmata, and Tarshiha. Iqrit's (Christian Arab) population
had been moved inland, to the Israeli Arab village of Rama.[118] A
few hundred (Christians) remained in Tarshiha; in Mansura, soon
to be completely cleared of Arabs, he found eighteen Christians
still in place.

The plan [is] to set up several agricultural settlements in the villages and,
in Tarshiha and other villages, to settle new immigrants who will . . . grow

[114] ND, 10 Nov. 1948.				[115] ND, 11 Nov. 1948.
[116] ND, 19 Nov. 1948 and 8, 17, and 18 Dec. 1948; and CZA, KKL 9/62,
'Summary of Talks with Mr. Y. Weitz in Tiberias on 18 Dec. 1948', by Y. Nahmani,
18 Dec. 1948.
[117] ND, 24 Dec. 1948.
[118] In Nov. 1949 Nahmani offered a detailed proposal to solve the problem of the
landless Iqrit villagers, who had been forcibly evicted to Rama by the IDF in Nov.
1948. He proposed that the transferees, numbering in all 416 souls, be given
possession of the lands of Rama villagers who had left the country in 1948—some
2,000 dunams in all, somewhat less than the lands they had been dispossessed of at
Iqrit (see CZA, KKL 9/329, Nahmani to Y. Weitz, JNF, Jerusalem, 2 Nov. 1949).

tobacco and cultivate the existing olive groves and fig trees . . . It is very important to put Jews in all the Galilee which is empty of inhabitants. The villages are rich with olives, vineyards, figs, etc. The weather is wonderful, healthy, and the land is good for tobacco.[119]

NAHMANI AND THE ARAB QUESTION AFTER 1948

The ambiguity or ambivalence that characterized Nahmani's thinking and actions during 1948 in all that concerned the 'Arab Question' was to manifest itself, sometimes in extreme fashion, during the following years. His activities in four areas are worth examining—the destruction of the Arab quarters of Tiberias; the planned transfer abroad of the Maghrebi villagers of Eastern Galilee and other Arab communities; the transfer inland of Khisas's remaining inhabitants; and the fate of the Arab villagers of Kirad al Ghannama and Kirad al Baqqara, in the Israeli–Syrian Demilitarized Zone

The Destruction of the Old City of Tiberias

From the end of May 1948, one of Nahmani's principal concerns was the levelling of much of the Old City of Tiberias. He appears to have been motivated by a desire to improve and renovate the city—by creating new throughfares and public parks in place of the dank alleys and hovels that characterized the site.[120] But the matter also was tied up with the question of a possible Arab return. Less than a month before, Nahmani had been an unequivocal, voluble advocate of the return of Tiberias's Arab inhabitants. No doubt the Arab states' invasion and the threat to Tiberias had contributed to his change of heart. Be that as it may, the destruction of parts—and soon, most—of the Old City would mean that there would and could be no Arab return, as the former inhabitants of the town would have nowhere to return to.

By late July, Nahmani's plans for the Old City of Tiberias were being translated by the local IDF units into action. The municipality was behaving lethargically, partly out of fear of incurring fresh financial responsibilities. But Nahmani had managed to persuade

---

[119] ND, 16 Dec. 1948. See also CZA, KKL 9/62, 'Summary of Talks with Mr. Y. Weitz in Tiberias on 18 Dec. 1948', by Y. Nahmani, 18 Dec. 1948.
[120] ND, 25 May 1948.

local IDF commanders of the necessity of the planned urban face-lifting. The army 'continued today to blow up houses in order to open streets in Tiberias. Now is the chance to renovate the city,' he wrote at the end of July.[121] But a lack of dynamite[122] and various bureaucratic snags held up the work for months. It was only renewed, though quickly completed, in early 1949. Throughout, Nahmani's role appears to have been pivotal. He advised, blandished, cajoled, organized, and lobbied. 'My plan is being implemented despite the interference of the city folk,' he jotted down in his diary in February. And on the 28th he wrote: 'Today also I devoted to the destruction of the city. I had to instruct the sappers to be careful in the destruction of the houses next to the churches . . .'.[123]

The Transfer Abroad of the Maghrebi Communities and Other Israeli Arab Villagers

As we have seen, already in January 1948 Nahmani had proposed the organized transfer of the Maghrebi Arab villagers out of the country. Several groups of Maghrebis, mainly Moroccans, had emigrated from North Africa and settled in Palestine in the middle of the nineteenth-century. They lived mainly in two clusters of villages—in Deishum, Sammu'i, 'Ammuqa, Al 'Ulmaniya, and Tuleil, around and North-east of Safad, and in 'Ulam, Ma'dhar, Kafr Sabt, and Khirbet Sha'ara, between Kfar Tavor and the Sea of Galilee. After the battles of the spring and summer of 1948 had ended and most of the Maghrebi villagers had fled the country, Nahmani took steps to 'finalize' this transfer. He sought formally to purchase the tracts of land from the villagers already in exile and buy out, on condition that they departed the country, those still left in the country. Nahmani's contact man with the Maghrebis was Emir 'Abd al Razek Jezraili, an effendi who apparently lived in Syria and, back in 1945, had sold land in Ma'dhar to the JNF.[124] He contacted Nahmani in September 1948.[125]

---

[121] ND, 27 July and 16 Aug. 1948.   [122] ND, 31 Aug. 1948.
[123] ND, 6, 18, and 28 Feb. 1949, 31 Mar. 1949, etc. For more detail on the destruction of Tiberias's Old City, see ISA PMO 5525 gimel and other entries in ND.
[124] Weitz, *Nahmani*, 104, Nahmani to Weitz, 27 June 1945.
[125] ND, 28 Sept. 1948.

On 18 December, in a meeting between Nahmani and Weitz, it was agreed that after Yoav Zuckerman, Weitz's land-purchasing agent in the Gedera area, and Gad Machnes met Jezraili (who was then, apparently, in Paris), explained the situation to him, and saw whether he was willing 'to deal with the transfer of the Maghrebi villagers to Syria or Morocco,' Nahmani would meet with him 'to determine the plan, the conditions, and the details' of the transfer.[126]

On 22 January 1949, 'Abd al Razek arrived at last in Israel. Nahmani and his guest discussed ways and means of contacting the Maghrebis still in the country and persuading them to sell their holdings and leave. Most of the remaining Maghrebis were no longer in their (now empty) villages and were temporarily living, along with other rural refugees, in a number of Galilee towns, particularly Nazareth. On 24 January, Nahmani and 'Abd al Razek travelled to Nazareth to seek out Maghrebi villagers. 'We found two or three [willing] to go to Transjordan and Syria to talk to [Maghrebis already in exile there] about moving to Morocco.' But Nahmani was not optimistic that anything would come of it.[127]

Further meetings between Nahmani, 'Abd al Razek, and some Israeli Maghrebis left the JNF official no more sanguine. Nahmani wrote that most of the Palestinian Maghrebis were already in exile in Jordan, Syria, and Lebanon, and were difficult to contact or make deals with. And the few left in Israel (mostly in Nazareth) 'were afraid of travelling to the Arab states lest they be charged with being [Israeli] spies, and the [Palestinian] Maghrebis in the Arab states would not dare to come to Israel for the same reasons.' Alas, until peace was reached between Israel and the Arab states, no real progress could be made, concluded Nahmani. As a result, whereas in the past Nahmani had been wont to distinguish between Maghrebis and 'regular' Palestinian Arabs, he now began to regard the exiles without such 'ethnic' differentiation. Indeed, he proposed that the refugee Maghrebi lands be lumped together with those of the other Palestinian 'absentees' and treated in the same way—i.e. expropriated, pure and simple. Israel would

[126] CZA, KKL 9/62, 'Summary of Talks with Mr. Y. Weitz in Tiberias on 18 Dec. 1948', by Y. Nahmani, 18 Dec. 1948.
[127] *Nahmani*, 255, entries for 22 and 24 Jan. 1949.

always be able, at some point in the future, to compensate them, if need be.[128]

But this still left the problem of the (small number of) Maghrebis still in the country. Nahmani continued intermittently to send out feelers: Even if not living in their old villages, these Maghrebis were still legally the owners of their lands, which the JNF coveted. Towards the end of 1949 he appears to have made contact and reached agreement with a number. Some apparently were interested in selling their holdings but staying on Israel, in their new domiciles; others were willing to sell and leave for Syria or Jordan. Altogether, Nahmani had made contact or reached provisional agreement with some twenty-five families, from 'Shajara, Hadatha, Kafr Sabt, Ma'dhar, 'Ulam, Dalata, and Sasa,' not all of them Maghrebis, owning some '2,000 dunams' altogether. Nahmani reasoned that if the JNF 'initiated appropriate treatment, this action might expand and cover hundreds of Arabs, and we could work it so that the bulk of them would agree to move to Transjordan or Syria.' Nahmani wrote that the Arabs were still living in uncertainty and anxiety about their status and future, and 'this feeling of theirs . . . should be exploited in order to obtain their voluntary agreement to leave the country and move to another [*sic*] Arab country.'[129]

Weitz responded that the Cabinet had approved—and presumably agreed to budget for—'the purchase of land from Arabs who are citizens of Israel, but who do not live in their permanent [i.e. former] places, if they intend to leave the country.'[130]

But Nahmani's efforts to acquire Arab land for Jewish settlements were not limited to legal purchase. In February 1949 he wrote to the Custodian of Absentees Property, Dov Shafrir, complaining that a number of inhabitants of the Circassian village of Kafr Kama, near Kfar Tavor, were cultivating plots of land that belonged or, rather, that had belonged, to relatives who had left the country during the war. As, by law, property belonging to

[128] *Nahmani*, 256, entries for 28 Jan. and 6 Feb. 1949.
[129] CZA, KKL 9/329, Nahmani to Y. Weitz, JNF, Jerusalem, 3 Nov. 1949. Nahmani wrote that 'the average' holding of these families was '2,000 dunams'. But it seems more likely that there is an error in the letter and that he meant a total of 2,000 dunams. Nahmani, incidentally, kept using the term 'Transjordan' long after that country had in 1948 formally changed its name to 'Jordan'.
[130] CZA, KKL 9/416, Weitz to JNF office, Tiberias, 7 Nov. 1949.

those who had left automatically reverted to the state ('absentees property'), these Kafr Kama residents were illegally cultivating the said plots and the state should lay hands on them. The plots were needed in order to 'round out' the allotments for Jewish settlements neighbouring on Kafr Kama, wrote Nahmani. Besides, the plots, totalling some 700 dunams, belonged/had belonged to 'inciters' (i.e. anti-Yishuv activists) in the village, who 'had tried on every occasion to emphasize their affiliation with the Arab nationalists'.[131]

The Case of Khisas

Nahmani's relations with Khisas, a small village near the northern tip of the Galilee Panhandle, dated at least back to the 1930s. A number of Khisas families had acted as go-betweens in JNF–Arab land-deals and, indeed, Nahmani himself ended up owning a tract of land formerly owned by a Khisas family. The villagers had traditionally been friendly towards the Yishuv and during the 1930s and 1940s had helped the Haganah in intelligence-gathering.[132] In December 1947, as we have seen, the Palmah raided the village, to Nahmani's chagrin. In March 1948, a number of villagers—headed by 'Atiyeh Juwayid—fled to Jewish Tiberias to escape from Arab nationalist militiamen, who had intended to arrest them for pro-Zionist activities. Nahmani arranged for their accommodation in a Jewish hotel. 'Atiyeh and his band later moved to Kibbutz Dafna, where they served as guards, and carried out raids into Lebanon and Syria for the IDF. Two of 'Atiyeh's sons subsequently served in the IDF.[133]

'Atiyeh and his kinsmen returned to Khisas towards the end of the war. The November 1948 IDF border clearing operations passed over Khisas; the village remained in place. But in early summer 1949 a rumour that some villagers were in contact with Syrian intelligence, the severing of a military telephone line, and a

---

[131] CZA, KKL 9/230, Nahmani to Shafrir, 23 Feb. 1949.
[132] CZA, KKL 9/403, 'To Whom it May Concern', by Yosef Nahmani, 14 Mar. 1952.
[133] ND, 24 Mar. 1948; and CZA, KKL 9/403, 'To Whom it May Concern', by Yosef Nahmani, 14 Mar. 1952.

general desire to clear of Arab communities a 5–10 kilometre strip along the border persuaded the IDF of the need for eviction.[134]

At midnight 5 June, the remaining fifty-five inhabitants of Khisas and the villagers from neighbouring Qeitiya, 2 kilometres to the South, together with the villagers of Ja'una, East of Safad, were forcibly 'and brutally' packed by the IDF on to trucks, 'with kicks [and] curses', driven South, and dumped on a bare hillside near 'Akbara, South of Safad.[135]

Nahmani, indignant and moved by the Khisas villagers' plight, three days later travelled to 'Akbara to visit the evictees. He jotted down in his diary: 'We saw the Arab families lying in the barren, fire-scorched field on the way to 'Akbara. It is shameful [*busha u'khlima*]—a disgrace to our government . . . God help a state that acts in such immoral fashion. Such foolish acts must be combated . . .'.[136] But, within days, his anger, seemingly, had changed focus, from indignation over the transfer itself to indignation over the 'sorry' manner of its implementation, which the Military Government's justifications could not paper over.[137]

On 14 June, Nahmani was moved to write directly to Ben-Gurion. The Khisas villagers had 'served our cause . . . and are worthy of special treatment . . . Without doubt the [operation] could have been carried out in a fair manner without hurting their feelings and without causing damage to their property and crops,' he wrote. The Khisas evictees, now stranded with the other evacuees on a barren hillside, had nothing on which to live and were having to sell off their cattle cheaply. Nahmani proposed that the Khisas villagers be allowed 'to return to gather their crops and, meanwhile, a suitable place could be found for them in one of the [other Arab] villages.' Nahmani proposed that they be resettled in the 'abandoned houses' in Maghar, North-west of Tiberias, from which some twenty–twenty-five families had fled. And if the Khisas villagers could not be allowed to reap their crops, they should be separated—and treated differently—from the villagers of Qeitiya and Ja'una.[138]

---

[134] HHA Baruch Rabinov Papers, 'Report of an Investigation about the Transfer of the Arabs of the Villages of Khisas, Ja'una and Qeitiya', Lt. Colonel Baruch Rabinov to IDF CGS General Y. Dori, 30 Aug. 1949; and Morris, *Birth*, 242.

[135] Morris, *Birth*, 242.   [136] ND, 8 June 1949.

[137] ND, 10 June 1949.

[138] CZA, KKL 9/403 Nahmani to Ben-Gurion, 14 June 1949.

Nahmani was appalled by the 'cynicism' with which Yehoshu'a Palmon, the Prime Minister's adviser on Arab affairs, had responded to his queries about the treatment meted out to the Khisas's Arabs. 'Atiyeh Juwayid and his clansmen had put their lives on the line for the Yishuv, and now 'we are treating them like cattle. Little reason, then, to wonder why the Gentiles treated the Jews so—there is certainly no reason to blame them [for such behaviour] after we behave even worse.' Nahmani reached agreement with Palmon that the evictees from Khisas should be moved to Maghar. He also proposed that the evictees from Ja'una and Qeitiya be moved off the hillside and resettled in the houses of the empty village of 'Akbara.[139]

But the evacuees from Khisas never resettled in Maghar. It is probable that Maghar's (remaining) Druse inhabitants opposed the idea; perhaps the evictees themselves refused to resettle there. Be that as it may, in July, the evictees, led by 'Atiyeh, were still petitioning the Israeli authorities to get them off the empty hillside and allow them to return to their village. Given their long-standing relations with the Yishuv, they felt, they should not be treated like the 'other' Arabs who had been removed from the border areas. And they reasoned that the signing of the Israeli–Syrian General Armistice Agreement (20 July 1949) should enable Israel to drop its fears and let them return to their homes and land.[140] Nahmani was also persuaded: There was 'now no just reason or logic preventing 'Atiyeh Juwayid and his men from returning to their homes and lands.' It depended, he wrote to Palmon, only on his, Palmon's, 'will and decision'.[141] At the same time, 'Atiyeh and his band petitioned everyone they could think of—Prime Minister, President, Knesset members, IDF generals, etc.

But none of the appeals and petitions seemed to help. Perhaps the fact that the Khisas and Qeitiya lands were immediately taken over for cultivation by neighbouring kibbutzim was an important factor in the decision against their return to Khisas; perhaps it was

[139] ND, 18 June 1949; CZA, KKL 9/403: Nahmani to Palmon, 19 June 1949, and 'Summary from a Visit to the Village of 'Akbara in the Safad District on 18 June 1949', signed Y Nahmani, N. Alexandrovsky, A. Hanukki, I. Friedman, and Hillel Landsman.
[140] CZA, KKL 9/403, 'Atiyeh Juwayid to the Speaker of the Knesset, Yosef Sprinzak, 24 July 1949.
[141] CZA, KKL 9/403, Nahmani to Palmon, 18 Aug. 1949.

the authorities' fear of creating a precedent. All the evicted villagers, of Khisas, Qeitiya, and Ja'una, eventually moved into the dilapidated houses at 'Akbara.

But 'Atiyeh and his clansmen, ten–eleven families in all, for years continued to seek redress—to be allowed to return to Khisas or, at least, to be given a better alternative site. And 'Atiyeh and his fellow villagers still had an important card up their sleeve— they still owned plots of land in Khisas, which the JNF coveted. As they were not proper 'absentees', their lands could not (or could not easily), in law, be confiscated. A stand-off ensued.

But by 1952, 'Atiyeh and his men had had enough. They were ready to give up all claims to return to their native village and were willing to exchange their patrimony in Khisas for lands of the absentees from Maghar in Wadi Rubadiya.[142] Nahmani, apparently, was instrumental in persuading 'Atiyeh and his men to give up the dream of a return and to accept the offered compromise. At the same time, the Khisas evictees refused to move into empty houses in an existing Arab village because, as they argued, 'the Arabs continue to regard them as traitors and sinners against the Arab cause'.[143]

With 'Atiyeh's agreement to give up the Khisas lands, the way was open for a resolution of the problem. Nahmani met Ben-Gurion, and the Khisas evictees at last received lands for cultivation in Wadi Rubadiya in exchange for their holdings at Khisas. The ten families settled and built houses in Wadi Hamam, just South of Wadi Rubadiya, some 7 kilometres North-west of Tiberias. Most of the menfolk, by May 1952, had found employment in neighbouring Jewish settlements (Migdal, Genossar).[144]

Kirad al Baqqara and Kirid al Ghannama

The Israeli–Syrian General Armistice Agreement of July 1949 had set up a string of 'Demilitarized Zones' along the old international border. Neither country was sovereign in the DMZs, though all of them were in territory to the West (that is, on the Israeli side) of the old international frontier. A number of Arab villages were left

---

[142] CZA, KKL 9/403, Nahmani to Palmon, 19 Mar. 1952.
[143] CZA, KKL 9/403, Nahmani to Ben-Gurion, 25 May 1952.
[144] CZA, KKL 9/403: Nahmani to Ben-Gurion, 25 May 1952; and S. Atiyeh, JNF office, Haifa, to Y. Weitz, JNF, Jerusalem, 4 Apr. 1965.

in the zones, their property and, indeed, existence protected by the provisions of the agreement and its UN supervisors.

The following years saw an intermittent struggle between Israel and Syria over control of the DMZs. By 1956, the DMZs, in effect, were divided between the two countries, with Israel getting the lion's share (in line with its military preponderance).

In the course of the years-long struggle, Israel gradually pushed out the Arab inhabitants of the DMZs, mostly to Syria. The focus of the struggle was the central DMZ, just South of Lake Hula, with its two Arab villages of Kirad al Baqqara and Kirad al Ghannama (the prefatory 'Kirad' apparently attesting to the Kurdish origin of their inhabitants).

On 31 March 1951, in the midst of one bout of the battles for the DMZs, in fact, as part of it, the IDF forcibly transferred the inhabitants—some 765 souls, all told—of the two villages inland, to the partly empty Israeli Arab village of Sh'ab, near Acre. The transfer ignited Nahmani's imagination. Two days later he shot off a letter to Weitz proposing

to use [i.e. exploit] the situation to send out feelers to the Arab landowners [of the Kirads] . . . to check the possibility of reaching a land-sale agreement and that they move to Transjordan or, alternatively, [reach agreement] on an exchange of land so that they receive [other plots] in Israel in place of their lands in the DMZ.

The Hula Valley lands were, agriculturally, among the best in the country, and of strategic importance besides. Nahmani suggested sending an agent to Sh'ab to sound out the evictees.[145]

Apparently he got the go-ahead. Nahmani moved quickly. Hillel Landsman and Avraham Hanukki, both of Kibbutz Ayelet HaShahar, who in the past had had contact with their neighbours in the Kirads, travelled to Sh'ab. They were extremely unhappy with what they found there, complaining to the Military Government that 'many of [the evacuees] are hungry.' They urged the military authorities to supply the evacuees with bread and flour and to give back the Syrian money (or its Israeli equivalent) confiscated from the evictees. But the worst problem was water: Not enough had been supplied, and apparently the evictees were coming to blows around the single accessible well. Hanukki and

---

[145] CZA, KKL 9/227, Nahmani to Weitz, 2 Apr. 1951.

Landsman pointed out that 'nothing could be done with' the evictees (presumably in connection with persuading them to sell their lands and/or move out to Syria or Jordan) so long as they were hungry.[146] Hanukki, who returned to Ayelet HaShahar the following day, reported that there was 'no point in beginning any negotiation' with the Kirads evictees so long as their situation in Sh'ab was not improved.[147]

But Hanukki, pressed by Nahmani and Weitz, returned to Sh'ab the following month, with a mandate to try to persuade the evictees to permanently resettle in Sh'ab and to sell or exchange their lands. Weitz had been asked/instructed to approach Hanukki in the matter by the Prime Minister's Office, in the person of Palmon, the adviser on Arab affairs. Nahmani and Hanukki had agreed, on 21 May, to first seek out and approach those evacuees who were interested in staying on in Sh'ab and to have them sign declarations to this effect, and, if possible, to conclude on the spot land-purchase or exchange deals.[148]

But, arriving later that day in Nazareth, Hanukki met Palmon's representative, Goel Levitzky, and was surprised to discover that Palmon opposed any land-purchase deals with the Kirads Arabs. Palmon apparently felt that such deals—which would mean Israeli expenditure—were superfluous as the landowners had already been kicked off the land and the land had, *de facto*, become Israeli Government property. Why pay for something which could be had for nothing?

Despite the conflicting instructions, Hanukki persevered and went on to Sh'ab and Shfar-'Am, where the Kirads evacuees were now dispersed. He found that the Government was employing a whole range of coercive measures, including petty and not so petty persecution, to demoralize the evacuees and to get them to bend to the Government's will—'arbitrary arrests, dispersion among various villages, separation of families, separation of property-owners from their property (cattle and sheep) . . . threats . . .'. All these had 'embittered' the evacuees 'and turned them into open or covert haters' of Israel.

---

[146] CZA, KKL 9/271, Landsman and Hanukki to the Military Government representative, Sh'ab, 3 Apr. 1951 (17:30 hours).
[147] CZA, KKL 9/227, Nahmani to Weitz, 4 Apr. 1951.
[148] CZA, KKL 9/227, Hanukki to Galilee Office, JNF, 23 May 1951.

Hanukki was 'certain that these measures would not achieve their purpose [i.e. agreement to stay in Sh'ab and relinquish their lands in the Kirads], at any rate, not more than could be achieved by persuasion and constructive means'. He threatened to quit if the Military Government did not change tack.[149] Nahmani immediately asked Weitz to intercede with Palmon, apparently seen as responsible for Israeli policy *vis-à-vis* the Kirads (though, without doubt, given the sensitivity of the DMZ issue, it was sanctioned directly by Ben-Gurion).[150]

Weitz's approach to Palmon seemed to have some effect. The latter instructed IDF Northern Command and the Military Government 'to grant all waivers [i.e. assistance]' to the Tiberias office of the JNF in its effort to purchase land from the Kirads evacuees.[151] But Palmon's letter was deliberately obscure, and resulted (probably as intended) in no real change of Military Government policy on the ground. Indeed, the following day, 25 May, Hanukki met Palmon and Levitzky in Acre and discovered 'that they do not see a need to change the way [i.e. methods] they had employed' and did not regard purchasing the Kirads lands as particularly important. Palmon rejected Hanukki's request to be allowed to stay in the area seven–ten days to try to make contacts and personally negotiate with the Kirads landowners. 'I realized that they [i.e. Palmon and Levitzky] had no idea or understanding about the methods [which need to be used] to purchase land from Arabs, and perhaps were unwilling [indeed] that we do so,' reported Hanukki, and announced he was throwing in the towel.[152]

'It is difficult to understand the business. [It is] like a babble of tongues,' Nahmani complained (of Palmon and what appeared to be his duplicity) to Weitz.[153] Weitz may have tried again with Palmon, but nothing changed. Indeed, within weeks, UNTSO forced Israel to allow back to the DMZ those Kirads Arabs who wished to return. Most did so. Only a small number decided to stay on in Sh'ab.

---

[149] CZA, KKL 9/227, Hanukki to Galilee Office, JNF, 23 May 1951.
[150] CZA, KKL 9/227, Nahmani to Weitz, 24 May 1951.
[151] CZA, KKL 9/227, Palmon to IDF OC Northern Command, Military Government Branch, etc., 24 May 1951.
[152] CZA, KKL 9/227, Hanukki to JNF Tiberias Office, 25 May 1951.
[153] CZA, KKL 9/227, Nahmani to Weitz, 30 May 1951.

But the bad blood created during the summer between Nahmani and Palmon resulted in Palmon sending a strongly worded complaint about the JNF official to the JNF head office. Palmon was offended by criticism of his actions which had appeared in one of Nahmani's reports. Nahmani seems to have referred specifically to 'acts of violence' against the Kirads evacuees in Sh'ab. 'No one likes criticism against himself, even if it is just, and Palmon is no angel,' wrote Nahmani. Palmon, after all, had been the cause of the failure at Sh'ab.

The JNF men in all parts of the country, myself among them . . . during [the] tense, difficult, and long period of the Mandate which was hostile towards us, and while there was a strong and aggressive Arab nationalist movement, [knew how] to get along with the authorities and the Arabs, and [suceeded in] emptying Arab villages of their inhabitants, voluntarily, despite the fact that they were protected by the law then existing, and to establish on the lands of these villages Jewish settlements, and, without doubt, we would have known how to make use of our experience in negotiating with the Arab landowners in the Hula [Valley; i.e. the Kirads], had it not been for the interference of inexperienced elements, who have governmental powers . . .[154]

Nahmani apparently continued during the following years to try to purchase land from the evacuees from the Kirads who had stayed on in Sh'ab.[155] But it was the Palmon line which eventually determined the fate of the Kirads. In October–November 1956, during the Sinai Campaign, the IDF evicted the remaining inhabitants of the two villages. Most, apparently, were pushed across the Syrian border; a few joined their relatives already in Sh'ab. The lands that had belonged to the two villages became Israeli property and were transferred to the control of the Government's Development Authority. 'As the Arabs have moved to Syria, they are absentees and [so] their land must be transferred' to the state, ruled the JNF official responsible.[156]

---

[154] CZA, KKL 9/227, Nahmani to Weitz, 5 Sept. 1951.
[155] CZA, KKL 9/227, Hiram Danin to Palmon, 19 Sept. 1952.
[156] CZA, KKL 9/385, H. Danin to A. Danin, JNF, Haifa, 25 Nov. 1956; and E. L. M. Burns, *Between Arab and Israeli* (London, 1962), 115–18.

CONCLUSION

The story of Yosef Nahmani and, particularly, his diary for the years 1947–9, sheds substantial light on a number of important issues and events: Zionist attitudes and behaviour towards Palestine's Arabs in the course of the war; the battle for Tiberias; relations between the local- and national-level leaderships and between the civilian and military authorities and institutions within the Zionist camp; the JNF's activities and role during the war; and the Zionist establishment's attitudes and behaviour towards the new State of Israel's Arab minority in the war's aftermath. The tale also highlights just how difficult, on the ethical plane, was the life of a key Jewish official who dealt with Arab affairs during a bitter civil and conventional war.

Yosef Nahmani was probably as close as one could get to a personification of the Zionist enterprise in the crucial decades, from the turn of the century to the establishment of the state. While not one of its national leaders, he was certainly a nationally known and respected figure, and fulfilled a number of important state-building functions, to do with land, defence, and Arabs. What he thought at different times more or less reflected the evolution in Zionist establishment thinking, and what he did, he did as its agent and representative. Land-acquisition ('Redemption of the Land'); the expansion of the Yishuv; the dispossession of Arabs; and, implicitly or explicitly, various mutations of transfer was what Nahmani, and the Zionist enterprise, were largely about in the 1930s and 1940s.

With the start of 1948, a number of historical processes came to a head in one giant explosion. But Nahmani, like most of the Yishuv, accepted the UN partition resolution and the large Arab minority earmarked for the prospective Jewish state that went with it. His desire to reduce its numbers was natural and understandable—but it was not comprehensive. At least for a time, he abandoned the notion of a general, agreed, voluntary transfer. The Jewish state would have to cope as best it could. As the war unfolded, he repeatedly bemoaned and berated Haganah behaviour, arguing that it would becloud future Jewish–Arab relations in the new state. He was particularly disturbed by what was happening on his home turf, in Tiberias: The Arab community wanted peace; the Haganah was behaving provocatively and pushing the Arabs into the hands of the war-mongers and extremists; it would all end badly. In the end came the explosion, and Tiberias, overnight, turned into a wholly Jewish city; the same was to happen in the rest of Eastern Galilee during the following weeks and months. Nahmani fairly quickly accepted this turn of events. By July, he was a clear opponent of a Palestinian refugee return.

But Nahmani, an important local figure in Eastern Galilee in general and in Tiberias in particular, for weeks and months seemed to function in a highly local manner and context, dissociated from the national framework of events and policies. It seemed for a while—in January–March 1948—to judge from Nahmani's words and actions, that Tiberias was cut off from the rest of Palestine and that its troubles unfolded in complete isolation. While Nahmani occasionally was in contact with the Yishuv's national leaders—Ben-Gurion, Shitrit, Yisrael Galili— he was by and large kept in ignorance of changes in national Yishuv policy and strategy with respect to the Palestinian Arabs, Tiberias, and important land-matters. He believed that Ben-Gurion was interested in 'limiting the conflagration' and keeping the Galilee quiet for months after this was true. He had no awareness of the Haganah's shift to the offensive in the first half of April 1948 or of its decision to conquer Arab Tiberias—and, in consequence, thought and did things which were out of kilter. For weeks after the Yishuv's leadership had more or less decided—at the end of April, start of May—to bar an Arab refugee return, Nahmani was still open to the idea of an Arab return to Tiberias. He was similarly out of step, months later, at least for a time, during the Khisas and Kirads transfer operations.

If Nahmani's divorce from national-level thinking, decisions, and policy was an occasional source of trouble and confusion, both for himself and with respect to the matters with which he dealt, his ignorance of and divorce from realities and developments in the security realm, during the war, was profound. He lived through most of the first half of the war with an (unjustified) depressing feeling of Jewish weakness and Arab strength, which to some degree guided or misguided his attitudes and actions. He frequently expressed himself, before April 1948, in terms of the impending 'annihilation' of the Jewish community. This feeling underlay, at least in part, his conciliatory approach towards the Arabs of Tiberias and his continuous castigation of the Haganah's provocative behaviour in the city as well as in the rural hinterland of Eastern Galilee. He attributed the breakdown of Jewish–Arab amity in Tiberias during February–early April 1948 mainly to trigger-happy Jewish troopers and officers, and 'primitive' and aggressive Sephardi townspeople. Like other civilian leaders in Tiberias and Eastern Galilee, Nahmani was not kept abreast of military developments by the local or Haganah national command, nor, usually, was he consulted in advance of specific actions. Indeed, the divorce was so complete that in summer 1948 he was not even informed in advance of or invited to the establishment ceremony of the Jewish settlement near Blida (Kibbutz Yiftah)— for which the JNF was forking out half the bill! No doubt this also reflected the growing marginalization within the burgeoning state bureaucracy of the JNF. During the final battle for Tiberias, in mid-April, we find Nahmani pulling in one direction—conciliation, coexistence, and the institution of a permanent cease-fire—while the Haganah has already decided on non-negotiation and decisive conquest.

The story of intercommunal relations in Tiberias between December 1947 and April 1948, as it emerges through the prism of Nahmani's diary entries, seriously throws into question the portrayal in traditional, 'Old' Zionist historiography of a peace-minded Jewish community prodded into militancy and conquest only by Arab provocation and extremism. It is possible that the pattern in Tiberias was not unique, and that at least to some degree it faithfully reflected developments during the December 1947–April 1948 period elsewhere in Palestine. There is need here for a great deal of impartial, detailed, local research.

Nahmani, to judge from his diary entries and correspondence, had a well-developed moral sense, which was repeatedly offended by Jewish military behaviour towards the Arabs in his region, starting with the December 1947 raid on Khisas, running through the IDF atrocities of October 1948, and ending with the eviction from Khisas in June 1949. His diaries are highly revealing about the 'dark side' of Israel's 'war of establishment'—the killing and

massacre of Arab civilians (at Khisas, Al Huseiniya, Khirbet Nasir
ad Din, Safsaf, Saliha, and Eilaboun); the expulsions; and the
pillage and looting that accompanied almost each Jewish conquest
of an Arab urban neighbourhood and town. On occasion, as with
(Galileean) Majdal and Khisas, Nahmani went out of his way
to try to protect Arab rural communities faced with Jewish
depredation.

Yet, for some perhaps unaccountably, Nahmani never really
traced connections between these events and his own beliefs
and activities, which for decades were geared to the gradual,
relentless dispossession—albeit 'voluntary' or semi-voluntary, by
legal means, and with appropriate pecuniary compensation—of
the Arab landowner, fellah, and tenant-farmer. Back in the late
1930s and early 1940s, he had supported a general transfer solution
to the prospective problem of the large Arab minority in the future
Jewish state. At the start of 1948, he moderated this to be
implemented only with respect to Maghrebi villagers, large
landowners, and tenant-farmers. But by the war's end, he was
again bent on transfer—legal and compensated, but transfer none
the less—with respect to as many of Israel's Arabs as would be
willing to go. This was the point of his repeated 'buy out and
transfer' proposals and of his actions with respect to the villagers
of Kirad al Ghannama and Kirad al Baqqara. Where his (moral)
sensibilities led to divergence from the views held by some of the
national leadership was over method: Hence his clash with the
'cynical' (in Nahmani's phrase) Yehoshua Palmon, the Prime
Minister's Arab affairs adviser and executive officer, over the
Kirads. Nahmani wanted to use suasion and blandishment, and
was willing to pay the villagers to agree to move to Syria or
inland to Sh'ab; Palmon (and, apparently, Ben-Gurion) preferred
persecution and coercion, and thought the way of persuasion and
purchase a waste of money and time. But the ultimate objective
was the same. Nahmani and Palmon were at one about the need to
transfer the Arabs of the Kirads.

However, Nahmani always maintained a soft spot in his heart
for Arabs who had co-operated or collaborated with the Zionist
enterprise—and frequently flailed the establishment's attitude of
'use and discard when finished' towards its helpers in the Arab
camp. He bewailed and protested against the treatment of the

'friendly' clan at Khisas in Summer 1949, and for years made sincere efforts to alleviate their plight—and ultimately succeeded. But here too, there was a measure of change and conformism in Nahmani's attitude. At first he demanded the evictees' return and resettlement in Khisas; but, within weeks, he bowed to Ben-Gurion's will and accepted the transfer, demanding only that the evictees' be properly and comfortably resettled, not left to languish on a barren hillside under a hot sun.

The essential dualism of Nahmani's thoughts and actions during 1947–9 leaves one with a paradox and a sense of wonder—and with a pointer to one of the keys to Zionism's success. And this is true on two levels: The conciliatory 'soft-line' rendered Zionism acceptable to the world community and world Jewry, and won their support; the 'hard-line' led to concrete, physical success in the encounter with the disunited surrounding Arab communities and world, who understood, and retreated before, superior power, efficiently wielded. At the same time, the coexistence in the Zionist 'soul', as in the Zionist establishment in general, of a morally sensitive 'soft-line' and an activist, security-minded 'hard-line', while occasionally confusing and disruptive, gave the Zionist enterprise an inner strength, certainty of purpose, and sureness of its essential justice that made it (relatively) unstoppable.

Fig. 3. Haifa in the 1940s

rmel

0   200   400   600   800 metres

Carmelite Sisters
Convent

French   Colony

Carmelites
Monastery

Stella Maris

BBAS STREET

Zeitoun

Kiryat
Eliahu

Templar or
German Colony

Bat Galim

Mediterranean Sea

See overleaf for FIG. 3: Map of Haifa in the 1940s.

6

Haifa's Arabs: Displacement and Concentration, July 1948

Before 1948, Haifa had had a population of 140,000—about half Arab and half Jewish. During the first months of the war, thousands of prosperous and middle-class Arab families fled the city. Tens of thousands more fled Haifa during and immediately after the Haganah conquest of the city's Arab neighbourhoods in April 1948. By July, only some 3,500 of the city's original Arab inhabitants remained.

During that summer, Haifa's remaining Arab inhabitants lived in political limbo. Although the city was part of Israel, by virtue of the United Nations General Assembly Partition Resolution of 29 November 1947 and in consequence of the Haganah's victory of 21–2 April 1948, a lack of clarity prevailed because of the continued presence in the town and its environs—the triangle bounded by Atlit, Ramat David, and Kurdani—of substantial British forces in this last enclave of the Mandate.

During the first week of May, after the battle and mass exodus, the Haganah withdrew the bulk of its troops from the city. The remaining Arab families scattered around the city enjoyed a period of relative calm. But immediately after the completion of the British military's evacuation of Haifa on 1 July, most of the city's remaining Arabs were ordered by the Israeli military governor, Major Rehav'am Amir (Zabledovsky), to pack their belongings, leave their homes, and 'concentrate' in the downtown Wadi Nisnas neighbourhood. A major eviction and moving operation, overseen and carried out by the IDF, got under way, and within ten days almost all the dispersed Arab families were summarily moved and installed in abandoned Arab houses and flats in Wadi Nisnas and along Abbas Street, a second and smaller area of concentration.

Why and how the concentration was carried out will be examined in the following pages. The examination, it is hoped, will shed light on Israeli attitudes and policies toward the Palestinian Arabs during 1948, and on the manner in which the civilian and military authorities of the new-born Israeli state reached and carried out decisions.

PLANS AND PROPOSALS FOR RELOCATION

The idea of concentrating Haifa's Arabs can be traced to a visit to
Haifa by David Ben-Gurion, the Jewish Agency chairman and
Prime Minister-designate on 1–2 May 1948. According to Yosef
Vashitz, a high-ranking member of Mapam and the Arab affairs
correspondent of the party's daily, *al-Hamishmar*, Ben-Gurion had
spoken during that visit of 'his plan regarding the future of the
Arabs of Haifa: (*a*) Their number would not exceed 15,000; (*b*)
two-thirds would be Christians, one-third Moslems; (*c*) all the
Christians would be concentrated in Wadi Nisnas; (*d*) the Moslems
would be concentrated in the Wadi Salib neighbourhood.'[1] According
to Vashitz, who was on the spot, during May and June local Haifa
Haganah / IDF officers tried to persuade Arab families dispersed
around the city to return to, or move to, Wadi Nisnas. 'The plan to
concentrate the Arabs was known to all the commanders,' Vashitz
wrote.[2] But not only the military were interested in concentrating
Haifa's Arabs. In late May, Avraham Ye'eli, the secretary of
Haifa's Arab Affairs Committee, informed his colleagues that he
had submitted a memorandum to Major Amir 'concerning the
delineation of boundaries for Arab residence'. The committee
would 'be able to act' once Amir 'gave his reply'.[3] The Haifa Arab
Affairs Committee had been appointed on 24 April 1948 by Tuvia
Arazi, a senior Haifa Haganah Intelligence Service officer. The
committee was composed of leading Haifa Jews who had Arab
connections and a knowledge of Arab affairs and was set up to look
after the interests of the city's Arab population. It was, in effect, a
subcommittee of the Situation Committee, the supreme authority in
Jewish Haifa until 21–2 April and a major advisory body thereafter.
The Arab Affairs Committee acted as an advisory body and, on

---

[1] HHA–ACP 10.95.10 (4), Vashitz to Secretariat of Mapam Centre (Tel Aviv),
5 July 1948. Ben-Gurion's plan for Haifa was to reverberate in internal Mapam
discussions for months. For example, Mapam's co-leader, Meir Ya'ari, on 26 July
1948, at a meeting of the party's leading military commanders and security officials,
spoke of Mapai's plan to leave '12,000' Arabs in Haifa. HHA, see M. Ya'ari at
,'Meeting of Mapam Defence Activists (protocols)', 26 July 1948.
[2] HHA–ACP 10.95.10 (4), 5 July 1948.
[3] ISA, JM, 5667/gimel, 25/2. 'Protocol of the Fifth Meeting of the Arab Affairs
Committee, Haifa', 27 May 1948.

occasion, as an executive body affiliated with and subordinate to the Haganah command in the city.

Ye'eli's interest, at least initially, in 'concentrating' Haifa's Arabs was not motivated by hostility or prejudice. Rather, he linked the need for concentrating the Arabs to a possible return of the Haifa Arab refugees to their former homes—about which, apparently, he was keeping an open mind. He put it this way:

It can be said against us [that is, the Haifa Arab Affairs Committee] that we have still not determined exactly within what boundaries we are willing to allow the Arabs to live in Wadi Nisnas and in Wadi Salib. Of course, the Arabs are not returning [to Haifa] for their own reasons, and from the statements of the people with whom we are in contact it is possible to understand that the reasons [for the Arabs not returning] are not linked [to the problem of the delineation of the Arab pale of residence in Haifa].

Ye'eli went on to explain that Arabs were not returning to Haifa because they feared that the Arab states intended to bomb the city and because they hoped to return on the coat-tails of a victorious Transjordanian Arab Legion. Still others, according to Ye'eli, 'were afraid to return because of the desolation prevailing in the [abandoned Arab districts of the city]'.[4]

But Ye'eli's explanation notwithstanding, the desire of the Jewish civil and military authorities to concentrate Haifa's remaining Arab population in one or two limited areas was in no way connected to a wish to see a return to the city of its tens of thousands of refugees. Rather the contrary was the case. By dint of the Arab evacuation during the last week of April, Haifa, almost overnight, had become a 'Jewish' city. The abandoned Arab neighbourhoods lay open and ready to accommodate the tens of thousands of Jewish immigrants now arriving at Israeli ports; a massive return of Arab refugees to Haifa would have meant many fewer houses for the newcomers.

But it was primarily security considerations that dictated the concentration of Haifa's Arab population. Collectively, Palestinians represented a potential fifth column inside the new-born state that was struggling for its life against invading Arab armies on three fronts. Individually, the Arab populace could produce anti-Israeli

---

[4] Ibid. Ye'eli was being less than frank here when implying that the Arabs, at this time, were not returning to Haifa because they simply did not want to. Many probably did not want to return, but others who did were barred from doing so by the Haganah.

spies, saboteurs, and subversives. The restriction of the 3,000 to 4,000-strong Arab community to one or two clearly defined small areas of habitation would vastly simplify the task of the Israeli security apparatus and substantially decrease the amount of manpower needed by the Haganah / IDF to 'supervise' the community. Haifa's Arabs, moreover, were now defenceless, prey to depredation, intimidation, and assault by such Jewish extremist groups as the IZL and LHI and by Jewish and Arab criminals. Concentrating the community would enable the Haganah / IDF and police to protect them more effectively. It was also felt that isolated Arab families dispersed in mainly Jewish districts or in largely abandoned Arab districts would feel more comfortable if moved to an all-Arab, fully populated neighbourhood. Problems of supplies and employment for the Arabs could also be more easily solved. 'Ghettoization' seemed to afford a simple, quick solution.

The solution, however, could not be effected while British troops remained in control of the last Mandate enclave in Haifa. This enclave was made up of several districts, including the German colony and the Carmelite Monastery of Stella Maris, in which some Arabs lived. The final departure of the British at the end of June 1948 served as a catalyst for Jewish plans to concentrate the remaining Arabs. As Ye'eli reported to a meeting of the Arab Affairs Committee on 1 July, it 'was clear to all of us that with the final departure of the English from Haifa, we would face [the problem of] moving the Arabs [to Wadi Nisnas and, if need be, to part of Wadi Salib]'.

On 1 July, the IDF General Staff ordered the Haifa District Command to carry out the transfer and concentration operation within five days. The army clearly wanted the operation completed before the end of the First Truce, on 8 July, when general hostilities were expected to resume. The order, as transmitted by Major Amir to the Arab Affairs Committee, specified concentrating the Arabs in one area only—Wadi Nisnas. The order caught the committee and Ye'eli by surprise. While he continued to believe that it was 'justified to concentrate the Arabs in one place both from the point of view of the military good and for their own welfare', he resented the speed and abruptness of the order and the fact that 'we were not consulted at all'. This cast doubt on the need for the continued existence of the Arab Affairs Committee. The members would have to make a 'spiritual reckoning', Ye'eli felt. 'One cannot gather up

3,000 persons like eggs. After all, there exist decades-old links between the Jews and many of the Arabs here. In the hastiness of the eviction, how will severe damage to and subversion of these links be avoided?' asked Ye'eli.

Ye'eli agreed that the army had to take into account its own interests—meaning security—'but in such matters it also ought to hear the opinion of others, [and on] how to carry out the thing in a satisfactory manner . . .'. Ye'eli noted that the IDF order asked the Arab Affairs Committee to 'assist in its implementation. But [the committee] was not given any opportunity to give its opinion about the operation it was being asked to carry out.' The army required that the committee provide accurate information about the number of Arabs and their location and about available housing in Wadi Nisnas, and assist in organizing workers and transport for the removal operation. Ye'eli concluded by saying that the committee, especially in light of the opening in Haifa of an office of the Ministry for Minority Affairs, had lost its *raison d'être* and must now weigh whether there was any point in its continued existence.

Vashitz, an Arabist and a committee member who lived in a kibbutz south of Haifa, thought that the committee should continue to exist, if only because the army in Haifa lacked an authoritative adviser on Arab affairs and would fail to take political problems into consideration. As for the eviction order, Vashitz felt that, given the five-day time limit to its implementation, there was 'no possibility of its being carried out in a humane manner', or perhaps at all. It would be preferable, he remarked bitterly, 'to say to the Arabs of Haifa that we regard them as enemies on whom we cannot depend and therefore—we should make them [all] prisoners of war'.

Haifa lawyer Naftali Lifshitz, the Trustee of Enemy Property and a committee member, said that he was 'sorry about the decision [to concentrate the Arabs] which would cause us harm in the wide world'. He saw no point, however, in appealing the order, because it would doubtless do no good. It was better to focus immediately on the task at hand, he said, and organize 'some 50 trucks [and] a lot of inspectors and labourers . . . and act swiftly', making sure that Arab interests would be protected. The meeting concluded with a statement by Major Amir, who was clearly embarrassed by the tone of the committee's criticism of the IDF order. He countered that the committee members had long known of the plan to concentrate the

Arabs. 'It was spoken of more than once', he said. The army had
allotted five days for the operation and 'twelve hours [had] already
gone by since the order was received . . . You will be responsible if
there is a hitch', he told the committee. The 1 July meeting wound
up with the Arab Affairs Committee reluctantly agreeing to assist
the army in the transfer operation in order to make it as clean and
humane as possible.[5]

The leaders of Haifa's Arab community, who included Deputy
Mayor Salah Shihadeh, Victor Khayyat (a millionaire, Spain's
honorary consul in the city, and a US citizen), and Tawfiq Tubi (a
lawyer and communist activist), were summoned to Amir's office
on the evening of 1 July. There they were informed of the plan—to
concentrate the Christians in Wadi Nisnas and the Muslims in Wadi
Salib. Amir led off by stating that he did not know Arabic and would
let Ye'eli explain what was happening. Ye'eli then conveyed the gist
of the IDF order to move the Arabs living in the Carmelite Monastery,
the Germany colony, and other districts to Wadi Nisnas 'to be
implemented by the fifth of (July)'. He asked the Arab representatives to assist in carrying out the operation, so that it could be
completed smoothly. The Arabs immediately protested. Tubi said:
'I see no reason, even military, that necessitates such a step. As I see
it, this is a political rather than military problem. The intention is to
create an Arab ghetto in Haifa. This was not expected by those who
remained here and accepted the existing regime . . . We expected
different treatment . . . We ask that the people [be allowed to]
remain in their places.' Bulus Farah (a Nazareth-born communist
leader) charged: 'This is racism! . . . If there are elements you are
afraid of—take steps to concentrate them, but [do not take steps]
against everybody.'

Amir. I see that you sit here and give me advice. But you were
    invited here in order to hear the Haganah [*sic*, IDF] Command's
    order and to provide assistance! I do not interfere with or take
    part in politics. I only implement orders. During [the past weeks]
    . . . I did all I could in these warlike circumstances to improve the
    conditions of life . . . [But] this is war [and] . . . I must carry out
    orders! I must make sure that this is carried out by the fifth of the
    month . . . I want this work to be carried out by people you

[5] ISA, JM 5667/gimel, 25/2, 'Protocol of the Seventh Meeting of the Arab Affairs
Committee, Haifa', 1 July 1948.

appoint and I will give them assistance . . . Though I am a soldier, I also have a heart and it pains me if someone is harmed unnecessarily. I understand and it pains me when a person must be uprooted from a place where he has lived for decades. But what can one do? I don't want to get into an argument because this is not my job. I flatly reject what was said about a 'ghetto' because this is not true. I do not intend to close off the area and seal it with barbed wire . . . No! People will continue their normal lives, but they will be concentrated in one place.

The meeting continued as follows:

Tubi. I take it that the decision is final and cannot be changed. We therefore waive argument, but has the commander considered that there are families that cannot afford the expenses of transfer . . .?

Amir. Tomorrow morning we will deal with the technical matters. I will take care of the vehicles and the benzine, but the people will pay [the other transfer expenses] . . . It is best for you that the matter end quickly, so long as it is in my charge . . .

Shihadeh. There are also Moslems.

Amir. The Moslems will be concentrated in Wadi Salib easily. There are only 174 Moslem families.

Ye'eli. Afterwards [you] will value this operation and see that the concentration is beneficial to you. When the schools open and life proceeds normally, you will learn that all this was only for your benefit. Now you see the thing as a sudden blow. Through the concentration you will also enjoy protection against robbery.[6]

On 3 July, a deputation led by the Greek Catholic Archbishop of Haifa and the Galilee, Georges Hakim, went to see Cyril Marriott, the British consul-general in Haifa, to protest the operation, which had already begun, and to attempt to mobilize British support to stop it.

'I hope it has never been your misfortune to receive a deputation in the circumstances in which I received the Arab deputation this evening', Marriott cabled the Foreign Office. The deputation, which included a number of clerics apart from Hakim, told Marriott that they had come to him because he represented 'his Brittanic Majesty, one of whose titles is Defender of the Faith (most of the

---

[6] Quoted from Tom Segev, *1949 Hayisra'elim Harishonim* (1949 The First Israelis) (Jerusalem: Domino Press, 1984), 69–71. Segev obtained from Amir a copy of a protocol of the 1 July 1948 meeting between Amir and Ye'eli and the Arab notables.

Arabs remaining in Haifa are Christians)' and because 'they now have nobody else to whom to turn'.[7]

Marriott was very angry with the Jewish authorities. He cabled London: 'In spite of [Jewish] assurances since the truce . . . that Arabs who choose to stay would have equal rights with other law-abiding citizens[,] Jewish military commander of Haifa has ordered the concentration of Arabs in Wadi Nisnas and Wadi Salib.' He noted that the operation had begun, with Arab refugee families encamped on the grounds of the Carmelite Monastery of Stella Maris being forcibly evicted and the area occupied by Israeli troops. Marriott complained that one of the consulate's clerks, Hazou, and a British passport-holder, Zammot, had both been ordered out of their homes. He subsequently complained to Haifa Mayor Shabtai Levy, and these particular evictions were stayed.

Marriott then persuaded Captain Eddy, the representative in Haifa of the UN mediator for Palestine, to meet the Arab deputation. Marriott and his American counterpart, Aubrey Lippincott, also took part in the meeting. Marriott had persuaded the Arabs to appeal to the UN representative not on 'humanitarian and sentimental grounds', but on the grounds that the eviction operation was a breach of the UN-sponsored First Truce then prevailing between Israel and the Arab states. Eddy, however, responded that he did not think a truce violation had been committed. Marriott demurred. 'The action of the Jews was a military action with a military purpose . . . I was satisfied that the Arabs were being moved to the [Wadi Nisnas] quarter where they would be a fire screen for the Jews. There was therefore a change in the military situation to the advantage of the Jews'—hence, a violation of the truce.

Marriott urged London to allocate a ship, the *Ocean Vigour*, for use by the '1,000' Arabs he believed now wanted to leave Haifa and embark for Beirut.[8] Marriott, and perhaps the Arab community leaders as well, were worried about the possibility of Arab air attacks after the termination of the truce. Wadi Nisnas and Wadi Salib, he cabled London, 'are near the Jewish quarter and apparently the intention of the [Jewish] military commander is to surround the Jewish inhabitants with Arabs so that these parts of the town may be

---

[7] PRO, FO 371–68568 E8994/4/31, C. Marriott to Foreign Office, 3 July 1948.
[8] PRO, FO 371–68568 E8963/4/31, C. Marriott to Foreign Office, 3 July 1948.

spared attack by air . . .'[9] That same day, in another cable, Marriott elaborated: 'There may be few survivors from the massacre I foresee . . .'.[10] While Marriott's language was characterized as 'somewhat forthright and outspoken' by senior Foreign Office official Lance Thirkell, the 'action of the Jews' in concentrating Haifa's Arabs and the eviction of the families from the Carmelite Monastery was seen as 'going a little too far'. Thirkell felt that the Israeli action should be 'questioned on humanitarian grounds', although he dismissed the idea that the UN mediator could or would do anything about it.[11]

As for Marriott's proposal to supply a British evacuation vessel, Thirkell recommended approaching the Ministry of Transport. A Foreign Office official, J. G. S. Beith, contacted a Transport Ministry official, who ruled that the *Ocean Vigour* was not available as it had previously been used 'for the transport of Jewish illegal immigrants' and was scheduled for refitting. In general, Beith thought that it would be 'far more suitable' for the Arab states to do 'something by way of shipping' rather than Britain, especially as there would be a question of 'where the refugees should go. If we took them off in a British ship, we should have to make arrangements for their reception in some Arab country.' In short, while Marriott's 'concern for these unfortunate Arabs [is] understandable,' said Beith, 'it is not desirable that HMG should involve themselves in this matter. . . . The question of succouring Arab refugees is a matter primarily for the Arab states. Should they wish to charter a British ship . . . we should, I think, agree but that is as far as we should go . . .'.[12]

Harold Beeley, another senior Foreign Office official, more or less concurred. He wrote that it was 'unlikely' that the Jews would agree to an Arab ship entering Haifa harbor to take out refugees and rejected Marriott's request for a British ship.[13] In the event, no

[9] Ibid, and 371–68568 E8994/4/31, C. Marriott to Foreign Office, 3 July 1948. Marriott's 'military geography' makes little sense. Placing Arabs in Wadi Nisnas and Wadi Salib would hardly have 'surrounded' the main Jewish areas of the city, which were to the south and up the slopes of Mount Carmel.

[10] Ibid. Marriott's appreciation of Arab air-power was greatly exaggerated and wholly undeserved. Arab aerial performance was poor in the extreme in the weeks after 15 May and was far from posing a serious threat to any city in Israel.

[11] PRO, FO 371–68568 E8963/4/31, Minute by Lance Thirkell, 6 July 1948.

[12] Ibid., Minute by J. G. S. Beith, 6 July 1948.

[13] Ibid., Minute by H. Beeley, 9 July 1948.

ship was needed. Although a few more Arab families may have left Haifa, the eviction to Wadi Nisnas did not precipitate a new mass exodus. The Haifa Arabs' appeals to Britain and to the United Nations had failed to halt the operation.

The Arabs then pursued a new avenue of appeal—to Haifa's mayor, Shabtai Levy, who, on 22 April, had issued the dramatic appeal from the Jewish side to the Arabs not to evacuate the city.

On 4 July, Levy cabled the Minister for Minority Affairs, Bechor Shitrit: 'In relation to the concentration of the Arabs in Haifa in one neighbourhood, in Wadi Nisnas alone, it is necessary that you come immediately for a few hours to Haifa.'[14] Shitrit's mandate was the welfare of the country's non-Jewish minority communities. He was informed of the eviction operation belatedly, apparently after it had begun. That day, either just before or just after receiving Levy's cable, Shitrit raised the matter in the Cabinet, submitting a question about 'the isolation of the Arabs in Haifa and Jaffa in special neighbourhoods'. (He also asked that day about a 'mass arrest of Arab villagers' and the destruction of Arab villages).[15] Ben-Gurion, as Defence Minister, responsible for the IDF, apparently ignored the question. The following day, Shitrit cabled Levy that he had raised the matter in Cabinet, but that there was 'no decision yet'.[16] 'No decision' meant failure, as the operation proceeded apace. Mayor Levy seems to have been troubled less by the operation itself than by its restriction of the Arabs mainly to the one area of Wadi Nisnas. Initially, he probably believed that the Arabs were to be moved to the two districts, in line with the original plans.

If Levy's appeal to Shitrit had failed, his intercession at the same time on the local level with Haifa IDF officers seems to have been successful. The eviction order against the wealthy Arab inhabitants of the Abbas quarter overlooking the German Colony was rescinded (probably on 4 July). According to Vashitz, the army initially agreed to allow only the wealthy residents of the area to stay put, but Vashitz intervened and succeeded in persuading Major Amir to adopt an 'egalitarian' approach. Some 50 per cent of the houses and

---

[14] HMA, 1374, S. Levy (Haifa) to B. Shitrit (Tel Aviv), 4 July 1948.
[15] KMA–AZP 9.9.1., 'Agenda for the Cabinet Meeting, 4 July 1948'.
[16] HMA, 1374, B. Shitrit (Tel Aviv) to S. Levy (Haifa), 5 July 1948.

flats in the Abbas quarter were then allocated to lower-class Arabs, who were chiefly from other districts.[17]

Thus, the plan to concentrate Haifa's remaining Arabs went through three stages: first, concentration in the two quarters of Wadi Nisnas and Wadi Salib, based on religious affiliation; second, concentration only in Wadi Nisnas; and third, concentration mainly in Wadi Nisnas, with an additional smaller area in the nearby Abbas quarter. When precisely Wadi Salib was dropped from the plan is unclear.

'GHETTOIZATION'

The transfer and relocation of the Arabs in and around Haifa—some 720 families—to Wadi Nisnas and Abbas Street began on 2 July and ended on 9 July. It was supervised by the Haifa Arab Affairs Committee, with trucks and troops supplied by the IDF. The Ministry for Minority Affairs, which in theory should have been involved, preferred to stand aside from what it obviously regarded as an unpleasant affair. Moshe Yitah, its newly appointed Haifa representative, made it clear to Ye'eli 'that he did not want to . . . cooperate in the transfer of Arabs as the start of the Ministry of Minority Affairs' activities in [Haifa]'.[18]

On 8 July, with the transfer almost complete, Vashitz and Ye'eli briefed the Arab Affairs Committee, in what the members had decided would be its last meeting; they had voted earlier for dissolution. At the meeting Ye'eli reported that the grounds of the Carmelite Monastery had been completely evacuated, Wadi Carmel 'almost completely', Wadi Jamal and Zaitun 'completely', the German Colony 'in large measure', and the old market-place 'completely'. He believed that the entire evacuation could be completed with a bit of effort within 'a few days'. The Jewish authorities—the Arab Affairs Committee, the IDF, and the municipality, all of which had lent various types of assistance—were also helped in carrying out the operation by an *ad hoc* eight-man committee of Arab notables, selected by each Arab community. It was composed of four Christian priests representing the different

---

[17] HHA–ACP 10.95.10 (4), Y. Vashitz (Haifa) to Secretariat of Mapam Centre (Tel Aviv), 5 July 1948.

[18] ISA, JM 5667/gimel, 25/2, 'Protocol of the Eighth Meeting of the Arab Affairs Committee (Haifa), 8 July 1948'.

denominations, with the Greek Catholic priest, Butrous Fakhouri, acting as committee chairman, and four secular members, including the two communist activists, Bulus Farah and Tawfiq Tubi, and Haifa's deputy mayor, Salah Shihadeh; Victor Khayyat acted as liaison between the committee and the Jewish authorities. The Arab committee's task was to oversee the removals and to allocate housing in Wadi Nisnas and the Abbas quarter.

Throughout the transfer, the members of the Arab Affairs Committee remained unhappy with the operation but carried it out to the best of their ability in the knowledge that, if they stood aside, the IDF would perform it in a manner that the Arabs would find still more unpleasant. In the middle of the operation, on either 6 or 7 July, the security authorities called a one-day halt and mounted a search for hidden arms among the Arabs. The operation's complexity, the late start, the originally planned five-day span, and the loss of a day in arms searches meant that most of the transfer was carried out in great haste and without even minimal preparation of the flats in Wadi Nisnas and, to a lesser extent, the houses in Abbas Street. 'The flats are filthy, like the streets. There is no water, no electricity, and there are no locks on the doors. There is no time to properly arrange the allocation of flats', Vashitz wrote on 5 July. In mid-operation, there was also a crisis over who was to bear the cost of the operation. 'The army says the Arabs must pay. The Arab [Affairs] Committee has the funds for it but these were impounded by the Minister of Finance and [the committee] is not empowered to spend the money. In effect, every side assumes that someone else will pay.' (The committee's funds derived from the proceeds of sold, abandoned Arab property.)[19]

The Arabs, according to Vashitz, were 'negative' about the whole operation. There was a natural reluctance to be evicted from one's home. Moreover, 'among the simple people, rumours abounded that the Arabs were being concentrated in order to slaughter them more easily, that this [that is, the ghetto] was a prison, etc. The leftists [among the Arabs] opposed [the operation arguing] that this was a political-racist operation and not [a military necessity, and was] designed to create an Arab ghetto in Haifa.'[20] Ye'eli, however,

[19] HHA–ACP 10.95.10 (4), Y. Vashitz (Haifa) to Secretariat of Mapam Centre (Tel Aviv), 5 July 1948.
[20] Ibid.

thought, or said he thought, otherwise. He was 'happy to note', on 8 July, 'that by the decision to settle Arabs also in Abbas Street the cogency of the contention regarding [the creation of] a ghetto was undermined as Abbas Street was not linked geographically at all to Wadi Nisnas'. But there remained the 'danger', according to Ye'eli, that the housing in Wadi Nisnas would be sufficient to accommodate all the Arabs in Haifa, thus making transfers to Abbas Street unnecessary. Ye'eli feared that, in that event, the army would insist that the Arabs be restricted to Wadi Nisnas alone, again raising the spectre of a 'ghetto'. 'I will demand from Rehav'am [Amir] that he fulfil the promise that he gave that he will widen the boundaries [of the Arab "pale of settlement", presumably to include Abbas Street].'[21]

Ye'eli and Vashitz had played leading roles in softening the blow of the transfer and concentration operation. But they disagreed on the operation's purpose and purport. Vashitz was convinced that its roots lay in Ben-Gurion's plans of early May, which were political in motivation and character—'a political act, aimed at creating a ghetto . . . while exploiting an appropriate military moment (*she'at kosher tzva'it*), which partially justifies the operation.'[22] Ye'eli thought that the operation was

essentially military [in nature], and it is also of benefit to the Arabs themselves. For weeks before the Army took the decision, I tried to persuade the Arabs voluntarily to concentrate and, by so doing, many of their affairs [that is, problems] would have sorted themselves out more easily. But they did not agree. Rumours were spread among them that they would be used as hostages; for example, if there was no water in [Jewish] Jerusalem [which depended on water pumped via Transjordanian-held Latrun], we would cut off their water and suchlike.

Ye'eli also remarked that while members of the *ad hoc* Arab transfer committee spoke in contacts with Jews of 'ghettoization', they 'denied this' when speaking of the concentration operation to their Arab constituency.[23]

Initially, the plan had been to settle Christians and Muslims separately. But this plan was scrapped when 'it became clear that there weren't many Moslems [left in Haifa] and that those who had remained were ready to go to Wadi Nisnas', Vashitz said. He

[21] ISA, JM 5667/gimel, 25/2, 8 July 1948.
[22] HHA–ACP, 10.95.10 (4), 5 July 1948.
[23] ISA, JM 5667/gimel, 25/2, 8 July 1948.

agreed, as one committee member remarked, that the Christian and Muslim Arabs of Haifa had always lived in largely segregated districts, but added that the Jews 'had no interest in forcing them to stay separate'.[24]

The Arabs offered no physical resistance to the operation and it was completed on 9 July without any outbreak of violence—resistance to the evictions, they felt, would have been fruitless. The operation, all told, cost P£15,000, the cost ultimately being borne by the Haifa Arab Affairs Committee after Lifshitz obtained Treasury approval for the expenditure. The operation was hampered throughout by lack of transport, and one day was lost when the army withdrew its trucks, which were needed for operational duties outside Haifa. 'The heat also caused laxity in the work', Major Amir maintained.

On 8 July, Amir was ordered by the General Staff to complete the eviction and transfer operation that day and was given additional trucks. Apparently, the IDF wanted the operation over before the army embarked on its offensives, which were scheduled to begin the following day, at the end of the First Truce. Amir more or less demanded that the Arab Affairs Committee make a final effort to complete the operation. Ye'eli balked, taking offence at Amir's peremptory tone. 'I do not accept many of Rehav'am's assumptions concerning the order he [*my italics, B.M.*] received concerning us as civilians . . . but we will continue to cooperate in the transfer because it is our duty towards the military command, taking account of the war situation in which we are found. Differences of opinion are for other times.'[25]

Vashitz summed up the operation on 5 July by writing that 'there is nothing bad which has not also in it something good'. While the concentration of Haifa's Arab community was, he believed, politically motivated, 'it had renewed [Arab] public life and created a basis for [renewed] internal economic life. Since the start of the concentration [operation], there have been many demands [by Arabs for permits] to open shops, workshops, coffee shops.' He assumed, in mid-operation, that if everything went off smoothly, without violence, 'tempers would [eventually] cool'. 'I believe', Vashitz wrote to the Secretariat of the Mapam Centre, 'that this [operation] is the most important act done with respect to the Arabs in the State of Israel.

[24] ISA, JM 5667/gimel, 25/2, 8 July 1948.   [25] Ibid.

Here it will be decided whether the State of Israel will be a democratic state or a feudal state with medieval customs and Nuremberg laws.'[26]

THE 'SPECIAL CASES'

The July concentration operation, which left most of Haifa's 3,500-strong Arab community in Wadi Nisnas and some dozen families in the Abbas quarter, was to have a sequel. Several dozen Arab families —all 'special cases'—had been passed over in July and had been left in their original homes around the city. Five months later, in December, the Defence Ministry—apparently for security reasons—decided that these Arabs should also be transferred to Wadi Nisnas. But the war was more or less over and the military no longer controlled Haifa. The army wanted the Ministry for Minority Affairs to handle the matter.

On 15 December, two Defence Ministry officers visited Moshe Yitah, the Minority Affairs Ministry representative in Haifa, and informed him that they had received orders 'to concentrate in Wadi Nisnas' the Arab families still dispersed around town—some '110–120', they said. Yitah asked the officers to return with an accurate, detailed list. They returned with a list of thirty-one families. According to Yitah, the list included families already living in Wadi Nisnas, families living in Wadi Salib (an area, he commented, originally earmarked for Arab residence), families with mixed marriages, and families of Arabs holding foreign citizenship. A few of the families, according to Yitah, were living outside Wadi Nisnas and Abbas Street by special individual dispensation of various Jewish institutions. Yitah promptly referred the matter to his superior, Minister for Minority Affairs Bechor Shitrit, who apparently had not been told of the 'special cases' by the Defence Ministry.[27]

Shitrit raised the question of moving these families at the 17 December meeting of the Ministerial Committee for Abandoned Property, a Cabinet body composed of the ministers of defence, foreign affairs, minority, finance, agriculture, and justice. This committee was responsible for the fate of all property of Arab refugees and, in some cases, for the fate of the refugees themselves.

[26] HHA–ACP, 10.95.10 (4), 5 July 1948.
[27] HMA 1374, M. Yitah (Haifa) to IDF Haifa District OC (Haifa), 19 Dec. 1948.

Shitrit reported that the Defence Ministry wished to move '120' Arab families. 'The Minority Affairs Minister is opposed to this and asks [that the committee] take a stand on the matter', records the protocol of the meeting.

The committee, chaired by Finance Minister Eliezer Kaplan, backed Shitrit and ruled that the 'Arabs could not be evicted without the matter being brought before [and approved by] the Ministerial Committee on Transfers [of Arabs from Place to Place]'.[28] Shitrit thereupon cabled Yitah that the ministerial committee had ruled that the Arab families could not be evicted and moved summarily by the Defence Ministry and that he should inform the Haifa IDF command to that effect.[29]

Yitah sent Shitrit's cable to the IDF Haifa District OC, and wrote that the security forces must henceforth consult the Minority Affairs Ministry 'before taking a serious decision', that the ministry must receive orders in writing from the district commander's office rather than learn of them orally, and that the current matter must be considered in light of the ministerial committee's decision, meaning that nothing could or should be done without the approval of the Ministerial Committee on Transfers.[30] The matter apparently ended there. Ben-Gurion did not bring up before the Ministerial Committee on Transfers the matter of transferring fewer than three dozen 'mixed' or 'foreign' families, and the dispersed families were left in place.

OPERATION SHIKMONA

The final British evacuation of Haifa at the end of June triggered not only the concentration of the city's remaining Arab population in Wadi Nisnas and the Abbas quarter, but also opened the way to Operation Shikmona—the destruction of parts of abandoned Arab neighbourhoods and buildings that were ruled unsuitable for accommodating new Jewish immigrants. The destruction, in part, followed blueprints of the city planning authority.

[28] ISA, FM 2401/21/aleph, 'Protocol of the Meeting of the Ministerial Committee for Abandoned Property', 17 Dec. 1948.
[29] HMA, 1374, B. Shitrit (Tel Aviv) to M. Yitah (Haifa), 19 Dec. 1948.
[30] Ibid., M. Yitah (Haifa) to IDF Haifa District OC, 19 Dec. 1948.

Previously, in May, the Haifa Arab Affairs Committee had considered the destruction of 'the Arab shack neighbourhoods in Halissa and Ard al-Ghamal for reasons of security and health'.[31] After committee members Ye'eli and Aharon Danin, however, had checked the cost of the prospective demolition work, estimated at some P£10,000, it was decided to abandon the operation. The committee was also swayed by the opinion of Yitzhak Gvirtz, a member of the national Arab Affairs Committee in Tel Aviv, who, on a visit to Haifa, told the Haifa committee that its funds were not designed for such a purpose.[32]

The planning for a face-lift of Haifa's Arab districts really began —as with most developments in the embryonic Jewish state—with Ben-Gurion, who on 16 June consulted with Uriel Friedland (later Shilon), the director of the Shemen factory and a member of the Haganah command in Haifa. Friedland said that there was 'need for demolition [of Arab houses] in Haifa for purposes of adjustment and construction, in line with city-planning [requirements] . . .'. Ben-Gurion agreed and 'urged this work forward immediately with the British evacuation'.[33] Operation Shikmona, carried out by IDF engineer units, got under way in various parts of Haifa during the third week of July, just after the start, on 19 July, of the Second Truce between Israel and the Arab states (which freed IDF units, including engineers, from front-line duties).

The demolition of houses was carried out, according to a complaint by Fred Khayyat, one of Haifa's Arab businessmen, 'without prior announcement, legal process, or promise of compensation'. Khayyat described how he had witnessed the demolition of buildings on Allenby Street and in Hamra Square: 'As far as I can see', he wrote, 'the destruction is being carried out to open up streets marked in the Haifa city planning blueprint', but without the usual procedure of legal expropriation and payment, or promise of payment, of appropriate compensation to owners. As Haifa was completely quiet, wrote Khayyat, the demolitions could not be justified on grounds of

[31] ISA, JM 5667/gimel, 25/2, 'Protocol of the Fourth Meeting of the Arab Affairs Committee, Haifa', 20 May 1948.
[32] Ibid. 'Protocol of the Fifth Meeting of the Arab Affairs Committee, Haifa', 27 May 1948.
[33] David Ben-Gurion, *Yoman Hamilhama-Tashah* [the war diary, 1948–9] (Tel Aviv, 1982), 522, entry for 16 June 1948.

security.[34] A stream of similar complaints by Haifa Arab notables to Mayor Levy[35] prompted the mayor to send a sharp letter on 30 July to Minority Affairs Minister Shitrit: 'I want to make it completely clear to you and the Cabinet that Haifa Municipality has no connection with these operations and, indeed, no formal knowledge of them. All we know is [from] complaints from the people and from hearing the echoes of explosions from parts of the city. Moreover, we do not know under whose orders these actions are being carried out and who is responsible for them.' Levy demanded that the situation be 'rectified' because 'a day will arrive when the owners of the property [that is, mostly Arab refugees] will demand compensation for their property and they will direct their suits at the municipality, believing that it was the municipality which was responsible for the development, expropriation and other projects'. The municipality refused 'material or moral responsibility for the demolitions'. Levy concluded his letter by stating that the municipality rejected absolutely any responsibility for finding housing for those whose houses were being destroyed.[36]

The first official notification any civil authority received from the defence establishment about the demolition operations in Haifa was apparently a telephone call from an officer, who identified himself as 'Barlas', to an official in the bureau of the Trustee of Enemy Property in Haifa on 3 August, about a fortnight after the start of Operation Shikmona. Barlas said he was 'in charge of opening King George Street' and warned that in two days the IDF would blow up two houses on Carmel Boulevard. The official from the custodian's office then called city hall, where municipal officials informed him that the municipality 'knew nothing about the operation'. The official—apparently not Naftali Lifshitz, the Trustee of Enemy Property in Haifa—then wrote to the IDF Haifa District Command and to the mayor saying that he did not know what the legal basis was for the destruction of 'state property'. As far as he could see, it

[34] ISA–MAM 298/82, F. Khayyat (Haifa) to Minister for Minority Affairs (Tel Aviv), 25 July 1948.
[35] HMA 556, Elias Koussa to S. Levy (Haifa), 21 July 1948; Basil Laham, Secretary to the Greek Catholic Archbishop of Haifa (Haifa) to S. Levy (Haifa), 1 Aug. 1948; G. Manjikian and W. Sarkissian, Armenian owners of 'Queen Shoes' (Haifa) to S. Levy (Haifa), 27 July 1948.
[36] HMA, 556, S. Levy (Haifa) to Minority Affairs Minister (Tel Aviv), 30 July 1948. There is a copy of this letter in JM, 5667/gimel, 25/3.

was 'illegal'. He complained both about the 'manner' in which he had been informed of the impending demolitions on Carmel Boulevard and about the destruction itself. 'All those responsible for this operation [Shikmona] will be responsible to the Trustee of Enemy Property and the Government of Israel', he concluded.[37]

The continuing demolitions·in Haifa through August and Levy's letter of complaint eventually prompted Minority Affairs Minister Shitrit to take action. On 22 August, he asked his colleagues on the Ministerial Committee for Abandoned Property to put the demolitions on the agenda of the committee's next meeting.[38] But Shitrit missed the meeting, which took place on 27 August, and his stand-in, Minority Affairs Ministry Director General Gad Machnes, failed to raise the subject.[39] Shitrit, however, persisted. At the Cabinet meeting of 1 September, he submitted a question, directed at Prime Minister and Defence Minister Ben-Gurion, about 'the destruction of the houses in Wadi Nisnas in Haifa, the eviction of Arab families from their homes in Jaffa', and other matters relating to Israel's minority communities. Ben-Gurion parried with an evasion and a deception. 'The Defence Minister answered that these matters belonged to the official responsible for the occupied territories.' The reference was apparently to General Elimelech Avner, the OC Military Government, which governed the territories Israeli forces had occupied that lay outside the 1947 UN partition boundaries of the Jewish state. But Haifa, where Jewish military rule had been lifted on 3 May, was not 'occupied territory'; it had been included in the Jewish state in the partition plan. In any case, as Minister of Defence, Ben-Gurion was ministerially responsible for and in charge of the Military Government, a branch of the IDF.

[37] HMA 556, an official signing 'in the name of the Trustee of Enemy Property' (Haifa) to IDF Haifa District OC, 3 Aug. 1948. The legal status of the property of Arab refugees was unclear at this time. *De facto*, it had been expropriated by the State of Israel—and much of it allocated, outright or on lease, to new immigrants, Jewish settlements, government ministries, and IDF units. *De jure*, a Custodian of Abandoned Property, later called the Custodian for Absentees Property, was appointed a few weeks earlier, in July. His task was to oversee and protect the property (houses, land, movable goods), and to oversee its temporary or permanent distribution and sale, and the funds gained from these actions.

[38] ISA, JM 5667/gimel, 25/3, B. Shitrit (Tel Aviv) to the ministers of defence, justice, finance, etc. (Tel Aviv), 22 Aug. 1948.

[39] ISA, FM 2564/13, 'Protocol of the Meeting of the Ministerial Committee for Abandoned Property', 27 Aug. 1948.

The Cabinet's agendas in 1948 were always full; the ministers never managed to cover all the topics listed for each session. Ben-Gurion could usually parry or defer answers to questions on sensitive subjects, especially when presented by a 'weak' minister, as Shitrit was, and when 'buried' inside a whole cluster of queries, as were Shitrit's about the Haifa demolitions.[40]

Shitrit had perhaps not received a satisfactory answer from Ben-Gurion on 1 September, but Haifa's Mayor Levy was at last officially informed on 8 September about Operation Shikmona, and apparently persuaded that all was for the best. On that day, Minister of Interior Yitzhak Gruenbaum visited Haifa and, in a private conversation in the mayor's office, gave justifications for the demolition operation. The gist of the explanation was that because the demolitions were being carried out by the military they could be justified as a military operation and, therefore, did not require compensation for property owners, as would have been the case had the normal city planning expropriation / demolition procedures been adhered to. A great deal of money—of which the State of Israel was short—had thus been saved.

Following the meeting, Mayor Levy wrote to Gruenbaum:

This large-scale operation, which is decisively changing the face of the city, is no doubt of great significance in bringing progress to the city, in accordance with the city building plans which have been prepared over the years. This courageous operation, carried out by the Army by order of the government, will save a great deal of money which the city would have had to pay in the form of compensation for the demolished buildings, had it attempted to carry out the operation by its own [usual] means.

But Levy still had a problem—one of the reasons for his letter—which was that the city urgently needed to clear away the rubble from the demolition sites. (The other reason, apparently, was the Cabinet's wish to obtain Levy's stamp of approval for Operation Shikmona.) Levy said he needed P£10,000 for this and asked Gruenbaum to supply the funds. To illustrate the problem, Levy wrote: 'The destruction of the Old City alone involves more than 300,000 cubic metres of waste . . .'.[41]

If Levy was at last convinced of the propriety and worth of

----

[40] KMA–AZP 9.9.1, 'Decisions of the Provisional Government', 1 Sept. 1948.
[41] HMA, 556, S. Levy (Haifa) to Minister of Interior (Tel Aviv), 8 Sept. 1948.

Operation Shikmona, the local Trustee of Enemy Property was not. At the end of September, Lifshitz against wrote to Levy and the IDF Haifa District Command that to the best of his knowledge, the demolitions—apparently still going on—were illegal and were being carried out without due process. He again condemned the operation and asserted that those responsible would eventually have to explain their actions to the government.[42]

But Lifshitz's protests were ineffectual. The operation, carried out by the IDF on Ben-Gurion's orders, had neatly and cheaply 'rearranged' Haifa, exploiting the background of war, a cowed Arab population unable to protest effectively, and the absence of most of the property owners.

CONCLUSION

The events in Haifa in July 1948 were a sequel to the fall of the Arab neighbourhoods and the evacuation of the vast majority of the city's Arab inhabitants in April, three months earlier. They illuminate first the nature of the Israeli decision-making processes concerning the Palestinian Arabs during the 1948 war; second, the basic divisions within the Jewish community—both between the military and the civilian bureaucracies and among the civilian officials—concerning policy toward the Arabs; and third, the events illustrate the pattern of Israel's treatment of its Arab minority during the war.

All wars are characterized by confusion, and 1948 was probably more confused than most, mixing, as it did, various aspects of guerrilla, civil, and conventional warfare. And for the Yishuv, the war's complexity was compounded by the simultaneous necessity of setting up and operating the machinery of modern government. A great deal of confusion reigned in policy-making *vis-à-vis* the Palestinian Arabs. Little had been foreseen or planned for, decisions were often taken extemporaneously and not necessarily by the bodies nominally responsible for each area. The fount of all authority was Ben-Gurion, and major decision-making in regard to the Arabs—whatever the trappings or dictates of normal democratic government—was in the hands of the defence establishment. A war for survival was on.

---

[42] Ibid., Trustee of Enemy Property (Haifa) to the Mayor, IDF Haifa District OC, 27 Sept. 1948.

Confusion reigned also in the concentration of Haifa's Arabs in Wadi Nisnas and the Abbas quarter and regarding Operation Shikmona. The Minister for Minority Affairs was bypassed or deceived, the Cabinet plenum ignored as the IDF went its own way and changed the face of Haifa. The city's municipal authorities were shunted aside or, in the case of Operation Shikmona, kept in the dark for weeks and months, the civilian Arab Affairs Committee was given its orders by the IDF rather than consulted in an operation that had clear civil as well as security aspects. In general, in both the concentration and demolition operations, a great divide can be discerned between the new-born state's military and civilian authorities in matters pertaining to the Arab minority population during the war. Decisions were made by the defence establishment, and the civil authorities were either kept in the dark or asked to assist in implementation only after the fact.

An indication that this was a wartime state of affairs and that matters would or might change, at least to a degree, once peace dawned, was afforded by the events of December 1948 (by which time all fighting in the north of the country had ceased), when the IDF tried to 'order' the Minority Affairs Ministry to organize the eviction and transfer of several dozen Arab and half-Arab families. The IDF was rebuffed by Minority Affairs Minister Shitrit after he had obtained the backing of a key Cabinet committee.

The events in Haifa in July 1948 also highlighted the division running through the Jewish civilian population concerning Israel's policy towards the Arabs. There were 'soft-liners' and 'hard-liners' (usually following party lines), with continuous argument and tension between the two groups. The hard-line usually won in 1948, both because it enjoyed majority support and because the background was one of a war for survival. The military argument may not always or wholly have been accepted, or even believed, but this was no time to give doubters their head or to take chances. 'Differences of opinion are for other times', as Ye'eli put it, but moral arguments continually surfaced and were heard, even though they did not usually prevail.

The July events in Haifa illustrate the pattern, in the first months of existence of the State of Israel, of the government's policy toward the Arab minority—military rule and arbitrary measures were the order of the day. The Palestinian Arabs, at least many of them, had fought against the emergence of the Jewish state, and those who remained behind to live in it were usually treated as potential fifth columnists or spies. Their treatment had to be primarily a function of security considerations and needs. The wartime situation, however, was exploited to legitimize and carry out various measures—summary eviction and transfers of population, destruction of property without due process or compensation—whose purport was not necessarily bound up with, or mainly tied to, security considerations. The requirements and considerations of the object —the Arab minority population—were not consulted or allowed to affect decision-making. It was war, and the Arab was the enemy.

7

The Harvest of 1948 and the Creation of the Palestinian Refugee Problem

During the 1947–9 Israeli–Arab war, which pitted two more or less agrarian societies against each other, an intense struggle developed, especially during May–July 1948, over the harvest. The struggle was won by the militarily stronger and better-organized side. While it was peripheral to the outcome of the major engagements of the war and of the war itself, it was important in a variety of ways in the creation of the Palestinian refugee problem and hence had a major bearing on the political outcome of the war.

As with the military and other political aspects of the war, the battle for the crops evolved gradually. In some localities, such as the Hefer Valley, neighbouring Jewish and Arab settlements at least initially adopted a live-and-let-live policy of mutual non-aggression; each allowed the other to cultivate and reap his crops. But in other areas, at first spontaneously, Arab and Jewish farmers-militiamen, caught up in the escalating guerrilla operations, attacked each other and each other's fields; the aim was to harass and inflict casualties, as well as to cause economic damage. By early spring 1948, fear and Jewish military pressure prompted Arab villagers in large numbers to begin moving out of the areas allocated to the Jewish State in the 1947 UN Partition Plan. The burning of fields and attacks on cultivators were among the pressures that led to the exodus. During May 1948, with most of the Arabs having left the Jewish-held areas, the Yishuv organized the harvesting of many of the abandoned Arab fields. Over the summer, in various areas, the often hungry and destitute exiles, playing a cat-and-mouse game with the IDF, infiltrated through Israeli lines back to their fields to salvage some of the crop. Jewish fears that, if allowed to succeed, these temporary, economically motivated forays would be transformed into a permanent refugee 'return' led to hard and fast orders to IDF units along the cease-fire lines to prevent such forays with fire.

Thus, the prevention of Arab refugees cultivating their fields coupled with the harvesting of the abandoned fields by the Jewish settlements became one aspect of the general policy, which crystallized during the summer, of preventing an Arab refugee return. The harvest by the Jewish settlements of the abandoned Arab fields created among the settlements an attachment to the newly acquired lands which, in turn, served to harden attitudes against a return of the refugees and contributed to the emergence of the vociferous and passionate 'agricultural lobby' against allowing a return, ever. This Jewish cultivation of Arab fields and the prevention of Arab harvesting continued through 1948 and early 1949, consolidating both the Jewish hold on the newly acquired lands and the refugeedom of Palestine's Arabs.

The first cases of intereference in the cultivation of fields appear to have occurred in southern Palestine in January 1948. While Arab guerrillas fired on Jewish settlements and traffic, and blew up the water pipeline supplying the relatively isolated Jewish outposts, Haganah retaliation often took the form of attacks on Arab farmers in the fields.[1]

As the Haganah attacks increased, the Arabs of the northern Negev (mostly Beduin) and of the northern Negev approaches became 'greatly worried and considerably impressed by the rumour of Haganah threats that the crop will be destroyed if they do not behave themselves', according to the British Gaza District Commissioner. But the threats, according to the British official, would prove an insufficient deterrent, as they 'will not stop [the Arabs from] taking every opportunity of killing such Jews as give them the chance'.[2]

The Jewish assessment of the situation was that the Arabs might resort to the same tactic. Hence Yosef Weitz, the Jewish National Fund Lands Department director who, as chairman of the Negev Committee, was the Yishuv's *de facto* civil governor of the Jewish settlements in the area, thought that the Jewish harvesting of the Jewish fields should be done 'as swiftly as possible, before the

[1] See e.g. PRO, CO 537–3855, CID Summary of Events, 23 Jan. 1948, Appendix, entry for 22 Jan. 1948, which tells of Fakhri Yunis Awad and Yusuf Darwish, two Arab farmers near Isdud (Ashdod) fired upon in their fields by unknown (presumably Jewish) assailants. Awad was killed and Darwish was slightly injured.

[2] PRO, CO 537–3853, 'Fortnightly Report 16–31 Jan. 1948', District Commissioner, Gaza, 3 Feb. 1948, and 'Fortnightly Report . . . 1–16 Feb. 1948', District Commissioner's Office, Gaza, 16 Feb. 1948.

Arabs' concluded their harvest and felt free to renew or increase their attacks on the Jewish fields. The Arabs' fear for their crops had led, apparently, to a falling off of attacks on the Jews. 'Generally, the *fellahin* of [the] Gaza [area] try not to get involved [in hostilities] against the Jews, as their most vital interest today is: To safeguard the crop of their fields, and to assure the possibility of an unhampered harvest.' The Gaza Arabs, and the northern Negev beduin, were rejecting 'until after the harvest' the importuning of the extremists to attack the Jews, according to a Haganah Intelligence Service (Sha'i) assessment in mid-February 1948. However, the assessment added that while many of the beduin were excusing their inaction against the Jews on the basis of fear for their crops, in fact 'most of them' simply were not interested in joining the *Jihad*.[3]

According to the British District Commissioner, R. J. P. Thorne, who was trying to restrain the Gaza Arabs, the 'moderates' were having a hard time controlling the 'hotheads'. He told the Arab community leaders that Arab attacks on the well-fortified Jewish settlements would be 'badly mauled' and that these 'would give the Jews the excuse they were looking for to burn Arab crops at harvest'. In early March, Ben-Gurion noted briefly that the Negev Brigade OC, Nahum Sarig, had reported that the *fellahin* were afraid that 'the Jews would burn their fields'.[4]

The Haganah retaliatory tactic of attack on Arab farmers and fields was not restricted to the south. In March, the British authorities repeatedly reported such attacks in the Galilee, noting that each community feared the burning by the other of their crops before harvest-time.[5]

---

[3] Yosef Weitz, *Diaries* (Tel Aviv, 1965) iii. 243, entry for 23 Feb. 1948; and Kibbutz Meuhad Archive, Palmah Archive (KMA-PA) (Efal, Israel) 109 aleph/204, '*Yediot Tene* (Haganah Intelligence Service daily reports) 16 Feb. 1948'.

[4] PRO, CO 537–3853, 'Fortnightly Report . . . 16–29 Feb. 1948', District Commissioner's Office, Gaza, 1 Mar. 1948 and David Ben-Gurion (DBG) *Yoman Hamilhama-Tashah* [Ben-Gurion's war diary, 1948–9] (Tel Aviv, 1982) i. 291, entry for 10 Mar. 1948.

[5] See e.g. PRO, WO 275–90, CRAFORCE to 17/21 L, 1 Para Bn, etc. 6 Mar. 1948, which cites Jewish attack on Al Samiriya, in the Beit Shean Valley, as an indication that 'Jews are preventing villagers from working on the lands' and PRO, CO 537–3856, CID Summary of Events, 3 Mar. 1948, Appendix 'B', entry for 2 Mar. 1948, which cites Jewish attack on farmers from the village of Qabba'a, southwest of Kibbutz Ayelet Hashahar. See also PRO, CO 537–3853, 'Fortnightly Report for the Period ended the 29 Feb. 1948', District Commissioner's Office, Galilee District, Nazareth. Other attacks were cited in Mar. by British observers near Deir al Balah,

It was in the Negev, where the wheat and barley fields ripened earliest, that a general policy of destruction of Arab fields was first considered. The imminence of the harvest prompted the Negev Brigade commanders in early April to request from Palmah Headquarters incendiary mortar bombs with which to set alight Arab fields. The options were discussed at a meeting between Yosef Weitz and the Negev Brigade commanders on 28 April. The brigade's troops could hamper the Arabs from harvesting some 100,000 dunams of crops, or agreement could be reached to allow the Arabs to harvest their crops in exchange for Arab agreement to a general cease-fire in the area. Or, if it was decided against allowing the Arabs to harvest their fields, perhaps the Jewish settlements could be allowed to harvest some of the Arab fields, with the proceeds eventually going to the Arab owners. Weitz himself thought 'that the Arabs should not be allowed to reap their fields.' The matter was clearly political, and no decision was reached. But Weitz persisted, and on 4 May wrote to Negev Brigade OC Sarig, either proposing or instructing that Jewish settlements whose fields had been destroyed by their Arab neighbours be allowed to reap the fields 'of the saboteurs' to the extent of their losses. Weitz took a similar line with regard to compensatory harvesting of Arab fields by Kibbutz Mishmar Hasharon in the coastal plain.[6] Thus the mutual destruction of fields was linked with the start of Jewish cultivation of Arab fields.

In some areas, neighbouring Arab and Jewish settlements concluded *ad hoc* agreements of mutual benefit to enable the harvesting on both sides to proceed unhampered. Arabs put out feelers to reach such agreements in the Hefer Valley and Baqa al Gharibiya areas of the northern coastal plain, as did the refugees from Al

southwest of Gaza, and (by Arabs on Jewish farmers), near Kfar Darom, to the east of Gaza. See PRO, CO 537–3857, CID Summary of Events, 23 Mar. 1948, entry for 21 Mar. 1948, and CO 537–3857, CID Summary of Events, 19 Mar. 1948, Appendix 'B,' entry of 18 Mar. 1948.

[6] *Hativat Hanegev Bama'aracha* (Tel Aviv, undated), 49, communication from Negev Brigade HQ to Palmah HQ, 5 Apr. 1948; Weitz *Diaries* iii, 274, entry for 28 Apr. 1948, and p. 377, Appendix No. 1, the Negev Committee to Nahum Sarig, OC Negev Brigade, 4 May 1948; and Labor Archive (Histadrut-Lavon Institute) 235/IV, 2251 bet, Yosef Weitz to Gad Machnes, 2 May 1948, and Mishmar Hasharon to the Arab Property Department (Committee), 21 Apr. and 29 Apr. 1948.

Kheiriya, east of Tel Aviv.[7] But far more common was mutual destruction, which by May had become widespread. Israel Galili, the head of the Haganah National Staff, briefly referred to it in his report on the military situation to the People's Administration (the Yishuv's pre-state provisional government, also known as the 'Thirteen') on 26 April: 'The arson of fields may start, and we will have to mete out arson for arson.'[8] In early May, as the crops ripened, the first reports came in of Arab depredations against Jewish fields in the centre and north of the country. The Golani Brigade reported an incident near Mahanayim, in the Jordan Valley; the Haganah's English-language radio station, Kol Hamagen Ha'ivri, on 7 May reported an attack on Jewish farmers in the fields of Kibbutz Hama'apil; on 9 May, the Yiftah Brigade reported cases of arson the previous day in the fields of the kibbutzim Dan and Dafna, in the Galilee panhandle.[9]

The intensification of the war in May, highlighted by the Arab invasion and the temporary Jewish shift to the defensive after the 15th of the month, coupled with the ripening of the summer crop, saw an intensification in the battle for the harvest. As with the war itself, so with the harvest—Jewish arms generally prevailed. From the Jewish side, the stress shifted (with the successive conquest of new formerly Arab-populated areas) from destruction of fields to the harvesting of the Arab crop; on the Arab side, the stress shifted from destroying Jewish fields to attempting to reach and reap as much as possible in the fields they had abandoned behind or near the Jewish lines.

The decision in principle to harvest as much as possible of the crop of the abandoned Arab villages was taken during the first days of May, probably by Ben-Gurion in consultation with his political and military advisers. An echo of that decision is to be found in the

---

[7] Referred to in LA 235/IV, 2092, 'Circular No. 10', the Samaria Settlements Bloc Committee, 24 Apr. 1948; KMA–PA 100/MemVavDalet/3–138, '*Yediot Tene* (Haganah Intelligence Service Information)' 24 Apr. 1948; 100/MemVavDalet/3–150, '*Yediot Tene* 6 May 1948'; and KMA–PA 100/MemVavDalet/3–154, '*Yediot Tene* 9 May 1948'.

[8] *Minhelet Ha'am*, (ISA, Jerusalem, 1978), protocol of the meeting of 26 Apr. 1948, p. 22.

[9] *Ilan Vashelah*, ed. Binyamin Etzioni (Tel Aviv, undated), 151; Central Zionist Archives, S25–8918, transcript of broadcast on Kol Hamagen Ha'ivri, 7 May 1948; and KMA–PA 109 Gimel/175, Palmah HQ Daily Report to the Haganah General Staff, 9 May 1948.

deliberations of the Yishuv's 'Arab affairs advisers'—who were members of or affiliated to the Jewish Agency Political Department's Arab Affairs Division and / or the Haganah Intelligence Service—with the coastal plain Arab affairs experts in Netanya on 9 May. Among the decisions reached were: 'the [Jewish] farmers [in the Coastal Plain] should be encouraged not to leave unharvested [Arab] crops and that the harvest constitutes part of the war effort . . .'. On the local operative level, the advisers decided that the fields of 'Ein Ghazal—a village not yet abandoned by its inhabitants whose lands lay near the Jewish settlement of Bat Shlomo—should also be harvested. But as these fields were rock-strewn and unharvestable by combine, it was proposed that the harvest be conducted, on behalf of the Yishuv, by the (Arab) villagers of Jisr Zarka, who had thrown in their lot with the Jews.[10]

During May, the Yishuv's settlement institutions, together with the local settlements bloc committees, organized the harvesting of tens of thousands of dunams of abandoned Arab fields—in the coastal plain, in the Galilee, in the Jerusalem Corridor and in the northern Negev approaches. The Agriculture Ministry together with the Arab Property Department (at first a branch of the Minority Affairs Ministry and, from June, part of the office of the Custodian for Abandoned (later, Absentees) Property), allocated the abandoned Arab fields in each area to local Jewish regional councils or settlements bloc committees, which, in turn, distributed them among the Jewish settlements in their region, according to farming capability and needs. In the northern coastal plain, the kibbutzim Gan Shmuel, Ma'ayan Zvi, Mishmarot, Ma'anit, and Ein Shemer jointly harvested over May and June the fields of Baqa al Gharbiya, Ad Dumeria, Arab Kabara, Ali Bek, Kafr Qari, Faras-Hamdan, and other Arab villages; in the Tel-Hai (Galilee panhandle) district, the kibbutzim Dafna, Dan, Kfar Giladi, and Amir, and private farmers from Rosh Pinna, harvested the crops from the fields of the abandoned Arab villages of Nabi Yusha, Qadas, Al Malikiya and the Hula Valley, and so on. Fields inaccessible to combines and other machinery were usually set alight. The Jewish harvest of the Arab fields was seen as 'crucial to the war effort', in

---

[10] David Ben-Gurion Archive (Sdeh Boqer), 'Summary of the Meeting of the Arab Affairs Advisors in Netanya,' 9 May 1948.

the phrase of Yitzhak Gvirtz, an Arab affairs adviser and head of the Arab Property Department, and brought in income to the Treasury (as the harvesting settlements had to pay the Treasury a set fee for each dunam reaped). Some of the Jewish settlements regarded the harvest as compensation for their material losses during the hostilities and balked at paying. The harvesting triggered possessiveness, and already during the summer, Jewish settlements appealed to the Agriculture Ministry, the Jewish National Fund, and other land-allocating bodies for permanent leaseholds and possession. The harvest of Arab fields in the early summer of 1948 thus became a major step in the process of Jewish acquisition and expropriation of the abandoned Palestinian Arab lands.[11]

The battle for the harvest became increasingly bitter. In the fighting between Kibbutz Ramat Hakovesh and the neighbouring village of Al Tira south-east of Netanya, the abandoned Jewish fields—in no-man's land between the opposing armies—magnetized the Arab villagers. The villagers attempted to collect the harvest and the kibbutzniks planted land-mines in the fields. 'It was a war to the finish', recalled a Jewish participant from the Alexandroni Brigade.[12] Similar local struggles raged elsewhere. On the western side of the Galilee panhandle, Arab *fellahin* stayed clear of the fields in no-man's land near the IDF front lines, and dared venture only into the more distant fields opposite Kibbutz Manara and only at night.'A great fear gripped them', recorded one kibbutz member. But, at the same time, the refugees were threatened by hunger. 'If they do not succeed in reaping their [abandoned] fields, it will be a very serious blow . . . The depression and confusion and bitterness among them is great. May these multiply.'[13] The same situation—and similar desperate attempts to infiltrate into fields near the front lines to reap the abandoned Arab crop—were reported at this time in the Hula

[11] LA 235/IV, 2082 bet, 'Circular No. 11', Samaria Settlements Bloc Committee, 24 May 1948, and 2251 bet, 'Things Said at a Meeting of Settlements Bloc Committees in Tel Aviv on 26 May 1948', unsigned but printed on the stationery of the Arab Affairs Ministry (the original name of the Minority Affairs Ministry); ISA, MAM 303/41, 'Report of the Department for Arab Property until the end of May 1948', undated, unsigned (but certainly by the department's director, Gvirtz, from early June); and ISA, AM Aleph/19/Aleph (part 1), 'Summary of the Meeting with the Arab Property Committee in the Tel-Hai District, 5 June 1948', unsigned, undated.

[12] *Hativat Alexandroni* (Tel Aviv: IDF Press), 106.

[13] LA 235/IV, 1630, '*Alei Manara*' (the Kibbutz Manara bulletin), No. 65, 4 June 1948.

Valley along the Syrian border, in the Samaria foothills and in the Gilbo'a area.[14]

One Palestinian Arab, who later became an historian, recalled these infiltration attempts during the summer to salvage the crop from abandoned fields. Elias Shoufani, from Mi'ilya, in the Galilee, was 14 at the time. The village's fields, mostly in the coastal area of Western Galilee, had fallen under Haganah control in May. Food supplies in Mi'ilya, which was conquered only six months later by the IDF, were

scanty . . . The villagers had no alternative but to attempt to collect the crops from the abandoned fields . . . The lure of food was irresistible . . . The trickle of individuals who began to infiltrate across enemy lines in June became a large scale nightly operation in August. Every day at around five o'clock long columns of farmers led their donkeys to the vicinity of the village watching posts and waited impatiently for the sun to set. With nightfall, they made their way through the curving valleys to the plains. All night long they cropped millet from the fields of Kabri and Zib [two abandoned Arab villages]. Before dawn, they loaded the night's crop on their donkeys and returned home.

Later, some of the villagers stayed in the fields during the days, lying low until nightfall, when they would resume reaping.[15]

The plight of the refugees, which was leading to the infiltrations to harvest abandoned fields, in early June was viewed with growing trepidation by the Yishuv's military and political leaders. This infiltration could lead 'in time to resettlement in the villages, something which could seriously endanger many of our achievements during the first six months of the war', stated one intelligence report.[16] The start of the First Truce, on 11 June, aggravated the problem; the temporary cease-fire, the Jewish leaders feared, might tempt, and enable, refugees to try to cross through the lines back to their fields and villages.

On 5 June, three powerful Yishuv executives—Yosef Weitz of the JNF, Elias Sasson, director of the Foreign Ministry's Middle East Affairs Department, and Ezra Danin, a senior figure in the

[14] ISA, FM 2570/6, 'Tsur' to Haganah Intelligence Service, 7 June 1948 and '*BaTziburiut Ha'Aravit*' (in the Arab Public), Middle East Affairs Department, Foreign Ministry, 11 June 1948.

[15] Elias Shoufani, 'The Fall of A Village', *Journal of Palestine Studies*, 1/4, 1972.

[16] ISA, FM 2570/6, '*BaTziburiut Ha'Aravit*', Middle East Affairs Department, Foreign Ministry, 11 June 1948.

Haganah's Intelligence Service (soon to be named a special adviser at the Foreign Ministry)—submitted a comprehensive proposal to Ben-Gurion pressing the government to decide against allowing a return of the Arab refugees to their homes. The three executives—who the previous month had set themselves up as the unofficial 'Transfer Committee'—outlined a whole range of steps to ensure that there would be no return of the Palestine Arabs (about 300,000–400,000 thus far) who had fled or been expelled from Israeli-held territory. The committee's second proposal (coming after one calling for the destruction of abandoned Arab villages) was 'to prevent all cultivation of land by [Arabs], including harvesting, collection [of crops], olive-picking . . . also during days of "ceasefire" '.[17]

This lobbying, coupled with the increase of harvest-oriented Arab infiltration and growing pressure by local military commanders for a clear-cut policy, resulted during June in repeated orders from Ben-Gurion and IDF OC Operations (and *de facto* chief of staff) General Yigael Yadin to all units to prevent a return of refugees and harvesting by Arabs of Arab fields 'if necessary by [light weapons] fire'.

The crystallization of Israeli policy in this connection is perhaps illustrated by a series of Negev Brigade communications. The unit stationed at T'kumah on 30 May, reported that Arabs were reaping fields some 600 metres away. 'Are we allowed to shoot?' the unit asked HQ. On 7 June the unit stationed at Kibbutz Be'eri informed HQ that it had 'stopped the Arab harvesting . . . We set alight piles of wheat. Several camels, asses and cows were killed . . .'. On 9 June, the unit at T'kumah informed HQ that it had that day sortied out to set fire to the fields of Abu Barjit. 'Again, the standing crop would not burn [but] the [stacked] piles [of crops] burned nicely', the unit reported. At Mishmar-Hanegev the same day the local Palmah unit attacked nearby Arab granaries.[18]

[17] ISA, FM 2564/19, 'Retroactive Transfer, A Scheme for the Solution of the Arab Question in the State of Israel,' by Yosef Weitz, Ezra Danin, and Elias Sasson, undated, presented to Ben-Gurion on 5 June 1948 and Y. Weitz to D. Ben-Gurion, 6 June 1948. For a full description of the activities of Yosef Weitz and the two 'transfer committees' that he chaired, see Essay 4 in the present volume and Benny Morris, 'The Crystallization of Israeli Policy Against A Return of the Arab Refugees, April–December 1948', in *Studies in Zionism*, 6/1, Spring, 1985.

[18] KMA-PA 110/2/tet-40, battalion logbook (Negev Brigade), entry for 30 May 1948; 110/2/tet-50, battalion logbook (Negev Brigade), entry for 7 June 1948; and 110/2/tet-51, battalion logbook (Negev Brigade), entry for 9 June 1948.

On 9 June, the Jezreel Valley District commander, in the name of the IDF General Staff, ordered all local units to prevent 'by force' an Arab return and Arab harvesting in their areas; a similar command apparently went out from the General Staff to all IDF units that day or in the following days. On 10 June, six Arab reapers were shot dead in the fields of Al Muharraqa, in the northern Negev. On 13 June, Arabs reaping their fields South of Kibbutz Gesher were fired on and forced to retreat eastwards across the Jordan River. On 15 June, Golani Brigade troops fired on Arab reapers near Zir'in in the Jezreel Valley and near Ghuweir Abu Shusha, North-west of the Sea of Galilee. Again, on 18 June, Golani troops fired on reapers near Zir'in. Reapers were driven off on 24 June, near Sheikh Qaddumi Hill, in Eastern Galillee. Jewish farmers were also attacked, near Kibbutz Mizra, in the Jezreel Valley, on 2 July 1948.[19]

On 13 June, General Yadin issued an order to IDF brigades to 'prevent completely' all Arab reaping in areas conquered by the IDF.[20] Yadin expanded on this order on 19 June: 'Every enemy field in the area of our complete control we must harvest. Every field we are unable to reap—must be destroyed. In any event, the Arabs must be prevented from reaping these fields.' According to the director of the Arab Property Department, Yitzhak Gvirtz, 'the army prodded us to immediately reap [the abandoned Arab fields], or else it would burn the crops, and we barely managed to prevent [the army] from doing so'. Gvirtz was writing about fields east of Tel Aviv, in the lower coastal plain, where the army maintained it could not prevent the nightly infiltration of the area by exiled Arab villagers bent on harvesting their fields because of the ban on shooting in force because of the truce.[21]

The General Staff's orders were 'explained' to the Negev Brigade units by Nahum Sarig on 15 June. Sarig wrote:

[19] HHA-ACP 10.95.10 (5), 'Levi,' OC Jezreel Valley District, to area commanders, 9 June 1948; KMA-PA 105/390, 'Sergei' (Nahum Sarig) to Palmah HQ, 11 June 1948; KMA-PA 109 Gimel/215, 216, 'Daily Report, 11 June 1948', Palmah HQ to **IDF** General Staff (covering 9–11 June 1948); *Ilan VaShelah*, p. 239, for harvesting incidents in the North, 13 June–2 July 1948.

[20] KMA-PA 105-422 and 109 dalet-220, Operations/Yadin to Harel, 7th, Negev brigades etc., 13 June 1948.

[21] KMA-PA 103/44, OC Operations to the brigades, 19 June 1948; and LA 235/IV, 2252, Y. Gvirtz to the Custodian for Abandoned Property, 2 Dec. 1948.

In the previous instructions concerning the Arab harvest, it was stressed that our actions in this field are of a political character and their aim is not the destruction of the crop for its own sake. We must [now] know that this approach has changed fundamentally [following] the start of the Egyptian invasion [of the Negev of 15 May]. The destruction of the Arab crop is a direct injury to the invader, [and] forces him [the invader] to worry about flour for the [local Arab] inhabitants, puts him under pressure of the local population and encumbers his transportation system.

Therefore, 'everything must be done to destroy the Arab crop . . .'.[22] Whether Sarig really believed that these were the main or only reasons for the General Staff / Operations general orders in June to destroy Arab crops and prevent Arab harvesting of crops is unclear. Perhaps in the Negev, more than elsewhere, such considerations played an important part in determining military policy *vis-à-vis* Arab crops and harvesting. But in the centre and north of the country, while such military considerations may also have been relevant, the thrust of the reasoning was political and strategic-political—to prevent a return of refugees for a variety of political and strategic reasons.

What was happening to the Arab fields and farmers was intermittently noted, and criticized, by foreign observers. But—unlike Ben-Gurion's internal Yishuv critics, from Mapam—these observers failed to grasp that these 'local' incidents were part of a national policy and design with a clear strategic-political goal.

The UN observers strung out along the front lines during the First Truce reported a number of incidents of IDF troops setting fire to Arab fields. Paul Cremona, the Special Representative of the UN Secretary General, on 23 June complained to Foreign Minister Shertok that these—he cited cases in Khulda, Deir Muheisin, and two other sites—constituted violations of the terms of the truce. Shertok replied three days later that 'no fire was set to Arab crops by Israeli troops. Crops did indeed take fire, but only by accident, the ignition having been caused by exhaust sparks from passing vehicles . . . and by the carelessness of drivers who threw off [*sic*] lighted cigarettes.'[23]

The problem, as the American chargé d'affaires to Damascus put

[22] Nahum Sarig to the units, 15 June 1948.
[23] ISA, FM 2416/9, Paul Cremona to Moshe Shertok, 23 June 1948 and M. Shertok to P. Cremona, 26 June 1948.

it, was that the 'Israelis refuse to permit refugees [to] return to their fields'. The problem of the Arab harvest, wrote Robert Memminger remained 'unsolved'.[24]

The matter was also brought up in the Israeli Cabinet, by Mapam's Agriculture Minister, Aharon Zisling, who throughout 1948 sniped at Ben-Gurion's policy towards the Palestinian Arabs, which Zisling, reflecting majority thinking in Mapam, thought tending towards expulsion. On 27 June, Zisling asked about rumoured plans to destroy forty abandoned Arab villages and about 'the burning of the standing crop' in various parts of the country. Ben-Gurion apparently did not reply. Two months later, the leaders of the Jewish kibbutzim of Ruhama, Nir-Am, and Dorot in the northern Negev complained that the army had burned the fields of beduin in their area who had been 'neutral' in the hostilities and that the exiled villagers of Huj, who had been 'friendly' towards the Jews, were being prevented from reaping their fields.[25]

These complaints, apparently, had, if any, only a marginal effect on Israeli behaviour. On 24 June a senior IDF liaison officer with the UN, Major Chaïm Herzog, reported to his commander, IDF Chief Liaison Officer with the UN Lieutenant-Colonel Baruch Komarov, that 'it was decided to somewhat ease [policy] concerning the harvest of Arab crops in no-man's land'. Herzog's discussion with the UN observers had focused on 'the infiltration of Arabs into our lines in order to reap [and] the burning of the Arab fields by our people . . .'.[26]

Be this as it may, in the main things remained unchanged: Arab crops were either burned or harvested by the Israelis, and Arab farmers were prevented from cultivating their fields—the abandoned ones in the rear of the IDF lines and those in no-man's land and near the Israeli lines. Major Herzog had a rather difficult conversation on the matter on 30 June with a senior UN observer in his sector.

[24] US National Archives (NA), RG 84, Jerusalem Consulate, Classified Records 1948, 800-Syria, Damascus (Memminger) to Secretary of State, 30 June 1948.

[25] KMA, AZP 9/9/1, 'Decisions of the Provisional Government', 27 June 1948; and ISA, FM 2564/9, Arye Farda (Dorot), Yaakov Gavri (Nir-Am), and Eliezer Frisch (Ruhama), to the Prime Minister and Defence Minister (Ben-Gurion), 4 Aug. 1948.

[26] ISA, FM 2426/5, Chaim Herzog to 'Baruch', 'Report on the Activities of the Liaison with the UN Observers in the Jerusalem–Tel Aviv Road Area', 24 June 1948.

Major Maliszewsky asked that the IDF permit the exiled Arabs of Abu Shusha, Deir Muheisin, Beit Jiz, and Beit Sussin (in the Latrun area) to be allowed to return to harvest their fields during the cease-fire. Herzog said 'no' and the UN man, according to the Israeli liaison officer, 'proceeded with his usual lecture on the inhumanity of war and the disgraceful conditions under which the poor Arabs were allowed to starve while we would not allow them to reap the harvest'. Herzog replied that 'this was war, and that also in accordance with the truce agreement, we were entitled to reap the Arab harvest in our areas. I was immediately informed in an indignant tone that this was sheer communism.' Herzog ended by saying that a 'concession' by Israel was possible on this point if the Arabs allowed the resumption of operation of the Latrun pumping station, which had traditionally pumped up from the Ras al Ayin spring much of Jerusalem's water supply. Nothing came of this. Herzog also turned down a request from the Father Superior of the Latrun Monastery to allow the Arabs of Beit Jiz and Beit Sussin to reap the monastery fields.[27]

On 3 July the Secretary General of the Arab League, Abdul Rahman Azzam (Pasha), formally complained to the UN Mediator for Palestine, Count Folke Bernadotte, about the Israeli prevention of Arabs' harvesting their fields behind Israeli lines. According to British diplomats in Cairo, Azzam had ordered Qawuqji's irregulars to shoot 'out of hand' Jews caught burning Arab fields.[28]

Bernadotte himself seems to have fundamentally misunderstood Israeli policy with regard to the harvest of the Arab fields. His reference to the problem in his interim or progress report of 16 September—which was to be his final report—on the Palestinian situation is misleading. 'The period of the first truce coincided with the ripening of cereal crops in Palestine. Since the front line ran almost entirely through land belonging to Arab cultivators, a great number of fields bearing crops [were] in no-man's land and in the vicinity of and sometimes behind Jewish positions [and this] often led the Jews to react by firing on the harvesters', he wrote. But this

[27] ISA, FM 2426/10, Vivien (Chaim) Herzog to 'Baruch', 'Report on a Meeting with Major Maliszewsky, UN Observer Latrun Area, and the Father Superior, Latrun Monastery, on June 30, 1948.'
[28] ISA, FM 2427/9, Abdul Rahman Azzam to Count Bernadotte, 3 July 1948; and PRO, F0371–68570 (E9283/4/31), British Middle East Office, Cairo, to Foreign Office, 9 July 1948.

'military' explanation held true only for Arab fields near and between IDF front line positions. The problem, as construed from Tel Aviv in mid-summer 1948, was essentially 'political' and policy on harvesting was bound up with decision-making about whether or not in general to allow an Arab refugee return. The decision against a return had crystallized, though not in definitive form, in mid-June, and the decisions against allowing Arab cultivation of abandoned fields and favouring Jewish harvesting of the abandoned Arab crops stemmed from it. Military considerations had little to do with it— except in the wider, strategic sense that a massive return of Arab refugees to their former villages and towns within Israeli-held territory could well strategically undermine the Jewish state.[29]

During the following months, hundreds of thousands of dunams of abandoned Arab fields were reaped by Jewish settlements in the north and centre of the country. From August, much of the abandoned land was formally leased out for periods of up to one year to the Jewish settlements. Along the cease-fire lines and in the Negev, most of which was only conquered by the IDF in October–December, IDF units regularly put Arab fields to the torch—sometimes as retaliatory measures though more often in implementation of a policy designed to prevent an Arab return or, as in the south, as part of the campaign to keep the area clear of potentially hostile Arabs. In early 1949, the government organized the harvesting of some 300,000–400,000 dunams of Arab crops in the Negev and northern Negev approaches.[30]

The prevention of the Arab harvest was also used as a tool of policy by the Israeli authorities *vis-à-vis* those Arabs who had preferred to remain in the Jewish state rather than go into exile. The

---

[29] See Benny Morris, 'Crystallization . . .', for a fuller discussion of this.

[30] See e.g. reports on Third Battalion raids on Arab Negev villages and their fields in September in KMA-PA 120, 12 (22 Sept. 1948) and 18 (29 Sept. 1948); and ISA, FM 2426/13, complaints from 5, 10, and 15 Nov. 1948, from Paul Mohn, the Personal Representative of Ralph Bunche, the Acting UN Mediator for Palestine, to Israel Foreign Ministry Director General Walter Eytan, about IDF prevention of Arab cultivation near the front lines. Mohn wrote, on 10 Nov., following IDF firing on cultivators at Al Midya and Ni'lin, on the central front: 'In view of the plight of the Arab civilians concerned, and in order to save them unnecessary hardships during the winter, UN observers have tried to make necessary local arrangements for the harvest, but they have met with difficulties from the side of the Israeli forces.' He asked Eytan to intervene—which Eytan subsequently did, without much success. On 15 Nov. Mohn warned Eytan that 'public opinion in the world' would not take kindly to Israel's treatment of the Palestinians, in connection with the harvest.

Middle East affairs experts at the Israel Foreign Ministry put it rather bluntly at the end of July, during the Second Truce: 'In many parts of the country the matter of collecting the harvest served as an important card in our hands. It was not without worth that the Druze in the north of the country [who had in April switched allegiance from the Arab to the Jewish side] were allowed to reap their crops while their neighbouring [Muslim] villages were barred from doing so and they are wandering around hungry.' The implication is that the Druze freedom to harvest their fields had been a factor in the retention of Druze loyalty by the Jewish side.[31] The same use was made by the Israeli authorities of the right to harvest in the case of Mahmoud al Mahdi, a Muslim, of Ijzim, in the Coastal Plain.[32]

In general, with many of the still-inhabited Arab villages (mostly in the Galilee) close to the front lines, Arabs were barred by the IDF and security services from cultivating their fields. Part of the problem was technical. The property of those who had fled the country now 'belonged' to the state. In the case of most of the villages—where all the inhabitants were no longer *in situ*—matters were simple; all the land 'belonged' to the state and could be, and was, distributed among Jewish settlements. But in Galilee, many villages remained at least partially inhabited; it was often difficult to distinguish between fields owned by those who had left the country (which now belonged to the state and could not be cultivated by the Arabs) and fields owned by villagers who had stayed put (which remained the possession of the villagers). But more important, the Arabs who had stayed put were placed under Military Government, and their freedom to move freely outside their villages was severely curtailed. The daily movement of villagers back and forth from village to fields (sometimes involving relatively great distances) was regarded by the authorities as a security risk or, at least, problem. The country was still at war with the Arabs; the Israeli Arab minority was seen as a bed of potential saboteurs, spies, and fifth columnists. Hence in most areas of the country, the Military Government and local IDF units found it simplest to forbid *in toto* Arab cultivation of

[31] KMA-PA 100/Mem VavDalet/1–22, '*BaTziburiut Ha'Aravit*', 20 July 1948.
[32] The case of Mahmoud al-Mahdi took up months of the time of Israeli Foreign Ministry and Defence Ministry officials. See ISA, FM 2570/1 for the protracted correspondence in the autumn and winter of 1948.

fields. At the same time, Jewish settlements began to cultivate fields of Arabs who had remained in the State. This is what happened, for example, to fields belonging to Shafa 'Amr inhabitants in November.[33]

The situation in the Galilee was summarized in April 1949 by the Mapai boss in Haifa, Abba Khoushy, in a speech to the party's Knesset members: in many villages, the Arabs were not being allowed access to their fields; some villages had remained 'without land'; their crops were being pillaged.[34]

Eventually, the Galilee lands were sorted out. Those belonging to absentees reverted permanently to the state, and were mostly distributed among the old and new Jewish settlements. And as the dust of the first Israeli–Arab war settled and the Military Government took efficient control of its wards, fears subsided and the Arab farmers still living in the state were allowed to resume cultivation of their fields.

But during 1948 and the early months of 1949, Israeli policy towards the Arab fields and the harvest of the summer and winter crops had contributed to the creation of the Palestinian refugee problem. The retaliatory policy of early 1948, involving the burning of Arab crops, had undermined rural Arab morale and self-confidence and to some extent impoverished Arab villagers; in some areas there was a lack of flour, or fears of an impending major shortage of flour. It certainly contributed to the readiness of the Palestinians to go into exile during the spring and summer. It is probable that at least some Haganah commanders understood that the arson of the fields would have this effect.

In May and June, a dual policy evolved in the Yishuv—to bar the Arab villagers, now in exile, from returning to harvest their fields and for the Yishuv to reap as much of the Arab crop as Jewish equipment and manpower allowed. What could not be harvested was destroyed. The policy effectively deepened the psychological and physical separation of the Arab *fellah* and tenant-farmer from

[33] ISA, MAM 302/83, Minority Affairs Ministry Haifa Branch office to the Minister for Minority Affairs, 9 Nov. 1948, and A. Hanuki, Agriculture Ministry, to the Minority Affairs Ministry, 28 Nov. 1948.

[34] ISA, Finance Ministry Papers 10/1/9, 'Protocol of the Meeting of the Leadership of the (Mapai Knesset) Faction together with Our Comrades in the Cabinet and Invited Guests on the Problem of Activity Among the (Israeli) Arabs', 26 Apr. 1949.

his lands and home, reinforcing his sense of, and existence as an, exile. In the Negev, still largely in Arab hands, the prevention by fire and sword of Arab harvesting was one direct cause of the Palestinian exodus. At the same time, the massive cultivation of the abandoned Arab fields by the Jewish settlements around the country forged an initial, powerful, and protracted link between these settlements and the newly cultivated fields. This link, within weeks, was to breed a sense of possessiveness which, in turn, led to demands for a permanent transfer of these lands into Jewish hands. The need, after the summer harvest, to sow the fields with winter crops and the state investment in seed-funds consolidated the hold of the state and the settlements on the abandoned lands. As agricultural pioneer and Mapai stalwart Shlomo Lavi put it in late July 1948: 'We have reaped the Arabs' fields and now a new [agricultural] year is upon us.' He proposed that the fields now be ploughed and sowed. 'We must not leave uncultivated fields', he told his Mapai colleagues. 'There is nothing more terrible for a farmer than to see fields of thistles, it is one of the greatest sins.' He suggested that the profit from the harvest could be given to the exiled landowners—if they resettled permanently in the Arab countries. Implicit in the appeal was the idea of permanent expropriation of the abandoned lands.[35]

The Jewish settlements and settlement associations, in which Lavi was a leading figure, during the summer became powerful interest groups militating against a return of the refugees. The day after Lavi's statement at the Mapai meeting, Reuven Cohen, a leading figure in the Kibbutz Meuhad kibbutz movement, one of the mainstays of Mapam, put one of the interest group's arguments very clearly:

The question is how to maintain the [Yishuv's] economy. One of the main things that could save us is extensive cultivation of [our lands] and, in addition, the cultivation of the Arabs' lands. This would mean an addition of about 1,000 dunams for each kibbutz . . . This is a plan and opportunity for additional income for the kibbutzim . . . The function of the [movement] is to press for the establishment of new settlements and to organize the settlement groups.

[35] LPA 23 aleph/48, protocol of the meeting of Merkaz Mapai (the Mapai Center), 24 July 1948, statement by Shlomo Lavi.

Cohen in this connection mentioned the abandoned Arab villages of Al Tira, Tantura, Buteimat, and Al Kafrin, all south or south-east of Haifa.[36]

The position taken by these powerful pressure groups (which provided the backbone of the defence establishment), in turn, hardened the Yishuv leadership's resolve, which effectively crystallized over the second half of 1948, not to allow a return of the refugees and not to give up any of the newly acquired lands.

Through the summer, autumn, and winter of 1948 the Israeli security forces prevented Arab cultivation of abandoned fields in the rear of the IDF lines and near them, and the cultivation of 'unabandoned' lands (those whose owners had stayed in Israel). In large measure the reason for this policy was military; constant movement across the borders by infiltrators invited and heralded trouble for the Jewish state. And such 'temporary' forays into Israel could well lead to resettlement by the refugees on a more permanent footing in the desolate villages, representing a strategic-political (fifth column) threat to the new-born Jewish state. Be that as it may, the policy and measures designed to prevent Arab cultivation of the abandoned fields served to consolidate the separation of the exiles from their lands, driving home the message that there would be no return, which, in turn, further demoralized the exiles and made it that much easier for Israel to keep them out. At the same time, the prevention of cultivation by Arabs still resident in the state and the takeover of most Arab fields by the Jewish settlements cannot but have persuaded some of the exiles that they would face an uncomfortable life if they did indeed return; and it may have persuaded some of those who had so far remained in Israel that life would be more pleasant, after all, in exile. It is possible that some of those who fled before the advancing IDF in October 1948 in the Galilee and Negev were at least in part motivated by the knowledge of what had befallen their cousins who had come under Israeli rule in the months before.

---

[36] KMA 1 bet/8/35, protocol of the meeting of the Kibbutz Meuhad Secretariat, statement by Reuven ("Vinya") Cohen, 25 July 1948.

8

The Case of Abu Ghosh and Beit Naqquba, Al Fureidis and Jisr Zarka in 1948— or Why Four Villages Remained

In the course of December 1947–August 1949, the great majority of the Arabs living within the territory that in the first Israeli–Arab war became Israel went into exile and became refugees. Most of these refugees were created during the bitter fighting of April–June and July 1948. Those who remained behind, becoming Israel's Arab minority, were concentrated almost exclusively in the areas that fell to Israeli forces towards the end of the war, in October–November, or were transferred to Israeli sovereignty through the Israel–Jordan General Armistice Agreement of April 1949, at war's end—the central and upper Galilee, the northern Negev (beduins), and the western foothills of Samaria (Umm al Fahm and Wadi Ara, At Taiyiba Baqa al Gharbiya, Kafr Qasim).

Nowhere was the clearing of Arab communities out of the Jewish State more thorough and complete than along the new state's two major highways, the Tel Aviv–Haifa road on the Mediterranean coast and the Tel Aviv–Jerusalem road running through what became known as the 'Jerusalem corridor'. The great majority of the Coastal Plain and 'corridor' Arabs fled over March–May 1948— out of fear, Jewish and Arab pressures, and Jewish attack and expulsion.

But there were four notable exceptions: the villages of Abu Ghosh and Beit Naqquba, west of Jerusalem, sitting astride the Tel Aviv–Jerusalem highway, and Al Fureidis and Jisr Zarka (also called 'Arab al Ghawarina), south of Haifa along the main Tel Aviv–Haifa coast road. These villages remained, and have grown and prospered along with Israel itself during the past forty years. Why these villagers were allowed by the Yishuv to stay put and what, if any, was the significance of these exceptions, will be examined in the following pages.

ABU GHOSH AND BEIT NAQQUBA

In late June 1948, during the month-long First Truce between Israel and the invading Arab states, the IDF's Harel Brigade, responsible for the Jerusalem corridor, made clear to the local Jewish settlements and to the national political leadership its desire and intention to expel the villagers of Abu Ghosh and Beit Naqquba before the resumption of hostilities, which all expected (and indeed occurred) on 8–9 July.

Abu Ghosh was regarded by the Yishuv as a 'friendly' (some Arabs might and did say 'collaborationist') village. Traditionally, its relations with neighbouring Kibbutz Kiryat Anavim—during 1948 the site of the HQ of various Harel Brigade units—were excellent. The village had occasionally sold arms to the kibbutz; it regularly provided the Jewish defenders—who included a Palmah company —with information about hostile Arab intentions, armaments, and alignments. During the Mandate, the Arab villagers repeatedly shielded or hid Jewish—both Haganah and LHI—militiamen and terrorists being sought by the British authorities. Throughout the 1936–9 Arab Rebellion in Palestine, Abu Ghosh defied the Arab irregulars (called by the Yishuv *knufiyot* or gangs) and in various ways assisted Kiryat Anavim. 'They worked together with the [British] army against the gangs', according to Ya'akov Lisser, the *mukhtar* of Kiryat Anavim.[1]

Abu Ghosh adopted the same attitude during the first months of the 1948 war, supplying Kiryat Anavim with 'small quantities of ammunition'. Other Arab villages treated the inhabitants of Abu Ghosh as 'enemies and traitors'.[2] Throughout the first months of the war, the villagers had displayed 'not only loyalty but a friendly attitude towards the Yishuv . . . [Jewish] convoys that were attacked found sanctuary in Abu Ghosh'. Kiryat Anavim requested funds

---

[1]   ISA, FM 2564/9, 'Memorandum of the Meeting on 6 July 1948 at the Police Ministry, between Mr. B. Shitrit, the Minister of Police and Minority Affairs, and Mr. Ya'akov Lisser, who Represents Kiryat Anavim in the Question of the Arabs of Abu Ghosh', 7 July 1948. But relations between Kiryat Anavim and Abu Ghosh were apparently not quite so consistently halcyon as later myth asserted. One kibbutz old-timer, writing in the settlement's volume recalling 1948, *Al Em Haderekh* (Kiryat Anavim Press, 1949), 5, states that 'we also suffered from Abu Ghosh not a little, though it [generally] displayed towards us good neighbourly relations . . .'.
[2]   ISA, FM 2564/9, 'Memorandum of the Meeting on 6 July 1948 . . .'.

from the Jewish Agency for Abu Ghosh, which was in economic straits, and during the following months supplied the village with provisions.[3]

Relations between Kiryat Anavim and Beit Naqquba—in effect a satellite village of Abu Ghosh—were never quite as good. The kibbutz had always coveted and repeatedly (and unsuccessfully) tried to buy tracts of land from Beit Naqquba. During the Arab Rebellion, Beit Naqquba apparently hosted Arab irregulars passing through and occasionally there had been sniping between the two communities.

During April and May 1948, Haganah units, spearheaded by the Palmah's Harel Brigade, fought bitter battles (operations Nahshon, Yevussi, Maccabi, and Bin-Nun A and B) against the irregulars and the Transjordanian army, the Arab Legion, for possession and dominance of the Tel Aviv–Jerusalem highway, the only lifeline to Jerusalem's besieged 100,000-strong Jewish community. In the course of the fighting, almost all the Arab villages in the corridor were depopulated, either by flight or Israeli expulsion. Abu Ghosh, and smaller Beit Naqquba, remained *in situ*, despite occasional requests by local Palmah commanders for permission to expel or nudge the villagers into at least temporary flight.

In early June pressure built up to expel Abu Ghosh. Yishuv intelligence sources reported that 'people from Abu Ghosh are giving information to the enemy, either willingly or under duress'. The continued presence of the villagers near IDF bases was causing 'demoralization'. Ya'akov Shimoni, of the Foreign Ministry's Middle East Affairs Department, an old Haganah Intelligence Service hand, thought that perhaps the time had come to 'expel [Abu Ghosh], while [maintaining friendship] with them', a position he had long advocated. But he added a caveat that the possibility of using Abu Ghosh for contrary, Yishuv intelligence purposes also needed examining.[4] But a week later, the caveat was removed, and Shimoni took action. On 15 June he met Lisser and another man named 'Segal' and concluded with them that 'on the eve of the renewal of hostilities, they would give forceful advice [to the inhabitants of the village] to pack up and leave. Meanwhile, they

---

[3] CZA S25-9.194, Kibbutz Kiryat Anavim to the Political Department of the Jewish Agency, 29 Apr. 1948.
[4] ISA, FM 2570/6, Shimoni to Eliahu Sasson, 9 June 1948.

would continue to adopt the usual attitude towards [the villagers] and would not say anything [to them].'[5] From the context, incidentally, it would appear that Shimoni had meant departure of Abu Ghosh's population to Arab territory rather than transfer inland, into the interior of the Jewish State.[6]

Meanwhile, more or less simultaneously, the local army command, probably led by Harel Brigade OC Colonel Yosef Tabenkin, also decided that the time had come for expulsion or transfer. 'The military believe that one must not leave inside our area an Arab village like Abu Ghosh with a population of 1,000 and [like] Beit Naqquba with a population of 300 . . . The army wishes to move the Arabs from Abu Ghosh and clean up the place [*lenakot et hamakom*].'[7]

Word of this quickly filtered out to Minority Affairs Minister Bechor Shitrit, who on 30 June raised the matter 'urgently' in the Cabinet. The proposal mooted, apparently, was to transfer the inhabitants of Abu Ghosh (and perhaps also of Beit Naqquba) to Jaffa, from which most of the original Arab population had fled out of fear and under the impact of the Irgun Zva'i Leumi (National Military Organization or 'Irgun') assault, in April and early May. Prompted by Shitrit and the two Mapam ministers, the Cabinet blocked the IDF resolve by deciding that only the 'Ministerial Committee for the Abandoned Area' (soon officially designated the Ministerial Committee for Abandoned Property) could decide on such an expulsion.[8]

But Harel Brigade, especially in view of the imminent renewal of hostilities, still wanted the villagers out. On 6 July, Lisser went to Tel Aviv to meet with Minority Affairs Minister Shitrit. Shitrit, who had apparently initiated the meeting, informed Lisser of the 30 June Cabinet decision that the fate of Abu Ghosh was in the hands of the Ministerial Committee for Abandoned Property. He asked Lisser for Kiryat Anavim's position.

Lisser declared that the kibbutz was 'of the opinion that the Arabs of Abu Ghosh and Beit Naqquba should be allowed to stay in their places . . .'. They were providing the Yishuv's forces with

[5] ISA, FM 2570/6, note on 'A telephone conversation', Shimoni to Eliahu Sasson, 15 June 1948.
[6] ISA, FM 2566/15, Y. Shimoni to B. Shitrit, 13 July 1948.
[7] ISA, FM 2564/9, 'Memorandum of Meeting on 6 July 1948 . . .'.
[8] KMA-AZP 9/9/1, 'Decisions of the Provisional Government', 30 June 1948.

information. He conceded that it was possible that they were also providing the enemy with intelligence. But he noted that, in April, the inhabitants of Abu Ghosh had voluntarily handed over to the Haganah the strategic police fort overlooking the village when the British departed.

Shitrit asked Lisser whether the Arabs of Abu Ghosh knew that the army wanted to transfer them. Lisser: 'They don't know about this—but I am preparing them for this psychologically.' At one point in the conversation, Lisser said that it was he who had proposed to Yitzhak Navon, the IDF intelligence officer responsible for liaison with Abu Ghosh and Beit Naqquba, that the villagers be transferred to Jaffa. Summarizing his position, Lisser said: 'I oppose, in principle, the transfer [of the Abu Ghosh population]—but we will not stand against the army if it decides differently.'[9]

But events were fast approaching a climax. On 6–7 July, the inhabitants of Beit Naqquba, 'including their children and women, their sheep and property (as much as they could take)' decamped, according to Shitrit 'after receiving an order from their Arab commander in Ein Karim to leave the place'.[10]

As to Abu Ghosh, '900 of the [village's] 1,000' inhabitants also left, 'though they received no expulsion order' from the Israelis (according to Shitrit). The inhabitants, wrote Shitrit, had left because of 'a state of mind' generated by the example of the evacuation of the women and children of Kiryat Anavim and the neighbouring kibbutz, Ma'aleh Hahamisha, in the days before the end of the First Truce. They were probably also influenced by the departure of their Arab neighbours from Beit Naqquba.

The army now pressed for the evacuation of the remaining inhabitants of Abu Ghosh and, on 11 July, issued a written expulsion order to this effect. Lisser, instructed by the army to tell the remaining Abu Ghosh inhabitants to leave, came to Shitrit to ask what to do. Lisser repeated his proposal that the population be transferred to Jaffa, if they could not remain in the

---

[9] ISA, FM 2564/9, 'Memorandum of a Meeting on 6 July 1948 . . .'.
[10] ISA, MAM 307/44, 'Information Concerning the Arabs of Abu Ghosh', by Bechor Shitrit, 12 July 1948, reporting on his meeting that morning with Ya'akov Lisser. The diary of Kiryat Anavim's area commander (ma'az) put the flight of the Beit Naqquba inhabitants on 8 July. See *Al Em Haderekh*, (Kiryat Anavim Press, 1949), 34.

village.[11] Shitrit thereupon wrote directly to Harel Brigade HQ saying that he had seen the order (file number 'kof-resh/7/16')—which stated that the evacuation of Abu Ghosh was 'necessary and urgent' and that 'every assistance' must be rendered to Lisser in carrying out the order. Shitrit informed Harel HQ that he had protested to Foreign Minister Moshe Sharett—obviously on the grounds that the army was acting contrary to the Cabinet decision of 30 June and without the authorization of the Ministerial Committee for Abandoned Property. Sharett, Shitrit told Harel HQ, 'informed me that the eviction should not be carried out so long as the Minister of Defence [David Ben-Gurion] had not ruled in the matter'. Shitrit ordered Harel HQ to ask for Ben-Gurion's ruling before taking any action. Should Ben-Gurion support the eviction, added Shitrit, it should be carried out with a minimum [amount of] discomfort for the inhabitants of this village . . . who, to some extent, had helped us, and we do not want it said that we demanded their evacuation'.[12]

But it appears that Lisser (or Shitrit) had not been completely frank about the reasons for the departure of the inhabitants of Beit Naqquba and of the bulk of the population of Abu Ghosh. The Harel Brigade expulsion order (of 11 July) regarding Abu Ghosh, indeed, had been formulated *after* the bulk of the inhabitants had left and, in any event, was not served. But the 900 had apparently left at least in part because they had also been strongly advised, if not actually ordered, to do so by Lisser himself and by Yitzhak Navon, the local IDF intelligence officer. Navon later recalled that he had gathered together (apparently in Kibbutz Kiryat Anavim around 5–6 July) representatives of both Abu Ghosh and Beit Naqquba and had told them that 'they must leave' (though they would be allowed back, he promised, when the fighting ended). Lisser, it appears, had told the villagers the same thing, either at the same meeting or separately.

The published version of the Kiryat Anavim area commander's diary from the period more or less confirms this, at least as regards Beit Naqquba. It states, in the entry for 8 July: 'The day before the

[11] ISA, MAM 307/44, 'Information Concerning the Arabs . . .', 12 July 1948. Shitrit passed on Lisser's explanation of why the 900 had abandoned Abu Ghosh to Shimoni at the Foreign Ministry. See ISA, FM 2564/10, Shitrit to Shimoni, 19 July 1948.
[12] ISA, MAM 307/44, B. Shitrit to Harel Brigade HQ, 12 July 1948.

end of the truce . . . Arabs from Beit Naqquba came to say goodbye. They are leaving. The parting was friendly and tearful. It is difficult to see friends in tears. But the military consideration [*hashikul hatzva'i*] is for departure . . .'. The implication is that the Yishuv's 'military consideration' was the overriding factor; the Kiryat Anavim diary contains no mention of an external Arab order for Beit Naqquba to evacuate. Nor—and I think this points to Kiryat Anavim's uneasy conscience regarding these events—does the published version of the diary contain any reference to or explanation of the evacuation of the bulk of the Abu Ghosh population.[13]

Among the Yishuv leadership in mid-July it was understood that the villagers of Abu Ghosh had been expelled by the IDF. Yosef Sprinzak, the secretary general of the Histadrut trade-union federation (later Speaker of the Knesset), heatedly condemned the 'expulsion' a few days later.[14] Mapam's Agriculture Minister, Aharon Zisling, also raised the matter in Cabinet.[15]

(Incidentally, several months later Kiryat Anavim was to deny that a 'promise'—that they would eventually be allowed to return— had been given to the villagers of Beit Naqquba: 'They left the village without receiving from us any promise regarding their future', the kibbutz later wrote the government.)[16]

In any event, Shitrit's actions (the 'halt' order, regarding the 100–150 remaining inhabitants of Abu Ghosh, to Harel Brigade HQ and his talk with Sharett in the matter) and Zisling's submission of the matter to Cabinet debate on 14 July, had had the necessary effect. Ben-Gurion specifically forbade an expulsion without his 'written authorization' and, in any case, had noted that the 'urgency' of the

---

[13] *Ha'ir*, 'Tzipor Achat Ba'etz', by Yehuda Litani, 11 Nov. 1983; interview in 1987 with Mihik Shapira, of Kibbutz Kiryat Anavim, who had heard the story of the two villages in 1948 from Lisser; and *Al Em Haderekh*, p. 34. It is possible that the inhabitants of Beit Naqquba had received *both* an order to evacuate from Arab military commanders in Ein Karim and 'strong advice' to the same effect from Lisser and Navon. But it is likely that the 'advice' given in the name of the Harel Brigade, which physically controlled the area, was the more potent of the two factors in precipitating the evacuation.

[14] See Histadrut Archive (Va'ad Hapo'el Building, Tel Aviv), protocols of the meeting of the Histadrut Executive Committee, 14 July 1948.

[15] KMA-AZP 9.9.1, 'Decisions of the Provisional Government', 14 July 1948.

[16] ISA, MAM 307/44, Kiryat Anavim to 'the Government Committee Dealing with Arabs', 30 Jan. 1949.

desired expulsion had faded as a result of the capture of the neighbouring Arab village of Suba (on 12 July). But, apparently, Ben-Gurion had indicated that he would approve the transfer—to Jaffa, not out of the country—of the remaining Abu Ghosh population should a military need recur.[17]

By early August, there were some 300 villagers in Abu Ghosh—consisting of the 100–150 who had stayed put and dozens of others who, in dribs and drabs, had infiltrated through the Arab and Israeli lines back to their homes. The area commander of Kiryat Anavim noted in his diary on 19 July that '200 Arabs had returned to Abu Ghosh'.[18] Meanwhile, the bulk of the village's 'refugees', camped out near Ramallah, were having a bad time. The locals treated them like traitors; a handful were even jailed.

As to the Arabs of Beit Naqquba, they had come to temporary rest in the abandoned village of Sataf, in no-man's land, to the south, 'under trees, because the Arabs had not allowed them to come over their lines, out of distrust and revenge'. The IDF had agreed to their staying at Sataf. The Beit Naqquba refugees had appealed, via Abu Ghosh notables and Lisser, to be allowed to return to their village or, at least, to come to Abu Ghosh. Lisser reported that the inhabitants of Abu Ghosh were willing to take in their brethren from Beit Naqquba.[19]

Shitrit asked Ben-Gurion for instructions.[20] The Prime Minister, responding through Cabinet Secretary Za'ev Sharef, evaded relevant reply: 'The people of Abu Ghosh had remained in their village', wrote Sharef, 'with the permission of the authorities.'[21]

Meanwhile, Lisser or Kiryat Anavim were busy playing a double game. While passing on to Shitrit the Beit Naqquba refugees' request to return, Lisser or fellow members from Kiryat Anavim had informed the army that the Beit Naqquba villagers were infiltrating into Abu Ghosh and settling in its abandoned houses. Kiryat

---

[17] ISA, FM 2564/10, Shitrit to Shimoni, 19 July 1948.

[18] *Al Em Haderekh*, p. 35.

[19] ISA, FM 2564/9, memorandum by Shitrit after a conversation with Lisser, 9 Aug. 1948.

[20] ISA, FM 2564/9, the Minister for Minority Affairs to the Prime Minister of Defence, 16 Aug. 1948.

[21] ISA, FM 2564/9, Cabinet Secretary to Minister for Minority Affairs, 30 Aug. 1948; ISA MAM 307/44, unsigned minute 'to the minister', 30 Aug. 1948; and ISA MAM 307/44, E. Chelouche to the Cabinet Secretariat, 9 Sept. 1948.

Anavim apparently hoped that the army would act to halt the influx of these refugees. Moreover, the kibbutz 'also proposed that the remaining Abu Ghosh villagers be transferred to Jaffa and thus end the problem of Arabs [living] on the main [Jerusalem–Tel Aviv] road, but this proposal did not at the time receive the requisite attention. The Arabs of Abu Ghosh, without hindrance, began to return to their village and with them, the Arabs of the village of Beit Naqquba.'[22]

Shitrit apparently got no direct reply from Ben-Gurion concerning the refugees' request to return. But the army, in the person of General Zvi Ayalon, OC Central Front, ruled in early September that it 'would not allow additional Arabs to enter Abu Ghosh as every additional Arab in our area is a superfluous burden'.[23] This view was shared by General Allon, the commander of the Palmah, and by Tabenkin, the commander of the Harel Brigade. Their attitude was that the Jerusalem corridor should remain 'clear of Arabs', at least for many years to come.[24]

Ayalon's attitude had in part been prompted by the continuous 'illegal' trickle during July and August of the Abu Ghosh refugees back to their home. This trickle also raised the hackles of Shimoni at the Foreign Ministry, who wrote to Shitrit that while he, too, was awaiting the Prime Minister's ruling regarding the refugees from both villages, the matter must not be solved by the unilateral, piecemeal return of the villagers as infiltrees. This 'disorganized' return must be halted.[25] But Lisser and Navon continued to lobby in Central Front HQ for formally allowing a return of the refugees, at least to Abu Ghosh (as the two had promised the departees in July).[26]

Meanwhile, many of the refugees from Abu Ghosh—the local army commanders apparently turning a blind eye—slowly made their way back to the village. By mid-January 1949, it was reported that the village, which had had 960 inhabitants before the war, now

---

[22] ISA, MAM 307/44, Kvutzat Kiryat Anavim to 'the Government Committee Dealing with Arabs', 30 Jan. 1949.
[23] ISA, MAM 307/44, HQ Military Government in the Occupied Areas to Minister for Minority Affairs, Defence Minister, Foreign Minister, 5 Sept. 1948.
[24] Interview in 1987 with Mihik Shapira, of Kibbutz Kiryat Anavim, who had heard from Lisser the Abu Ghosh and Beit Naqquba story.
[25] ISA, FM 2564/9, Y. Shimoni to the Minister for Minority Affairs, 25 Aug. 1948.
[26] Interview in 1987 with Mihik Shapira.

had 600, which included 60 originally from Beit Naqquba and 50 from another smaller, abandoned satellite village, 'Ein Rafa.[27]

By early 1949, Kiryat Anavim appears to have resigned itself to the permanent repopulation of its neighbour, Abu Ghosh. But it persistently lobbied against the government allowing the Beit Naqquba refugees to be allowed to stay in Abu Ghosh or to be allowed to return to their original village: 'In our opinion, it is illogical to allow the return of the inhabitants of the village [of Beit Naqquba, resident in Abu Ghosh, 97 in number] for the following reasons: (a) The village of Beit Naqquba is indeed too close to our kibbutz. (b) If the village is "renewed", our [kibbutz] will be surrounded on two sides.'

Kiryat Anavim proposed the resettlement of the refugees of both Beit Naqquba and Abu Ghosh in the nearby abandoned village of Khirbet al 'Umur. (It was unclear whether the kibbutz, when speaking of Abu Ghosh 'refugees', was referring only to those villagers who were still living outside the village or also to those who had remained throughout or had already returned to Abu Ghosh.)[28]

Kiryat Anavim's opposition to the return of the Beit Naqquba refugees to their village was strongly backed by the local Jewish regional council, on which sat representatives of Kibbutz Ma'aleh Ha'hamisha and other settlements.[29]

Kiryat Anavim's stand was only in part based on 'security' considerations. The kibbutz also wanted Beit Naqquba's lands. The problem was that the handful of Beit Naqquba refugees now living in Abu Ghosh continued to cultivate their lands, 'and it is to be assumed that they look forward to the day on which they will be able to return to their homes. It seems that so long as the Beit Naqquba inhabitants remain near their abandoned village, they will continue to maintain contact with their village, and the members of Kiryat Anavim will not be able to take over and cultivate the village lands.' Reporting this, the Interior Ministry official responsible for the Jerusalem District recommended that the Beit Naqquba villagers

[27] ISA, MAM 307/44, Shlomo Asherov to Gad Machnes, 17 Jan. 1949.
[28] ISA, MAM 307/44, Kvutzat Kiryat Anavim to 'the Government Committee Dealing with Arabs', 30 Jan. 1949.
[29] ISA, MAM 307/44, Judean Hills Settlements Bloc Committee to the Minister for Minority Affairs, 12 Nov. 1948.

residing in Abu Ghosh be moved 'somewhere . . . far away'.[30]

There remained a further problem—the nearby satellite village of 'Ein Rafa. Some ten families—'35 souls'—had either never abandoned it or had returned to their homes during the preceding months. The Interior Ministry official noted that the place had become a way-station for Arab infiltrees through the Jerusalem corridor and that 'the men of the new [Jewish] settlement of Misgav Palmah [subsequently named Kibbutz Tzuba, next to the abandoned Arab site, Suba] were very interested in ['Ein Rafa's] lands'. The official recommended that the ten families be moved to 'another Arab area'.[31] But his recommendation was never acted upon. 'Ein Rafa remains to this day.

Over the months, the bulk of Abu Ghosh's inhabitants returned to their homes, the army and civil authorities in this case turning a blind eye to the influx of Arabs. But sometime during the second half of 1949, as part of the government's increasingly hard-line policy *vis-à-vis* Arab infiltrators, the authorities decided to put an end to the continued, piecemeal infiltration of Abu Ghosh and Beit Naqquba refugees back to Abu Ghosh. (All such illegally returning refugees were regarded as illegal residents, and liable to arbitrary deportation.) Those who had made it back to Abu Ghosh by March–April 1949 were left alone (even though they had not been in the country during the autumn 1948 census and were not necessarily in possession of official ID cards). But the more recent infiltrators were targeted for expulsion. In a series of more or less brutal search-and-expulsion operations, police and IDF units descended upon the village, identified and rounded up infiltrees, and pushed them over the border into Jordan.

Following one such round-up, in early July 1950, the inhabitants of Abu Ghosh sent off an emotional appeal to Knesset members, political parties, and journalists. In their 'open letter', the inhabitants charged that the Israelis had repeatedly 'surrounded our village, and taken our women, children and old folk, and thrown them over

---

[30] ISA, MAM 307/44, A. Bergman (Biran), Jerusalem District Commissioner, to 'the Government Committee for the Settlement of Dispossessed Arabs', 16 Mar. 1949.

[31] ISA, MAM 307/44, A. Bergman, Jerusalem District Commissioner, to 'the Government Committee for Settling Dispossessed Arabs', 16 Mar. 1949.

the border, and into the Negev Desert, and many of them died in consequence, when they were shot [trying to make their way back across] the borders'. So far, the inhabitants had held their peace.

But we cannot remain silent in face of the latest incident last Friday, when we woke up to the shouts blaring over the loudspeaker announcing that the village was surrounded and anyone trying to get out would be shot . . . The police and military forces then began to enter the houses and conduct meticulous searches, but no contraband was found. In the end, using force and blows, they gathered up our women and old folk and children, the sick and the blind and pregnant women. These shouted for help but there was no saviour. And we looked on and were powerless to do anything save beg for mercy. Alas, all our pleas were of no avail . . . They then took the prisoners, who were weeping and screaming, to an unknown place, and we still do not know what befell them.

On 11 July, taking heed of the press and public criticism that the affair had sparked, which included a Knesset debate and vote (won by the coalition), Ben-Gurion jotted down in his diary:

[Jerusalem District Commissioner Avraham] Biran and the chief of police came to me concerning the round-up in Abu Ghosh. In June [should be, July] 1948 there were 180 souls in the village . . . Today there are more than 800 souls. In the round-up, 105 persons were caught, mostly children and women, [and] a minority of men. That is the method of infiltration—they first send women and children, afterwards comes the male. There are thieves and smugglers in the village. According to [Moshe] Perlman, there are 300 infiltrators in the village; 150 were left alone, 150 must be expelled; only 105 were caught, there are another 45 [to catch and expel] . . . There were no acts of cruelty in the round-up. The infiltrators caught were handed over to the army for expulsion.

The incident also sparked some soul-searching within the Cabinet. Foreign Minister Sharett wrote that

with all the logical and relevant justification for the wholesale round-up, which included women and children, it is a fact that forcible expulsion of women and children stirs up the public and perturbs its conscience. The public will not countenance such measures for long and it is well to take note of this . . . Therefore, the battle against the infiltrators must be waged in ways that will not lead to a public rebellion against the government . . .

Sharett proposed that the government act with greater vigour and immediacy against infiltrators, so that they do not amass in each village and do not manage to reside in the village for a year and longer before the authorities act against them. He also cautioned against expelling women and children; 'only adult males' should be expelled.

Sharett was able to discover a silver lining in the affair: 'One must comment that the fact that there was, among the public, a display of moral sensitivity is praiseworthy and I am certain that none of us would like to see in our public a complete lack of moral sensibility regarding such issues of humanity.'[32] In the end only several dozen Abu Ghosh families remained in exile, as refugees, in the Ramallah area in the West Bank.

But as the months wore on, the Beit Naqquba 'refugees' living in Abu Ghosh outwore their welcome. The Abu Ghosh leaders wanted them out. But their homes in Beit Naqquba 'had been given to new [Jewish] immigrants from Yugoslavia' and their orchards—apples, pears—were being cultivated by Jews 'who were not allowing the Arabs of Beit Naqquba to enjoy the fruits of their trees'. The Agriculture Ministry recommended that they be resettled near Lydda or Ramle, where there were empty, abandoned, semi-intact Arab houses. But the Arabs of Beit Naqquba refused to budge, demanding that they be resettled on their lands some distance from Abu Ghosh and from their original village, to which, they gradually understood, they could never return. So, by common consent, the Beit Naqquba refugees were allowed to stay on in Abu Ghosh.[33]

For fourteen years the refugees from Beit Naqquba lived in Abu Ghosh. Then, starting in 1962, with the permission and encouragement of the Israeli authorities, they gradually moved to a new site, named 'Ein Naqquba, on some of their lands south of the Jerusalem–Tel Aviv highway. After 1967, some Beit Naqquba refugees who had lived in refugee camps and villages in the West Bank, around Bethlehem, were also allowed back into Israel, and joined their

[32] 'An Open Letter to the Inhabitants of Israel', 25 Ramadan 1369 (10 July 1950), by the inhabitants of the village of Abu Ghosh, in HHA kaf-90-1/6; Ben-Gurion diary, 11 July 1950, in David Ben-Gurion Archive. Sdeh Boqer; and Foreign Minister Moshe Sharett to the advisor on special affairs, Reuven Shiloah, 14 July 1950, in ISA, FM 2402/12.

[33] ISA, AM 591, Avraham Hanuki, secretary of the Agriculture Ministry, to 'the Committee for Refugees next to the Prime Minister's Office', 2 Nov. 1949; A. Hanuki to the Adviser on Arab Affairs, the Prime Minister's Office, 28 Feb. 1950; and Moshe Levin, in the name of Zalman Liff (Lifshitz), the Adviser to the Prime Minister on Land Matters, to the Custodian of Absentees Property, 16 Mar. 1950.

brethren at the new village site. The site overlooks their old village
site, today the Jewish settlement of Beit Nekofa.[34]

AL FUREIDIS AND KHIRBET JISR AZ ZARKA

In May 1948, the large Arab village of Al Fureidis south of Haifa
and the small, former beduin village of Jisr Zarka ('Arab al
Ghawarina), five kilometres to the south, along the Tel Aviv–
Haifa highway, surrendered to the Haganah without a fight. The
surrender had been preceded by orders to Al Fureidis, in late April,
by the Arab Liberation Army, the foreign Arab volunteer force
assisting the Palestinians against the Yishuv, to evacuate its 'women
and children . . . and to be ready to completely evacuate [the
village]'.[35] The local Arab command was clearly worried by the
prospect that the village would be attacked by the Haganah and fall,
and/or that the inhabitants might agree to surrender and live under
Jewish rule.

When the Arab inhabitants of the northern Coastal Plain began
to leave their villages in April, out of panic, or under Jewish
or Arab pressure, the inhabitants of Al Fureidis and Jisr Zarka
'also wanted to abandon their villages out of fear of coming to harm,
but under the influence of the heads of the *moshavot* [Jewish private
farmers' settlements] of Zikhron Ya'akov and Binyamina, they
stayed in their places, after being promised that they had nothing to
fear'.[36]

Before 1948, relations between Al Fureidis and Jisr Zarka and
the neighbouring Jewish *moshava* of Zikhron Ya'akov, one
of the country's main wine-producing centres, had been generally
good. The villages supplied the *moshava* with field-hands for its
vineyards. During the first months of the war, snipers from Al
Fureidis occasionally fired on Jewish traffic on the main road. But in
general, peace prevailed between Zikhron and its Arab neighbours.

By early May, with the Haganah clearly on the ascendant, Al
Fureidis (and two nearby villages, As Sindiyana and Sabbarin)

---

[34] *Ha'ir* 'Tzipor Achat Ba'etz', by Yehuda Litani, 11 Nov. 1983.
[35] KMA-PA 100/MemVavDalet/3—150, 'Yediot Tene, 6.5.1948.', referring to
24 Apr. 1948.
[36] ISA, MAM 307/31, the Minister for Minority Affairs to the Ministers of
Defence, Agriculture, and Labour, 25 June 1948. Shitrit was reporting on a meeting
he had had on 24 June 1948 with local leaders from Zikhron Ya'akov and Binyamina.

decided, according to Haganah intelligence, 'not to allow the entry of foreign [Arab] forces and not to serve on any account as a base for the [Arab] Liberation Army . . .'. Moreover, Al Fureidis was 'willing to live in peace with its [Jewish] neighbours . . .'.[37] Within days, the village surrendered to the Haganah, giving up its arms. The inhabitants of Jisr Zarka had surrendered to the Haganah a few days earlier. A meeting of Haganah intelligence officers immediately afterwards ruled against expulsion, instructing that 'the village is to be treated in accordance with the guidelines laid down regarding a surrendering village'.[38]

But within weeks, the presence of the two villages in the northern Coastal Plain, in an area completely cleared of Arabs during the previous months, began to irk the local IDF unit, the Alexandroni Brigade. The IDF, complained Abba Shechter, the 'mayor' of Zikhron, Shalom Burstein, a member of the vine-growers association, and Asher Schumann, the chairman of the Agricultural Committee in Binyamina, wanted to prohibit the inhabitants of the two villages from 'moving around'. The problem, the delegation of local Jewish leaders told Shitrit, was that Al Fureidis (with a population of some 500–600 supplied the two *moshavot* with 129 workers; Jisr Zarka supplied an additional, smaller number. 'The agricultural work in Zikhron Ya'akov and Binyamina is based mainly on hired [Arab] labour.' In the past, workers from the two villages had worked in the Zikhron and Binyamina fields together with youngsters from the *moshavot*. But the Jewish youngsters were all mobilized in the army, 'and now the farming in the two *moshavot* is dependent on the work of the Arab labourers from the nearby [villages]. If these workers are expelled or arrested, the farms will remain without workers and agriculture will be seriously jeopardised.'

The Alexandroni Brigade OC, Dan Epstein, and the district commander, Yitzhak Shemi, were now preventing the villagers from reaching the Jewish fields and vineyards. The local Jewish leaders had proposed to Shemi that the villagers be restricted to their villages by curfew during the nights but that they be allowed to

---

[37] KMA-PA 100/MemVavDalet/3—154, 'Yediot Tene 9 May 1948'; see also ISA, MAM 307/31, Minister for Minority Affairs to the Ministers of Defence, Agriculture, and Labour, 25 June 1948.

[38] David Ben-Gurion Archive, 'Summary of the Meeting of Arab Affairs Advisers in Netanya', 9 May 1948.

go to work in the daylight hours, after being issued with ID cards. 'But he naturally rejected this', the Jewish leaders complained. And, above everything, hovered the threat of a permanent solution —a mass expulsion. If the villagers are expelled, 'the heads of the *moshavot* will appear as breakers of promises'. Moreover, the promises were given, said the local Jewish leaders, only after they 'had consulted with the defence forces'. In other words, the local IDF commanders had approved the Zikhron and Binyamina leaders' appeals to the inhabitants of Al Fureidis and Jisr Zarka to stay and, at least implicitly, had endorsed the assurances that no harm would come to them if they did so.

The local leaders were apparently persuasive. Two days after their meeting with the Minister for Minority Affairs, Shitrit appealed to his fellow ministers, including David Ben-Gurion, 'to delay for four weeks any action aimed at the removal of the inhabitants of these villages or their detention as prisoners [an option apparently threatened by the Alexandroni Brigade officers] . . .'.[39]

Shitrit won the support of Mapam. Mordechai Bentov, the Minister of Labour, proposed that the police (who were controlled by Shitrit himself) be placed in charge of the two villages. 'I don't think the security forces have any legal basis for carrying out these mooted actions [that is, expulsion or detentions]', he said.[40]

The following day the matter came up for decision in the Cabinet, apparently tabled by Shitrit. There was 'a plan to transfer the Arabs of Fureidis and Ghawarina'. The ministers decided that Arabs were not to be 'transferred from place to place without the decision of the committee for the abandoned area', that is, the Ministerial Committee for Abandoned Property, which met for the first time a fortnight later.[41]

But the approaching end of the First Truce—as with the Harel Brigade and Abu Ghosh and Beit Naqquba—fired the Alexandroni Brigade into action. On 7 July, the day before the truce ended, Epstein decided 'to end the Ghawarina affair. He intends to transfer them to the Arab area [that is, outside the state] or to a prisoner-of-war camp.' The reason for the precipitate decision, according to the

[39] ISA, MAM 307/31, the Minister of Minority Affairs to the Ministers of Defence, Agriculture, and Labour, 25 June 1948.
[40] ISA, MAM 307/31, M. Bentov to B. Shitrit, 29 June 1948.
[41] KMA-AZP 9.9.1., 'Decisions of the Provisional Government', 30 June 1948.

brigade's Arab-affairs adviser, Shlomo Zucker, was that 'a gang had visited and run amok' in Jisr Zarka. The adviser despatched an 'urgent' cable to the 'IDF General Staff / the Department for Arab Affairs' to step in and halt the prospective expulsion.[42]

Shitrit, to whom the adviser had sent a copy of his cable, the same day contacted Alexandroni HQ to try to find out what was going on, but failed to locate the relevant officers. His only comment was that he opposed transferring the inhabitants of Jisr Zarka to Al Fureidis—an option not actually mentioned in the adviser's cable.[43] Two days later the adviser clarified matters: 'The gang's rampage . . . was directed against villagers and was aimed at robbery.' (The gangsters got away with I£700). In his confused response, the adviser seemed to express support for transferring the Ghawarina, should the need arise. But, meanwhile, expulsion had been stymied.[44]

No sooner had the problem of the Ghawarina died down, however, than the bigger problem of Al Fureidis surged again to the surface. In mid-July, the IDF was heavily engaged on all three fronts against the Arab armies—the Arab Liberation Army and the Syrian Army in the north, the Arab Legion in the centre, and the Egyptian Army in the south. The resulting tension also encompassed Alexandroni, which remained fairly inactive but poised to repel a possible thrust towards the coast by the Legion or the Iraqi Army stationed in Samaria. Alexandroni clearly wanted Al Fureidis—behind the lines and sitting astride a major highway—out.

In early July, the brigade's Arab-affairs adviser journeyed to Jaffa—where the IDF Intelligence Service was headquartered—to take advice. He then recommended, in view of the lively and 'undesirable' illegal movement of infiltrators back and forth around Al Fureidis, that ID cards be issued to the inhabitants, that a police

---

[42] ISA, MAM 307/48, Arab-affairs adviser / Alexandroni Brigade, to General Staff / Department for Arab Affairs, 8 July 1948.

[43] ISA, MAM 307/48, Shitrit to the adviser for Arab affairs, Alexandroni Brigade, 9 July 1948.

[44] ISA, MAM 307/48, Arab-affairs Adviser / Alexandroni Brigade to the Minister for Minority Affairs, 12 July 1948. Mapam may also have had a hand in removing the expulsion threat. At the meeting of the Histadrut Executive Committee on 14 July, Moshe Erem, a Mapam representative, referred to 'an Arab village near Zikhron Ya'akov' that, 'with great trouble, we succeeded' in saving from expulsion, 'for the time being'. See the protocols of the Histadrut Executive Committee meeting of 14 July 1948, Histadrut Archive.

station be established in the village, and that a permanent nightly curfew be imposed.[45] This advice was promptly acted upon: Alexandroni notified the Agricultural Committee at Zikhron, Binyamina, and Hadera that it intended to institute a curfew in Fureidis and Jisr Zarka 'and to prevent them by this means from going to work in Zikhron and its environs unless the farmers pay the army 580 [should read 850] mil per day as wages [1,000 mil = I£1], from which 500 mil will be paid the Arab worker and 350 mil will go to the army'.[46] The meaning was clear: either the Jewish farmers pay the army 350 mil per day per Arab worker or the army would completely seal off the villages, thus depriving the *moshavot* of their vital field hands.

The Zikhron farmers appealed once again to the Ministry for Minority Affairs. The implementation of the edict 'would do grave harm to the agricultural work of the *moshava*'. The farmers demanded that the edict be annulled or that its implementation be deferred 'at least until after the grape-gathering'.[47]

Shitrit raised the matter at the meeting of the Ministerial Committee for Abandoned Property the same day. The ministers ruled that 'this matter is under the jurisdiction of the Minister for Minority Affairs. The committee rejects [the idea] . . . and empowers the Minister for Minority Affairs to act accordingly.'[48] Shitrit then wrote to Alexandroni, expressing the ministerial committee's

astonishment . . . If the presence of the Arab workers endangers security, then the 350 mil the army will receive for each worker will not eliminate this danger, and if their presence is not dangerous to security, then there is no reason—indeed, it is prohibited—to impose on the [Jewish] farmers a payment, which is in the nature of a tax . . . Such an action is certainly illegal.

[45] ISA, MAM 307/48, Arab-affairs adviser / Alexandroni Brigade to IDF General Staff, etc., 10 July 1948.
[46] ISA, MAM 307/31, Minister for Minority Affairs to Alexandroni / Shlomo Zucker, 13 July 1948.
[47] ISA, MAM 307/48, H. Ariav, Secretary General of the Farmers Association of the Land of Israel, to Gad Machnes, the Director General of the Ministry for Minority Affairs, 13 July 1948.
[48] ISA, FM 2401/21 aleph, 'Protocol of the Meeting of the Ministerial Committee for Abandoned Property that Took Place in the Kiriya [the Government compound, Tel Aviv], on Friday, 13 July 1948'.

Shitrit went on to forbid the brigade from 'uprooting any Arab worker from his place without an order to this effect from the Minister of Defence'.[49]

To recap for a moment: in late June, the Alexandroni Brigade had sought to expel the inhabitants of Al Fureidis and Jisr Zarka. But prompt intervention by the agricultural notables of Zikhron and Binyamina, driven by economic considerations, and the support of the Minority Affairs Minister—who obtained Cabinet backing—had blocked an expulsion. Yet Alexandroni still wanted the two thorns in its side removed. No doubt the constant movement of Arabs to and from the two villages—in part between the villages and areas to the north still under Arab occupation, such as the Al Jaba–Ijzim–'Ein Ghazal triangle—perturbed the brigade. The outbreak of fresh fighting on 8–9 July, with the end of the First Truce, seemed to provide an opportunity. The brigade informed the Jewish farmers that the presence of the two Arab villages and the free movement of its menfolk to and from work in the Jewish fields and vineyards was troublesome. The villages would either have to be placed under a round-the-clock curfew or the Jewish farmers would have to pay the army for its security services. The thinking behind this seems to have been that in either case, the Zikhron and Binyamina farmers would be forced to adjust to the idea of dispensing with the Arabs' labour: either the curfew would physically keep the field-hands away or the 'tax' would make their services prohibitively expensive. The local Jewish farmers could then be expected to lose interest in the fate of Al Fureidis and Jisr Zarka and Alexandroni would be free, at last, to expel the villagers.

Shitrit's letter of 13 July failed to impress Alexandroni's commanders. Two days later they placed Al Fureidis and Jisr Zarka under quarantine, barring all entry to and exit from the two villages until further notice. The brigade's Arab-affairs adviser promptly complained to Shitrit that a local commander had acted without his knowledge or approval and registered his disagreement with the action: the Ghawarina and Fureidis

are not so dangerous that they must be placed under complete quarantine . . . It is possible that there was need for some sort of action to increase

[49] ISA, MAM 307/31, Minister for Minority Affairs to Alexandroni / Shlomo Zucker, 13 July 1948.

their isolation from the unconquered villages [Jaba, 'Ein Ghazal, and Ijzim] and the Triangle [the Palestinian-populated area of Nablus, Jenin, and Tulkarm] but this could have been done in a more fair and humane way.[50]

Meanwhile, the deputy brigade commander, Binyamin Goldstein, also wrote to Shitrit (and to Ben-Gurion), explaining Alexandroni's actions. The two villages, he declared,

endanger security in the district, through constant infiltration to and from them. Security [considerations] compel me to impose constant surveillance on them, and this can be done in two ways: (A) To remove them from our area to the Arab-held area. (B) To keep them under constant surveillance . . . I had to take the second course . . . The difference in the wages will cover the costs of supervising them.

Alternatively, wrote Goldstein, the villagers could be 'held as prisoners-of-war', and could be employed by the Office of the Custodian for Absentees Property picking fruit or reaping crops. The problem, implied Goldstein, was as much economic as military: without work, the villagers would be penniless and would have to be maintained by the army. Alexandroni lacked the funds for this.[51]

Shitrit backed down. Perhaps Ben-Gurion had told him to lay off Alexandroni, it was military business. But the quarantine galvanized the Zikhron farmers into action. A delegation of plaintiffs duly arrived at Shitrit's doorstep on 16 July.

Shitrit. I raised the matter in the Cabinet and sent [Alexandroni] a letter.

The farmers' delegation. From yesterday they imposed a quarantine on the village. What does the minister think?

Shitrit proposed that they pay out the 850 mils per day per worker (with the army getting 350 mils) and that the farmers then ask the Treasury and Shitrit himself for a refund. 'I'll fix the matter', he promised. 'If the Treasury won't pay you, I tell you to go ahead and sue [the government or army].'

The farmers were not pleased. They wanted instant action: 'The vineyards are ready for harvesting . . .'.

[50] ISA, MAM 307/48, Arab-affairs adviser / Alexandroni Brigade to Minister for Minority Affairs, 15 or 16 July 1948.

[51] ISA, MAM 307/48, Binyamin Goldstein, Alexandroni Brigade, to the Minister for Minority Affairs, the Prime Minister and Minister of Defence, and the Minister of Finance, 17 July 1948. Zucker, in his letter to Shitrit of 15 or 16 July, had written that Fureidis 'lacked provisions to maintain themselves even for one week'.

Shitrit. I'll write today to the Prime Minister.[52]

The Zikhron farmers must have felt that not much had been achieved. Niether was the Minority Affairs Ministry's effort to mobilize the Finance Minister, Eliezer Kaplan, against Alexandroni any more successful. 'The question . . . was raised in Cabinet . . . I will be happy to learn from you what is the situation', Kaplan wrote vaguely and irrelevantly a few days later to Machnes, the Director General of the Ministry for Minority Affairs.[53]

The affair, at this stage, was also to have repercussions within Mapam. It was raised by both Meir Ya'ari and Moshe Erem, party leaders, at a meeting on 26–7 July of Mapam's defence officials and senior IDF officers. Erem said that the quarantine of the two villages meant that they would lack for food. He blamed an unnamed party member—who was a senior officer in Alexandroni, perhaps Goldstein—for what was happening. The unnamed Mapam officer had told him that the villages constituted 'a Fifth Column' and that supplying them with food was like 'giving supplies to the enemy'. Yet Zucker, said Erem, 'who was not a member of our party', thought that the whole quarantine was 'exaggerated and that there is no need to seal them off'.[54]

A fresh and ominous twist to the affair was introduced on 26 July, when two General Staff / Operations officers appeared at the district headquarters in Netanya and told the Alexandroni staff to 'prepare to transfer the inhabitants of [Fureidis and Jisr Zarka] to the Arab[-held] area at 1800 hours'. The local district commander, 'Naftali' (perhaps Shemi), 'refused and said that he must receive the order from his direct superior Binyamin [Goldstein]'. Goldstein, for his part, delayed carrying out the order until consulting with Zucker, the Arab-affairs adviser. Zucker 'opposed the operation' and promptly informed Shitrit of what was going on.[55] The expulsion was stymied.

[52] ISA, MAM 307/48, 'The Minister's Interview with a Delegation from Zikhron Ya'akov', 16 July 1948.

[53] ISA, MAM 307/48, Gad Machnes to the Minister of Finance, 18 July 1948; and E. Kaplan to Machnes, 26 July 1948.

[54] Hashomer Hatzair Archive 10.18, 'Protocols of the Meeting of Mapam Defence Activists', 26–7 July 1948.

[55] ISA, MAM 307/48, Arab-affairs adviser / Alexandroni Brigade to the Ministry for Minority Affairs, 27 July 1948.

But the IDF quarantine and its possible alternative, the 850 mils arrangement, remained. At the end of July, following the end, on 18 July, of the second round of Arab–Israeli hostilities and a change in the strategic situation in the area, a compromise agreement was at last hammered out between the army and the local Jewish farmers, with the Minority Affairs Ministry advising, and perhaps mediating, from the sidelines. The subject of the agreement—the inhabitants of Al Fureidis and Khirbet Jisr az Zarka—did not participate in the discussions. The crucial meeting took place on 27 July, with the chairmen of the Zikhron Ya'akov and Binyamina local councils (Abba Shechter and M. Paicovitch), the IDF district commander (Yitzhak Shemi), the district police commander (Yitzhak Ressner), the IDF district intelligence officer (Binyamin Winter), and local kibbutz leaders participating.

All present noted the history of good relations between the two villages and their Jewish neighbours and the villages' resistance to the Arab 'gangs'. The main security problem during the previous weeks had been the infiltration back and forth between the two villages and the still unconquered Arab villages of the so-called 'Little Triangle' (Jaba, 'Ein Ghazal, and Ijzim). But the 'Little Triangle' had fallen to Jewish attack earlier that week; the villagers had fled and / or been driven out. The problem of infiltration between the hostile villages of the 'Little Triangle' and Al Fureidis and the Ghawarina had thus disappeared. The situation had changed.

The local leaders and the IDF district commander, Shemi, agreed that henceforward, the inhabitants of the two villages would be allowed to work in Zikhron Ya'akov and Binyamina in the vineyards and the wine press; they would be transported to and from work in organized fashion in vehicles; the adult male hands would be paid 600 mils per day (with '400 mils for women, [and] 300 mils for children'); the Jewish farmers would be responsible for and pay the costs of the transportation; the farmers would pay the army an additional 75 mils per male, adult hand 'for guarding the village[s], and for providing supplies for and development of the village[s]'. The money was to be handed to IDF-appointed supervisors whose work was to be regulated by the Minority Affairs Ministry. The two villages were to receive their supplies from Zikhron Ya'akov and Binyamina until shops were set up in the villages. The *moshavot* were also responsible for the medical care of the villagers. The villagers were to be allowed to cultivate their fields (from which the quarantine had previously barred them).[56]

At the beginning of August, Erem visited the area to see how the agreement was being implemented. 'The workers are travelling to work every day in organised fashion, the supervisors registering the workers when they leave [home] and upon their return.' The supervisors were paid the 75 mils per head per day. During his visit, Erem encountered a truck 'bringing the workers back to Al Ghawarina; it was full and crowded [with] (70 persons), to the point of danger . . .'. Erem reprimanded the driver; the Arab passengers, for their part, complained that men and women were being transported tightly packed together—'they feared possible harm to family relations'. In Fureidis, Erem learned that beside the village's 700 permanent inhabitants, the village contained 215 refugees from nearby Tantura, conquered by the Haganah and abandoned by its inhabitants in May. The refugees were receiving their supplies from the Fureidis villagers and at their expense. The refugees had no housing and lived out in the open. The village had no school or teachers. Twice a week, it was visited by a Jewish doctor. The villagers complained that they had sown wheat in the abandoned fields of Tantura but that the army had then reaped the crop.

In Binyamina, the Jewish farmers complained that the villagers did not need the 'busing' and could make their way to the fields by foot. 'They argued that the security situation west of the *moshavot* was not problematic and therefore the matter of transport was superfluous.' They also thought the 75 mils charge unnecessary. But Erem said the transportation arrangement and the 75 mils payment were irreversible. He summed the matter up by saying that 'the arrangement added a pleasant chapter to the [history of] good neighbourly relations [in the area]'. Binyamina and Zikhron Ya'akov were thus providing funds for the development of the two Arab villages. The meeting between Erem and the Binyamina farmers

---

[56] ISA, MAM 307/48, 'Memorandum on the Meeting with the Shomron [Samaria] Settlements Bloc Concerning the Inhabitants of the Villages of Fureidis and Al Ghawarina', by Moshe Erem (the Mapam leader and Minority Affairs Minister official responsible for the agreement), 1 Aug. 1948 (the meeting took place on 27 July 1948).

ended on a cheerful note, Erem recorded: Binyamina would carry out the agreement.[57]

Thus was resolved the 'problem' of Al Fureidis and Jisr Zarka. The army had failed to dislodge the two villages, which to this day, having grown and prospered, overlook the Tel Aviv–Haifa highway.

CONCLUSION

The stories of Abu Ghosh and Beit Naqquba and Al Fureidis and Jisr Zarka in 1948 are instructive in a number of ways about Jewish–Arab relations and about Yishuv decision-making concerning Arab communities during the first Israeli–Arab war.

One notes clear, common patterns. In both areas, the local Haganah / IDF command (Harel and Alexandroni brigades), in varying degrees backed by the high command, strongly desired the removal of the villages, which were regarded by the military as thorns in their side. They wanted Arab-clear areas behind the front lines and along the vital roads under their supervision. In both areas, during the First Truce and, even more pressingly, during the subsequent 'Ten Days' of hostilities (9–18 July), the army made efforts, albeit falling short of outright expulsion, which was forbidden by the political echelon, to obtain the removal of the villages.

In the Jerusalem corridor, the tactic was one of pressure and 'advice' to leave, with the military using the local 'good guys'— Lisser and Navon—to persuade the villagers to decamp. The inhabitants of Abu Ghosh, and perhaps also those of Beit Naqquba, were promised that they would be allowed to return to their homes when the hostilities subsided. The villagers of Beit Naqquba were apparently—simultaneously—ordered by local Arab commanders to evacuate. Subsequently, the army tried, by and large unsuccessfully, to bar the return of the villagers—from both sites—to their homes in Israeli territory.

In the coastal plain, the local command and high command alternated between efforts to expel the inhabitants of Al Fureidis and Jisr Zarka outright and more subtle methods of making the

[57] ISA, MAM 307/48, memorandum on 'The Visit to Fureidis and the Ratification of the Agreement by the Binyamina Agricultural Committee', by Moshe Erem, 2 Aug. 1948.

villagers' continued life under Israeli rule unpleasant or impossible. (Not being allowed to work in the neighbouring Jewish fields or to cultivate their own fields would have meant economic strangulation.) The quarantine and its alternative, the 350 mil tax, both seem to have been ultimately designed to obtain the villagers' removal. In Al Fureidis and Jisr Zarka—far less of a war zone in July than the Jerusalem corridor—the army proved completely unsuccessful.

In both areas, the Arabs' *summud* (to use a later term for holding tight to their lands)—when backed by important local or national elements within the Yishuv—proved stronger than the army's will to uproot them.

In general, in 1948, where Arab communities fled at the first hint or whiff of grapeshot, there was no problem and the Yishuv was happy. But where Arab communities held tight *after the end of hostilities in a specific area*, the Jewish establishment, which had no master plan or agreed and public policy, and was riven by dissent, occasionally proved unavailing. There were a handful of politicians and officers who as a matter of course on political and / or moral grounds opposed expulsion. There were many others who, though they might have been satisfied, not to say happy, to see Arabs flee in panic, would have been embarrassed to be seen to be involved in forcibly uprooting Arab communities.

Happily for the Yishuv, most of the Arabs who became refugees in 1948 fled out of fear or panic before or during Haganah / IDF attack on their villages, thus freeing the Jewish officers and officials at each site from confronting the dilemma of expelling or leaving in place an Arab population. One can fairly say that when Arab communities in 1948 did not flee and / or were not expelled before or during their conquest, and the issue came up for debate in civilian bodies, meaning the Cabinet or its committees, and in the Jewish political parties, then ideology, morality, and embarrassment coalesced to stymie the army's desire to expel (where that existed). Outright expulsions such as occurred along the Lebanese border in November (Iqrit, Bir'im, Nabi Rubin, Tarbikha) were carried out by the army *without Cabinet knowledge, debate, or approval* —though, almost inevitably, they received *post facto* Cabinet endorsement. ('Eilaboun, from which the inhabitants were expelled by Golani Brigade units at the end of October, was an exception, due largely to the villagers' Maronite faith and affiliations: there, subsequently, the Cabinet approved the exiled villagers' return).

In the cases dealt with here, clearly, the main reason for the army's failure to uproot the communities in both areas was local Jewish pressure and intercession. That intercession was founded largely on the decades-long history of mutual non-belligerency or outright friendship and collaboration between the neighbouring Jewish and Arab settlements. Without this basic amity or, at least, trust, born in the 1930s and early 1940s, the intercessions of June–July 1948 are inexplicable. (Nor, indeed, is the non-flight of the four villages, earlier, in April–May—as almost all their Arab neighbours decamped into exile—understandable without taking into account that basic foundation of trust in the Jews, in Jewish godwill, and in promised Jewish protection.)

But this local Jewish 'protection' or intercession—by Kiryat Anavim *vis-à-vis* Abu Ghosh and by Zikhron Ya'akov and Binyamina *vis-à-vis* Al Fureidis and Jisr Zarka—to be cogent and successful, required national, Cabinet-level endorsement. This was provided, in both cases, by Minority Affairs Minister Bechor Shitrit, whose job was to care for the lot of the country's remaining Arabs, and by the Mapam ministers and officials (Aharon Zisling, Mordechai Bentov, and Moshe Erem). Shitrit, it can be surmised, continuously frustrated, ignored, or contumaciously defied by the army in all that concerned the uprooting of Arab communities during 1948, was probably happy to discover one or two sites still with Arabs and to which he could afford effective protection. The Mapam ministers and officials, likewise, saw in Al Fureidis, Jisr Zarka, and Abu Ghosh (if not Beit Naqquba) good grounds upon which to exercise their moral-ideological fervour. They believed in or, at least, espoused the possibility of, Jewish–Arab coexistence; and here were villages which one could protect at no expense to Mapam or its kibbutzim.

The combination of Shitrit and the Mapam ministers proved effective in frustrating the army's expulsive will; neither the colonels nor Ben-Gurion, even if he was expulsively inclined, could gainsay the past friendliness or collaborationism of the villages in question.

It is worth noting that in both areas the army acted or attempted to act in July in limited defiance of the will of the political leadership. The Cabinet or Cabinet Committee for Abandoned Property may have ruled that Arab villagers were not to be expelled or otherwise moved about without Cabinet-level or the Defence Minister's authorization. But, while there were hostilities, the army continued to go its own way, at least in limited fashion. It could not, perhaps, forcibly expel the inhabitants of Al Fureidis and Jisr Zarka. But it half-heartedly tried to (the tale of the two General Staff/Operations officers) or at least adopted a course that it hoped would have the same evacuative effect. And in the Jerusalem corridor, the army helped nudge, if not actually engineer, the departure of the Abu Ghosh and Beit Naqquba villagers.

Jewish 'protectionism', in both cases, ultimately stymied the army's will. But in the case of Al Fureidis and Jisr Zarka, this 'protectionism' wasn't merely or, indeed, mainly a matter of sentimental goodwill or political morality. Rather, the farmers of Zikhron Ya'akov and Binyamina, to judge by their statements, were primarily driven by economic self-interest. Past Jewish–Arab friendliness or non-belligerency was background; the wine harvest of summer 1948 was pressing foreground. Indeed, at one point the Jewish farmers baldly asked the authorities at least to allow the field-hands to stay for the summer, until the harvest was over, perhaps implying that they would not be troubled overmuch if an expulsion occurred thereafter.

And in the Jerusalem corridor, too, economic interests were at play, at least in all that concerned the relations between Kiryat Anavim and Beit Naqquba. The kibbutz was bent on obtaining its neighbour's removal and lands. Once the villagers decamped, Kiryat Anavim was in the forefront of those opposing Beit Naqquba's return. But the protection afforded Abu Ghosh, both by some elements within the kibbutz (Lisser), and by the politicians, to some extent came to encompass Beit Naqquba's inhabitants or at least those who had ended up in Abu Ghosh in the second half of 1948. (The main village, Abu Ghosh, thus seemingly exercised an indirect protective function over its satellite. The same pattern may also have occurred with Al Fureidis and Jisr Zarka: the Zikhron and Binyamina farmers were mainly exercised over the fate of Al Fureidis; the protection afforded that village was then somehow extended to cover the smaller village, Jisr Zarka.)[58]

---

[58] It is worth noting that the documents contain more than a trace of a hint that at

In any case, the campaign by Kiryat Anavim and the army against Beit Naqquba was only partially successful: the villagers' return to their former site was blocked, but uprooting those provisionally resettled in Abu Ghosh proved beyond the kibbutz or army's powers. The intervention of the politicians was effective; the cessation of hostilities severely curbed the army's freedom to oust or move about Arab communities. By 1949, military necessity could no longer be compellingly argued.

least some members of Kiryat Anavim through 1948 also desired the permanent removal of Abu Ghosh. Lisser himself apparently in June 1948 sired the idea of transferring its inhabitants to Jaffa. In January 1949, the kibbutz wrote to the authorities in a tone suggesting only reluctant acquiescence in the continued existence of Abu Ghosh as their neighbour. Perhaps here, too, long-term security-mindedness was joined by economic considerations.

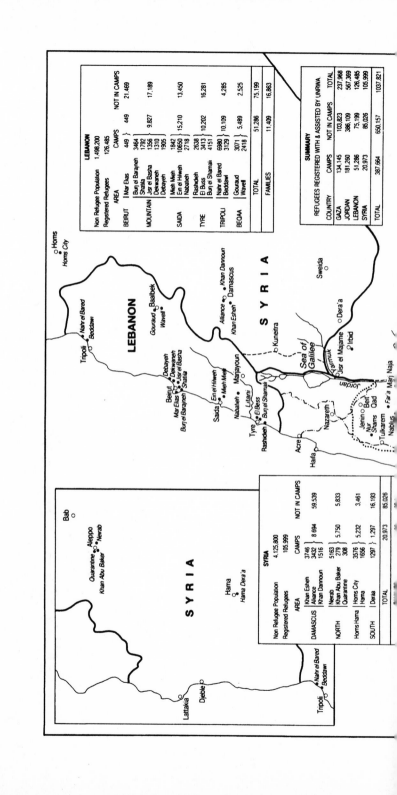

LEBANON

Non Refugee Population 1,498,200
Registered Refugees 126,485

AREA		CAMPS		NOT IN CAMPS
BEIRUT	Mar Elias		449	21,469
			449	
MOUNTAIN	Burj el Barajneh	3464		17,189
	Shatila	1792		
	Jsr el Basha	1356	9,827	
	Dekwaneh	1310		
	Debayeh	1905		
SAIDA	Meh Meh	1842		13,450
	Ein el Hilweh	10650	15,210	
	Nabatieh	2718		
TYRE	Rashdeh	2638		16,281
	El Buss	3413	10,202	
	Burj el Shamali	4151		
TRIPOLI	Nahr el Bared	6980	10,109	4,285
	Beddawi	3129		
BEQAA	Gouraud	3071	5,489	2,525
	Wavell	2418		
	TOTAL		51,286	75,199
	FAMILIES		11,409	16,863

SUMMARY

REFUGEES REGISTERED WITH & ASSISTED BY UNRWA

COUNTRY	CAMPS	NOT IN CAMPS	TOTAL
GAZA	134,145	103,823	237,968
JORDAN	181,260	386,109	567,369
LEBANON	51,286	75,199	126,485
SYRIA	20,973	85,026	105,999
TOTAL	387,664	650,157	1037,821

SYRIA

Non Refugee Population 4,125,800
Registered Refugees 105,999

AREA		CAMPS		NOT IN CAMPS
DAMASCUS	Khan Esheh	3746		59,539
	Alliance	3432	8,694	
	Khan Dannoun	1516		
NORTH	Nerab	5163		5,833
	Khan Abu Baker	279	5,750	
	Quarantine	308		
Homs Hama	Homs City	3576	5,232	3,461
	Hama	1656		
SOUTH	Dera	1297	1,297	16,193
	TOTAL		20,973	85,026

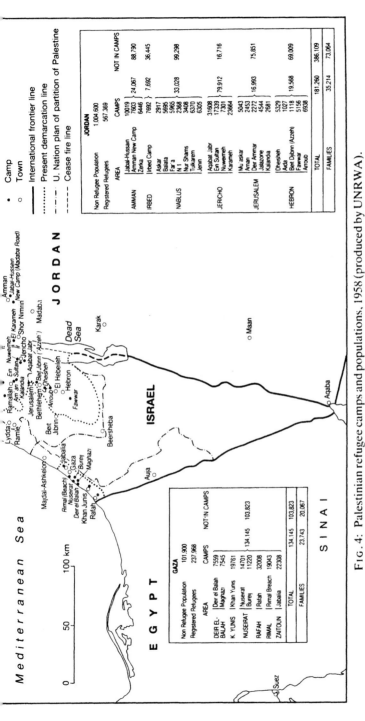

FIG. 4: Palestinian refugee camps and populations, 1958 (produced by UNRWA).

See overleaf for FIG. 4. Map showing Palestinian refugee camps and populations, 1958.

9

The Initial Absorption of the Palestinian
Refugees in the Arab Host Countries,
1948–1949

THE FIRST WAVE

The Palestinian Arab exodus began in December 1947, within days of the UN General Assembly passage of the Partition Resolution for Palestine and the start of Arab–Jewish hostilities around the country. The first wave of exiles, who numbered several tens of thousands over December 1947–March 1948, was largely drawn from the urban middle classes—relatively wealthy families from Jaffa, Haifa, and Jerusalem, some with second houses in Lebanon, Nablus, or Amman, who preferred to be out of harm's way for the duration of the conflict. In most cases, they were not compelled to emigrate by Jewish order, pressure, or victory in the field; often, as in Haifa and Jaffa in the first months of the war, the hostilities were relatively minor and these families, if at all, were only remotely threatened. Exile promised enhanced comfort and safety. Few of them thought that exodus would turn into refugeedom, and that their towns, houses, and lands would be conquered and permanently occupied by the Jews; many probably expected the armies of the Arab states to intervene, make short shrift of the Haganah and the emergent Jewish state, and restore them to their towns and property, which, as the months passed, gradually fell under Jewish control.

The arrival in Sidon and Beirut, Ramallah and Nablus, Amman, Cairo, and Alexandria of this first wave of refugees apparently passed without excessive difficulties; the numbers were relatively small, the influx stretched out over months, and the exiles' money oiled the proceedings. There were no major problems of accommodation or sustenance; most had relatives to stay with, second houses, or money to pay for hotel rooms and keep. And the hosts, like the exiles, never conceived of the influx as permanent; within weeks or months, they would be returning to Palestine. It occurred probably to no one on the Arab side at this stage that the war would definitively and radically transform the demography of Palestine to the detriment of the Arab population.

HOSTING THE SECOND WAVE

But things changed dramatically during April and the first half of May, with the Haganah switch to the strategic offensive and the Jewish conquest of most of the Arab-populated areas allotted to the Jewish state in the partition plan. Jewish pressure on the Arab villages of the coastal plain, and the Haganah conquest of parts of Arab Jerusalem and the Jerusalem corridor, Tiberias, Haifa, the Hula Valley and the Galilee panhandle, Jaffa and its environs, Beisan, and Safad, sent some 200,000–300,000 urban and rural Palestinian Arabs fleeing to the safety of the surrounding Arab states (Lebanon, Syria, Egypt, and Transjordan) and the Arab population centres of Gaza, Nablus, Ramallah, and Hebron. These refugees—driven by panic, fear of injury or death in the hostilities, wartime economic privation, and Jewish pressures and expulsion orders—also did not conceive of exile as anything but a temporary expedient or condition. But this second and major wave of refugees, by sheer weight of numbers and chronological concentration, posed a new and radical problem for the Arab host governments, municipalities, and local inhabitants.

Lieutenant-General Gordon MacMillan, the British GOC Palestine, already before the fall of Arab Haifa wrote of the 'suffering' of the Arabs of Samaria (the Jenin–Tulkarm–Nablus–Ramallah area) from the 'enormous influx of refugees from Galilee'. The locals (as well as the refugees) were hit by shortages of food and petrol.[1]

Tens of thousands of the Galilee (and Haifa) Arabs fled to Lebanon, where the influx, in May, was reported by the British Legation to be 'aggravating the shortages existing in certain essential commodities, especially cereals and oil products'. Petrol was in short supply and the Lebanese Government stopped the fuel ration to Palestinian-registered cars; Palestinian car-owners were forced to use the black market. In June, much was made in the Lebanase press of the suffering and death of refugees on the roads to Lebanon

---

[1] CPV/4/9, 'The General Position in Palestine' by Lt.-General MacMillan, 21 Apr. 1948.

and, according to one French agent (who doubled for Israel), the refugees in Lebanon wanted to end the war at any price 'as they had reached the limit of their endurance'.[2]

The arrival in Egypt during April of what were the first major batches of refugees gave rise to problems, solutions, and attitudes which were soon to characterize most of the host countries. More than 1,100 reached Port Said from Jaffa and Haifa between 25 and 29 April, arriving mostly in 'small steamers, fishing smacks, rowing boats and caiques'. About 270 of these, many of them women and children, arrived in 'open rowing boats, without sails' and without food. The Egyptian authorities placed them in quarantine and Port Said inhabitants took up a collection of funds and food for them.

A 'special quarantine camp' was set up to accommodate some of the refugees at Port Fuad (across the Suez Canal from Port Said), but 'a considerable number' were taken in by local Egyptian families. According to the American Consulate in Port Said, 'many' of the refugees had come with quantities of Palestinian banknotes 'and some of them have been found in possession of narcotic drugs (hashish) which they intended to sell in Egypt'. But there were more serious problems. 'The fact that many of the Arab refugees are of military age and able to bear arms tends to have a dampening effect on the enthusiasm of prospective Egyptian volunteers for military service with the Arab armies. "Why should we go to Palestine to fight while Palestine Arab fighters are deserting the cause by flight to Egypt?" some of them have been heard to remark', reported the consulate. Moreover, 'anti-British feeling' had increased in Port Said as a result of the influx, because the refugees were charging 'that the British are supporting the Jews and neglecting the defence of the Arab population in Palestine'.[3]

The problem of the refugees generating anti-British feelings among Arab host populations was to crop up increasingly through 1948, causing serious concern in Whitehall about Britain's position in the various host countries. Already in February 1948, the High

---

[2] PRO, CO 537-3986, [Beirut Legation] Summary for the Month of May, 1948; and ISA, FM 2408/16, 'An excerpt from information given by Yosef Sabagh, an agent of the French Consulate in Tiberias and Safad, who had just returned from Lebanon, 24 June 1948.'

[3] NA, Record Group 84, Jerusalem Consulate, Classified Records 1948, 800— Refugees, John P. Robertson, Vice Consul, US Consulate, Port Said, Egypt, to State Department, 29 Apr. 1948.

Commissioner for Palestine, Sir Alan Gordon Cunningham, reported
to London that Transjordan's King Abdullah—with whom he had
lunched that week at Shuneh—had complained about the 'exodus
of Palestine Arabs into Transjordan [saying] . . . they were all arriving
thoroughly anti-British and, hence, might give him trouble'.[4]

Egypt's Moslem religious leaders, meeting as the *Ulema* in Cairo
on 26 April, called on the Arab governments to 'take action' (that
is, to go to war) to liberate Palestine and, meanwhile, 'to give
asylum to Arab refugees from Palestine'. In Egypt, two new camps
were readied for the absorption of refugees, at Kantara and Abbassia,
on the banks of the Suez Canal; most of the 1,600 refugees who had
arrived by sea at Port Said between 2 and 8 May were sent there.
Local Egyptian relief organizations were still supplying food and
clothing, but 'they do not appear to be as enthusiastic now as they
were with the first arrivals'. Quarrels had erupted between the
refugees and the local population. And a rumour had surfaced that
the relief-organization officials intended to visit the camps and
ask the able-bodied among the refugees to join volunteer units to
'fight the Jews. If the men refuse, the Committee [of representatives
of the relief organizations] will request the Government [of Egypt]
to send them back to Palestine.' Some middle-class Egyptians
had reportedly threatened that if the Government did not send
them back, 'they will place them on caiques and send them back
by force . . .'.[5]

Similar sentiments surfaced in Transjordan. 'Some rich [refugees]
have come to Amman and the fact that they are seen frequenting
the banks is causing trouble and ill feeling, the Transjordan folk
seeing no reason why their men should go to Palestine to fight for
the Palestinians, who got their wealth by selling their land to the
Jews', wrote one British observer from Transjordan in mid-June.
She also remarked that money and relief workers were urgently
needed to take care of the mass of poor refugees.[6]

[4] PRO, FO 371–68537 (E3291/4/31), Sir A. Cunningham to J. M. Martin,
Colonial Office, 2 Feb. 1948.
  [5] PRO, FO 371–68371 (E5528/11/65), Sir Ronald Campbell, Cairo (British
Middle East Office), to Foreign Office, 30 Apr. 1948; and NA, Records Group 84,
Jerusalem Consulate General, Classified Records 1948, 800—Refugees, Philip
Ernst, US Consul, Port Said, to US Embassy, Cairo, 13 May 1948.
  [6] Jerusalem and East Mission Papers (JE&EM), Box LXXIII/1, Winifred
A. Coates, El Husn, Transjordan, to 'Mabel' (Jerusalem), 15 June 1948.

Palestinian leaders tried to combat this ill-feeling towards the refugees. Suleiman Tukan, a pro-Hashemite dignitary from Nablus, on 11 June on Amman Radio comprehensively defended the refugees by charging that the Arab states were 'responsible' for the plight of the Palestinians as they had not heeded the Palestinians' cries for help. The essence of Tukan's defence was that the Arabs had not fled the country of their own free will. Be that as it may, Tukan appealed to the refugees of the Samaria and Hebron districts to return to their homes; the appeal may have been the price Tukan had had to pay the Transjordanian authorities for allowing him to broadcast his 'defence' of the refugees.

The start of the First Truce between Israel and the Arab States on 11 June also apparently spurred the Syrians to try to 'push' their refugees back across the border, back to the abandoned Arab villages in the (Galilee Panhandle) Hula Valley. Israeli intelligence assessed that Damascus had adopted this policy 'to remove from itself the economic and organisational burden [of their upkeep]' and 'to introduce a Fifth Column [back] into the Jewish areas cleared [of Arabs]'. Meanwhile, the Syrians were providing at least some of the refugees with food supplies.[7]

The IDF, of course, had received orders—stemming from both tactical military and strategic-political considerations—to halt with fire the return of refugees back into Israeli-held territory.[8] Local IDF intelligence officers in various sectors of the country believed that Arab refugees were infiltrating back into Israeli-held territory mainly to harvest the summer crops rather than to permanently resettle in their former villages. The refugees were driven by 'real hunger'. The situation of the refugees along the Israeli–Syrian border was so desperate that they braved IDF bullets to foray into the fields in the Galilee panhandle during the nights. Some refugee farmers even returned at night to water their fields 'in the hope that they will manage to plant vegetables on [for?] their return to their village with the [start of the] truce'. IDF Intelligence warned that the process, if allowed to go on, would eventually result in the

---

[7] KMA-PA 100/MemVavDalet/1—9, *Batziburiut Ha'Aravit* (in the Arab public), Foreign Ministry Middle East Affairs Department, 11 June 1948. Copy also in ISA, FM 2570/6; and ISA, FM 2408/16, 'An Excerpt from Information Given by Yosef Sabagh . . .'.

[8] See Ch. 7 in the present volume.

refugees indeed permanently resettling in Israel.[9] The IDF duly
barred the refugees from returning to Israeli-held territory.

THE THIRD WAVE AND THE STATE OF THE REFUGEES DURING THE SUMMER OF 1948

The majority of the 300,000 refugees who had left Israeli-held
territory by the 15 May invasion of Palestine by the Arab armies fell
under the control, and became the immediate responsibility, of
King Abdullah and his government; his army, the Arab Legion, had
occupied most of the Nablus–Ramallah–Jericho–East Jerusalem–
Hebron area. Sir Alec Seath Kirkbride, the British Minister to
Amman, grasped the significance of the events and sensed what was
to come in terms of the refugees. 'It is not even possible to foresee
how the Transjordan authorities are to provide food and shelter
during the coming winter' for the thousands 'now living in destitution,'
he wrote to Foreign Secretary Ernest Bevin. The refugees themselves, he added, were 'becoming increasingly vocal' in demanding
an end to the war 'at all costs'. Their demand, he thought, was
'based on the assumption that if hostilities cease, they will be able to
return to their homes in the Jewish areas. [But] why the Jews should
permit them to do so, now that events have solved the most difficult
problem which originally faced the Jewish state, that of a large Arab
minority, it is difficult to see. In fact, the Arab world is likely to be
faced with the resettlement of these refugees and not with their
repatriation . . .' The Arab leaders had never 'anticipated' the mass
flight of the Arab population, 'often without there being any
imminent threat', from their homes in the areas allocated to the
Jews under the partition plan, he added as an afterthought.

Kirkbride's letter to Bevin sparked the first major internal Foreign
Office debate about what could be done for or about the Palestinian
refugees. Lance Thirkell thought that the International Refugee
Organization, which, he said, had 'done so much to help Jews to get
into Palestine', could help the 'unfortunate Arabs who have been

---

[9] KMA-PA 100/Mem VavDalet/1—9, *Batziburiut Ha'Aravit*, Foreign Ministry
Middle East Affairs Department, 11 June 1948; and ISA, FM 2570/6, 'Tsur' (the
code name of a local intelligence officer) to Haganah Intelligence Service, 7 June
1948. The IDF duly barred the refugees from returning to Israeli-held territory.

pushed out incidentally. Singularly little has been heard of the fact that the Jewish incursion into Palestine has produced an exodus of 300,000 refugees. I should have thought that this would have had some [anti-Israeli] propaganda value.' David Balfour also thought the IRO could help. But A. W. Wilkinson minuted: 'The IRO has insufficient funds to take on any more refugees and doesn't deal with "internally displaced" people.' She rejected Thirkell's and Balfour's comments that the IRO had helped Jews get to Palestine and said that, in fact, the organization had assisted in the resettlement of European Moslem refugees. H. Beeley commented that in Palestine the issue was not really one of 'internal displacement'.[10]

The '10-days fighting' (between the end of the First Truce and the beginning of the Second Truce) in mid-July both highlighted and exacerbated the plight of the refugees. A further 100,000 Palestinians joined the ranks of the exiles, the bulk of them expelled by the IDF from Lydda and Ramle to the Transjordanian-held part of Palestine (Latrun–Ramallah–Qalqilya–Jericho). The massive, concentrated influx (on top of the defeat administered to the Arab Legion) shook Abdullah's kingdom. The British colony in Amman considered evacuation, but rejected the idea after Legion commander General John Glubb said he was 'not pessimistic' about keeping order in the city: 'it may be possible to keep Amman Suk [marketplace] and Palestinian refugee elements under control'. Abdullah and Glubb wanted to 'end hostilities' but were 'frightened' of the reaction of the other Arab states and of 'public feeling'. There had been several anti-British and, implicity, anti-Abdullah demonstrations in Amman and elsewhere in the country.[11]

Transjordan's refugee problem had 'become acute' and the government was unable to cope. A rough idea of the situation in July in Ramallah, a town of about 10,000 and the first major way-station of the Lydda–Ramle refugees, is provided in a message from the municipality to King Abdullah, transmitted via the Arab Legion's radio communications system and monitored by Israeli intelligence: 'Seventy thousand people are scattered in the streets, the great

---

[10] PRO, FO 371–68570 (E9239/4/31), Sir A. Kirkbride, Amman, to E. Bevin, Foreign Office, 2 July 1948 and attached minutes by FO officials.

[11] PRO, FO 371–68575 (E9723/4/31), C. M. Pirie Gordon, Amman, to Foreign Office, 18 July 1948; and NA 501 BB. Palestine/7–1548, U.S. Legation, Amman to Secretary of State, 15 July 1948.

majority of them impoverished [and] suffering from a major lack of basic goods and water, constituting a serious health hazard', reported acting mayor Hanna Khalaf. 'The municipal council beseeches Your Highness to issue [an order] to the city of Ramallah to evict [the refugees] as the city cannot cope.' Abdullah answered unsympathetically that the city must display 'patience towards your brothers', and that relief would soon be on its way. A graphic description of the situation in the town was provided by an English-language Ramallah radio broadcast:

The smell is beginning to be bad, in so many places [said the reporter-observer], and what can the girls do with small brooms of twigs, in classrooms now holding three hundred people? Look at the dignified families in the [olive] groves and rooms, attempting to make privacy for themselves with stretched out blankets and dresses . . . Look at the women washing clothes and baking some precopis flour for their hungry families . . . There won't be a drop of flour left in Ramallah in three days . . . There are seventy thousand people to feed . . . Transjordan rushed over dates, flour and bread, but it is a drop in the ocean . . .

Seen from Tel Aviv, the refugees constituted a major burden for the Transjordanian authorities, particularly the military, clogging roads, requiring food and shelter, diverting Arab Legion resources and energies, as well as undermining the morale of the local population in the towns north and west of Jerusalem.[12]

Towards the end of July thousands of Lydda–Ramle refugees moved from Ramallah, eastwards, into Transjordan, to Amman. There, too, most were housed in school buildings (the schools were recessed for the summer vacation) or camped out in olive groves and private gardens. One British observer, Winifred Coate, a school headmistress, found them 'lying on old sacks and rags', destitute. They lacked bedding and cooking utensils. 'Life out of doors like this does not seem unnatural to many of them who were accustomed to go out and camp in their vineyards at this time of

[12] NA 501 BB. Palestine/7–1548, Amman to Secretary of State, 15 July 1948; ISA, FM 2569/13, 'From Monitoring the Legion Wavelength', 21 July 1948; PRO, FO 371–68578 (E10440/4/31), Sir H. Dow, British Consul-General, Jerusalem, to Foreign Office, 19 July 1948, enclosing text of Ramallah Radio broadcast, undated; and ISA, FM 2569/13, the Research Department (the Foreign Ministry's intelligence department), to Y. Shimoni, acting director of the Foreign Ministry Middle East Affairs Department, 19 July 1948.

year, but this is in the middle of Amman and is most unsuitable in a town', she commented.[13]

The US vice-consul in Amman, Wells Stabler, towards the end of July reported that the Transjordanian estimate of Palestinian refugees in Transjordan (east of the Jordan River—in Amman, As-Salt, Zarka, and Irbid) stood at '80,000–100,000', and Abdullah had felt obliged to close the kingdom's frontiers to additional refugees. The British estimate at this time, based on figures provided by Glubb, was about 56,000 refugees in Transjordan proper and some 70,000–100,000 in the areas west of the Jordan River occupied by the Arab Legion.[14]

How were the Transjordanian authorities coping with the refugees? Coate thought that 'the people of T.J.[Transjordan] had risen to the occasion rather better than might have been expected, as they have no experience of the kind of organisation needed'. In Amman, two ladies' welfare societies had raised funds. In Zarqa, a 'Ladies Committee' had doled out to each family 'a small packet of rice and sugar and tea and a piece of soap; also the most destitute had been given one blanket per family'. But this order of voluntary assistance, as Coate realized, was 'only a drop in the bucket of the great need'.

Coate, friendly with the Transjordanian finance minister's wife, appears to have been well-informed, at least as regards the refugees east of the river. They were getting, at the end of July, two small loaves of bread per head per day from the government. In addition, pregnant women and some children were getting milk. The government planned, she said, to hand out 300 mils (about six shillings) per month per head to cover other necessities; but she probably treated this information sceptically in light of Transjordan's poverty.[15]

The scepticism of the British consul in Amman, Pirie Gordon, was more comprehensive and far-seeing. 'I doubt whether Transjordan Government is capable of preparing any plans for organizing the

[13] J&EM LXXIII/1, Winifred Coate, principal, CMS Girls' School, Amman, to 'Mabel' Jerusalem, 30 July 1948; and ISA, FM 2569/13, 'Hiram' to Foreign Ministry Research Department, 19 July 1948.

[14] NA, Record Group 84, Jerusalem Consulate General, Classified Records 1948, 800—Refugees, Amman (Stabler) to State Department, 26 July 1948; and PRO, FO 371–68576 (E10219/10006/4), Amman (C. M. Pirie Gordon) to Foreign Office, 29 July 1948.

[15] J&EM LXXIII/1, Winifred Coate, Amman, to 'Mabel' Jerusalem, 30 July 1948.

future relief, and in any case the main difficulty lies in the burden imposed on the country's minute financial resources', he wrote. The local authorities foresaw starvation and the outbreak of epidemics if nothing substantial was done, quickly. And he was not particularly impressed by the level of public generosity displayed. In one Transjordan district, with 16,000 refugees, he wrote, the local authorities had managed to raise by public subscription only P£1,800. 'In Amman suggestion that merchants should contribute has been flatly rejected and an offer of funds of the Supreme Moslem Council and of the Ramle municipality approximately a total of P£90,000 has so far come to nothing because the Arab banks who hold these accounts prefers [sic] to have no funds available.' Meanwhile, prices had shot up, and the refugees themselves had quickly run out of savings and were begging or hungry; 'there has been a marked increase in crimes against property', Pirie Gordon added.

In short,

being idle, homeless, bereft of all their possessions and discontented with the relief efforts made on their behalf[,] the refugee communities in Amman and Salt at least, are fertile breeding grounds for embittered and opposed sentiments . . . Britain is accused as usual of being mainly responsible for their plight. The Arab rulers are held guilty of misleading them and involving them in the loss of their farms and settled lives. Local authorities regard them as a menace to the peace and security of the country and believe that communists are at work amongst them agitating against established order here,

wrote Pirie Gordon.[16]

In the Transjordanian-occupied part of Palestine, the situation was no better. Sir Hugh Dow, the British consul-general in Jerusalem, reported that 'local efforts to deal with the problem are largely uncoordinated and limited to bare emergency measures by local authorities and social committees . . . The main requirements of Arab refugees still inside Palestine are food, water, blankets and clothing. As the autumn approaches, the need for the two last named will increase and also for temporary or permanent housing . . .' Dow was thoroughly disgusted with the Arab governments' attitude to the refugees: they appeared less concerned with providing relief than getting rid of the 'refugee incubus'.

[16] PRO, FO 371–68576 (E10219/10006/4), Amman (Pirie Gordon) to Foreign Office, 29 July 1948.

Dow suggested that the 'best' solution for the problem of the refugees from the Jewish areas would be their resettlement in Arab countries. Israel would pay for the abandoned Arab lands and other property in Palestine, and the money would go towards compensating individual refugees and towards 'the resettlement of the poorer refugees'. At the same time, fund-raising in Britain ('a Lord Mayor's Fund') could cover the cost of repatriating Palestinians to Arab or Jewish-held areas of Palestine ('though they should not be encouraged to do so', commented Dow). Dow said that the Lord Mayor's Fund should be administered by Britain rather than the Arabs (a suggestion with which Pirie Gordon concurred). He added, however, that one should expect Arab League opposition to the scheme 'since it will have a purely humanitarian and practical object and will not fit in with their political desire to rid themselves of refugees in their territories in the first place . . . and to send large Arab populations back into Jewish areas as a nucleus for future trouble'.[17]

Dow was reacting to a cable from W. E. Houstoun-Boswall, the British Minister in Beirut, who on 21 July had proposed the establishment of a Lord Mayor's fund as 'a spontaneous act on the part of the British public to show their sympathy and friendly feelings for the Arabs' and to counter the trend in the Arab countries of vilification of Britain as a betrayer of the Arab cause. Houstoun-Boswall, like many other British diplomats in the Middle East at the time, was at best dismissive of the Palestinians, who had chosen 'to run away rather than fight'; by their 'general exodus', he had written, the Palestinians had 'shown themselves to be rather contemptible and perhaps not so deserving of sympathy . . .'. But Britain must act charitably, to show that the British remain the Arabs' 'best friends'.[18]

The American assessment of the state of the refugees west of the Jordan River was at first somewhat more sanguine—'Condition . . . not yet desperate'; it forecast complete destitution 'shortly', followed by 'hardship and danger to health' with the onset of winter. But an on-the-spot inspection by consular officials a fortnight later, in mid-August, produced a far darker picture. The Ramallah area

---

[17] PRO, FO 371–68576 (E10235/4/31), H. Dow, Jerusalem, to Foreign Office, 29 July 1948 and (E10219/10006/4), Amman (Pirie Gordon) to Foreign Office, 29 July 1948.
[18] PRO, FO 371–68575 (E9992/4/31), Houstoun-Boswall, Beirut, to Foreign Office, 21 July 1948.

was flooded with some 100,000 refugees, or almost twice the number of the normal local population. 'Condition refugees appalling . . . Live along sides road under trees . . . Housing facilities or even tents not available . . . Nights become very cold mid-September and rains start soon after . . . Water supply . . . precarious . . . water probably contaminated . . . Definitely possible that water supply may give out completely before end August.' The Trans-jordanian Government was daily distributing 250 grams of bread per day per refugee (half the amount east of the Jordan). The doctor accompanying the consular officials ruled that this represented about 600 calories per day and was 'insufficient [to] sustain life for long'. Moreover, 'sanitation practically nonexistent . . . no hospital beds available', little vaccine left for immunization against typhoid, and none at all against typhus, smallpox, diphtheria, and cholera. While 'good weather and good luck', to date, had left the adult death-rate normal, and only twenty suspected cases of typhoid, one of diphtheria, and one of meningitis had been reported, the worst was to be expected with respect to health during the following weeks. The consul general summed up the situation thus: 'Complete lack of organization apparent. Local authorities overwhelmed by magnitude problem and admit own inability cope with situation. No funds or qualified personnel available for organizing camps, food distribution, sanitation and immunization programs etc.'[19]

The situation was no better north of Ramallah. Major Hackett-Paine, a former British liaison officer with the Transjordanians, in mid-August toured the Iraqi-controlled Samaria District (the Nablus–Tulkarm–Jenin 'triangle') and found the state of the refugees—who he was told numbered in the District between 100,000 and 120,000—'very bad' and their morale 'very low'. Most lived in the open, under trees, in caves, and in unfinished houses; few had blankets and there was insufficient food. A major health problem was expected when the rain came. Most blamed the British for their plight 'and their hatred for us plus America and the Arab League is unbelievable'. As well, since the fall of Lydda and Ramle, 'Abdulla's name is just plain dirt'. Hackett-Paine, too, pleaded for British relief aid (to be channelled not through the Arab League).

---

[19] NA Record Group 84, Jerusalem Consulate General, Classified Records, 1948, 800—Refugees, John MacDonald, US Consul-General, Jerusalem, to Secretary of State, 27 July 1948 and John MacDonald to Secretary of State, 12 Aug. 1948.

The Foreign Office's Lance Thirkell thought the major's report 'ungrammatical and over-emotional' but that it conveyed well the 'acute misery' of the refugees in Samaria. Another Foreign Office official minuted: 'We may be hated now but that is nothing like the hatred which the Jews are laying up for themselves in the future if they don't allow these people back.'[20]

The great majority of the Palestinian refugees at this time—as in future decades—were concentrated in Transjordan and in the Transjordanian-held eastern areas of Palestine; smaller groups had moved to Egypt, Lebanon, Syria, and Iraq.

By August, according to Jefferson Patterson, the US chargé d'affaires, there were some 14,000 refugees in Egypt, dispersed in private homes and in the makeshift camps along the Suez Canal and in Cairo. 'All are reported to be in great need', he reported. He had been informed that Egypt was considering expelling its Jewish community and confiscating their property 'in order to provide aid and houses for the Palestine Arab refugees'; Egyptian officials denied this. The Egyptian press, he reported, was 'indignant' at the world's silence about the plight of the refugees. There were another 50,000 refugees in Egyptian-occupied Palestine, mainly concentrated in the Gaza area.[21]

In Lebanon, mainly concentrated in camps outside Sidon, near Lake Kar'oun in the eastern Bek'a Valley and at Bint Jbail, just north of the Israeli border, were some 50,000 refugees. The government was providing each with 10 kilograms of flour and three Lebanese pounds per person. Part of this was covered by a grant to the Lebanese Government of E£100,000 from the Arab League. The Lebanese were pressing UN Mediator for Palestine Count Folke Bernadotte to obtain Israeli permission for their repatriation. The Lebanese Christians viewed this massive influx of Moslems as a serious threat and 'would resist any attempt to [permanently] resettle refugees in Lebanon,' reported the British Minister, Houstoun-Boswall. He agreed with Dow's assessment that the solution to the refugee problem would ultimately have to be resettlement in the

---

[20] PRO, FO 371-68677 (E11504/10748/31), copy of Hackett-Paine's report covering note from HM Consulate General, Jerusalem, to Eastern Department, Foreign Office, 25 Aug. 1948, and minutes by several FO officials.
[21] NA, Record Group 34, Jerusalem Consulate General, Classified Records 1948, 800—Refugees, Patterson (Cairo) to Secretary of State, 7 Aug. 1948.

Arab countries, 'but Lebanon for obvious reasons would have to be excluded from any such scheme', he thought.[22]

By the end of July, only some 200 Palestinian refugees had reached Iraq. But Iraq, according to its Prime Minister, was about to receive another 5,000 (mainly from the 'little triangle' of Jaba, 'Ein Ghazal, and Ijzim, an originally Iraqi-controlled Arab enclave in Palestine's coastal plain conquered by the Israel Defence Forces during the Second Truce). The Iraqis, according to the British Legation in Baghdad, had made no provision for the refugees and had raised no public funds on their behalf.

Another 70,000 refugees were camped out, in poor condition, in Syria, mostly along the border with Israel. Both Iraq and Syria were already being targeted by senior British diplomats in the Middle East (as by Israeli officials) as the most appropriate sites for the permanent resettlement of most of the refugees. As a senior official in the British Middle East Office in Cairo put it, 'in Iraq and Syria . . . there are sufficient latent resources . . . to support a population several times the present numbers. In fact, in Iraq rapid progress in development is to a considerable extent dependent on an increase in population.' Of course, such argumentation was presented most forthrightly by British representatives in precisely those countries —such as Egypt and Lebanon—on which the burden of the refugee influx, be it for political, economic, or demographic reasons, weighed most heavily.[23]

Two major factors emerged from the cursory British and American diplomatic investigations in late July and early August 1948 of the Palestinian refugee situation. The conditions of their existence were, by and large, 'appalling'—'worse than anything he had ever seen', according to Bernadotte—and most of the Arab states were doing little, if anything, for their relief. As the Transjordanian Prime Minister told Kirkbride, Abdullah's appeal to his fellow Arab leaders for aid had secured only 'unfulfilled promises of money from Saudi Arabia and the Yemen'. Abdullah and his Prime Minister agreed, according to Kirkbride, that 'some of the Arab

---

[22] PRO, FO 371–68576 (E10232/4/31), Houstoun-Boswall (Beirut) to Foreign Office, 28 July 1948.

[23] PRO, FO 371–68576 (E10234/4/31), Richmond (Baghdad) to Foreign Office, 31 July 1948; (E10235/4/31), minute by Lance Thirkell, 4 Aug. 1948; and FO 371–68578 (E10456/4/31), BMEO (Cairo) to Foreign Office, 3 Aug. 1948.

states best able to bear a heavy burden . . . are doing the least of all . . .'.[24]

Something obviously had to be done. British Foreign Secretary Bevin felt that the key lay in the hands of the Arab states themselves. On 13 August he sent a forceful cable to Britain's posts in the Middle East stating: 'I am by no means convinced that the Arab States, and particularly those who can best afford it, are using their resources to the best advantage for the relief of Arab refugees.' He instructed the British diplomats to inform the Arab governments that 'more could and should be done by the Arab States themselves. His Majesty's Government realise that the main concern of the Arab States is that the refugees should be allowed to return to their homes and that they wish to do nothing to prejudice this possibility.' But even if this became possible, much time would elapse before implementation could conceivably take place; meanwhile the refugees were living in misery. Bevin particularly feared the outbreak of major epidemics. He called on the Arab states to supply funds and equipment for the relief of the refugees, a course which might persuade the powers outside the Middle East also to come forward with assistance; and he proposed that a local, Middle Eastern refugee relief organization be set up, to co-ordinate the efforts on behalf of the refugees.[25]

A similar feeling surfaced during July, August, and early September among Bernadotte and his staff, as it gradually became clear to them that Israel had no intention of allowing a return of the refugees to their homes. Bernadotte had the UN secretary general send Sir Raphael Cilento, the Australian director of the Division of Social Activities in the UN's Department of Social Affairs, to investigate the situation of the refugees. Cilento toured Transjordan and in early August reported on their condition. Bernadotte subsequently formulated a three-stage plan for refugee relief: (1) Immediate

[24] PRO, FO 371–68677 (E1088/4/31), Chapman Andrews (BMEO, Cairo) to Foreign Office, 16 Aug. 1948; and FO 371–68677 (E11025/10748/31), A. Kirkbride (Amman) to Foreign Office, 18 Aug. 1948.
[25] PRO, FO 371–68578, Foreign Office to Cairo, Baghdad, Beirut, Jidda, Damascus, Amman, BMEO, etc., 13 Aug. 1948.

relief of absolute basic needs, (2) relief from September to December, in conjunction with a thorough study of the problem, and (3) a long-range programme, covering January–September 1949. At the same time, he began personally to solicit assistance for the immediate relief of the refugees from dozens of governments and international bodies, asking for funds from the wealthier states, cereals from cereal exporters, and so on. Within his administration, a Disaster Relief Project (later called Refugee Relief Project) was set up, headed by Cilento, to co-ordinate these efforts and to oversee the distribution of the contributions. But Bernadotte was assassinated in Jerusalem by Jewish terrorists on 17 September, and Cilento's organization proved substantially ineffective, given the lack of any major contributions from the wealthier Western states and the lack of effective organization and generosity by most of the Arab states. Britain, for example, had supplied thousands of tents. For weeks these remained unopened and unused in a warehouse in Beirut, where the major relief-supplies bottleneck existed, due to a mixture of corruption and inefficiency. Money was not forthcoming and basic foods, water, medicines, doctors and medical facilities, tentage, clothing, and bedding all remained in very short supply or nonexistent through August and September in most of the refugee communities.

In late September an official of the International Committee of the Red Cross toured the refugee centres in Lebanon, Syria, Trans-jordan, and Palestine and reported that, despite the 'hullabaloo' surrounding international contributions, the 'tragic fact is that substantially nothing in food or goods have reached refugees up to October 1' apart from the direct aid proffered by the Arab governments and local communities. Stanton Griffis, the US Ambassador in Cairo, found the situation 'extremely delicate' in view of the almost complete absence of any US government or private contributions. Such aid was 'vital', said the ambassador, as the refugee issue had moved to the top of the Arab agenda in negotiations about a possible solution to the Middle East conflict.[26] Griffis felt very strongly about the refugees, not only within the context of American vulnerability and US interests in the Middle East. In December 1948, he was appointed by the UN secretary general the first

---

[26] NA 501. BB Palestine/10–648, Cairo (Griffis) to Secretary of State, 6 Oct. 1948.

director of UN Relief for Palestine Refugees in the Near East, effectively replacing Cilento. As his adviser, Griffis appointed Dr Bayard Dodge (former president of the American University of Beirut).

A similar message reached the State Department from Amman, where Stabler reported that, with the onset of rain, the condition of the some '200,000' refugees in Transjordan proper and in Transjordanian-occupied Palestine was 'severely deteriorating'. Transjordanian resources were too meagre to cope and, thus far, the only relief supplies to have arrived through the UN was a 'small amount [of] powdered milk for children and pregnant women . . . Immediate relief is not only of importance from humanitarian standpoint, but also as essential factor in arriving at satisfactory solution Palestine problem based on Bernadotte's conclusions [in his Interim Report and 'plan' of mid-September]. This running sore of refugees will make Arab acquiescence therein [that is, in the plan] more difficult and odious as it will remain evidence of UN inability cope with complicated yet urgent problem.' Stabler warned that further delay in the provision of relief 'can only result in appalling number of deaths'. He strongly urged the State Department to pressure the UN to begin providing the necessary supplies.[27]

The sense of urgency and pressure from the field culminated, for the US Government, with the cable of 17 October to the President and the Secretary of State from the new US Special Representative to Israel, James McDonald. Of the 'approximately 400,000 refugees', he wrote, an estimated '100,000 old men, women and children who are shelterless and have little or no food' would die when the rains came. The refugee problem was reaching 'catastrophic proportions and should be treated as a disaster'. The UN relief machinery was 'both inappropriate and inadequate' and had led to 'gross inefficiency and wastefulness'. Immediate action, guided by a comprehensive programme of relief, was needed to 'avert horrifying losses'. The present system of getting the relief from the contributor through the UN machinery to the countries and then the individual refugees was a failure, with wastage *en route* estimated at as high as '90 per cent'. McDonald recommended the immediate transfer of the whole relief operation to the hands of the Red Cross. McDonald believed the

[27] NA 501. BB Palestine/10–148, Amman (Stabler) to Secretary of State, 10 Oct. 1948.

UN administration, Israel, and the Arab states could be persuaded that such a change would be in everybody's interest.[28] The obvious anarchy in the relief efforts and the growing suffering of the refugees, issuing in increased international (mainly American) pressures, prompted the UN General Assembly resolution of December 1948 setting up the United Nations Relief for Palestine Refugees in the Near East (UNRPR). The UNRPR co-ordinated with and acted through the International Committee of the Red Cross, the League of Red Cross Societies, and the American Friends Service Committee in the distribution of the relief supplies. The Red Cross was given 'jurisdiction' over the refugees in Israel and the Transjordanian-occupied parts of Palestine; the League of Red Cross Societies, over Transjordan, Syria, and Lebanon; and the American Friends Service Committee (Quakers), over the Egyptian-occupied Gaza District. The UNRPR effectively replaced the Disaster Relief Project. In turn, in December 1949 the UNRPR was succeeded by the United Nations Relief and Works Agency for Palestine Refugees in the Near East (UNRWA), which took over and ran the refugee camps during the following decades.[29]

HOSTING THE FOURTH WAVE, THE WINTER OF 1948–1949
AND ORGANIZAING THE FIRST CAMPS

The refugee situation took a major turn for the worse towards the end of 1948, with the successful Israeli offensives of October and December 1948–January 1949, resulting in the flight of a further 150,000–200,000 Palestinians, most of them to the Gaza area.

In early November 1948, the Gaza Strip turned almost overnight into the worst hit district of Palestine. Some 210,000–230,000 refugees from the southern coastal plain and the northern Negev now packed an area (roughly 25 miles long by 5 miles wide) previously inhabited only by 60,000 local inhabitants. The first weeks were chaotic. The bulk of the refugees, after a lengthy trek from the north or east, came to rest 'under trees or just along the road . . .', reported UNICEF official Dr P. Descoeudres, who

[28] NA 501. BB Palestine/10-1748, Tel Aviv (McDonald) to Secretary of State (and President), 17 Oct. 1948.
[29] See Don Peretz, *Israel and the Palestine Arabs* (The Middle East Institute, Washington, DC 1958), 8–13.

visited the Strip on 11–12 November. One observer, who visited the Strip between 9 and 11 December, reported that in and around Gaza town now lived 60,000 refugees in addition to the original population of 25,000. 'They pack sidewalks, take up the vacant lots and the public market, occupy barnyards, and generally seem to fill in every empty space . . . They live in churches, mosques, schools . . .'.[30]

But already, a small proportion of the refugees—probably directed by Egyptian officers—had taken up residence in camps. By mid-November some 20,000 refugees had moved into the former British Army camps at Bureij and Nuseirat, south of Gaza, filling the ramshackle buildings and tents set up alongside the buildings in the camp compound. During a visit to Bureij, one observer described the refugees ensconced in the camp's former mess hall: 'It was about 50 feet wide and 120 feet long. There must have been 800 people in the place. They had staked out little cubicles for themselves using rags or flattened gasoline tins to make the borders between the family groups. Everyone was very dirty and cold. In one cubicle we saw a group of ten people . . . looking at an old woman on the floor who had just died.'[31] At Nuseirat camp, part of which had served in Mandate days as a military prison, families of seven or nine persons lived in each 'one-prisoner cell', six by eight feet in size. The original roofs had vanished, but the Egyptian Army had installed makeshift canvas and tin roofing 'which does not keep out the cold but does help lessen the amount of rain entering each room'. The wooden covers installed in the central latrines were immediately removed by the refugees and used for firewood.

During the following weeks the refugees, initially diffused, clustered together in new concentrations, which gradually became, under Egyptian Army and UNRPR management, organized camps. Altogether, eight large organized camps emerged in the Strip (Jabalia, Beach, Nuseirat, Bureij, Maghazi, Deir al Balah, Khan Yunis, and Rafah). In the new refugee camp, outside Khan Yunis, south of Bureij, with a 'supposed 40,000' population, the refugees lived initially fifteen to twenty per tent in tents originally intended for seven soldiers. There was a major shortage of tents, which was to plague the Gaza refugees at least until February 1949.[32] In Rafah, with some 30,000 refugees in mid-December, only 4,000 lived in a tent-camp, with 'the rest huddled wherever they can find any kind of shelter'.[33] The problem of shelter sorted itself out over December 1948–January 1949, as the bottlenecks in Beirut were unclogged and tentage began to flow to the Strip. By the start of March 1949, some two months after the Quakers took over the refugee relief operations in the Gaza Strip, a senior American Friends Service Committee (AFSC) figure was able to report that 'all refugees [in the Strip] are now under some kind of shelter, mostly tents'. But still more tents were needed, to reduce the overcrowding.[34]

In the early November 1948 days in the Gaza Strip, the refugees endured appalling conditions. Apart from shelter, the supply of food, water, medical services, and clothing were the primary problems. One American Red Cross official, R. T. Schaeffer, reported that 'thousands of refugees have fallen by the roadside from starvation' and there was widespread dysentery. The Egyptian Army, recovering from the series of defeats and routs that ended on 9 November, barely had time or resources for refugee relief. A UN official, F. G. Beard, reported that the Egyptian Army and the Cairo-based Arab Higher Refugee Council had been 'grossly negligent'.[35] The Egyptians initially, in early November, distributed some flour and rice to the refugees. The Strip's military governor said he had received E£12,000 which he had used for this purpose. But by mid-November the supplies had apparently run out and the refugees were receiving no food rations from the Egyptian authorities, according to foreign observers on the scene. Indeed, all the observers reported that, the moment they reached a refugee encampment or

[32] AFSC, Foreign Service 1948, Palestine, 'Memorandum', Gillespie Evans to Ambassador Stanton Griffis (Cairo), 26 Dec. 1948; 'Confidential Memorandum', John Devine to Ambassador Stanton Griffis (Cairo), 13 Dec. 1948; and 'Memorandum', Gillespie Evans to Ambassador Stanton Griffis (Cairo), 26 Dec. 1948.
[33] AFSC, Foreign Service 1948, Palestine, 'Confidential Memorandum', John Devine to Ambassador Stanton Griffis (Cairo), 13 Dec. 1948.
[34] AFSC, Foreign Service 1949, Palestine, 'Report of Clarence E. and Lilly Picket on their Visit to the Middle East', 3 Mar. 1949.
[35] NA 501. BB Palestine/11–1648, Cairo (Patterson) to Secretary of State, 16 Nov. 1948; and 501. BB Palestine/12–748, Cairo (Patterson) to Secretary of State, 7 Dec. 1948.

concentration, 'we were surrounded by crowds of mothers bringing their children and begging for food, and adolescents and men, threatening with doubled fists . . . stating they were starving'; the observers were 'smothered . . . with entreaties for food'. According to the International Red Cross doctor who treated the Gaza refugee population, 'at least ten children died from starvation each day in the camps' in mid-November. There was no milk ration for children.[36]

A month later, in mid-December, the situation had somewhat improved. In Bureij camp, with some 13,500 refugees, each person was receiving two and a half kilograms of flour per ten days (the Arab Higher Refugee Council having sent 1,000 tons and Australia, via th UN, another 500 tons). 'There are no prostrate people visible such as one read about in the famines in India and China,' reported one observer. But of the 10,000-odd refugees clustered in the Khan Yunis area, 'no more than half . . . [were] receiving the flour ration. The rest [were] begging for Egyptian Army leftovers, stealing oranges, or spending whatever money they have brought with them.' The Egyptian military governor in the Khan Yunis area 'seems to have very little interest in the problem', reported one western observer.[37]

But by the end of the month, the food situation seems to have stabilized, with most or nearly all the refugees receiving regular food rations. Most of the refugees had been issued with Egyptian identity cards and each card-holder received two and a half kilograms of flour per ten days (roughly half a pound of bread per person per day). Bakeries had been set up, with the refugees bringing in unbaked loaves and paying the baker one piastre (1,000 piastres to an E£) per twenty loaves. In the Gaza area, Egyptian soldiers apparently routinely gave away to the refugees one loaf of bread of the four they drew as their daily food allowance. The Egyptians, funded by various UN agencies and private contributions, maintained this level of nutrition of the refugees (about 600 calories per day) until January–February 1949 when, under the

---

[36] AFSC, Foreign Service 1948, Palestine, 'Report of a Visit by Dr Descoeudres to Southern Palestine, Nov. 11–12, 1948', 13 Nov. 1948. Beirut; and NA 501. BB Palestine/11–1648, Cairo (Patterson) to Secretary of State, 16 Nov. 1948.

[37] AFSC, Foreign Service 1948, Palestine, 'Confidential Memorandum', John Devine to Ambassador Stanton Griffis (Cairo), 13 Dec. 1948.

Quakers' management, the daily refugee diet rose to 1,800 calories per day. The Quakers were distributing about 200 tons of food per day, six days a week.[38]

Powdered milk also began to reach at least some of the child refugee population by the end of December. There was a milk distribution centre at Bureij camp, operated by the Red Cross. A western observer, arriving at the end of one distribution session (which he described as being handled 'in an extremely haphazard fashion'), spoke of 'children holding old beer bottles and tin cans . . . clamouring at the window and passing their containers through it to be filled'. By March 1949 milk was reaching all the refugee children through twelve fixed distribution centres.[39]

In certain areas of the Strip lack of water emerged as a major problem. In Rafah, in mid-November, the local inhabitants were selling the refugees water 'for 20 piastres a liter'.[40] In mid-December at Maghazi camp, south of Bureij, the 3,000 refugees had water, 'but often at some distance and in inadequate quantity'.[41] By the end of December, the Egyptian Army had installed in all the camps 'water tanks made from former British boilers and petrol tanks' and water was trucked in and distributed for two hours each day.[42]

The refugees' lack of clothing was another general problem, one which became more acute as the fall weather changed to winter. The refugees arrived in the Strip over October–November with very little baggage and very few clothes. The Egyptian military governor of Khan Yunis, Captain Nagui Amin Sallam, at the end of December defined the shortage of clothes as more 'urgent' than food. The Egyptian officer in charge of refugee affairs in the Strip, Captain Wahid, said that the combination of poor nutrition and lack of clothes would make the refugees 'easy prey' to pneumonia and

[38] AFSC, Foreign Service 1948, Palestine, 'Memorandum', Gillespie Evans to Ambassador Stanton Griffis (Cairo), 26 Dec. 1948; and AFSC, Foreign Service 1948, Palestine, 'Report of Clarence E. and Lilly Pickett on their Visit to the Middle East', 3 Mar. 1949.

[39] Ibid.; ibid.

[40] AFSC, Foreign Service 1948, Palestine, 'Report of Visit by Dr Descoeudres to Southern Palestine, Nov. 11–12, 1948', 13 Nov. 1948, Beirut.

[41] AFSC, Foreign Service 1948, Palestine, 'Confidential Memorandum', John Devine to Ambassador Stanton Griffis (Cairo), 13 Dec. 1948.

[42] AFSC, Foreign Service 1948, Palestine, 'Memorandum', Gillespie Evans to Ambassador Stanton Griffis (Cairo), 26 Dec. 1948.

other diseases. Most of the refugees cut up blankets distributed by the relief organizations and turned them into 'coveralls . . . in which [they] . . . live and sleep'.[43]

Medical services in the Strip remained appalling through November–December 1948 and, indeed, into 1949, until the activation of AFSC-directed teams. At the end of 1948 the Red Cross representative in the Strip, Dr Pflimlin, estimated that 120 refugees were dying each night, mostly from starvation and dysentery. An Egyptian doctor, who refused to treat serious cases among the refugees, was quoted as saying: 'After all, this is the season for dying.'[44] Dr Pflimlin and a local Arab doctor were the only doctors regularly treating the refugees during November. Pflimlin, who was Swiss, was assisted by a Swiss nurse. A second nurse joined him in December. The doctors had almost no medical supplies.[45] In December, Egyptian army doctors occasionally visited the camps and dispensed treatment to the sick but there were no regular hours and no medical centres or clinics in any of the camps. An American observer reported that, for all his efforts, Dr Pflimlin '[has] not made any noticeable dent in the [refugees' medical] problem'.[46] Local doctors, of whom there were only a handful, were apparently unwilling to treat destitute refugees without payment.

There were several small hospitals in Gaza—one run by the Red Crescent, another by Dr Hargreaves of the proselytizing Church Mission Society—but these had been established with the Gaza Strip pre-1948 local population in mind, and from November 1948 only a handful of beds were set aside for serious refugee cases. The problems of hospitalization in the Gaza Strip were made more acute by the renewed IDF offensive of 22 December 1948–6 January 1949, in which dozens of local inhabitants and refugees—especially from the mortared Maghazi camp—were killed and injured. A western observer who visited the Red Crescent Hospital in Gaza on

[43] AFSC, Foreign Service 1948, Palestine, 'Memorandum', Gillespie Evans to Ambassador Stanton Griffis (Cairo), 26 Dec. 1948.
[44] NA 501. BB Palestine/11–1648, Cairo (Patterson) to Secretary of State, 16 Nov. 1948, and 501. BB Palestine/12–748, Cairo (Patterson) to Secretary of State, 7 Dec. 1948.
[45] AFSC, Foreign Service 1948, Palestine, 'Report of Visit by Dr Descoeudres to Southern Palestine, Nov. 11–12, 1948'. 13 Nov. 1948, Beirut.
[46] AFSC, Foreign Service 1948, Palestine, 'Confidential Memorandum', John Devine to Ambassador Stanton Griffis (Cairo), 13 Dec. 1948.

23 December reported that it was 'completely unheated and unlighted' and that the injured from the mortar attack overflowed on to the hospital porch. The hospital was staffed by two Arab doctors and a handful of 'completely untrained interns'. There was a shortage of 'everything', according to the hospital director.[47]

But, despite the almost complete absence of medical care or supplies and the onset of winter, the refugees' health situation was not as bad as western observers expected, in large measure because of what these observers defined as the refugees' natural 'hardiness'. Indeed, after the initial death toll of November 1948, it was not clear that infant, child, or adult mortality rates among the Gaza refugees from the beginning of 1949 were any higher than among the indigenous Gaza population. Some of the refugees were inoculated by the Egyptian Army against smallpox and typhoid, and no epidemics broke out during the first crucial winter months of November and December 1948 or during the first months of 1949. By February–March 1949, the refugee population's health was adequately assured by the Quaker-run teams of doctors and para-medics.[48]

Although the refugee concentrations in Transjordan and Trans-jordanian-held parts of Palestine had not been substantially increased by further fighting after the summer of 1948, conditions there too had deteriorated, mainly because of the advent of winter. The commander of the Arab Legion, General Glubb, in December wrote from Amman to J. Baker-White, MP, that 'many died in the night', after the first rain of the season. Down the road from his house eleven refugees were living in a quarry. Glubb had sent them blankets 'but their little boy of about four . . . during the night died all the same'.

The Transjordanian authorities, in concert with the UN refugee officials, had during the autumn moved tens of thousands of refugees from the Ramallah–Hebron hill-country, where snow occasionally fell in winter, to the warmer Jordan valley; about 30,000 were living

[47] AFSC, Foreign Service 1948, Palestine, 'Memorandum', Gillespie Evans to Ambassador Stanton Griffis (Cairo), 26 Dec. 1948.
[48] AFSC, Foreign Service 1948, Palestine, 'Report of a Visit by Dr Descoeudres to Southern Palestine, Nov. 11–12, 1948', 13 Nov. 1948, Beirut; and AFSC, Foreign Service 1949, Palestine, 'Report of Clarence E. and Lilly Pickett on their Visit to the Middle East', 3 Mar. 1949.

in refugee camps (and another 5,000–6,000 elsewhere) around Jericho by December.

Glubb complained at the start of December that the Jericho area refugees were getting 'no food'. This was inaccurate. According to British officials on the spot, the Transjordanian Government was distributing flour sufficient for 225 grams of bread per refugee per day, and food was arriving from the UN relief agency. More than 1,000 half-pints of milk were being prepared from powder and distributed daily for infants and nursing mothers. Two kilograms of potatoes and chunks of cheese had been distributed to each person, and a shipment of olive oil, tinned meat, and margarine had been received and was to be distributed. A shipment of 1,000 blankets had also arrived and largely had been distributed.

The Jericho camps, according to British officials, were being run efficiently by a Belgian Red Cross official, Dr Depage, but suffered from a basic lack of funds to cover such expenses as 'milling of wheat, sanitation, water supply, warehousing . . . and transport'. A Danish field hospital unit—with staff—was due to arrive, but meanwhile Depage suffered from lack of medical personnel. There were Arab doctors in Jericho but 'they were not willing to work without some form of payment' and Depage had no money.

Depage had probably created the first major experiment in organized camp life for the refugees in Palestine, a model camp. An attempt had been made to place people from the same villages together, in blocks. Arabs were given various jobs in the camp administration and cleanliness was enforced. And it appeared to work, as far as it went. But in January 1949, lack of supplies from the Disaster (Refugee) Relief Project, which had employed Depage, administrative changes, including Depage's removal, and unemployment resulted in major violence. Discontented refugees ransacked Jericho's Jordan Hotel, killed an Arab Legion officer, and wounded several people. The refugees had heard that relief money was being used to throw a party at the hotel. The camp was cordoned off by Legion armoured cars, searched, and placed under curfew. Dow, the British consul-general in Jerusalem, pressed for funds to employ and pay at least some of the camps' male population, 'paid employment [being] a most important psychological factor in maintaining the morale of male refugees and preventing them from lapsing into anarchy and Communism'. The Red Cross, which had taken over the camps from the UN organization, apparently peferred bringing in its own staff to using local workers.[49]

The situation in the Nablus area, controlled by the Iraqi military, remained unchanged. 'To turn to Nablus from Jericho is to sink from Day No. 1 of the creation back into chaos', wrote Dow. The refugees in the Nablus–Tulkarm area refused to move to warmer Jericho. The consul-general believed that they were being encouraged in this course by local officials and merchants, who stood to gain by their continued presence (charging those with money exorbitant prices and siphoning off some of the relief money destined for the refugees). The local authorities maintained that there were 128,000 refugees in their area; Dow thought the figure inflated, and implied that the inflated figure stemmed from a desire to receive more relief. At least three refugees were dying each day in the immediate vicinity of Nablus, according to the mayor. There was only haphazard local distribution of food and milk and there were no tents. 'The Iraqi army with . . . 1 line of [Communications] of 1,500 miles are unwilling and probably unable to do anything about them. There is flour in the Bazaar but the refugees cannot afford it.' The municipal authorities wanted the Transjordanian Government to administratively take over the Nablus area but the Iraqis, 'for reasons of prestige', refused to relinquish any authority. The consul-general recommended that a refugee camp be set up east of Nablus and that relief supplies only be given to those refugees who agreed to move to the camp.[50]

But the whole concept of the refugee camps (whether run directly by a UN agency or by the Red Cross), almost from the start was understood to be politically dangerous and insufficient. Cilento, who more or less supervised the establishment of the camps, told a

[49] PRO, FO 371–68633 (E16038/10748/31), Glubb Pasha (Amman) to J. Baker-White, MP (London), 2 Dec. 1948; FO 371–68683 (E16264/10748/31), R. A. Beaumont (Consulate-General, Jerusalem,) to B. A. A. Burrows, Foreign Office, undated, c. 15 Dec. 1948; FO 371–68683 (E16344/10748/31), Sir H. Dow (Jerusalem) to Foreign Office, 21 Dec. 1948; FO 371–75417, Sir H. Dow (Jerusalem) to Foreign Office, 16 Jan., 1949; and NA 501. BB Palestine/12–2748, 'Minutes of Fifth Meeting with Voluntary Agencies.' Beirut, 3 Dec. 1948. Avi Plascov, in *The Palestinian Refugees in Jordan, 1948–1957* (Frank Cass, London, 1981), 66–7, briefly describes the switch from tents to huts—in fact, to relative permanency—of the Jericho area camps over 1949–50.

[50] PRO, FO 371–68683 (E16344/10748/31), Sir H. Dow (Jerusalem) to Foreign Office, 21 Dec. 1948.

gathering of representatives of voluntary relief organizations in Beirut in early December that the 'camps are not a good idea if their establishment leads to permanency or to an intensification of the feeling of isolation and frustration, which is the tendency of many of the refugees; nor are they good if they remain merely areas for the distribution of goods without any purposive trend towards a final solution'. The outbreak in Jericho in January 1949 had illustrated the danger the camps constituted to law and order, and perhaps to government, as well, in the Hashemite kingdom. A permanent solution, all understood, was possible in one of two ways: Repatriation to Israel or resettlement in the Arab states. A third possibility, of combining the two, was in fact a variation on the idea of resettlement in the Arab countries as, if Israel refused to accept and adopt the principle of repatriation (as was the case), it would certainly not accept more than a very small number of repatriates as part of any political deal with the Arabs.[51]

'THE REFUGEE THREAT' AND THE POSSIBILITY OF ORGANIZED RESETTLEMENT IN THE ARAB STATES

By the start of 1949, most US diplomats in the Middle East understood that repatriation was out of the question as Israel, simply, refused to take back the refugees. And some, such as James McDonald, had come around to the Israeli view that the alternative, of organized resettlement in the Arab countries, was indeed preferable. As William Burdett Jr., the new US consul-general in Jerusalem (who was generally unfriendly to Israel), put it: 'Political-security best served by settling refugees in Arab states. Return refugees [to Israel] would create continuing minority problem and form constant temptation both to uprisings and intervention by neighbouring Arab states.' It was the height of the Cold War and Burdett, like most other American officials, was keenly aware of the revolutionary, 'pro-Communist' potential of the hundreds of thousands of disgruntled, ill-fed, ill-housed, and stateless refugees: 'USSR may capitalize on opportunity', he wrote. Unlike most of his peers, Burdett thought that the organized resettlement of the refugees could focus on Transjordan and the Arab occupied parts of Palestine (Samaria, the

[51] NA 501. BB Palestine/12-2748, 'Minutes of the Fifth Meeting with Voluntary Agencies,' Beirut, 3 Dec. 1948.

Hebron Hills, and the Gaza district). His thinking was based primarily on his knowledge or intuition that the other Arab states—principally Syria and Iraq—would not agree to absorb any more refugees than they already had. But permanent absorption in Transjordan and the Arab-held parts of Palestine, he argued, would necessitate large-scale development schemes, including irrigation projects in the Jordan Valley, road construction, fisheries, phosphate production, and potash plants, which would provide employment. All this could be done only if the Western states poured in a lot of money.[52]

But Israel and most American officials preferred to focus on Iraq and Syria rather than Transjordan and Palestine, as the best sites for the resettlement of the refugees. The head of the US Legation in Jidda, Saudi Arabia, wrote that while, under Arab League pressure, the Saudis might accept 'a token number of Arab refugees', the kingdom would refuse to take any substantial number. There were both economic and political reasons, the latter weighing the more heavily. Saudi agriculture could absorb none and the oil industries could absorb only a handful. But more important, 'the entry of a significant number of Palestinians . . . could not help but have far-reaching political implications . . . [because] the Palestinians, under British tutelage, grew accustomed to at least a semi-free press and other beginnings of democratic institutions. They would doubtless find it most difficult to accept the situation in Saudi Arabia where the rule is absolute . . .' Hence, the senior American diplomat felt that it was neither in the Saudis' nor America's interest to press the king to take in more than a token number of refugees. As repatriation to Israel was to be ruled out, resettlement in Arab countries, 'principally Iraq and possibly Syria', should be planned. The US would have to foot the bulk of the bill, he felt. In the absence of an

[52] NA 501. BB Palestine/2-949, Burdett (Jerusalem) to Secretary of State, 9 Feb. 1949. Already in Aug. 1948 US diplomats were warning of the 'Communist' revolutionary potential of the Palestinian refugee communities. On 24 Aug., Keeley, the US Minister in Damascus, after a tour of camps in Syria wrote that the refugees were unquestionably 'ripe for Communist indoctrination'. See NA Record group 84, Jerusalem Consulate General, Classified Records 1948, 800—Syria, Keeley (Damascus) to Secretary of State, 24 Aug. 1948. See also NA 501. BB Palestine/3-2849, Beirut (Mark Ethridge, US representative on the Palestine Conciliation Commission) to Secretary of State (and, at his discretion, to the President), 29 Mar. 1949, for Ethridge's assessment of the refugees as a threat to the stability of the Arab host regimes.

organized resettlement scheme, the refugees would 'remain a canker in the Near Eastern states and [a threat to] American relations with them for some time to come'.[53]

Similar resistance to the permanent absorption of Palestinian refugees was expressed by Lebanon, which by the start of 1949 had 90,000–120,000 on its soil. Economically, they were an 'unbearable burden'; Lebanon suffered from 5 per cent unemployment and could offer almost no employment to the Palestinians. The US Beirut Legation concurred: 'It is difficult to see how present economic conditions in Lebanon will permit any significant absorption of refugees.' But even more important was the political aspect. 'The absorption of an alien population amounting to as much as 10 per cent of the native population . . . would create a Moslem majority and turn the entire political complexion of the country.' The Beirut Legation also pointed to Iraq and Syria, after appropriate agricultural investment and development, as the best sites for the refugees' relocation.[54]

A similar focus on Syria and Iraq for the refugees' permanent resettlement was to be found in Israeli planning at this time for the refugees' future. The proposal of the 'Transfer Committee' (set up by the government to smooth the path of the Palestinians' permanent relocation outside Israel), submitted to the Israeli Government at the end of November 1948, contained long sections detailing the absorptive capacity of the two countries. For months thereafter, committee members Ezra Danin, a senior Foreign Ministry official, and Yosef Weitz, director of the Jewish National Fund's Lands Department, promoted schemes for the absorption of the refugees in Syria, Iraq, and, to a lesser extent, Transjordan and for their employment by foreign companies with interests in the Middle East, primarily the oil corporations.[55]

The problem, however, was that Syria, with some 80,000 refugees, and Iraq, with 4,000–5,000, wanted no more. Those already in Iraq could be employed in road construction, if funds were found for such projects, wrote the American Embassy in Baghdad; their

[53] NA 501. BB Palestine/1-2149. American Legation, Jidda, to Secretary of State, 21 Jan. 1949.
[54] NA 501. BB Palestine/2-449. American Legation, Beirut, to Secretary of State, 4 Feb. 1949.
[55] For details see Ch. 4 in the present volume.

continued presence would have only a 'negligible effect' on the country. But Iraq's policy was that even these 'should be returned to Palestine'. As to additional refugees, economically—with appropriate international investment in agricultural development schemes —it was 'conceivable'. But socially and politically, it would be extremely problematic. 'Despite their common Arab culture, Palestinians would be regarded as foreigners and an influx of them would not be welcome either in the towns or in the agricultural areas of Iraq. They would be likely to form another unassimilated, discontented minority group', wrote the American Embassy. The Embassy, in short, reflecting Iraqi Government opinion, thought that 'the presence in Iraq of many thousands of victims of the clash between Arabs and Jews would be certain to keep the Palestine issue burning alive for generations. In the interest of long-range security in the Middle East, the Embassy recommends therefore that every effort be made to ensure . . . that refugees who so desire be returned to their homes [in Palestine] . . . '. The Iraqis, then, wanted no more refugees, for economic and social-political reasons. Neither did the Syrians.[56]

But it went deeper than that, and this applied to Iraq as well as all or most of the Arab states, as the American representative to the Palestine Conciliation Committee, Mark Ethridge, understood. A major reason for the Arab unwillingness to properly absorb and resettle the refugees at this time was rooted in their struggle against Israel rather than in internal political or economic and social considerations. The Arabs saw in the '700,000 or 800,000' refugees a 'political weapon against the Jews. They feel they can summon world opinion [against Israel] even if some refugees die in the meantime.' The Arabs sought the refugees' repatriation, both as a demand of justice and as a means to subvert the Jewish state. Hence, it was better to leave the refugees for the time being in squalor and living impermanently than to support and implement resettlement schemes in Arab countries which would neutralize, and perhaps ultimately solve, the problem. Moreover, the refugees camped along Israel's borders (rather than in faraway Iraq), the Arab leaders told Ethridge, would provide the 'core of [an] irredentist movement that will plague all Arab states and provide basis for con-

---

[56] NA 501. BB Palestine/2–749, Baghdad to Secretary of State, 7 Feb. 1949.

tinual agitation to the point that there will be no possibility of having anything more than [Arab–Israeli] armistice in the Middle East'.[57]

So it was that the Palestinian Arab refugees, numbering between 600,000 and 760,000, remained *in situ*. Unwanted as repatriates by Israel and unwanted as new immigrants by the larger Arab countries, the refugees remained by and large where they had initially come to semi-permanent rest—mainly in and near the main Arab towns of Samaria and the Hebron Hills, Jericho and Transjordan, and the Gaza District, and, in smaller numbers, in Lebanon and Syria.

Through 1948 the refugees suffered; hundreds, perhaps thousands, died. Their initial absorption by the Arab states and by the eastern Palestinian and Gazan communities, and the Iraqi, Transjordanian, and Egyptian armies that controlled these areas, was anarchic and thoughtless. As most of the refugees reached these areas in the spring and summer of 1948, the need for reasonable, rain-proof accommodation was not immediately apparent. Life in olive groves, caves, private gardens, and unfinished buildings and garages was possible, given the temperate climate. Moreover, for months most of the refugees and the Arab local and national leaders continued to believe that the refugees' lot was temporary, and that they would soon be returning to their homes. Few were able to think of non-return as a realistic prospect, or to suit their thinking and actions to what was and would be needed if the Palestinians' refugeedom was to become permanent. Lastly, the Arab states—poor, corrupt, and highly disorganized, by Western standards—throughout 1948 were involved in a major war with Israel, their main energies and thinking focusing on the war effort rather than on the alleviation of the refugees' misery. The refugees were a side-issue, and were regarded mainly as an added burden for the Arab armies and states. The alleviation of their physical plight was left largely in the hands of local Arab authorities and voluntary committees, though in Transjordan, Transjordanian-occupied territory, and Lebanon, the state provided a basic quantity of food for daily sustenance, but little else. There was unhappiness about the influx of refugees in various localities; they brought filth, disease, and demoralization.

[57] NA 501. BB Palestine/3–2849. Beirut (Ethridge) to Secretary of State, 28 Mar. 1949.

Why should Egyptian and Transjordanian boys fight for the rights
of Palestinians who had fled without a fight? some argued. Good
ladies organized to give aid, blankets, food, money. But local
merchants and, apparently, officials exploited the refugees, hiking
prices and siphoning off a proportion of the international and local
relief contributions.

Attempts by Arab governments, such as Syria and in some areas,
Transjordan, to get the refugees to go back were not pressed home.
And, in any case, Israel was firmly resolved, from June 1948, not to
allow the refugees to return, either in dribbles or *en masse*. Attempts
by refugees to return were repulsed by fire. Moreover, many of the
refugees, during the summer and autumn of 1948, preferred to stay
put for some of the same reasons that had prompted them to leave
Israeli-controlled areas in the first place—fear of the Jews and
unwillingness to live as a minority in a Jewish state. Some, at least
for a time, expected to return to their homes in the wake of
conquering Arab armies.

International relief efforts on behalf of the refugees were slow off
the mark, partly also because of a belief that the refugees would
soon be repatriated. But as winter approached and everyone grew
to accept that repatriation was not on the cards, tent camps were set
up to accommodate the refugees. From the first, these were regarded
—by the international relief bodies and the Arab host countries—
as a temporary arrangement; the danger of the presence of hundreds
of thousands of disgruntled, poorly fed and poorly housed refugees
to the Arab host regimes was clear to all. By the winter, and only
just, the UN and the other international agencies had overcome the
bureaucratic muddle and the bottlenecks in Beirut and elsewhere,
and a minimal if sufficient amount of relief aid began reaching the
refugees. The UN managed to put its act together with the belated
formation of the UNRPR, and the Arab states, armies, and municipalities during the winter of 1948–9 were almost completely
relieved of the burden of care for the basic physical necessities of the
refugee communities.

But this was seen by the international community as merely a
temporary situation, which required a major political initiative and
solution. Pressures on Israel to allow back all or a large number of
the refugees increased over the winter and spring; but, given its
victories over the Arabs, so did the new state's strength, and its

ability to resist such pressures successfully. Repatriation was just not on. But neither, it turned out, was its alternative, organized resettlement in the larger (and largely under-populated) Arab countries—the solution by the start of 1949 favoured by Israel and most senior American and British officials (who also wanted to see Israel take back some refugees, if only as a political gesture of conciliation towards the Arabs). In the course of the summer and autumn of 1949, Iraq, Syria, and the other major Arab countries resisted the dangled bait of large economic aid linked to readiness to absorb large numbers of refugees. They had good economic, social-demographic, and internal political reasons, the latter—the threat of revolutionary destabilization—apparently predominating. But also, as Ethridge perceived, there was a need born of the context of conflict with Israel—to use the refugees as a weapon against the Jewish state. The hundreds of thousands of refugees, if left in misery, would continue to demand repatriation, and would find support for this in the international community. If allowed back, they could destabilize the Jewish state. If not allowed back, their existence would eat at world support for Israel and would ignite an endless and violent irredenta, which would leave the Arabs and Israel in permanent conflict. Ethridge pressed for American pressure on Israel to take back some 250,000 of the refugees to neutralize this irredentist-political threat and to do at least partial justice to the Palestinians. But Israel, having won the war and got rid of its potentially destabilizing, large Arab minority was in no mood for compromise on the matter, a compromise seen by almost all of Israel's security-minded leaders as in itself a mortal threat to the country's well-being. The refugees remained in the camps.

10

The Transfer of Al Majdal's Remainng Arabs to Gaza, 1950

The Arab town of Majdal, next to the site of the Second Millennium BC Philistine port of Ashkelon or Ascalon on the Mediterranean coast between Jaffa and Gaza, had a population of about 10,000 at the start of the 1948 war. By October, thousands more—refugees from other parts of Palestine—lived in its streets, groves, and public buildings. During Operation Yoav, which began on 15 October, the IDF repeatedly shelled and bombed the town and, on 4 November, conquered it. Majdal's Egyptian army garrison, and much of the population, had fled the town already on 30 October.

The occupying Israeli force was ordered by OC Southern Front, General Yigal Allon, to expel the town's remaining Arabs. But the local commanders baulked, and the order was never carried out.[1] Something over 1,000 remained, their number growing to 2,400–2,700 in the following two years. The increase was due primarily to infiltration of refugees back into the town from the Gaza Strip, and in smaller measure to movement to the

[1] HHA–ACP 10.95.10 (6), notes written by Aharon Cohen during the meeting of Mapam's Political Committee, 11 Nov. 1948; and ISA, FM 2436/5bet. 'About the Eviction/Evacuation [*pinui*] of Migdal-Gad's Arab Inhabitants', 22 Oct. 1950, an unsigned two-page memorandum, probably by officials of the Israel Foreign Ministry's Research Department. Shimon Avidan, the 1948 commander of the IDF's Giv'ati Brigade, which conquered Majdal (interviewed on 22 Nov. 1990), did not recall receiving any order from Southern Front (i.e. later Command) to expel the Arab inhabitants of Majdal. On the contrary, he relates that just before his troops entered the town, a delegation of weavers slipped through the lines and came with a white flag to his HQ and asked to be allowed to remain *in situ*. 'As the IDF needed uniforms, and as Majdal's weavers were good craftsmen, I agreed. But when Giv'ati entered the town, the troops found no Arabs. Majdal was empty,' he recalled.

This is contradicted by the available documentary evidence, which says that something over 1,000 Arabs remained in the town. The Arabs may have hidden and the Giv'ati troops probably did not spend much time looking for them. In any event, the troops did not round them up and expel them.

town of remainder communities of Arabs from elsewhere in the South and to births.

During the 1948–9 period, Allon 'demanded . . . that the town be emptied of its Arabs'. New Jewish immigrants began moving into Majdal in 1949, settling in the abandoned Arab houses. The immigration absorption and settlement authorities wanted as many empty Arab houses as possible; the IDF did not want an Arab-populated town near Israel's frontier with Egypt. At the start of 1950, the IDF General Staff or its Southern Command formally requested government authorization for the eviction of Majdal's Arabs.[2]

The interdepartmental government Committee for Transferring Arabs already in February 1949 had decided in principle on the need to clear the town of Arabs. But Israel, at the time, was seeking admission to the UN, and the matter was deferred.[3]

The IDF's demand for the transfer of Majdal's Arabs was based on (*a*) a desire to put a stop to the ceaseless, troublesome infiltration back and forth between the Gaza Strip and Majdal; (*b*) Majdal's position as a 'source of information and refuge for Arab infiltrators' and as a way station for infiltrators from the Strip bound for Ramle, Lydda, and Jaffa; (*c*) the desire of Majdal's Arabs to see 'the return of Arab rule in their city' (a hint at the Fifth Column potential of this community); (*d*) the costs of maintaining an efficient military government in the town to oversee the Arab population and the costs of maintaining the Arab community, many of whom were unemployed and destitute; and (*e*) the assessment that the continued presence of Arabs

---

[2] ISA, FM 2436/5bet., 'About the Eviction . . .'.

[3] ISA, MAM 1322/22, 'Protocol of the Ninth Meeting of the Committee for Transferring [Arabs]', 25 Feb. 1949; and entry for 23 Feb. 1949, CZA, A-246/14, pp. 2584–5. The Committee for Transferring Arabs (sometimes also referred to in the documentation as the 'Committee for Transferring Arabs from Place to Place') was set up at the end of 1948 as an interdepartmental body consisting of representatives of the Interior Ministry, the Agriculture Ministry, the police, the Defence Ministry, and the Jewish National Fund (Yosef Weitz). Its task was to resettle in new sites Arabs who had been displaced by the hostilities but still lived in Israel. In the course of 1949–50, the committee, with the army's 'help', resettled 'remainder communities' from such Galilee villages as Khisas, Ja'una, and Qeitiya in 'Akbara; from al Bassa and Kabri in Mazra'a; from Kafr 'Inan and Farradiya in Tur'an; and from Saffuriya in ar Reina.

necessarily 'politically and militarily weakened [Israel's] hold over the town and its environs'.[4]

In early 1950, the government—perhaps in a formal Cabinet decision—approved the orderly transfer of Majdal's remaining Arabs to sites inside Israel, with the largely abandoned former Arab towns of Ramle and Jaffa being earmarked for their absorption.[5]

During the spring of 1950 Majdal's Arabs were repeatedly informed by the Israeli military governor, Major Yehoshua Varbin, and his assistant and liaison officer with the Arabs, Uri Chechik, that they would shortly have to evacuate the town. As a UN investigator put it in a report later, in early September: 'They have been warned two or three times that they all would have to leave Al Majdal within a [*sic*] near future.' An initial convoy of Majdal residents—some 200 souls originally from the village of Qatra displaced to Majdal during the war—were transferred in June or July to Ramle and resettled there in abandoned Arab houses.[6]

---

[4] ISA, FM 2436/5bet., 'About the Eviction . . .'. Three months before the transfer, an intelligence officer of IDF Southern Command reported: 'The town of Majdal serves as a centre for smuggling, infiltration and robbery for the whole area. A great number of the town's inhabitants directly assist the gangs . . .' (Capt. Yehoshua Nishri, command security officer, Southern Command/Intelligence, to Operations Officer Southern Command, 17 Mar. 1950, IDFA $\frac{2539/50}{14}$).

A few months earlier, the town's military governor, Major Yehoshua Varbin, complained to the Military Government Headquarters that infiltration had substantially increased during the winter months, with large bands, some of them armed, reaching the Majdal area: 'They steal everything they can lay hands on. Every night they penetrate the Majdal urban area.' Varbin reported that an Arab was arrested after attempting to rape the wife of the local government doctor. She had been wandering in a derelict area on the outskirts of the town after a quarrel with her husband (Varbin to Military Government, 25 Dec. 1949, IDFA $\frac{721/72}{843}$).

[5] ISA, FM 2436/5bet., 'About the Eviction . . .'. The Histadrut official, E. N. Mul, on 25 Oct. 1950 wrote to Reuven Burstein (LA IV-219-163) that on 5 Oct. 1950 he had learnt that the government 'already in January 1950' had decided to evict Majdal's Arabs, the operation to be carried out by the ministries of agriculture and labour. Mul was probably referring to the meeting in Tiberias on 14 Jan. between Ben-Gurion, Sharett, and a number of senior officials, including Yosef Weitz, the director of the Lands Department of the Jewish National Fund. According to Weitz's cryptic diary entry (Y. Weitz, *Yomani*, iv. 68–9, entry for 14 Jan. 1950), the purpose of the meeting was to discuss 'the transfer of Arabs in Israel: Majdal, Zakariya . . . It was decided that this would be carried out without coercion. It was also decided that land would be bought from owners desiring to leave the country.'

[6] ISA, FM 2436/5bet.: Major V. H. Loriaux, acting chairman Israel–Egypt

But at some point that spring, General Moshe Dayan, the new IDF OC Southern Command, decided to direct the evacuation of Majdal's Arabs out of Israel, toward the Egyptian-held Gaza Strip, rather than to sites inside the country. Dayan at this time supported the transfer out of the country of all of Israel's Arab minority. He received authorization for the transfer to Gaza from Prime Minister and Defence Minister David Ben-Gurion at a meeting between the two men on 19 June. According to Dayan's memoirs, Ben-Gurion set only one condition, 'one which I, too, had in mind . . . that we would make the transfer only if the Majdal Arabs themselves agreed to it'.[7] The transfer to Gaza began, in fact, five days earlier, on 14 June. No written order to carry out the transfer apparently was issued by Dayan or the IDF General Staff—everything was conducted by word of mouth. And the operation, contrary to the military norm, was never given a name or codename.[8]

In his memoirs Dayan was to present the transfer as a joint initiative of the Majdal Arab leaders and himself. He wrote: 'After talking to them, I found that the majority wished to move to the Gaza Strip . . . while some wanted to go to other towns inside Israel. I thought this an admirable solution.' The Egyptians, too, according to Dayan, were agreeable to this solution.

Dayan had to overcome both a certain (unexplained) 'sluggishness' on the part of the IDF General Staff and, more problematic still, objections by the Histadrut, the powerful, Mapai-dominated trades union federation.[9] When it came to the crunch, the Histadrut did not in principle oppose the transfer of Majdal's

Mixed Armistice Commission, to UNTSO Chief of Staff, 4 Sept. 1950; and General Dayan to IDF Chief of General Staff (General Yigael Yadin), ? (probably early) Oct. 1950. Dayan wrote that the 'military governor's semi-official announcements concerning the evacuation of Majdal by all its Arab inhabitants' was among 'the precipitating factors' (*gormim medarbenim*) in the eventual exodus.

[7] Moshe Dayan, *Story of My Life* (London, 1977), 160–1, and *Avnei Derekh, Autobiographiya* (Tel Aviv, 1976), 96; and Aluf Ben, 'Halchu Le'Aza', *Ha 'Ir*, 23 Sept. 1988. Ben's is the best investigative-journalistic piece published to date on the Majdal transfer. Ben interviewed many of the protagonists, including Varbin, Chechik, Palmon, and Hassan Hijazi. For Dayan on the transfer of Israel's Arab minority, see the protocol of the meeting of Mapai Secretariat and Knesset faction, 18 June 1950, Labour Party Archive (Beit Berl).

[8] Ben, 'Halchu Le 'Aza'.

[9] Dayan, *Story of My Life*, 160–1.

Arabs, but it tried to exclude from the transfer Arab families who, in a sense, had thrown in their lot with the Histadrut and Israel.

Soon after the IDF conquest, the Histadrut began to look at the town's Arab community as 'a subject of experiment for all our economic activity among the Israeli Arab [minority] . . . a laboratory . . . [for co-operative economic ventures] . . .'.[10] Already in April 1949, the Histadrut's Economic Department and its Bureau for Co-operation with Arab Workers had proposed that a weaving co-operative, with 200 workers and 100 looms, be set up among the Majdal Arabs, who, traditionally, were expert weavers.[11] The Histadrut also planned an associated agricultural co-operative. By September–October, the co-operative enterprise (called in Hebrew *ira ovedet*), directed by Histadrut officials, began donning 'skin and bone'. Arab family heads began to sign up and by March 1950, the Histadrut had mobilized some 100–110 families.[12] The co-operatives were to be set up either in Majdal itself or on nearby lands East of the town and were to include both weavers' workshops and an agricultural element, with twenty-five dunams of land for co-operative farming and one dunam per family for a house and a garden vegetable plot.[13]

Following the start of the transfer of Majdal's Arabs, the Histadrut moved swiftly to obtain the government's support for the venture. The trade union federation specifically sought government assurances that the Arab families joining the co-operative would be excluded from the transfer plans. On 7 August, a representative of the Histadrut's Executive Committee, E. N. Mul, travelled down to Majdal and met Chechik, who was running the transfer. Chechik assured Mul 'clearly and emphatically' that the army's policy was not to expel from Israel any Majdal Arab who wished to stay and not to prevent anyone from joining the co-operative. Indeed, the army was excercising

---

[10] LA IV–219–163, E. N. Mul to Reuven Burstein, Histadrut Executive Committee, 25 Oct. 1950.

[11] LA IV–219–163, 'Proposals of the Economic Department and the Co-operation Bureau for Arab Workers', to the Ministry of Labour, 27 Apr. 1949.

[12] LA IV–219–163: Mul to Burstein, 25 Oct. 1950; and 'The Activities of the Economic Section of the Arab Department', an undated memorandum, probably from Mar. 1950.

[13] LA IV–219–163, 'Minutes of the Meeting of the Co-operatives Committee in Migdal in the Office of the Economic Section on 21 August 1950'.

great 'caution' and forbearing from using any 'pressure' on the Arabs, asserted Chechik.[14]

Similar assurances were forthcoming from the policy-making echelon. On 20 August 1950 Mul met the prime minister's adviser on Arab affairs, Yehoshua Palmon, who expressed his support for the co-operative venture and gave his agreement to the lease of a patch of land outside Majdal on which the co-operative could be set up. Palmon's views, which were repeated later on various occasions, that the weavers' co-operative members were to be excluded from the transfer and that, indeed, no Majdal Arab who wished to stay would be forced to leave, were presented by him as official Cabinet policy.[15]

Meanwhile the transfer continued. It was conducted in an orderly manner, with three local Arab dignitaries helping the military government with the registration of the transferees, the sale of their property, and the transport arrangements. According to Chechik, the Arab dignitaries assisted the Israelis in persuading the successive batches of transferees to leave for Gaza.[16] None of the transferees sold their houses or land, which, like the real estate of the 1948 refugees, passed into the hands of Israel's Custodian for Absentees Property.

The Majdal Arabs were transported to the border in Israeli trucks and buses in convoys that left from the town hall. Most were pressed to sign, and signed, a form saying that their departure was voluntary, and renouncing property rights and the right to return. At first, there was only a trickle of departees. There were a few departures in July. Then the pace picked up. The vast majority of the town's Arab community left in September and October.

Thirty-eight Arabs left for Gaza in the first convoy, on 14 June, and seven more left that day for Jordan. Another 36 left for Gaza on 18 June; 115 went on 23 July; 165 on 8 August; 146 on 23

---

[14] LA IV–219–163, Mul to Burstein, 25 Oct. 1950.

[15] Ben, 'Halchu Le 'Aza'.

[16] LA IV–219–163: 'Minutes of the Meeting of the Co-operative Committee in Majdal in the Office of the Economic Section on 21 August 1950'; and Y. Palmon to Y. Varbin, 6 Oct. 1950. Palmon's role in the affair is hinted at in the contemporary Histadrut documents. In Ben, 'Halchu Le 'Aza', the author quotes Palmon as telling him: 'I persuaded them [i.e. the Majdal Arabs] to leave . . . I and others told them there would be a war . . . So they got up and left . . . I brought the matter before the Cabinet for approval, and [the Cabinet] decided in favour [of transfer].'

August; 192 on 30 August. During August, another 79 Majdalites left for Jordan. That month, Ben-Gurion recorded in his diary: 'The Arabs are fleeing Migdal-Gad. 1,500 are left. They are going to Gaza and Hebron. The Egyptians are receiving them. They are being allowed to sell their possessions and to exchange money.'[17] On 4 September, 145 left for Gaza; on 11 September, 119; on 19 September, 115; on 26 September, 194; on 2 October, 201; on 9 October, 374; and on 12 October, 229. Only some 20 Arab families were left in Majdal; 17 of them belonged to the Histadrut co-operative. They were 'depressed, hungry and completely shattered'. Most of them soon moved to Lydda, the rest to Gaza.[18]

A web of interlocking internal-Arab and external, mostly Israeli-organized, factors underlay the emigration to Gaza. Israeli spokesmen, especially in public, at the time stressed the internal-Arab factors. In internal correspondence in the governmental bureaucracies, a more balanced note was normally struck, though the internal factors usually received pride of place. But newly available documentation, especially from the months September–October 1950, gives far greater prominence to the external, Israeli-inspired factors, including systematic intimidation, as the primary cause of the Arabs' departure.

But first let us review the internal-Arab factors. Clearly, as in 1948, there was a psychological domino effect at work in Majdal in 1950. Israeli observers in the autumn were to assert that the initial transfer in June–July to Ramle, inside Israel, of the 200 Majdal Arabs, originally from Qatra, had had a catalytic effect, 'triggering among the remaining inhabitants of the city a growing tendency to leave',[19] much as, in 1948, the flight of the inhabitants of one urban neighbourhood or village triggered the flight of the inhabitants of nearby neighbourhoods or villages. Certainly, the registration for departure to Gaza by one family affected and ate away at the staying power of their neighbours, relatives, and

---

[17] ISA, FM 2436/5bet., 'About the Eviction . . .'; and entry for 24 Aug. 1950, David Ben-Gurion diaries, in DBG Archive (Sde Boker).
[18] ISA, FM 2436/5bet., 'About the Eviction . . .'; and LA IV–219–163, Mul to Burstein, 25 Oct. 1950.
[19] ISA, FM 2436/5bet., 'About the Eviction . . .'. This point was also made in ISA, FM 2436/5bet. by Major Yehoshafat Harkabi in his notes, appended to Harkabi to Ziama Divon, 24 Sept. 1950.

friends. Few wanted to be 'left behind' or 'left alone' to face the Israelis and life under Israeli rule.

Moreover, most of Majdal's Arabs during the period November 1948 to June 1950 had felt cut off from their family members and friends who had fled to Gaza during the 1948 war. In a wider sense, living in Israeli-ruled Majdal they had felt cut off from the Arab world. Two years as an abject, isolated, ghettoized minority community had induced in Majdal's Arabs a collective depression and sense of purposelessness. Dayan, in October 1950, put it this way:

> Much time has passed and the chances of a quick [Israel–Arab peace] settlement have weakened. Most of the [Majdal] families have members in Gaza and even in Egypt . . . No less than the separation of the families, there pressed upon the Arabs of Majdal their lowly and debased social condition. From free men and masters among their people they have turned into a miserable community living in a lifeless town. With all the difficulty of life in the Gaza Strip, the social and national feeling of the Arabs living there is better than that of the Arabs in Majdal.[20]

The condition of the families dismembered by the war and exodus of 1948 was exacerbated by the rigid guidelines Israel applied in its, at the time, much-vaunted 'Family Reunion Programme'. The scheme, a sop designed to parry Western demands for Palestinian refugee repatriation, provided for the orderly return to Israeli territory on humanitarian grounds of exiled relatives. The bulk of Majdal's inhabitants had relatives in Gaza. But, according to one Israeli Foreign Ministry official, 'Israel interpreted the concept of "family", in this context, in the narrow European sense [i.e. parents, wife, and children] and not according to the wide, Arab-oriental definition which included in the family brothers, sisters . . . uncles, etc.'[21] So Majdal's Arabs could not expect to be reunited with most of their family members in Majdal—leaving only the option of exodus and reunification in Gaza.

The Majdal Arabs suffered from unemployment—perhaps in part engineered by the Israeli authorities in order to persuade

---

[20] ISA, FM 2436/5bet., Dayan to Chief of General Staff (Yadin), ? (probably early) Oct. 1950.
[21] ISA, FM 2436/5bet., 'About the Eviction . . .'.

them to leave[22]—and from relative poverty. Like all Israelis at the time, they endured food rationing. But, unlike the Jewish population, the Majdal Arabs to a great degree subsisted on handouts from the authorities.

To turn to the external factors, not all were Israeli-organized or Israeli-inspired. For example, in contrast with the prevailing unemployment in Majdal, there was, reportedly, a 'flowering of the weaving industry' in the Gaza Strip, under Quaker tutelage. Many Majdalites were weavers and, in moving to Gaza, expected to find ready employment there. The Israeli authorities during the summer and autumn of 1950 often spoke of the Gaza weaving boom and pointedly announced that those moving to Gaza would be allowed to take their looms with them.[23]

During the spring and summer of 1950, the Arabs of Majdal lived in fear of the eruption of a 'Second Round' of Israeli–Arab hostilities. Egyptian propaganda and deliberate Israeli rumour-mongering—by Chechik and Varbin through their Arab agents in Majdal—combined to promote this fear. As an Israeli Foreign Ministry official put it in September 1950: 'we helped [foment] the panic and the general [depressed] feelings by [use of] black propaganda [*ta'amulat lahash*]'.[24] The Arabs feared that, living close to the Israeli–Egyptian frontier, they might be caught in the crossfire in an eventual war. Worse still, perhaps, they feared that their possibly victorious Arab brothers, overrunning Majdal, might consider them 'traitors' who had co-operated with the Israeli authorities. Some Israeli sources even speak of the Majdal Arabs' fears, against the backdrop of the outbreak, in June, of the Korean War, of being harmed in a Middle Eastern offshoot of a third world war.[25]

As to the Israeli-organized measures, Dayan at the time informed his superior, IDF Chief of General Staff Yigael Yadin,

---

[22] This is implied in Ben, 'Halchu Le 'Aza'.

[23] ISA, FM 2436/5bet.: 'About the Eviction . . .'; and Dayan to Chief of General Staff (Yadin), ? (probably early) Oct. 1950.

[24] ISA, FM 2474/13aleph., US Department, Israel Foreign Ministry, to Israel Embassy, Washington, etc., 17 Sept. 1950; and ISA, FM 2436/5bet., 'About the Eviction . . .', for Egyptian 'Second Round' propaganda.

[25] ISA, FM 2436/5bet.: 'About the Eviction . . .'; Harkabi to Divon, 24 Sept. 1950; and S. Sverdlov, 'Here are the Numbers of Arabs who Moved from Migdal-Gad to Gaza and Transjordan', a one-page memorandum, 24 Sept. 1950.

that he 'had heard . . . no complaints from the [Majdal] Arabs about the Israeli authorities and their day-to-day treatment. Indeed, I found that they had great personal faith in the military governor and his staff . . .'.[26] And an Israeli Foreign Ministry official asserted: 'It is not right [to say that] the Arabs of Majdal were expelled . . .'. True, Israel had used black propaganda to encourage departure. 'But no other measures [to induce flight] were taken. No Arabs were ejected from Majdal by force . . .'.[27] But these contemporary qualified denials of deliberate Israeli flight-inducing measures are misleading and disingenuous.

Through the spring, summer, and autumn of 1950, Israeli officials in Majdal repeatedly 'informed' the local Arabs that they would have to leave.[28] And a cluster of direct methods of intimidation were also sporadically, and with increasing frequency over September–October, brought to bear. Already in early August, when representatives of Majdal's military government were busy reassuring Histadrut representatives that no one was being forced to leave, the frightened locals had hinted at 'pressure' being employed against them (though they were cautious about going into specifics). The pressure was directed particularly against the members or potential members of the Histadrut co-operatives. By the end of September, only thirty-four Arab families were still signed on. According to the Arabs, after each Histadrut delegation visit to the Arab ghetto, Chechik would call in the Arab heads of families and tell them that they 'should place no hope in the Executive Committee [of the Histadrut] that it would save them' and that 'the army . . . would suddenly . . . throw them out and deposit them somewhere in the Galilee without a roof over their heads and without food'. In other words, it were best that they leave for Gaza in an orderly fashion.

Mul wrote in late October:

Since mid-September, the pressure of the [military] government on the Arabs has been increasing. Most of the Arabs have been called . . . personally to the representative of the government one or more times and

[26] ISA, FM 2436/5bet., Dayan to Chief of General Staff (Yadin), ? (probably early) Oct. 1950.
[27] ISA, FM 2474/13aleph., US Department, Israel Foreign Ministry, to Israel Embassy, Washington, etc., 17 Sept. 1950.
[28] See n. 6, above.

he asked them in a vague and suspicious way: Where are they going? To Gaza or Hebron . . .[29]

But the intimidation and 'nudging' to leave went beyond pointed or vague verbal threats. From the beginning of September the military government stopped supplying the Arabs with food rations. 'The lack of flour weighed heavily on the [remaining] Arabs . . .', wrote Mul. From the beginning of October, the soldiers who guarded the Arab ghetto regularly 'knocked their rifle butts against the doors of Arab houses and shouted: "Get out of here, infiltrators! Yallah, go to Gaza!" They also used to fire at night into the air.'[30]

One day Chechik appeared in the house of the agricultural co-operative's secretary, Muhi ad Din Daoud, and told his wife 'that her husband refuses to leave for Gaza and threatened her that if her husband would not agree to leave town then the army would come and throw him across the border'. On 8 October representatives of the military government visited the homes of the remaining Arabs and confiscated whatever food they found.

The following day Hassan Hijazi, the secretary of the weavers' co-operative, was summoned to the military government headquarters and told to stop dealing with the co-operative's affairs and to stop telling the members that they would be allowed to stay in the country. 'No Arab will remain,' he was told, though he himself would be allowed to move to Lydda.

The intimidation of Majdal's Arabs was coupled with a deception of visiting Israeli officials and press, much of which, throughout, wrote (and perhaps believed) that the transfer was completely voluntary.[31] 'Usually, after each visit by Histadrut representatives in Migdal [i.e. Majdal], Uri Chechik used to go about the town and tell all the Arabs that no visitor would save them. Migdal would be cleared of all Arabs . . .'. On 8 October, the local Arab schoolmaster was summoned by Varbin and

[29] LA IV–219–163, Mul to Burstein, 25 Oct. 1950.

[30] Ibid. See also Ben, 'Halchu Le 'Aza', with Varbin recalling his use of these measures. Such tactics had been used by Southern Command troops the year before to intimidate into flight the Arabs at Faluja and Iraq al Manshiya (see Morris, *Birth of the Palestinian Refugee Problem, 1947–1949*, 243–5).

[31] See e.g. in Ben, 'Halchu Le 'Aza', a reproduction of an article entitled 'I Saw Nice Arabs' (*ra'iti 'aravim neh'madim*) by H. Ben-Adi, from *Ma'ariv*, 15 Oct. 1950, describing the last, 12 Oct. transport, to Gaza.

ordered immediately to close his school. After some brow-beating, the headmaster agreed. But the following day, a group of journalists visited the town. Varbin again called in the headmaster and ordered him to reopen the school. A day or so later, the headmaster was again ordered to close the school—this time for good.[32]

The intimidation of the Arabs by the local military authorities grew as the transfer neared its climax, in late September and early October. The army, meaning Dayan, had set itself the goal of completely clearing out the Arabs. At the same time, the more resolute Arabs and those who had decided to throw in their lot with Israel, mainly the members of the Histadrut co-operatives, clung on with increasing desperation. The hard core of weavers was reluctant to leave. The army was compelled to raise the level of intimidation. Hence the outcrop of threats and menaces in the last weeks.

The army's actions were contrary to the promises made to the Histadrut—which were stated government policy: That Arabs wishing to stay would be allowed to do so, especially the members of the co-operatives. The army's actions in September and early October, as the last transports were leaving Majdal, were countered by growing Histadrut intercession on behalf of the remaining co-operative members, which, in turn, triggered anti-Histadrut action by the military.

By the end of September dozens of families which had signed on in the spring and early summer had succumbed to IDF pressures and had left or decided to leave for Gaza. On 29 September, Mul went to Palmon and extracted from him a letter ordering the Majdal military authorities to abide by the government's policy, which was to allow Arabs who wished to stay to do so. Mul then went to Varbin, who agreed that the thirty-four families still registered for the co-operatives would be allowed to stay and that the army would only carry out government policy.[33]

On 4 October Palmon told another Histadrut official, Ya'akov Cohen that it had been 'decided not to use any pressure or

---

[32] LA IV–219–163, Mul to Burstein, 25 Oct. 1950. Mul gives a day-by-day, blow-by-blow account of the intimidation.
[33] Ibid.

coercion against those Arabs who would wish to stay in Migdal.' But Cohen then travelled down to Migdal where he was informed by Chechik that 'Migdal would be emptied of all its Arabs in eight to ten days. This was the order given to him and he would carry it out in full'. He proposed that the Histadrut forget the co-operative enterprise as he was 'certain that [the Arabs] would all move to Gaza'.

Cohen responded that the Histadrut could not agree to this breach of a government assurance. He presented Chechik with a list of fifty families and demanded that no pressure be put on them to leave. Chechik, seemingly beating a tactical retreat, agreed. But he added that his 'agreement might be of short duration as it is possible that he would get a [new] order running contrary to the spirit of this agreement and he would have to carry it out'.[34]

On 6 October Cohen and Mul again saw Palmon and persuaded him to issue a second letter to Varbin setting out governmental policy toward the co-operatives and its members (and towards Majdal's other remaning Arabs).

Palmon wrote: 'I again stress that, regarding the residents of Majdal who are members of [the Histadrut co-operatives] and also non-members, who do not wish to leave Israel and move to Gaza, they must not be forced to do so. I have made this promise again to Comrade Mul . . . I ask again that you act accordingly.' Mul left for Majdal and presented the letter to Varbin.[35]

But two days later, on 8 October, the Histadrut was again informed by its Arab wards in Majdal that the military governor was pressuring all and sundry to leave, saying that 'nothing could help them . . . All without exception would have to go.' A Histadrut representative was despatched to Majdal the following day. He reported back that the complaint was accurate: The military were pressing everyone to leave and several families had already signed the 'voluntary' transfer form. One co-operative member, Abu Halawe, had been arrested and had subsequently

---

[34] LA IV–219–163, untitled, undated, unsigned seven-page memorandum on the last days of Arab Majdal, clearly from mid-Oct. and in Mul's handwriting.

[35] Ibid.; and LA IV–219–163, Palmon to Varbin (in Mul's handwriting), 6 Oct. 1950.

signed the form, reported the Histadrut representative.[36] That night, soldiers broke into Hijazi's house.[37]

The Histadrut made one last effort to save the members of the co-operatives. On 10 October Mul, Cohen, and a third Histadrut official travelled down to Majdal. The IDF sentries posted at the entrance to the Arab ghetto refused them entry. After a long run-around, involving an intercession by Palmon with Varbin, Mul and Cohen were eventually allowed to enter the ghetto. The Histadrut officials assembled the families who had initially signed on and informed them that those who wished would be allowed to remain. Sixteen family heads signed up again. Then 'an armed soldier appeared [at the door] and demanded that Comrade Mul accompany him . . . When they left the house, General Moshe Dayan appeared and approached Comrade Mul and demanded that he leave the Arab area.' Mul complied, following Dayan out. Dayan then turned to Mul and said that the Histadrut 'was pulling in a direction contrary to his own operations; he, the general, was trying to liquidate the Arab area in Migdal . . . Comrade Mul said that he was acting with government agreement and in accordance with [Histadrut] Executive Committee instructions.' Dayan said he would instruct the military not to allow the Histadrut representatives to enter the Arab area. Mul asked 'about the fate of the thousands of pounds invested by the Histadrut in the co-operatives'. Dayan ignored the remark.[38]

According to Dayan's recollections, Histadrut Secretary-General Lavon at this point went directly to Ben-Gurion. Perhaps in consequence, the Deputy Chief of General Staff, Makleff, on 11 October, ordered Dayan to suspend the transfer operation. Two days later, according to Dayan's autobiography, Dayan had it out with 'Lavon and his people' in Ben-Gurion's presence at the Prime Minister's Office in Jerusalem. Dayan (according to his memoirs) 'explained that those wishing to remain in Israel—including the

[36] LA IV–219–163, untitled, undated, unsigned seven-page memorandum on the last days of Arab Majdal, clearly from mid-Oct. and in Mul's handwriting.

[37] LA IV–219–163, note entitled 'For the secretary general's logbook', undated, unsigned, in Mul's handwriting, setting down the gist of events in the second week of Oct.

[38] LA IV–219–163, untitled, undated, unsigned seven-page memorandum on the last days of Arab Majdal, clearly from mid-Oct. and in Mul's handwriting, and Mul to Burstein, 25 Oct. 1950.

weavers—could do so' and would be moved to Ramle, Nazareth, or Haifa. 'Ben-Gurion, despite Lavon's anger . . . agreed.' The agreement meant approval of an Arab-free Majdal. Dayan had won.[39]

But to return to the complex of external, Israeli-organized factors, which, at least in the run-up to the start of the transfer and during its first months, fell short of physical intimidation. Dayan described these pressures and inducements thus:

There was no easing by Israel of restrictions . . . [on the Majdal Arabs' freedom of] movement, on their employment in the areas far away from the town and in the restoration of their property, [and this] led the Arabs to the conclusion that in the existing circumstances (so long as there was no peace) there was no chance of the lifting of the restrictions and of a change in their treatment by the Israeli authorities.[40]

Most of the grinding external pressures (and the inducements) that over the months wore down the Majdal Arabs' will to stay and tempted them to move to Gaza were economic. We have already noted the cut-off of rations, especially of flour, from September. At the beginning of September, Major V. H. Loriaux, a UN truce-observer and sometime acting chairman of the Israel–Egypt

[39] Dayan, *Avnei Derekh*, 96. Dayan's recollection of the event makes little sense. By 11 Oct., the transfer to Gaza was almost over; by 13 Oct., when the meeting with Lavon in Ben-Gurion's office allegedly took place, it had been completed (the last transport had left on 12 Oct.). Hence, if there was an argument, it was over thoroughly spilt milk. It is probable that Lavon interceded on 11 Oct., following the Mul–Dayan run-in in Majdal the previous day, and that Ben-Gurion agreed to the remaining members of the Histadrut-sponsored co-operative being moved to a site inside Israel rather than to Gaza. It is possible that the three-sided meeting—Dayan–Lavon–Ben-Gurion—occurred that same day. But Dayan's memoirs would still be a distortion as they suggest that on 11 Oct. the transfer had not yet taken place and that the finishing touches were being put to the plan whereas in fact the transfer was already all but over. Dayan also misrepresents his own part in the affair. Interestingly, in the English-language version of *Avnei Derekh*, entitled *Story of My Life*, 160–1, Dayan offered a somewhat different description of the affair, omitting all dates. Thus, Lavon's intercession is said to have occurred before the transfer began. The implication then would seem to be that it occurred as early as June—putting a completely different complexion on things. If Dayan's implied June dating is correct, then Ben-Gurion, from the start, supported the removal from Majdal of all the town's Arabs, including the Histadrut co-operative's members—which was contrary to the government's policy throughout, as repeatedly stated by Palmon.
[40] ISA, FM 2436/5bet., General Dayan to Chief of General Staff (Yadin), ? (probably early) Oct. 1950.

MAC, interviewed some of the evacuees shortly after they reached the Gaza Strip. He was told that the Majdal Arabs, soon after being warned that they would shortly have to leave their town, were charged '1,650 Israeli pound[s] for drinkable water (it was free of charge previously)'. Loriaux was also told of 'delays'—before September—in the distribution of rations. The Arabs, Loriaux was told, had been penned in in their ghetto, behind barbed wire and military checkpoints, and were rarely allowed out. They had little or no contact with the neighbouring, growing Jewish population.[41]

A month later, after further interviews with Majdal evacuees in the Gaza Strip, Loriaux reported that Majdal orange-grove-owners had not been allowed by the Israelis to sell their produce (perhaps partly in order to bar competition with Jewish orange-producers) and had received no compensation. 'But they were . . . [allowed] to cultivate vegetables on an allotment in the groves and eventually [to] sell the surplus.'[42]

The most persuasive, positive inducement to departure, apparently, was Israel's willingness to exchange the Majdal Arabs' Israeli pounds on a one-to-one basis with British Mandate Palestine pounds, which were still in use in the Gaza Strip. The

[41] ISA, FM 2436/5bet., V. H. Loriaux to Chief of Staff, UNTSO, 4 Sept. 1950.
[42] ISA, FM 2436/5bet., V. H. Loriaux to Colonel Bossavy, Chairman of the Israel–Egypt MAC, 3 Oct. 1950. Loriaux at some point complained that there had been cases of Arabs who had refused to move to Gaza being jailed. Israel denied this. In a formal note to Bossavy, an Israeli representative on the MAC, Captain Johanan Mannheim, wrote: 'Regarding the 7 Arabs who according to the statement were put in prison for refusing to sign a declaration stating their willingness to go to Gaza, I have been informed that in fact 7 Arabs were arrested in connection with certain violations of security laws. Their arrest had no connection with the transfer of Arabs to Gaza. This is proven by the fact that although these Arabs have long since been released, they have not been transferred to Gaza.' See ISA, FM 2436/5bet., Mannheim to Bossavy, 16 Oct. 1950.
On the basis of Loriaux's reports, UNTSO chairman General William Riley wrote that the reasons underlying the Majdal Arabs' agreement to move were: 'A. Since occupation of Majdal by Israel, Arabs are kept in special quarters. B. Shopkeepers not allowed to renew stock. C. Proprietors not allowed to enter their houses, lands or groves. D. Arab rations are inferior to Israeli rations. E. Rumours are spread amongst Arabs that Majdal will become military [i.e. war] zone. F. Many Arabs wished to stay, but found living conditions impossible through continuous vexations' (see UN Archives (New York), DAG–1/2.2.5.2.0–1, Riley to Andrew Cordier, Executive Assistant to UN Secretary-General, 13 Sept. 1950). Riley's cable was written before the climactic stage of the intimidation and transfer took place.

rate at the time in Egyptian-controlled Gaza was I£3.5 or I£4 for each Mandatory pound. The departing Majdal Arabs, who had amassed Israeli pounds during the previous two years, by 22 October had changed I£160,000–I£170,000 into Mandatory pounds at this highly favourable exchange rate, 'which turned them', according to Israeli officials, 'into rich men in the Gaza Strip and enabled them to purchase property and to deal in commerce'. Each Arab family head was allowed to take out of Israel 120 Mandatory pounds. Moreover, these new refugees knew that as a matter of course they would receive help from the absorbing UN agencies upon reaching the Strip, without regard for their relatively favourable financial situation.[43]

It seems that the Israeli authorities also helped the Arabs sell those possessions that they had decided not to carry with them into exile. 'The possibility of selling the moveable possessions at very high prices facilitated the Arabs' departure,' was how Dayan put it at the time. He estimated that each family sold some I£50–I£80 worth of goods,

and sometimes more. The Yemenite [Jewish] inhabitants of Majdal and other places, new immigrants, are paying fantastic prices—I£10 for a used blanket, I£16 for a shabby, small cupboard, I£4 for a small chicken, etc. The reason for this is the difficulty in obtaining these goods in the marketplace and not knowing the value of money . . . With the money the Arabs received for their goods in Majdal, they will be able to buy other [goods] in Gaza and also live for a long time on the difference . . .[44]

Dayan in October 1950, in his letter to Yadin, summed up the internal-Arab and external Israeli-organized impulses behind the transfer to Gaza thus:

I think that the evacuation of Majdal's Arabs is a natural phenomenon of a pointless situation on the one hand and convenient conditions . . . for emigration on the other. The mass impetus to go which took hold of the whole community also contributed to this. It is worth noting that the emigrants are not depressed and that their relations with the authorities and the many preparations for the transfer are characterized by a light-

[43] ISA, FM 2436/5bet., 'About the Eviction . . .'; and ISA, FM 2474/13aleph., US Department, Israel Foreign Ministry, to Israel Embassy, Washington DC, 17 Sept. 1950.
[44] ISA, FM 2436/5bet., Dayan to Chief of General Staff (Yadin), ? (probably early) Oct. 1950.

hearted spirit and, almost, conviviality. The Arabs understand that in the absence of a permanent peace there is no point to the present situation and they do not blame the local authorities in Majdal.[45]

Dayan's explanation of what had happened, stressing the internal-Arab factors and belittling the external Israeli-facilitated factors in the exodus, was tailored to suit the government's official version of events—that the transfer was completely voluntary and that no coercion had been employed. But as the quoted Foreign Ministry and Histadrut documentation shows, this explanation is highly inadequate, especially in relation to September–October 1950.

The ongoing transfer during the summer of 1950 prompted a measure of debate in Israeli political circles and some condemnations, especially on the left. Leaders of the Israel Communist Party repeatedly visited Majdal and tried to persuade the Arabs to stay put. They particularly inveighed against a transfer to other sites inside Israel, where, said the Communists, the Majdalites would be prey to the whims of local Israeli officials. The Communist intervention proved ineffective.[46]

The transfer was also regarded sceptically in Mapam, the left-wing (and largest) opposition party. The initial ambiguity of the summer—was the emigration really voluntary?[47]—by late September turned to criticism of the government[48] and, by mid-October, to open vilification of the 'criminal' expulsion from Majdal.[49] But apart from some strong language in the pages of *'Al HaMishmar*, Mapam's daily newspaper, the party took no action.

Only the Histadrut, as we have seen, actively lobbied and interceded with the military to leave in Majdal at least those Arab families that had volunteered for its co-operative ventures.

[45] ISA, FM 2436/5bet., Dayan to Chief of General Staff Yadin, Oct. 1950.

[46] ISA, FM 2436/5bet., 'About the Eviction . . .', 22 Oct. 1950; and entry for 24 Aug. 1950, Ben-Gurion diaries, DBG Archive. The Communist intercession may have been counter-productive.

[47] See e.g. *Al Hamishmar*, 'Encouragement' (*'idud*) by Y. Vashitz, 23 Aug. 1950.

[48] See e.g. *Al Hamishmar*, 'In the Shadow of Doubt' (*beTzel haShema*) by Shabtai Kaplan, 25 Sept. 1950.

[49] See e.g. *Al Hamishmar*, 'From Encouragement to Command' (*me'Idud leTzav*) by Y. Vashitz, 10 Oct. 1950 and (editorial) 'A Crime' (*ma'aseh pesha*), 13 Oct. 1950.

A curious feature of the transfer was the relative docility with which the Egyptians initially reacted to it. The Egyptians, at least before September, appear to have believed that the transferees had moved to Gaza of their own volition. Certainly the Egyptians that summer behaved as though they were reluctant to heat up their relations with Israel. According to Dayan's memoirs, the Egyptian MAC representative, Colonel Mahmud Riad, 'readily agreed' to co-operate when Dayan first broached the idea of the transfer.[50]

But fairly soon after the first large convoys reached the Strip, the evacuees began to complain that they had 'been compelled to leave . . . Some declared that they have been expulsed [*sic*] from their house on behalf of Israeli families.'[51]

These complaints may have prompted the Egyptians' first hesitant raising of the matter at the meeting on 15 August of the Egypt–Israel MAC, a good two months after the transfer had begun. The Egyptians complained that the Israelis were dumping the refugees on their border without prior notification or co-ordination. The Egyptian representative said: 'We complain against [moving] all these people to our side. You are forcing us to accept them. We cannot refuse to take them, because we are human. All what [*sic*] we want is a previous notice from you when you send them, so that we can be ready to meet them.'[52]

Thenceforth, Israel gave the Egyptians advance notice of each convoy, and Egyptian officials and trucks were ready to meet the transferees at the frontier crossing at Kilometre 95. One Israeli official later wrote that 'the fact that the Egyptian army came to receive them at the border served for those still remaining [in Majdal] as further confirmation that the decision of the departees was justified.'[53]

But the matter was not to end there. Fuelled by reports from his observers (such as Loriaux), the UNTSO Chief of Staff, Lieutenant-General W. B. Riley, United States Marine Corps, on 21 September issued an unusual public condemnation of the

---

[50] Dayan, *Story of My Life*, 160–1, and *Avnei Derekh*, 95–6.

[51] ISA, FM 2436/5bet., V. H. Loriaux to Chief of Staff, UNTSO, 4 Sept. 1950.

[52] ISA, FM 2436/5bet., Harkabi to Divon, 24 Sept. 1950; and ISA, FM 2592/18, M. S. Comay (Tel Aviv) to E. Elath (London), 6 Nov. 1950.

[53] ISA, FM 2436/5bet., 'About the Eviction . . .'.

ongoing 'expulsion'. He wrote that his officers' investigation had revealed 'that the Arabs alleged they had no desire to go to Gaza, but were required [by Israel] to sign a statement agreeing to go to Gaza, never to return to Israel and abandoning all property rights'. Riley was moved to take this public stand both by the continuing transfer from Majdal and by the simultaneous Israeli expulsion, in early September, from the Negev into Sinai of hundreds (or 4,000, according to UN observers) of members of the Azazme beduin tribe.[54]

Israel reacted by denying that the Majdal Arabs had been or were being expelled: 'No pressure has been brought on any Arab' to leave Majdal, Israel declared. (As to the Azazme, Israel argued that they were troublesome 'infiltrees', not legal residents of the country, and therefore Israel had every right to deport them.)[55]

Riley's statement and Egyptian unease soon prompted Cairo to formally complain about the 'expulsion' from Majdal (and of the Azazme—and linking the two made the Israeli-argued voluntarism of the Majdal transfer that much more dubious) at the UN Security Council and in the Israel–Egypt MAC. On 17 November 1950 the Security Council condemned Israel on both counts and on 30 May 1951 the MAC called on Israel to repatriate the 1950 Majdal transferees. Israel, of course, rejected the decision and, indeed, denied the Arab–UN charges. As Captain Johanan Mannheim, Israel's representative on the MAC, put it:

The transfer of Arabs from Majdal was initiated by the Arabs themselves who were desirous of joining their families in Gaza . . . There can be no . . . justification of the word 'expelled' used in the Egyptian complaints. Not a single Arab has been forced to go to Gaza . . . There is no justification for the complaints regarding distribution of rations. The Arabs received the same rations as the Jewish inhabitants. [Israel instituted an austere, universal regime of rationing following the 1948 war.] Any delays in distribution were equal to [*sic*] both. The complaint that the Jewish population were receiving 7 eggs per week and the Arabs 2, is completely false. The general ration is 2 eggs per week. The complaint regarding payment for water is also false. Any payments were made for arrears of taxes, and were collected by the Arab local council.[56]

[54] ISA, FM 2402/12, 'General Riley's Statement on the Expulsion of Beduin', 22 Sept. 1950, Israel Foreign Ministry Memorandum.   [55] Ibid.
[56] ISA, FM 2436/5bet., Captain Johanan Mannheim to Colonel Bossavy, 16 Oct. 1950.

Many of the Majdal refugees apparently soon after reaching Gaza changed their minds and wanted back. Conditions in the Strip's refugee camps, despite the Quakers' and UN's efforts, were dismal. Perhaps, too, fellow Palestinians and Egyptian officials incited them. But the road back was now firmly barred. Israel had attained an Arab-free Migdal and was in no mood to accede to a return to the status quo ante.

Dayan stressed that there was no possibility of agreeing to the return of Arabs, even the smallest number, to the city. The matter is linked to the question of a return of property, and is intimately linked to the infiltration situation in that area [which involved a great deal of theft, smuggling, acts of robbery, and the occasional murder of Jews by Arab marauders from the Gaza Strip].

Dayan thought that if the UN bodies persisted in calling for the return of the Majdal refugees, 'Israel would have to reject all the candidates for return during the joint [Israeli–UN] investigation [of each candidate] which we would have to demand'. (The MAC had ruled in favour of the return to Majdal of those Arabs the committee would deem 'had the right to return'. The legal adviser of the Israel Foreign Ministry, Shabtai Rosenne, suggested that this proviso 'would possibly provide a basis for instituting a preliminary investigation and [enabling] the rejection of people [that is, candidates for return] during the investigation'.)[57]

On 14 October 1950, two days after the last transport departed for Gaza, Dayan issued an official letter of thanks to Varbin. He commended Varbin's and Chechik's 'devotion' to duty and expressed the certainty that 'Migdal-Gad would become a large Jewish city; the Jews who will live in it will undoubtedly be unaware of your part in the city's development . . .'. A few weeks later, in the Kassit coffee shop in Migdal-Ashkelon, Dayan, Varbin, Chechik, and the other officers and officials involved in the transfer celebrated the successful operation and the end of military government in the town.[58]

One last item of business remained—the allocation of the empty Arab houses. The Migdal-Gad (or Migdal-Ashkelon) municipal

[57] ISA, FM 2439/8, S. Rosenne to Foreign Ministry Director General, 20 May 1951; and ISA, FM 2438/6, Lt.-Col. Michael Hanegbi to IDF Staff Officer in charge of MACs, ? Feb. 1952.
[58] Ben, 'Halchu Le 'Aza'.

council, set up in July 1950, soon focused on the problem. How was Ashkelon to insure that the abandoned houses would not be taken over by enterprising Jewish squatters? There was an acute housing shortage in the town, with many new Jewish immigrant-settlers residing in makeshift tent-camps. Might these hard-pressed settlers try to move into the abandoned Arab houses in anarchic 'invasions and counter-invasions' (as had happened in 1948 with the abandoned Arab dwellings in some neighbourhoods of Jaffa and Haifa)?

'There is a need', said municipal council chairman Ephraim Tsur, 'to [falsely] announce that there are no flats [available] in the town. The houses that have become available [it should be said] are almost uninhabitable, all is ruin and desolation.' Tsur and the other council members sought to distribute the abandoned houses in an organized, logical fashion—with priority going to public servants such as doctors and teachers. The councillors proposed that the empty flats be 'guarded' to keep out potential 'invaders' until the desired allocation could be affected.[59]

The empty dwellings, those deemed appropriate for Jewish habitation, were gradually distributed to the selected functionaries. Interestingly, during its meetings in July, August, September, and early October 1950 the council never once debated or discussed the ongoing Arab exodus from the town. Perhaps the matter came up in informal talks, but there is no mention of this in the carefully written and preserved council minutes. Perhaps there was a feeling of uneasiness, a sense of moral dubiousness about the whole enterprise. Only once does one catch a whiff of the subject in the official minutes, in a brief reference on 18 October, six days after the completion of the transfer. On 13 October *Al Hamishmar* had published an editorial, entitled 'A Crime' (*ma'aseh pesha*), condemning the transfer. That same day, the municipal council had received a letter from the secretariat of a nearby kibbutz, Zikim, which was affiliated to Mapam, asking that Migdal-Ashkelon allot the kibbutz some of the abandoned dwellings. The kibbutz, suffering from a housing shortage, wanted tham as homes for their retired old-timers.

Tsur, the town council chairman, referred in the same breath to

[59] Ashkelon Municipal Archive (AMA), protocol of the municipal council meeting of 4 Sept. 1950.

the Zikim request and the *Al Hamishmar* editorial: 'They [that is, Zikim] were not averse to demanding part of the fruits of the crime that we committed, and they explained, using Zionist argumentation, why they deserved some flats specifically in Migdal-Gad. It is, of course, clear to us that Migdal-Gad cannot solve the problem of the absorption of parents of neighbouring kibbutzim.'[60]

CONCLUSION

Majdal officially became Ashkelon in 1956, after passing through some nominal stations—Migdal-Gad and Migdal-Ashkelon. The three-sided (Israel, Egypt, and UN) debate over whether the Arab departure had been 'voluntary' or 'coerced' by then was something of an irrelevance. The UN calls for a return were never heeded and the Majdal transferees were fated to linger on, for decades, indefinitely, in Gaza's grim, grimy refugee camps.

What is clear is that after a year and a half of bureaucratic foot-dragging, the IDF in 1950 wanted this last concentration of Arabs in the southern coastal plain to leave, and engineered their departure. The Majdal Arabs' own uneasiness at life as a ghettoized minority, under military rule, hemmed in by barbed wire and sentries and a pass system, dependent on Israeli handouts, largely unemployed and destitute, cut off from their relatives in Gaza and from the Arab world in general, served as preparatory background. In the foreground, which became increasingly stark and insistent as the summer of 1950 wore on, were the well-tried measures of persuasion and pressure, including minatory rumour-mongering and outright threats of eviction, exercised by the Israeli military authorities. When these proved insufficient with the remaining hard-core of Histadrut-protected inhabitants, the army availed itself, in September and early October, of cruder methods—shooting in the night, threatening behaviour by the soldiery, unpleasant early-hour-of-the-morning

---

[60] AMA, Protocol of the municipal council meeting of 18 Oct. 1950. The *Al Hamishmar* editorial called for 'the punishment of those responsible for the crime . . . Are we like Sodom?'

visitations, a cut-off of rations, frequent summons, and occasional arrests. The use of these methods was hidden from the Israeli public and, probably, lacked Cabinet authorization.

To sweeten the pill, the military government offered some fulsome carrots in the form of financial incentives (a favourable Israel pound for Mandatory pound exchange rate, help in the sale of possessions, and assurances of employment and UN assistance in the Gaza Strip).

Until Israel's Defence Ministry and Cabinet records are opened, the exact decision-making processes behind the Majdal transfer will remain unclear. Certainly IDF Southern Command—Dayan and Varbin—were the scheme's architects and executors. It is likely that the police and General Security Service seconded the idea. Palmon, the Prime Minister's aide, appears to have played a deceitful, facilitatory role. But whether the Cabinet ever formally approved the transfer to Gaza or merely a transfer of Majdal's inhabitants to other Arab centres inside Israel is uncertain.

What is certain is that Dayan wanted to transfer the Majdal Arabs to Gaza and received Ben-Gurion's (and Treasury)— backing. There was no serious, or perhaps any, opposition to the transfer by Mapai's coalition partners inside the Cabinet, and the external opposition, by elements in Mapam and the Histadrut, proved ineffectual. Most if not all the ministers probably perceived the transfer as an important Israeli interest, in terms of demography (less Arabs), day-to-day security (less infiltration back and forth across the Gaza border), strategy (no Arab population concentration to serve as a way station for invading Egyptians), and immigration absorption and town-planning (more space for Jewish settlers and one less problem in building or rebuilding Ashkelon).

Less clear and understandable is the initial Egyptian response to the transfer. A fuller understanding of Egypt's role must await the opening of the Egyptian state papers for the period. For now, one may conjecture that Cairo, at least initially, in June–July 1950, really believed that the emigration was completely voluntary. It was only in August that they appear to have changed their minds, and began speaking of an 'expulsion'. Similarly, UNTSO only in late September—with Riley's public statement of 21 September— raised a hue and cry. But by then it was too late. The condemnations did nothing to halt the final stages of the transfer. The transports, still, curiously, co-ordinated with the Egyptians, kept arriving at the Kilometre 95 ('Erez') checkpoint on the Gaza border until Majdal-Ashkelon became a completely Jewish town.

SELECT BIBLIOGRAPHY

Primary sources

American Friends Service Committee Archive (AFSC), Philadelphia.

David Ben-Gurion Archives (DBG Archives), Sdeh Boqer, Israel.

Central Zionist Archives (CZA), Jerusalem, Israel. Papers of the Political Department of the Jewish Agency, protocols of the meetings of the Jewish Agency Executive and of the Jewish National Fund Directorate, Avraham Granovsky Papers, manuscript notebooks of Yosef Weitz diary, etc.

Sir Alan Cunningham Papers (CP), Middle East Centre Archives, St Antony's College, Oxford.

Hashomer Archive, Yosef Nahmani Diary and Papers, Kfar Gil'adi.

Hashomer Hatza'ir Archives (HHA), Givat Haviva, Israel. Papers of the Kibbutz Artzi, Mapam (Political Committee, Mapam Centre protocols), Aharon Cohen Papers (HHA–ACP), Meir Ya'ari Papers, etc.

Histadrut Archive, Va'ad Hapoel Building, Tel Aviv.

Archive of Ihud Hakibbutzim Vehakvutsot, Kibbutz Hulda.

Israel State Archives (ISA), Jerusalem. State papers of the Agriculture Ministry (AM), Foreign Ministry (FM), Justice Ministry (JM), Minority Affairs Ministry (MAM), Prime Minister's Office (PMO).

Jabotinsky Institute (JI), Tel Aviv. Papers of the IZL, LHI, Revisionist Movement, and Herut Party.

Jerusalem and East Mission Papers (JEM), Middle East Centre Archives, St Antony's College, Oxford.

Kibbutz Meuhad Archives (KMA), Ef'al, Israel. Papers of the Kibbutz Meuhad (protocols of meetings of the movement and Ahdut Ha'avodah institutions), Aharon Zisling Papers (KMA–AZP), Palmah Papers (KMA–PA).

Labour Archives (LA) (Histadrut), Lavon Institute, Tel Aviv.

Labour Party Archives (LPA), Beit Berl, Israel.

National Archives (NA), Washington DC, State Department Papers.

Public Record Office (PRO), London. Papers of the Cabinet Office (CAB), Colonial Office (CO), Foreign Office (FO), and War Office (WO).

United Nations Archives (UN), New York.

Yosef Weitz Papers, the Institute for Settlement Research, Rehovot.

350   *Select Bibliography*

Individual kibbutz archives—Mishmar Ha'emek, Ma'anit, etc.
Municipal archives in Israel—Haifa (HMA), Tiberias, Ashkelon.
Interviews with Yigael Yadin, Yitzkah Ben-Aharon, Yehoshua Palmon, Ya'acov Shimoni, Moshe Carmel, Eliezer Be'eri (Bauer), Binyamin Arnon, Aharon Bar-Am (Brawerman).

Published primary sources

BEGIN, MENACHEM, *Bamahteret, Ketavim* (In the Underground, Writings and Documents), 4 vols. (Tel Aviv, 1959).
BEN-GURION, DAVID, *Behilahem Yisrael* (As Israel Fought) (Tel Aviv, 1952).
—— *Medinat Yisrael Hamehudeshet* (The Resurgent State of Israel), 2 vols (Tel Aviv, 1969).
—— *Yoman Hamilhama-Tashah, 1948–1949* (DBG-YH) (The War Diary, 1948–1949), 3 vols., ed. Gershon Rivlin and Elhannan Orren (Tel Aviv, 1982).
DAYAN, MOSHE, *Avnei Derekh, Autobiographiya* (Tel Aviv, 1976).
—— *Story of My Life* (London, 1977).
Israel State Archives / Central Zionist Archives, *Te'udot Mediniot Ve'diplomatiyot, December 1947–May 1948* (Political and Diplomatic Documents, December 1947–May 1948), ed. Gedalia Yogev (Jerusalem, 1980).
Israel State Archives, *Te'udot Lemediniut Hahutz shel Medinat Yisrael, 14 May–30 September 1948* (Documents on the Foreign Policy of the State of Israel, May–September 1948), vol. i, ed. Yehoshua Freundlich (Jerusalem, 1981).
Israel State Archives, *Te'udot Lemediniut Hahutz shel Medinat Yisrael, October 1948–April 1949* (Documents on the Foreign Policy of the State of Israel, October 1948–April 1949), vol. ii, ed. Yehoshua Freundlich (Jerusalem, 1984).
Israel State Archives, *Te'udot Lemediniut Hahutz shel Medinat Yisrael, Sihot Shvitat-Haneshek im Medinot Arav, December 1948–July 1949* (Documents on the Foreign Policy of the State of Israel, Armistice Negotiations with the Arab States, December 1948–July 1949), vol. iii, ed. Yemima Rosenthal (Jerusalem, 1983).
Israel State Archives, *Te'udot Lemediniut Hahutz shel Medinat Yisrael, May–December 1949* (Documents on the Foreign Policy of the State of Israel, May–December 1949), vol. iv, ed. Yemima Rosenthal (Jerusalem, 1986).
WEITZ, YOSEF, *Yomani Ve'igrotai Labanim* (My Diary and Letters to the Children), vols. iii and iv (Tel Aviv, 1965).
—— (ed.) *Yosef Nahmani* (Tel Aviv, 1969).

Selected Secondary works

ASSAF, MICHAEL, *Toldot Hit'orerut Ha'aravim Be'eretz Yisrael U'brihatam* (The History of the Awakening of the Arabs in Palestine and Their Flight) (Tel Aviv, 1967).

'AV, NAHUM, *HaMa'avak 'al Tveriya, HaRishona LeShihrur BeMilhemet Ha'Atzma'ut* (The Struggle for Tiberias, the First [City] Liberated in the War of Independence (Tel Aviv, 1991).

AVIDAR, YOSEF, 'Tochnit Dalet (Plan D)', *Sifra Veseifa*, 2 (June 1978).

BANAI (MAZAL), YA'ACOV, *Hayalim Almonim, Sefer Mivtze'ei Lehi* (Unknown Soldiers, the Book of LHI Operations) (Tel Aviv, 1958).

Be'einei Oyev, Shelosha Pirsumim Arvi'im al Milhemet Hakomemiut (In Enemy Eyes, three Arab publications on the War of Independence), Israel Defence Forces, General Staff/History Branch (Tel Aviv, 1954). The book, translated into Hebrew by Captain S. Sabag, is composed of lengthy excerpts from Mahammed Nimr al Khatib, *Min Athar al Nakba*, Kamal Ismail al Sharif, *Al Ihwan al Muslemin fi Harb Falastin*, and Mohammed Ghussan, *Ma'arak Bab al Wad*.

BEGIN, MENACHEM, *The Revolt* (London, 1964).

BURNS, E. L. M., *Between Arab and Israeli* (London, 1962).

CARMEL, MOSHE, *Ma'arachot Tzafon* (Northern Battles) (Tel Aviv, 1949).

Carta's Atlas of Palestine from Zionism to Statehood, ed. Jehuda Wallach (Jerusalem, 1972, 1974).

Carta's Historical Atlas of Israel, The First Years 1948–1961, eds. Juhuda Wallach and Moshe Lissak (Jerusalem, 1978).

COHEN, AHARON, *Yisrael Ve'ha'olam Ha'aravi* (Israel and the Arab World) (Tel Aviv, 1964).

ESHEL, ZADOK, *Hativat Carmeli Bemilhemet Hakomemiut* (The Carmeli Brigade in the War of Independence) (Tel Aviv, 1973).

—— *Ma'arachot Hahaganah Be'Haifa* (The Haganah Battles in Haifa) (Tel Aviv, 1978).

GABBAY, RONY, *A Political Study of the Arab–Jewish Conflict: The Arab Refugee Problem (a Case study)* (Geneva and Paris, 1959).

GLUBB, SIR JOHN, *A Soldier with the Arabs* (London, 1957).

Hativat Hanegev Bama'arachah (The Negev Brigade during the War) (Tel Aviv, c.1950).

Hativat Givati Bemilhemet Hakomemiut (The Givati Brigade in the War of Independence), ed. and compiled Major Avraham Eilon (Tel Aviv, 1959).

Hativat Givati mul Hapolesh Hamitzri (The Givati Brigade Opposite the Egyptian Invader), ed. Major Avraham Eilon (Tel Aviv, 1963).

Hativat Alexandroni Bemilhemet Hakomemiut (The Alexandroni Brigade in the War of Independence), Gershon Rivlin and Zvi Sinai (Tel Aviv, 1964).

Ilan Va'shelah, Derekh Hakravot shel Hativat Golani (Tree and Sword, the Route of Battle of the Golani Brigade), ed. and compiled Binyamin Etzioni (Tel Aviv, c.1951).

ISRAEL DEFENCE FORCES, GENERAL STAFF HISTORY BRANCH, *Toldot Milhemet Hakomemiut* (History of the War of Independence) (Tel Aviv, 1959).

ITZCHAKI, ARIEH, *Latrun, Hama'aracha al Haderekh Leyerushalayim* (Latrun, the Battle for the Road to Jerusalem), 2 vols. (Jerusalem, 1982).

KAMEN, CHARLES, '*Aharei Ha'ason: Ha'aravim Be'medinat Yisrael, 1948–1950*', ('After the Catastrophe: the Arabs in the State of Israel'), *Mahbarot Lemehkar U'lebikoret* (Notebooks on Research and Criticism), 10 (1985).

KIMCHE, JON and DAVID, *Both Sides of the Hill* (London, 1960).

LAZAR (LITAI), HAIM, *Kibush Yaffo* (The Conquest of Jaffa) (Tel Aviv, 1951).

LORCH, NETANEL, *The Edge of the Sword, Israel's War of Independence, 1947–1949*, rev. edn. (Jerusalem, 1968).

MILSTEIN, URI, *Toldot Milhhemet Ha'Atzma'ut, HaHodesh HaRishon* (The History of the War of Independence, The First Month) (Tel Aviv, 1989).

Mishmar Ha'emek Ba'ma'aracha (Mishmar Ha'emek in the War) (Tel Aviv, 1950).

MORRIS, BENNY, *The Birth of the Palestinian Refugee problem, 1947–1949* (Cambridge, 1988).

NAZZAL, NAFEZ, *The Palestinian Exodus from Galilee, 1948* (Beirut, 1978).

NIV, DAVID, *Ma'arachot Ha'irgun Hatz'va'i Ha'leumi* (Battles of the IZL), 6 vols. (Tel Aviv, 1980).

ORREN, ELHANNAN, *Baderekh el Ha'ir, Mivtza Dani* (On the Road to the City, Operation Dani) (Tel Aviv, 1976).

PERETZ, DON, *Israel and the Palestine Arabs* (Washington, DC, 1958).

PORATH, YEHOSHUA, *The Emergence of the Palestinian–Arab Natinal Movement 1918–1929* (London, 1974).

—— *The Palestinian Arab National Movement 1929–1939* (London, 1977).

Sefer Toldot Hahaganah (The History of the Haganah), 3 vols. subdivided into 8 books, ed. Shaul Avigur, Yitzhak Ben-Zvi, Elazar Galili,

Yehuda Slutzky, Ben-Zion Dinur, and Gershon Rivlin (Tel Aviv, 1954).

Sefer Hapalmah (The Book of the Palmah), 2 vols., ed. and compiled Zerubavel Gilad together with Mati Megged (Tel Aviv, 1956).

SEGEV, TOM, *1949 Ha'yisraelim Harishonim* (1949, The First Israelis) (Jerusalem, 1984).

SHIMONI, YA'ACOV, *Arviyei Eretz Yisrael* (The Arabs of Palestine) (Tel Aviv, 1947).

SHOUFANI, ELIAS, 'The Fall of a Village', *Journal of Palestine Studies*, 1/4 (1972).

TEVETH, SHABTAI, *Ben-Gurion and the Palestinian Arabs* (Oxford, 1985).

INDEX

Index